Ruling the World

Ruling the World tells the story of how the largest and most diverse empire in history was governed, everywhere and all at once. Focusing on some of the most tumultuous years of Queen Victoria's reign, Alan Lester, Kate Boehme and Peter Mitchell adopt an entirely new perspective to explain how the men in charge of the British Empire sought to manage simultaneous events across the globe. Using case studies, including Canada, South Africa, the Caribbean, Australia, India and Afghanistan, they reveal how the empire represented a complex series of trade-offs between Parliament's, colonial governors', colonists' and colonised peoples' agendas. They also highlight the compromises that these men made as they adapted their ideals of freedom, civilisation and liberalism to the realities of an empire imposed through violence and governed in the interests of Britons.

Alan Lester is Professor of Historical Geography at the University of Sussex and Professor of History at La Trobe University. He is the author of *Imperial Networks: Creating Identities in Nineteenth-Century South Africa and Britain* (2001) and the co-author of *Colonization and the Origins of Humanitarian Governance: Protecting Aborigines across the Nineteenth-Century British Empire* (2014).

Kate Boehme is a Leverhulme Early Career Fellow at the University of Leicester. She has published on South Asian history in a number of journals, including the *Journal of the Royal Asiatic Society*.

Peter Mitchell is a writer and historian from Newcastle. He is the author of *Imperial Nostalgia* (forthcoming).

Ruling the World

Freedom, Civilisation and Liberalism in the Nineteenth-Century British Empire

Alan Lester

University of Sussex and La Trobe University

Kate Boehme

University of Leicester

Peter Mitchell

CAMBRIDGE
UNIVERSITY PRESS

CAMBRIDGE
UNIVERSITY PRESS

University Printing House, Cambridge CB2 8BS, United Kingdom

One Liberty Plaza, 20th Floor, New York, NY 10006, USA

477 Williamstown Road, Port Melbourne, VIC 3207, Australia

314–321, 3rd Floor, Plot 3, Splendor Forum, Jasola District Centre, New Delhi – 110025, India

79 Anson Road, #06–04/06, Singapore 079906

Cambridge University Press is part of the University of Cambridge.

It furthers the University's mission by disseminating knowledge in the pursuit of education, learning, and research at the highest international levels of excellence.

www.cambridge.org
Information on this title: www.cambridge.org/9781108426206
DOI: 10.1017/9781108584227

© Alan Lester, Kate Boehme and Peter Mitchell 2021

First published 2021

A catalogue record for this publication is available from the British Library.

ISBN 978-1-108-42620-6 Hardback
ISBN 978-1-108-44489-7 Paperback

For Patricia Joan Lester, 1940–2019

Contents

Figures

Maps

Acknowledgements

This book's origins lie in a research project, 'Snapshots of Empire'. I would like to thank the Leverhulme Trust for providing the necessary funding and Kate Boehme and Peter Mitchell, the research fellows who worked so professionally and collegially in The National Archives and the British Library, to lay its foundations.

I am very grateful to Mandy Banton, who shared her phenomenal expertise in the Colonial Office records, and to Penny Brook and Antonia Moon of the British Library, who helped enormously with the East India Company and India Office research. Clare Anderson, Dan Clayton, Ann Curthoys, John Darwin, Saul Dubow, Catherine Hall, Amanda Nettelbeck, Steve Legg and Sujit Sivasundaram all provided constructive feedback as the project progressed, for which I am very grateful.

The book was contemplated and written alongside a tenure as Research Professor in History at La Trobe University. I would like to thank my wonderful colleagues there, and especially Katie Holmes and Kerry Nixon, for their hospitality. There I helped see through to completion the late and greatly missed Tracey Banivanua Mar's PhD students, Crystal Mackinnon, Nikita Vanderbyl, Lucy Davies and Jessica Horton. It was a pleasure working with them and my co-supervisor, Liz Conor. I have benefitted greatly from their insight.

Thanks also to both the universities of Oxford's and Cambridge's Global and Imperial History seminars and the History seminar series of La Trobe, the University of Leicester, the University of Melbourne, Deakin University, Monash University, the University of Queensland, Flinders University, University of New South Wales, the University of Adelaide and the University of Sydney for opportunities to test out ideas and approaches in this book. Clare Anderson, James Belich, Leigh Boucher, Joy Damousi, John Darwin, Lisa Ford, Kate Fullagar, Anna Johnston, Amanda Nettelbeck, Lynette Russell and Tiffany Shellam all provided opportunities for helpful discussion, as did Luke Gibbon at the Foreign and Commonwealth Office. Anne Curthoys and Amanda

Nettelbeck very kindly read through drafts and their advice and corrections are greatly appreciated. Johanna Skurnik helped greatly by providing material from her own postdoctoral research. Thanks also to the Uckfield Dads Club for their stimulating debate.

Alan Lester

Introduction

I am the only Professor in England of my art – the art of understanding everything connected with the Constitution, Charters and Laws of some forty Colonies.

James Stephen, Permanent Under-Secretary, Colonial Office, 1845

When James Stephen, chief civil servant at the British government's Colonial Office, returned to his desk after the Christmas break in late December 1837, among the first despatches confronting him contained news of the rebellion of French- and English-speaking settlers in the colonies of Lower and Upper Canada. Through the first four months of the New Year, while he continued to be preoccupied with potential revolution in the Canadas, he also intervened in a debate between the lieutenant governor and governor of the Cape Colony over treaties with the Xhosa people on the eastern frontier, mediated a challenge to the authority of the Justice of the Peace in Port Natal and responded to the first reports of the Dutch-speaking Voortrekkers' mass emigration across the Cape Colony's border – all in southern Africa. At the same time Stephen resisted a massive land grab and extension of sovereignty in New South Wales, approved new measures for surveying the coastline in South Australia and agreed reluctantly to the establishment of a mounted police force to punish Aboriginal people attempting to drive back invading Britons in the Australian colonies. He worried about the seizure of eleven British subjects by a chief neighbouring Sierra Leone and advised caution about Belgium's establishment of a colony adjoining the Gold Coast in West Africa. He forwarded appeals for more troops from Gibraltar in the Mediterranean and from Heligoland in the North Sea, and consulted with the Foreign Office over how best to greet the Egyptian Pasha's envoy, on his way to London to study British artillery innovations. All the while, he was acutely conscious that the date set four years beforehand for the final emancipation of Britain's slaves in the Caribbean colonies, the Cape Colony and Mauritius, was looming. He had yet to advise who exactly was to be freed, and how.

It would have been quite remarkable if Stephen and his colleagues in imperial governance were able to concentrate on any one of Britain's colonies in isolation, or any one governmental agenda, for any substantial period without interruption. And yet colonial and imperial history is written for the most part as if they did. This book is based upon an appreciation of what it was to govern the most diverse and extensive empire that there has ever been, everywhere and all at once.

Writing the Empire

Until relatively recently, most historians of each of Britain's former colonies wrote across a reasonably broad span of years, but within a field of vision impeded by modern national borders. Historians of Australia were interested in how Australia emerged as its own nation from the separate colonies established by Britons from the late eighteenth century. They implicitly imagined the British Empire operating on an axis solely connecting the Government Houses of Australia with officials like Stephen in London. Stephen and his colleagues in the imperial government were relevant only insofar as they thought of Australian colonies. The multiple ways in which Australia was shaped through its connections with other parts of the empire that Stephen administered, and the gamut of factors that limited the span of Stephen's attention to Australian affairs, did not get a look in.[1] Such blinkers also applied to historians of each of Britain's other colonies.

In recent years, colonial historians' field of vision has broadened considerably, with a spike of interest in transnational and trans-imperial connections. This work, described at the time of its origin as the 'new imperial history', has provided one foundation for this book. Another is the longer standing interest of imperial historians in the administration and governance of the British Empire.

Since the 1990s a body of work driven mainly by women has helped reconfigure imperial history writing, largely by focusing on different questions from those asked by the predominantly male historians of imperial administration. Setting aside the conventional interest in how Britain acquired, governed and then lost an unprecedentedly large and diverse empire, feminist historians like Catherine Hall, Kathleen Wilson, Antoinette Burton and Mrinalini Sinha have been more concerned about the effects of British rule on colonised people, and the ways in which it fostered new patterns of thought about national identity, race, class and gender.[2] For them, trying to identify the 'driving forces' of empire was a less productive pursuit than exploring its effects on the ways that people relate to one another.[3] Colonial relations were forged not only by imperial administrators but by subjects of different status, gender and identity, pursuing many contradictory projects, connected across the globe by different kinds of networks.[4] The actors in historical change were of high and low status, men and women, coloniser and colonised, white and of colour. They remade both Britain and its colonies through the connections that they forged.[5] Such connections are fundamental to this account.

This is not to say, however, that all the elements of this imperial ensemble had equal opportunities to influence the lives of others. It was the task of the men who governed the British Empire to try to manage its chaotic assemblage of people and the infrastructures that connected them. These men exercised an influence out of proportion to their numbers. The policies that they pursued and the violence that they could draw upon to enforce them, conditioned millions of imperial subjects' lives in enduring ways. Men like Stephen, the politicians they served and the governors they appointed, could decide who was to be freed from slavery and who was not; who would participate in elections for colonial governments; who could trade freely and in what items; what rights of legal representation and of education certain people could enjoy; what terms of employment could be offered to whom and, in the final resort, who should be killed and who should live. In the nineteenth century their decisions on these and other matters had unprecedented global reach. While much of the recent scholarship on colonial connections, quite rightly, has shifted the attention away from these elite white men, they are the central figures in this account. This book is concerned above all with the ways that they exercised their responsibility of government in multiple colonies simultaneously.

One might expect that more conventional imperial historians, preoccupied with how Britain acquired, administered and lost its empire, would have had a better appreciation of the range of issues and places with which these men engaged on a daily basis. But for the most part, they seem to have assumed that the empire was governed, if not one place, then one agenda at a time.[6] In one way this book harks back to an old fashioned approach to imperial history, focused for the most part on its records of administration and its governing men. In other ways it is quite different. It not only looks at those records and their originators afresh, with an eye to the simultaneity of governance everywhere in the Empire at once; it also attends to the effects of these men's decisions for colonised subjects around the world.

The conventional, administratively – oriented, approach to imperial history has been dominated by the notion of an 'official mind', articulated by Ronald Robinson and John Gallagher from the 1950s to the 1980s. Their essential argument was that the British government could have had an empire at much lower cost had it stuck to the kind of free trade imperialism that we will deal with in Part I. This enabled Britons to exercise considerable influence over parts of the world such as South America and China without their formal colonisation, in large part through 'gunboat diplomacy'. The fundamental question for Robinson and Gallagher was, why go to all the expense of imposing and maintaining colonial governments around the world when you could obtain British prosperity and influence without them? Their answer was that 'circumstances overseas, rather than central policy, had governed the timing and decided the forms of imperial intervention in different regions'.[7] The 'official mind' – the shared sensibility and understanding of the men who governed the British Empire – was crucial in determining when and where a shift from informal to formal empire was needed. Those who developed careers as imperial officials, often in multiple colonies, were the ones who had to decide how best to represent local conditions, to respond to periodic local crises, and to recommend action. Influential men in London like James Stephen shared that sensibility and cooperated with the 'man on the spot' to govern an otherwise chaotic empire coherently. The key to understanding the British Empire was to unlock the decision-making process of these men: to get to grips with their official mind set.

This book shares some features of Robinson and Gallagher's approach. Our cast of characters largely comprises the kinds of figures who populate their account. Like Robinson and Gallagher's work, much of the action in this book takes place in Britain's colonies, rather than in London, and it deals with the relations that settlers, governors and occasionally philanthropists maintained with Indigenous populations there. We seek, however, to integrate these imperial men's actions more fully with the concurrent politics of Britain, and with the effects of their policies on colonised subjects.

A new integrative model of imperial expansion and decline was formulated in the late 1980s by Peter Cain and Anthony Hopkins. Whereas Robinson and Gallagher had seen the deliberations of governing 'men on the spot' as the primary motor of imperial expansion, Cain and Hopkins located it firmly back in Britain. 'Gentlemanly capitalism', emanating above all from Britain's financial heart in the City of London, was the driving force of interaction between Britain and its colonies. 'Putting the metropolitan economy back at the centre of the analysis', they declared, 'makes it possible to establish a new framework for interpreting Britain's historic role as a world power'.[8] British imperialism was the result of a new marriage (often literally) between those with traditional, landed status and the financial capitalists of the City of London. Cain and Hopkins enlisted parts of both the informal empire (Latin America, Persia and China) and formal empire to make the case that, behind the scenes, the interests of gentlemanly capitalists were at work.[9] Their argument launched other imperial historians on investigations of the financial and commercial manipulation impelling particular imperial episodes. We see the merit in doing so. For example, we highlight the restructuring of the East India Company and the means by which its shareholders were protected during the 1830s as being fundamental to the subsequent history of British India. But one of the most common grounds for criticism of Cain and Hopkins' thesis, which we share, is its relentlessly British focus. As Tony Ballantyne points out, 'viewing the empire and its history from London . . . returns indigenous people to the margins of history'.[10]

David Fieldhouse drew attention to the long-standing problem of 'the imperial historian' noted by Ballantyne: how to write about such vastly different places, processes and people as those contained within the nineteenth-century British Empire at the same time? Fieldhouse's answer was to specialise in the 'interactions' between the British 'core' and its 'peripheries'. The imperial historian, assumed to be male, would be located 'in the interstices of his subject, poised above the "area of inter-action" like some satellite placed in space, looking, Janus-like in two or more ways at the same time' and giving 'equal weight to what happens in a colony and in its metropolis . . . intellectually at home in both'.[11]

Fieldhouse admitted that 'no one person can satisfy all these requirements', simply because of the amount of historical material that would have to be processed if we were to examine in detail Britain and some forty other countries across any extended period. Our own attempt to encompass this question of being everywhere and all at once is to examine imperial governance everywhere and in much greater detail, but primarily during certain moments or snapshots. We think that this approach also enables us to shed light on the key developments that shaped imperial relations in the intervening periods.

John Darwin's is the latest large-scale attempt to examine the governance of the British Empire. Rather than focusing only inwardly on the deliberations of the British, Darwin relates their empire's fortunes to major geopolitical shifts enacted by other powerful actors across the world. In particular he is preoccupied with how the British global 'system' was subject to an unexpectedly rapid collapse in the mid twentieth century. Understanding this involves an appreciation of rival European powers' actions, of Japanese imperial ambitions and of the USA's role as Britain's ambivalent partner and rival. Our focus is on an earlier period than Darwin's – one of imperial growth, crisis and consolidation rather than dismantlement. But Darwin's argument that the motive forces of British imperial history need to be cast wider even than the vast extent of the British Empire itself still holds. British imperial governance was being rebuilt at the beginning of our period after wars with revolutionaries in the USA, France and Haiti. Americans' support for Canadian rebels was reinforcing an antipathy to republican democracy among the governing elite. Throughout, our cast of characters was preoccupied with the difficulties of maintaining contact between Britain and India across Ottoman-ruled Egypt, and both steam and telegraphic communication relied on striking a fine balance between cooperation and competition with other European empires.

Perhaps the most significant external driver of British imperial affairs in this account is Russia, or rather, British perceptions and fears of Russian imperial expansion. Anxiety about Russian encroachment, especially on India's north-western frontier, repeatedly propelled the men who governed the British Empire into more extreme behaviours, the effects of which were felt in other parts of that empire. It was not so much the Colonial Office, nor even the East India Company or India Office, which generated this anxiety, but the Foreign Office. Aside from being a complex governmental entity in its own right, Britain's empire was a weapon to be wielded and defended, almost at any cost, within that department's foreign policy. An interdepartmental view of imperial governance is therefore just as important as an inter-imperial one. As we will see in Part III, for example, Foreign Office preoccupations with Russian influence in the Balkans and Afghanistan in 1878–9 not only cost additional tens of thousands of lives; they also deflected the Colonial Office's priority of settler colonial confederation.

Imperial historians like Robinson and Gallagher and Cain and Hopkins tried to isolate the main driving force behind Britain's empire and Darwin encourages attention to rival empires too. However, there has, as yet, been no account of how the British Empire, in all its complexity and diversity, considering all of its relevant offices and all of its colonies, was governed at any one time. In this book, we see how the men who governed that empire broadly sought security, prosperity and the pursuit of certain ideals in the national interest, but we identify no one motor of imperial expansion nor any key principle behind imperial governance. As one of the Colonial Office's most senior and longest serving officials, Thomas Elliot wrote:

What has to be solved [in imperial governance] is not one problem, but many. I despair of discovering ... any self-acting rule, which shall be a substitute for the judgement and firmness of the Ministers of the Crown. ... They will doubtless always be guided by a policy, but they can hardly expect to despatch such complicated and arduous questions by a single maxim. To deal with cases on their merits, to labour patiently against opposition in some quarters, and to welcome and reciprocate co-operation from others: these, in so wide and diversified a sphere as the British Colonies, appear to me tasks and duties inseparable from the function of governing, which can never be superseded by the machinery of a system, however ably conceived or logically constructed.[12]

If we are to understand imperial governance, we cannot confine ourselves to the pursuit of any particular organisational logic, and we must resist the quest for the 'main' driving force. We also have to go beyond the imaginations of the men who governed. Even the arch imperialist Winston Churchill recognised that 'our claim to be left in the unmolested enjoyment of vast and splendid possessions, mainly acquired by violence, largely maintained by force, often seems less reasonable to others than to us'.[13] Our focus in this book may be on the elite white men in charge of the empire, but their view of the world that it shaped cannot be the only one that we narrate.

The British Empire generally seemed a 'good thing' to the men who governed it. It does to certain well-known British politicians and popular historians today. In part this is because, as Darwin points out, colonised people often remarked that British rule was preferable to the alternatives at a time of rampant European imperialism. Jeremy Black's appreciation of the legacies of the British Empire is premised on this notion that it was a less vicious empire than all the others. Black provides a litany of things that people other than Britons did that were worse than the things Britons did: the atrocities of societies and polities occupying the territories that Britain later governed, the brutality of the empires that predominated before Britain's, and which ruled concurrently elsewhere, and the violence and incompetence of the post-independence governments that took over once the British left. 'In practice, as a ruler of Caribbean colonies', Black argues, 'Britain was less harsh than Spain in Cuba. As a ruler of settlement colonies, Britain, in Canada and New Zealand, was less harsh than the USA; although the situation in Australia was less favorable for the indigenous population than that in Canada. ... Britain was far less totalitarian than the Soviet Union or Nazi Germany'.[14]

Perhaps the best known moral defence of the British Empire from Niall Ferguson makes the same point, arguing that Britain's legacy as an imperial power, however blemished by slavery, famine and atrocity, is forever redeemed by its sacrifice in order to defeat the Nazis.[15] For Black, Winston Churchill's call for the distinctiveness of Britain's empire can be read as its reality. Churchill asked 'Whether we are to model ourselves upon the clanking military empires of the Continent of Europe ... or whether our development is to proceed by well-tried English methods towards the ancient and lofty ideals of English citizenship?' Of course, the answer was that Britain's Empire should be (and in Black's eyes was) distinguished by the 'regular, settled lines of English democratic development'.[16]

Both Black and Ferguson go further than the argument that British imperial rule was comparatively benign. They also assert that it left a generally positive legacy for humanity. Ferguson argues that it 'acted as an agency for imposing free markets, the rule of law, investor protection and relatively incorrupt government on roughly a quarter of the world. . . . There therefore seems a plausible case that empire enhanced global welfare'. The cultural underpinning of these achievements was, apparently, the idea of liberty. 'What is very striking about the history of the Empire is that whenever the British were behaving despotically, there was almost always a liberal critique of that behaviour from within British society. Indeed, so powerful and consistent was this tendency to judge Britain's imperial conduct by the yardstick of liberty that it gave the British Empire something of a self-liquidating character. Once a colonized society had sufficiently adopted the other institutions that the British brought with them, it became very hard for the British to prohibit that political liberty to which they attached so much significance for themselves.'[17] For Black, the British Empire 'arose in the context of modernity and the Enlightenment as broadly conceived'. It 'came with promises of the rule of law, participatory governance, freedom, autonomy and individualism, to at least some of [its] members. Moreover these ideas subsequently spread in [its] area of power, as with the abolition of slavery and the spread of democracy.'[18]

These ideals, of a better empire than all the others, and even of an empire that worked for the benefit of all its subjects, were undoubtedly adopted and enunciated by the men who governed the British Empire. This book is structured around three of the terms that these men used most often to articulate them: freedom, civilisation and liberalism. In Part I, our largest section, we focus on the foundational idea of freedom, as applied in emancipation from slavery, the pursuit of free trade and the right of self-governance. In Part II, we see how the men who inherited that idea sought to impose the benefits of Britain's advancing civilisation on often reluctant subjects in the 1850s. In Part III, we highlight the ways in which they adapted the liberalism that they had forged from these principles of freedom and civilisation for the wider world in the later nineteenth century. Departing from Ferguson's and Black's approaches, however, we also highlight the disavowal that lay at the heart of these liberal ideals.

Two systemic features of imperial governance persistently contradicted its expressed ideals in practice: racial distinction and violence. It is because of these fundamental characteristics that the aspirations and protestations of the men who governed the empire cannot realistically be read as its reality. The principles of freedom, civilisation and liberalism that motivated them were dissolved in a solution of violent racism through which British power was applied. Even the most benevolently inclined governing men found it impossible to extract pure and universal solutes from that application. In our three periods of detailed analysis alone, the extent of the violence inflicted upon people of colour by the agents of British imperial governance is astonishing. We can state with some confidence that British forces killed in total over a million people in the First Afghan War and the First Opium War (1838–42), the suppression of the Indian Uprising and the Second Opium War (1856–8), and the Second Afghan War and wars for South African confederation (1878–80).[19] A Colonial Office clerk might well say that 'There are points on which mere military expediency must clash with consideration of policy & humanity & in such cases the military expediency must be very strong or it should give way', but killing on a scale greater than any contemporaneous empire was essential to establish the sway of British 'policy & humanity' around the world in the first place.[20]

Even in territories long administered by Britain, as Churchill recognised, the ongoing threat of violence, against people of colour in particular, remained an essential backstop for governance without consent. In 1859, the same Thomas Elliot who pointed to the lack of any overarching governing logic conducted a review of how much military force was required to retain each of Britain's colonies. Their varying racial composition was critical to his calculation. 'They are exposed ... some more and others less', he wrote, 'to perils from Natives ... in certain Colonies, [the] population is British, in others foreign; in part of them it is wholly white, in part almost wholly coloured, and in many it consists of a large proportion of both. ... Is it surprising with Colonies of such an infinite variety of condition, that ... their demands for military assistance should be different?'[21] Elliot's premise derived from the correspondence of governors like Henry Ward in Ceylon, who explained that 'an Oriental People is swayed by impulse, and checked only by its habitual submission to power. So long as we have that, small disputes, which are of frequent occurrence between Planters and Natives ... are easily settled. ... But when we have not the power, there is always a risk of ... serious collisions.'[22]

For officials like the evangelical James Stephen in London, the governance of empire could be mainly a theoretical question. Imperial governance was something that could and should have right, as well as might, on its side. It should improve the prospects, both material and spiritual, of Britain's subjects around the world, regardless of race. The problem was that empire necessarily entailed the denial of other people's self-determination, the use of violence to sustain that denial and, in the settler colonies, the mass eviction and subjection of prior inhabitants on behalf of British emigrants. Imperial officials in London might complain that settlers, and even occasionally governors, contradicted their liberal ideas and undermined their benevolent intentions in the colonies. They might, accordingly, condemn their distant compatriots as acting in a manner unbecoming Britons. Later generations of Britons might blame the destruction of Indigenous societies on people who came to be identified as Australians or Canadians, rather than Britons overseas. Every time they did so, they disavowed the nature of the British Empire. It was premised, as empires always have been, on taking possession and control of other peoples' lands, and on the reduction of alien peoples, by one means or another, to a subordinate position for the national benefit.

Everyday administration of the British Empire, as will see in abundance in this book, was completely saturated with racial differentiation. To give one, rather quirky, example, the idea of differing racial capacity extended even to the care of lighthouses. 'While I should have no scruple whatever in entrusting to natives properly trained the care of the lighthouses at Colombo, Galle, and Trincomalie', the governor of Ceylon wrote in 1879, 'I think that the entrusting to natives the care of such important and at the same time such isolated lighthouses as the Great and Little Basses, requires grave consideration. I find upon inquiry in India and Singapore that in the Madras Presidency natives (Asiatics) have not been placed in sole or partial charge of any lighthouses. And the light houses throughout the Straits have a European or Eurasian in charge. In Hong Kong a Light of the Fourth order is said to be in charge of Chinese only, under frequent supervision. But Chinese are so far superior to the bulk of other Orientals in steadiness and intelligence that the successful employment of Chinese in any pursuit is by no means a guarantee that the employment of other Orientals in the same pursuit would be equally successful.'[23] Throughout the empire, one of the most consistent features of British governance was its assumption that people of colour were 'not yet qualified by education and property to command the respect of the country'.[24] It may be comforting for Britons today to hear that 'it became very hard for the British to prohibit' their imperial subjects 'that political liberty to which they attached so much significance for themselves'.[25] Unfortunately it is not true. The Victorian British were, for the most part, quite comfortable with the denial of that same liberty to people of colour. Their successors surrendered it only late in the twentieth century, and only very reluctantly, in the face of colonised peoples' ever more assertive demands for it.

Examining the British Empire's governance during our selected moments enables us to appreciate how the men in charge sought to manage concurrent and often contradictory processes: the emancipation of Britain's slaves alongside the assuaging of settlers' demands for colonial expansion in the 1830s; the dissemination of British civilisational norms alongside the denial of other people's self-determination in the 1850s, and the belief in a uniquely liberal empire alongside multiple wars of aggression in the 1870s. When we examine how the empire was governed everywhere and all at once, the trade-offs between these simultaneous imperatives are inescapable.

Just as imperceptibly gradual changes in a growing child appear stark only when one sees her after a year or two has passed, so the subtle alterations in the temper of the British Empire's governing men, the nature of their policies and their means of communication appear more evident after intervals of around twenty years. The moments we have chosen to examine imperial governance are 1838, when the British Empire was in the midst of rapid expansion and reorientation after the loss of the American colonies and the end of the Napoleonic War; 1857, when its consolidation was blighted by interlocking crises around the world; and 1879, when a new generation of confident and ambitious imperial men sought to transform the world in Britain's liberal image.

These three years, examined in all their complexity, enable us to narrate some of the most significant developments of the Victorian Empire as whole. They include the ending of slavery and the rise of free trade doctrine, repeated Indian famines and the Uprising of 1857, the First and Second Afghan Wars, the First and Second Opium Wars, the Great Xhosa Cattle Killing and the Anglo-Zulu War, mass emigration from the British Isles, the self-governance of settler colonies in North America, Australasia and southern Africa and the devastation of Indigenous societies. We focus on the officials and politicians in London and the governors in the colonies who sought to manage and direct these events and the ways that they mediated between other interests, including Parliament and lobbyists in Westminster, British public opinion, emigrant British settlers, Indigenous collaborators, colonised peoples threatening and effecting resistance, and other imperial powers including France, the Ottoman Empire, the Qing Empire, Germany and the USA. We see British imperial policy as the accommodations and trade-offs that governing men reached within this global assemblage of actors, connected by different technologies in each of our years, everywhere and all at once, as they acted broadly in pursuit of national prosperity, security and values.

In the first four decades of the nineteenth century, which we cover in Part I, we suggest, the men who governed the empire were preoccupied with the theme of freedom. If a growing empire was to be governed most effectively, which kind of people should be allowed what kinds of freedom? What should happen when the freedom of colonisers conflicted with the freedoms of other imperial subjects? Which people were suitable for coercion into doing what kinds of work, where and for whom? Who was entitled to a say in colonial government and who was not? This is the largest of the three sections because it serves to introduce colonies, processes and people that are picked up again in Parts II and III.

Around the middle of the Victorian period, which we address in Part II, a more pressing issue arose that was directly related to the questions of freedom pondered in the 1830s. To what extent should Britons impose their own civilisation on others whom they now ruled? When colonial subjects resisted, was it right to use violence against them, assuming that it was for their own long term benefit? What kinds of violence and against whom could be reconciled with a progressive and beneficial empire? What kinds of technological and bureaucratic innovations would enable British governance to be sustained and better integrated around the world? Part II highlights these broader issues during a critical year of starvation in southern Africa, renewed war over free trade in opium in China and rebellion in India.

Later in Queen Victoria's reign, these established concerns with freedom and civilisation converged around the older, contested and incoherent idea of liberalism. An emerging liberal governmental consensus at home, however, was counterpoised with its seeming opposite, imperialism, overseas. To what extent should a progressively more liberal from of government, founded on individual rights and responsibilities, be extended to subject peoples of colour? What kind of individual characteristics were attached to race? What scale of violence did the spread of what officials believed was inherently beneficial British governance justify? Part III visits these questions in 1879, identifying an ever-widening gap between most Britons' perception of their empire and most imperial subjects' experiences of it.

Imperial Governance

The Colonial Office, where James Stephen and Thomas Elliot laboured in early 1838, administered the Crown and settler colonies in North and

Central America, Africa, Australasia, parts of Asia and pockets of Europe. This was about half of the British Empire. Until the 1860s, imperial administration took place in three London buildings. Stephen's premises at the Colonial Office was at 14 Downing Street, the top end of the prime minister's cul de sac in Whitehall, since demolished. Despite its global reach, the building was 'trembling on the verge of ruin' when our account begins in 1838, and would be condemned as unsafe the following year.[26] Its basement library, full of European travel accounts of distant lands, specially commissioned maps, theoretical disquisitions on colonisation, missionary periodicals, manuals for surveying and colonists' published letters, was prone to damp, and its staff of around twenty-five worked in dingy conditions.[27] As part of a polemical attack on James Stephen, the MP and journalist Charles Buller provided a colourful description of the office and its *modus operandi* in 1838:

There are rooms in the Colonial Office with old and meagre furniture, book cases crammed with Colonial gazettes and newspapers, tables covered with baize, and some old and crazy chairs scattered about, in which those who have personal applications to make are doomed to wait until the interview can be obtained. . . . These are men with Colonial grievances. . . . One is a recalled Governor, boiling over with a sense of mortified pride and frustrated policy; another . . . a merchant, whose property has been destroyed by some job or oversight; . . . another, a widow struggling for some pension, on which her hopes of existence hang; and perhaps another is a man whose project is under consideration. Every one of these has passed hours in that dull but anxious attendance, and knows every nook and corner of this scene of his sufferings. . . . Some give vent to their rage, when, after hours of attendance, the messenger summons in their stead some sleek contented looking visitor, who has sent up his name only the moment before, but whose importance as a Member of Parliament, or of some powerful interest or society, obtains him an instant interview. . . . These chambers of woe are called the Sighing Rooms; and those who recoil from the sight of human suffering should shun the ill-omened precincts.[28]

The second office from which imperial governance emanated was the much grander Leadenhall Street headquarters of the East India Company. The Company effectively ruled the other half of the British Empire. Whereas, in 1838, Stephen sought to administer thirty-two colonies dispersed across the Atlantic, Pacific and Indian Oceans, the East India Company governed much of subcontinental South Asia as well as colonies in the Middle East and Southeast Asia. East India House was a palatial neo-classical building in the City of London's financial centre some two miles to the east of Whitehall. Built in the 1720s it had been extensively remodelled in the 1790s, with large warehouses stretching back behind the façade housing commodities imported from India.[29] The main part of the Leadenhall Street interior could not have provided more of a contrast with the Colonial Office's dingy and cramped premises. Large airy meeting rooms enabled the Company's directors and shareholders to assemble for their lengthy deliberations and directors could emerge from their grandly furnished offices to stroll around its hall, courtyard and garden.

The Company was no longer in its heyday, however. Its administrative establishment, housed in less salubrious offices out of the visiting shareholders' sight, had been severely reduced in recent years. The 400 clerks of the 1790s had been cut to around 100 by 1838, although the Company's bureaucracy was still more than double the size of that available to Stephen.

The third element of the imperial government in 1838 was an unprepossessing townhouse just opposite the recently fire-ravaged Houses of Parliament at Westminster Hall, in Cannon Row. This was the office of the Board of Commissioners for the Affairs of India. More commonly referred to as the Board of Control, this committee of six government appointees and its president oversaw the activities of the East India Company on behalf of the government. The Board of Control's establishment in London may have been far more modest than that of the Company, but by 1838 it had the power not only to veto the directors' decisions, but to send the Company's considerable Indian military force to war where it considered that the national interest was at stake.

These three offices were situated within a complex of other governmental departments and buildings, located mainly in Whitehall, which also had a direct bearing on imperial affairs. The Foreign Office, in equally precarious premises next door to the Colonial Office in Downing Street during 1838, dealt with relations with other European and imperial governments whose colonial territories abutted British colonies or straddled the sea routes connecting them. Missives and minutes shuttled regularly between the neighbouring offices, especially during crises involving other states' threats to British imperial interests.

Both the Colonial Office and the Board of Control maintained necessary but often tense relationships with the Treasury, whose approval was vital for any plans of colonial expenditure from the British Exchequer. This department would be especially important when large government subsidies or guarantees were required, as they were for the disruptive technologies of steam in the 1830s–40s and telegraph in the 1850s–80s, which promised better imperial communications. Each office also liaised regularly with the Admiralty and the Army in Horse Guards, in an attempt to secure its preferred distribution of imperial military forces and transport capacity.

During the first half of the nineteenth century the administrations of each of the Colonial Office's thirty to forty colonies, and of each of the East India Company's three presidencies, based in in Calcutta (Kolkata), Madras (Chennai) and Bombay (Mumbai), were brought together as a rather loose and ill-defined 'imperial' government in these London offices by a worldwide infrastructure of sail ships, harbours and ports. Steam technology began to transform that infrastructure in the late 1830s, adding the need for coaling depots, but imperial governance remained dependent on the vagaries of current and wind, unreliably scheduled ship departures and arrivals, and feats of navigation.

An exchange between the governor of Mauritius, William Nicolay and the Colonial Office early in 1838 illuminates the arbitrariness of the communications system. Nicolay complained that he had received official notification of Queen Victoria's accession a full month after the news had already infiltrated the colony through military orders from the War Office, in the correspondence of local businessmen with investors in Liverpool and Bristol, and with the prior arrival of the London newspapers. The governor blamed the Colonial Office practice of accumulating its replies to separate despatches for a period of up to a month before despatching them in a single mailbag. He begged that James Stephen's staff adopt the practice of the 'Horse Guards, War Office, &c. because the mode adopted by those offices is to forward their letters singly, by post, and not to make them up in Separate Bags'. Stephen's reception was frosty. He told Nicolay, who was apparently suffering from an 'excess of zeal', that:

The difficulties . . . which . . . attend the endeavours of this Department and of the Post Office, to send every despatch by the earliest ship which may sail . . . are perhaps greater than may have occurred to your mind. Merchant Vessels are simultaneously advertised as about to sail from London, Liverpool, Bristol, Glasgow, and other ports; and it generally happens that the actual time of their departure cannot be stated with any degree of certainty, until immediately before they sail. . . . Moreover, it frequently happens in consequence of the chances incidental to navigation, that vessels do not arrive at their destination in the order . . . in which they may have successively left England. For example, my despatches which you received in the course of last year by the steam ships 'Atalanta' and 'Berenice', which left this country – the former nearly six weeks and the latter a month later than the ships 'Ino' and 'Patriot', arrived at Mauritius seven and ten days earlier than those which were conveyed by the latter vessels . . . I mention these particulars in order to satisfy you that no vigilance or activity can altogether prevent the occasional delay to which you allude in the receipt of official intelligence, especially from this Country, where there are numerous Ports at considerable distances from each other, whence the means of conveyance proceed to the Colony at uncertain periods.[30]

Together with the ability of its officials to wield paper, pen and ink effectively, this fragile and highly contingent system of navigation by sail was all that brought an understanding of the empire to the appointed officials who sought to govern it from London. In Part II we will see how the development of steam engines, on both ships and rails, altered the regularity, predictability and pace of these communications, while also enhancing British military capabilities. By 1857, when steam was enabling new forms of imperial power and reach, telegraphic communication was also beginning to impact upon the imperial administration, although the East India Company and Foreign Office adopted it well ahead of the Colonial Office. In Part III, focused on 1879, telegraph features as the standard means of governmental communication. However, its reach was still highly uneven, which had disastrous effects for governmental coordination in southern Africa. Revisiting the British Empire in these three snapshot moments enables us to highlight the ways that these technological developments impacted on its governance, and, in turn, how imperial governmental investment facilitated technological change.

In the world beyond Britain the geographical spheres administered by the different offices in London overlapped. Until 1858 the East India Company governed a number of territories within the Indian Ocean region and along the strategically vital route between Britain and India, as well as India itself. It administered these territories most directly through the three presidencies. The separate governors of Calcutta, Madras and Bombay, with the former having precedence, reported to the Company's directors in Leadenhall Street, who reported in turn to the Board of Control in Cannon Row. Each of the presidencies also correspond directly with governors elsewhere administered by the Colonial Office, and each presidency indirectly governed the princely states that were dispersed between Company-owned territories. The Company was an eastward facing sub-empire in its own right, with its own fiscal, military and judicial establishments, its own training colleges – Haileybury near Hertford in England and Fort William in Calcutta – and even its own jargon. By 1857 it had its own telegraph training school at Stevenage. However, even by 1838 the British government had clipped its wings substantially.

Following the beginning of the Company's transition in the mid eighteenth century from a commercial enterprise into a territorial power with revenue-raising potential, its directors had been flooded with appeals to act as patrons in the appointment of young British men eager to enrich themselves in its employ, and from private trade, in India. The scandals associated with the subsequent looting of India had prompted greater governmental oversight. From 1794, private traders were entitled to use

Company ships in competition with the Company. Even though the Government of India Act of 1833 had confirmed the Company's administrative and political functions in India, it had also removed its remaining trade monopolies and divested it of its commercial functions. In 1838 private traders exclusively used its fleets, competing for Indian Ocean markets and supplies. The 1833 Act also centralised the three Indian presidencies' powers under the governor-general in Council in Calcutta. In London, it shored up the Board of Control's authority over the Company. We will examine these changes in more detail in the next chapter.

Despite the differences between Crown Colony and East India Company administrative structures, the men who governed the British Empire from Downing Street and Leadenhall Street exchanged ideas, shared clubs, institutions and events on the social calendar, and were often related. A man governing one colony or presidency might well have a father, brother, uncle, cousin or nephew concurrently serving in a senior role in another. These men also frequently travelled between the colonies and territories administered by the different offices and sometimes served in each of the offices themselves.

Charles Grant, later Lord Glenelg, for instance, whose father was a prominent East India Company trader, and who was born in India, presided over the Board of Control when it turned the East India Company from a commercial concern into the proxy British government of India in 1833. He then oversaw James Stephen as secretary of state at the Colonial Office, seeing through the completion of Caribbean slaves' emancipation in 1838. Herman Merivale moved from being Stephen's successor at the Colonial Office to an equivalent role in the India Office (to which the East India Company transitioned after 1857), and Henry Bartle Frere carved out his career in India as a Company officer before lending his belligerent talents to the Colonial Office in southern Africa. Individual governing men could apply their enterprise relatively seamlessly between Colonial Office and East India Company bureaucracies. Outside of governing circles, hundreds of propertied British men and women in the 1830s also had a stake in both halves of the empire, owning shares in the Company as well as enslaved people in the Crown colonies.

This book's extensive cast of characters demonstrates the dense sets of familial, social and military connections between the men who governed the two major spheres of the Empire. Above all these imperial men circulated vast quantities of paper among themselves. James Stephen described a typical day in Downing Street being 'diligently enough spent in keeping back the flood of papers from deluging us'.[31] 'Papers! papers! papers!', he once wrote, 'I live amongst them, & shall soon become a mere bit of blotting paper myself'.[32] There were enough papers to compel successive structural works to shore up the Colonial Office's floors as they creaked under the weight of files, and ultimately to hasten the move to new premises in Whitehall. Enough to propel the literary careers of Charles Lamb, John Stuart Mill and Thomas Babington Macaulay, all of whom were employed at different times in the Company's administration at Leadenhall Street.

Each of the London offices governing the empire worked to an irregular rhythm, geared to the periodic arrival and departure of ships carrying mail to and from the colonies and presidencies. In 1838 the communications infrastructure of the Colonial Office and East India Company were interdependent, despite their separate spheres of governance. Malta, administered by the Colonial Office, was a vital relay point in the transmission of despatches from the Indian presidencies.[33] There was often slack in the administrative system of each office. James Stephen felt obliged to write a memo to his Colonial Office staff in the early 1840s reminding them to turn up for work by 11:00 am at the latest and not to leave before 4:00 pm, restricting themselves only to a two- to three-hour lunch break in the meantime. However, the offices did work more intensively when Parliament was in session, demanding the latest intelligence of colonial affairs. Clerks would be kept till late at night to process the correspondence when a mail packet arrived, or in anticipation of an appropriate vessel departing. Between 1813 and 1829, the East India Company's clerks at Leadenhall Street handled 14 414 folios of correspondence from India. Their processing was not exactly streamlined. Snap Courts of the Company's directors and shareholders were called when packets of letters arrived at Leadenhall Street. Each Court meeting would begin with a lengthy reading of all correspondence received, irrespective of subject or importance. The court would adjourn for a few hours while the directors' committees conferred, and upon their return, replies, decisions and paragraphs would be considered for inclusion in draft outgoing despatches. These drafts were either voted upon or laid by for a week or two so that all members of the Company in London could see them. Once voted on, messengers carried them to the Board of Control over in Westminster, which either approved them or suggested amendments. The Board also reserved the right to send its own despatches to India in the name of the Company.

In a debate on India in 1822, Lord Canning mentioned a single military despatch accompanied by 119 papers and containing 13 511 pages. One of the 'established clerks', responsible for analysing, rather than merely copying, these papers, was Charles Lamb, who worked in the office for thirty years until the late 1820s, exceedingly busy at certain times but 'free to write long letters at work' during the interludes. He later claimed that his published works 'were my recreations; my real works may be found on the shelves in Leadenhall Street, filling some hundred folios'.[34] James Mill authored his influential *History of British India* before joining the office and with no prior experience of the subcontinent. After making his name for his denunciation of 'rude' and 'backward' Indian culture and calling for British-imposed reform, Mill was appointed assistant (later chief) examiner of correspondence, a post which he held until his death in 1836. His son John Stuart Mill, the leading liberal of the nineteenth century, carried on the family tradition and, in 1838, was working for the Company's Secret and Political Department.

Men of Empire

At the salubrious Leadenhall Street building, the Chairman of the East India Company's governing Board of Directors, overseeing John Stuart Mill's work in 1838, was Sir James Lushington. A former Tory Member of Parliament, he had joined the Company as a cadet in 1796 and, after fighting under Arthur Wellesley, the future Duke of Wellington, in a number of its conquests of Indian states, been promoted to the rank of Major-General by 1837. His deputy was Sir Richard Jenkins, another former Tory Member of Parliament who had also worked to great acclaim for the Company in India. Jenkins' scholarship on Indian literature and governance saw him elected fellow of both the Royal Geographical Society and the Royal Society. He believed that the ideal 'Company man' should possess 'a knowledge of the languages, and an acquaintance with the manners and habits of the Natives. ... He unites with these qualifications a degree of mildness and temper, particularly calculated to succeed in business with natives and to ensure their confidence and good opinion.'[35] Jenkins' prior conduct in India, though, had not exactly been pacific. He had commanded Company troops in the capture of Nagpur and believed that Arthur Wellesley's older brother Richard, who was the Company's governor-general, had not gone far enough in crushing Maratha resistance to British rule.

Lushington and Jenkins were the Company's point of liaison with the Board of Control. In 1838 its president was the colourful John Cam Hobhouse (Baron Broughton), friend of Lord Byron, admirer of Napoleon (despite the death of his own brother at Quatre Bras), nonconformist and a radical who had been imprisoned at Newgate in 1819. As a younger man Hobhouse had accompanied Byron on his visit to Albania and Greece and helped copy edit *Childe Harold's Pilgrimage*. Acting as Byron's best man, he had recognised the poet's reluctance to marry and sought to persuade the minister not to perform the ceremony, thus alienating himself from the bride, Annabella Milbanke. After the 1832 Reform Act Hobhouse had become more moderate and Whiggish in his politics. Prime Minister Melbourne is thought to have liked him in part because he had discouraged Byron from eloping with his late wife, Lady Caroline Lamb. With Melbourne in post again in 1834, Hobhouse was offered his former job at the War Office but chose the Presidency of the Board of Control instead. As such, he was the Cabinet member responsible for the government of India and all of the associated territories. He was a figure around whom a number of our governing men socialised in 1838.

Without the need for consultation with shareholders or oversight from a separate government department, the decision-making process at the Colonial Office was more focused than that of the East India Company. By 1838, James Stephen's personal influence was especially significant. As permanent under-secretary, he reviewed every piece of correspondence received from the Crown colonies. He then drafted many of the official replies that were signed off by the secretary of state. It is largely through his handwritten notes on the back of governors' despatches that we access 'the Colonial Office view' of the empire in the late 1830s.

Described as a 'shy workaholic', such was Stephen's imagined influence that waspish colonists and metropolitan opponents like Edward Gibbon Wakefield, who found him uncompliant with profitable schemes of emigration, nicknamed him 'Mr Over-Secretary' or, as Buller had him, 'Mr Mother Country'.[36] Stephen thought his own capacities rather more limited. He was aware that the vagaries of imperial communication compelled considerable discretion for governors of varying ability. Governors were sent out with instructions gleaned from what Stephen and his clerks knew about their destination from their predecessors, but these men, appointed through patronage, largely with military backgrounds, tended to set Colonial Office guidance to one side as they familiarised themselves with their new environment. They became effectively autocratic rulers, their actions mitigated in some colonies only by the executive councillors whom they themselves nominated and, occasionally, elected assemblies of colonists, most of whom could vote on, but not amend, legislation.

Some idea of Stephen's background is essential to understanding the way he ran the Colonial Office in 1838. In 1783 his father, also named James, had travelled to join family in the Caribbean colony of St Kitts. Upon his arrival Stephen senior witnessed a blatant miscarriage of justice as four enslaved men were scapegoated for a murder obviously committed by a white man. He became an ardent anti-slavery campaigner. James Stephen junior lived on St Kitts for five years with his parents, after which an attack of smallpox permanently weakened his eyesight. Much of his writing thereafter would be through dictation, although the helpful marginalia found on office correspondence was his own. Trained at Cambridge and in London as a lawyer, he married Jane Catherine Venn. Her father was John Venn, rector of Clapham and one of the founders of the Church Missionary Society (CMS). Stephen would serve on the missionary society's committee, advocating Christian conversion for the 'heathen' subjects of empire. The family, including Jane, was a hub of the Clapham Sect of evangelical reformers and anti-slavery activists nicknamed the 'Saints' by those who mocked their earnestness.

Stephen's role included all three functions of government – legislative, judicial and executive. He had started out at the Colonial Office in 1813 as a legal adviser, reviewing all acts passed in the colonies for consistency with British law. At the same time he maintained a more lucrative private practice. His work for the Colonial Office increased during the 1820s as commissions of inquiry fanned out to make their recommendations on both the established colonies and the ones newly captured from France and its allies in the Revolutionary and Napoleonic Wars. The combination of assimilating their voluminous reports, continued private practice and the birth of a son led Stephen to a breakdown in 1822. He recovered in part by dropping the private practice, working thereafter solely in imperial administration. He was appointed assistant under-secretary in 1834 and permanent under-secretary in 1836. During the next two years he had extensively reorganised the department's procedures.

In 1838 Stephen sat at the apex of a hierarchy of clerks receiving, copying and forwarding papers from the colonial governments. At any one time he had at his disposal an establishment that was far smaller in scale than that of the East India Company administration: roughly twenty-five Colonial Office employees, including seventeen clerks, a counsel, librarian and assistant librarian, a registrar and his assistant, a précis writer and two office keepers. There were also two porters and a housekeeper, Maria Phillochody, who was the only woman employed in the office, and had been for more than thirty years.

Stephen himself was the reference point for consistency in imperial administration. He was renowned equally for his dedication to the work and his inability to delegate. He would apply himself to the minutiae of every despatch from every colony for ten or eleven hours solid, six days a week, confessing that 'it is only by starvation and seclusion that I am able to get through it'. 'To me', he wrote to his wife Jane, 'a colony is as turtle-soup is to an alderman, daily fare & hardly palatable'.[37] As an evangelical Christian, Stephen was driven in this work by a view of historical change as 'the progressive fulfilment of the Supreme Will'. He believed that

Britain's newfound opportunity to govern an enlarged Empire 'must be regarded as one of the most impressive movements of Divine Providence in the government of this world'. He saw his role in imperial administration as entirely compatible with his affiliation to the CMS: 'he who should induce any heathen people ... to recognize the authority of [God] would confer on them a blessing exceeding all which mere philanthropy has ever accomplished'.[38]

Stephen's reputation for influence above and beyond his station as a civil servant was perhaps most deserved on questions of slavery in the Caribbean. Unsurprisingly he aligned with the evangelical anti-slavery campaign. Even before he was appointed assistant under-secretary, his attention to the detail of the various codes reluctantly passed by West Indian legislatures to 'ameliorate' the conditions of enslaved people led to them being declared inadequate by the colonial secretary. As prime minister, the conservative Duke of Wellington objected to government reports authored by this 'partisan of abolition'. In the next chapter we will see how Stephen's office attempted to manage the aftermath of the emancipation of slaves from 1833. For now we can note that the secretary of state responsible for drafting the necessary legislation, Lord Stanley, had admitted his inability to address the complexities involved. Stephen's response was to dedicate an entire weekend to producing the twenty-six-page bill which finally saw an end to legalised slavery in the British Empire. It was one of two occasions in his life when he worked on the Sabbath.

Stephen may have been tremendously influential, but he alone never determined Colonial Office policy. He reported to two politicians. The under-secretary of state, George Grey, was, like Stephen, a committed evangelical who had established a private legal practice. He, however, had been elected as a Whig MP in 1832. First appointed under-secretary for the colonies within Melbourne's government in 1834, he had come to the role again the following year after a few months out of office. The under-secretary's role included reading and drafting despatches for the secretary of state, and potentially being a channel of communication between colonial governors and the secretary of state. Grey also became the Colonial Office spokesman in the House of Commons in early 1838, when his secretary of state was elevated to the Lords. It was Grey who defended the policies that Stephen had played a part in devising in Parliament. Later, as home secretary, Grey would play a highly controversial role in developing *laissez faire* British policy towards the Irish Famine, and a more emollient one in the handling of the Chartist Movement.

Grey in turn reported to Charles Grant, secretary of state for war and the colonies. Elevated to the peerage, he became known as Lord Glenelg. Glenelg was another evangelical and anti-slavery reformer. His father, also Charles Grant, had been impoverished during the previous century because his family had sided with the Scottish Jacobites against the English Crown. Grant senior had set himself the mission of restoring the family fortune and alighted upon a position with the East India Company as the most effective route. Starting out as a cadet in the Company's army and continuing as commercial resident buying goods in India to ship home to Britain, he had ended up a Company director and member of Parliament. Prompted by the deaths of his two daughters from smallpox within nine days of each other in 1776, which he regarded as punishment and warning from God, he had also become a well-known philanthropist, a member of Venn's Clapham Sect and a prominent supporter of William Wilberforce's campaigns to abolish the slave trade and evangelise India. He was a co-founder, with Stephen's father-in-law, Venn, of the CMS. Given the close connections between Stephen, Venn and Glenelg's father, and their common commitment to evangelical and anti-slavery causes, it is no surprise that the Colonial Office of the late 1830s was identified by its critics with a very particular ideological orientation referred to, scathingly, as 'Philanthropic'.

Glenelg himself had been born in Bengal towards the end of his father's rise through the Company ranks. At one point it looked as if he might be appointed governor-general of India, but, via the Board of Trade and then the Board of Control, he ended up at Downing Street in 1838 in charge of the Crown colonies instead. Unlike his Whig assistant, Glenelg was a Tory, in fact the first Tory supporter of Catholic emancipation to hold office. His political career had been one of vicissitudes associated not only with frequent changes of government but also allegations of incompetence, which seem unfair.

Glenelg was appointed to the Colonial Office in 1835 when Melbourne became prime minister. He had already had a tough time of it at the hands of political opponents and the press. He never married, and Thomas Babington Macaulay once described him as having a 'feminine mind'. Allegations vaguely connected with homosexuality swirled around him and powerful people made enemies with him. They included the royal family, after he refused to sanction government expenditure on a new dress for Queen Adelaide. After a Cabinet working dinner in 1833, both Melbourne and Glenelg had fallen asleep and another minister suggested blowing out the candles and leaving them. The cartoonist John Doyle (known as H.B.) got wind of the story and produced a lampoon of the sleeping minister. Glenelg was then nicknamed 'His Somnolency' by the *Times*. When the Canadian uprisings broke out a joke went around that the news 'must have cost him many a sleepless day'.[39]

In his capacity as colonial secretary, though, Glenelg could be decisive and full of moral conviction. A case in point was his brave decision to return territory wrested by British colonists and soldiers from the amaXhosa on the eastern frontier of the Cape Colony in 1834–5. Although we must remember that he was assisted by a government austerity drive, he did so in the face of outraged opposition from the governor and most British settlers, and in the midst of their campaign to portray themselves as innocent victims of amaXhosa aggression. The effect was to grant chiefdoms in what became the Ciskei region a reprieve from colonisation for another ten years. James Stephen's own judgement of Glenelg was that his 'real and only unfitness for public life arises from the strange incompatibility of his temper and principles with the rules of action to which we erect shrines in Downing Street'.[40]

Stephen greatly influenced Glenelg's decision-making in 1838, but his influence was tempered both by the chain of responsibility in the Colonial Office and the occasional tension between his personal convictions and his sense of professional duty. As an evangelical, for instance, Stephen opposed the employment of Indian indentured labourers to supply shortfalls after the emancipation of enslaved people in the West Indies. He believed that these 'idolaters trained from infancy in the barbarous and obscene rites of Hindoo superstition' would contaminate a place where freed slaves were just beginning to emerge into the light of Christian civilisation.[41] But this personal view would have to be set aside in the interests of reconciling emancipation with the continued supply of labour. It was just one of the trade-offs informing imperial policy during 1838. Towards the end of his career, in 1845, Stephen might have joked that he was 'the only Professor in England of my art – the art of understanding everything connected with the Constitution, Charters and Laws of some forty Colonies'. But as a younger man he confessed that 'had I the understanding of Jeremy Bentham himself I should distrust my judgement as to what is really practicable in such remote and anomalous Societies'.[42]

The British Empire in 1838

What of those 'anomalous societies' themselves? In 1838, the Colonial Office administered thirty-two colonies. Britain's military forces had seized eight of these from other European governments between 1792 and 1815 in the French Revolutionary and Napoleonic Wars. The newest colony was South Australia, where the British government claimed sovereignty in 1836 after lobbying from a private company seeking profits from organised colonisation (Map 0.1). The fact that two of the major

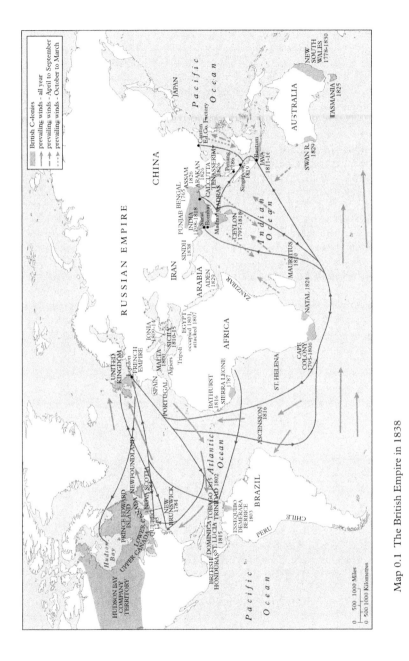

Map 0.1 The British Empire in 1838

investors in the South Australian venture, George Fife Angas, a former trader in mahogany from British Honduras, and Jacob Montefiore, son of a merchant to Jamaica, had both just received compensation for the loss of slaves owned in the Caribbean, indicates how the British Empire was shifting its centre of gravity in the 1830s. Those who had invested in colonial enterprises including slave based production systems across the Atlantic were turning their attention more to the Indian and Pacific Oceans, and from slavery to settlement. During the course of the year that shift would be propelled further, in part by Joseph Montefiore's brother, Jacob Barrow. He had invested some of the family's funds in a trading venture to New Zealand and gave his advice that its islands should be colonised to a House of Lords Committee. At the end of 1838 the committee recommended that a British consul be sent there as a prelude to the declaration of British sovereignty. The New Zealand Company would move quickly to organise the voyage of the first organised emigrants in May 1839.

For much of the eighteenth century, the government department for War and the Colonies had been preoccupied with the administration of colonies across the Atlantic. Although the American colonies had been lost by the 1780s, the sugar-producing colonies of the Caribbean continued to contribute hugely to the exchequer as well as to the fortunes of many British families.[43] The accrual of wealth, both from production in the West Indies and from the slave trade which brought captive labour there from Africa, had enabled substantial investment in Britain's industrial, commercial and agricultural enterprises. The nation's pioneering industrial revolution was indebted in no small part to the role of investments in the slave trade and industrial-scale plantation across the Atlantic.[44] By the 1830s, though, things were changing. The movement for the abolition of the slave trade and then slavery itself, along with the acquisition of new colonies from old enemies, was causing imperial preoccupations to shift.

In Australia there was vast terrain where Britons might escape their apparently overpopulated isles and settle in greater numbers. As South Australia and the Swan River colony in Western Australia received their first shiploads of free settlers, New South Wales and Van Diemen's Land (modern day Tasmania) were transitioning from sites of penal incarceration to lands of opportunity for British emigrants. In Australia's southern coastal fringes, Aboriginal people faced orchestrated invasion.

The First Nations of British North America were more familiar with rival European presences in their midst, and had signed treaties as military allies of either the British or the French. In the 1830s, the remaining British colonies on the Continent continued to compete for settlers with the independent USA to their south, but there was unrest among French speakers in Lower Canada (Quebec) and English-speaking settlers in Upper Canada (Ontario), and continuing anxiety about the balance between rule from London and colonists' self-determination. Threatened by a repeat of the American Revolution among Canadian settlers and by the precedents set by the successful Haitian slave revolution, as well as the French Revolution much closer to home, however, most of the men who governed the empire were still wary of anything smacking of democratic rights.

The Empire was far greater than the sum of these parts administered by the Colonial Office (which the War and Colonial Office was generally called once most of its military functions had been split off in the 1820s). Ireland had been considered an intrinsic part of the United Kingdom of Great Britain and Ireland since 1801, but it was still colonised. Its Catholic population had been freed of discriminatory laws in 1829, but it was not until 1832 that Catholics could be elected members of Parliament. The franchise was based on a property threshold which excluded most Catholic Irish freeholders. The majority of landowners were Anglo-Irish, many of them absentees living in England off the rent paid by Catholic tenants who were also forced pay tithes to the Protestant Church of Ireland.

The 1.5 million square miles to the west and north of the Canadian colonies, across which the Hudson's Bay Company (HBC) conducted its fur trade, was also beyond the Colonial Office's authority in 1838. Although the HBC operated as a de facto government in some respects, its sovereignty was patchy and dependent on continual, delicate diplomacy with independent First Nations.

Since the late seventeenth century the behemoth of the East India Company had succeeded in overcoming competition from rival European outfits to dominate trade from the East Indies. It had also become the rent-raising government of large swathes of India. It was not only the slave traders and plantation owners of the West Indies who had financed Britain's emergence as a pre-eminent global power, but also those who had invested in the Company and reaped the rewards of its transition to rent extractor. In the 1830s some 300 Britons are known to have owned enslaved people in the West Indies and also to have had close personal or financial connections to the East India Company. Its investors included the HBC, which had put £10 000 into its shares in 1732.[45] After 1833, the Company continued to pay dividends to its investors, but these were now drawn almost exclusively from the rent that it returned to Britain as the dominant governing entity in India rather than from commerce.

In 1838 the British Empire included the vast territories in India itself and around the Indian Ocean administered directly by the East India Company, but also India's various princely states. These were governed by hereditary Indian rulers but kept effectively under the Company's indirect rule through the appointment of Company Residents, who advised on internal governance, and the replacement of rulers where the Company considered it necessary. Finally, we might also add to our map of the 1838 empire the protectorates of the Ionian Islands, which were overseen by the Foreign Office to ensure strategic oversight of the Mediterranean, along with the Gibraltar garrison, maintained in case of conflict among the European powers.

This empire had been reconfigured by Britain's failure in the American War of Independence and successes in the French Revolutionary and Napoleonic Wars. The territories seized in the wars against France and its allies had offset the prior loss of the American colonies and helped effect the shift eastwards and southwards in the empire's centre of gravity. They also rendered the population of Britain's colonial possessions much more diverse. By 1838 the British government had acquired responsibility for former French, Dutch and Spanish colonists in the Indian and Atlantic Oceans as well as the Mediterranean, with their different legal systems, languages and labour practices.

By allowing emigrant settlers to expand old colonies and develop new ones in North America and Australia, the government had also been forced to confront the question of the rights and responsibilities of First Nation and Aboriginal populations resisting the invasion of their land. By 1838 the men appointed to oversee the empire from London had been grappling with the problem of how these disparate places and their peoples could be rendered into a *British* Empire for some twenty years.

One innovation, introduced by secretary of state Lord Bathurst, was the requirement for colonial governors to compile 'Blue Books' of statistical information, in standardised formats, through which, periodically, Colonial Office officials could update themselves on colonial developments. That greater quantitative grasp of empire came along with the gathering of new qualitative material too. In 1819 a commission of inquiry was sent to gather information and report on the penal colony of New South Wales. After one day of parliamentary work in 1822, the Colonial Office despatched more commissions to a further eighteen colonies, including all the new acquisitions. The commissioners were men with legal or military backgrounds, largely with prior colonial experience. Men like John Thomas Bigge, a barrister who had studied Spanish law at Madeira before being appointed chief justice of Trinidad, a colony seized from Spain in 1797. Travelling alone, in pairs or in small groups, each assigned to one or more colonies, these men were tasked to interview local people, conduct their own fact-finding journeys and report and recommend on law, governance, economy and labour relations.

The colonial commissioners' work took place after the abolition of the trans-Atlantic slave trade and during the ensuing campaign for the emancipation of those still held in slavery in the Caribbean colonies and in the new colonies of the Cape, Mauritius and Ceylon. They faced an overriding and particularly thorny issue. Much of the economic productivity of the empire relied upon large quantities of enslaved labour working in hot, unhealthy and unpleasant conditions in subtropical regions, producing sugar, tobacco, molasses, cotton, cinnamon, wine and other commodities. As we will see in the next chapter, the question of how a sufficiently pliable and inexpensive, yet freely recruited, labour force would replace an enslaved one was paramount, not just for the commissioners, but also for the East India Company, and for the British imperial economy as a whole.

As well as the rights of a freed labour force, the commissioners were concerned with the rights and freedoms of Britons migrating to the colonies. They were doing so in ever greater numbers after the cessation of the Revolutionary and Napoleonic hostilities, which had tied up a great proportion of British men in the fighting as well as interrupting travel and settlement across the Atlantic and Indian Oceans. In the 1830s, Edward Gibbon Wakefield was publicising a prospectus for more systematic colonial settlement, persuading Britons to think of colonial emigration no longer as a programme of 'shovelling out' paupers and convicts, but as a far more enticing prospect: a once-in-a-lifetime opportunity for all classes to build newly prosperous lives on supposedly empty lands such as those of Australasia. By 1838 a new government department had been created to promote and govern such emigration. Much of the debate about colonialism in Britain at this time was about the extent to which these new communities of Britons abroad should be able to govern themselves, how free they should be to trade in the produce that they garnered, and how they should engage with the Indigenous peoples whose lands they were invading.

Although the commissioners' intention was to gather evidence largely from colonial bureaucrats, they were inundated with unsolicited complaints from enslaved people, 'free blacks', convicts and formerly French, Dutch and Spanish colonial subjects as well as British settlers.[46] The cacophony of voices and interests to which they were exposed in this new, dispersed and diverse empire enlarged the sphere of their enquiries beyond any anticipation. The sheer volume of correspondence required to convey their reflections and recommendations not only forced returning ships lower in the water, and encouraged James Stephen's breakdown, it also necessitated a reformed and enlarged administration in Downing Street.

It was not only the overseas colonies that were in a state of flux as we proceed in Part I to take our first snapshot of the British Empire in 1838. The preceding six years had been among the most tumultuous in British parliamentary history. In reforming British governance, imperial govern-ance too, was reoriented. The passage of the Reform Act in 1832 had marked the culmination of a sustained campaign by workers demanding parliamentary reform and the extension of the franchise, and years of vigorous debate among Tory and Whig elites about the extent of electoral representation necessary to ward off more violent, revolutionary change.[47] 'When reform did come, it was not as a result' solely 'of a long and continuous build-up of pressure', however, but rather a conjunction of developments at home and overseas in 1830 and 1831. These included deepening economic distress and agrarian unrest, parlia-mentarians' fear of contagion from the 1830 revolutions in France and Belgium, and recent precedents for overturning seemingly immutable exclusions, with repeal of the Test and Corporation Acts and Catholic emancipation. Together, these rapid changes 'rendered the idea of a complete reshaping of the previously inviolate House of Commons imaginable and even inevitable' in 1831–2.[48]

The Whig prime minster Earl Grey's declared intention in seeing through the new bill for parliamentary reform was far from radical. It was to do 'as much as is necessary to secure to the people a due influence in that great council in which they are more particularly represented ... guarding and limiting it, at the same time, by a prudent care not to disturb too violently, by any extensive changes, the established principles and practice of the constitution'.[49] The Representation of the People Act was approved by Parliament and received royal assent on 7 June 1832. As a result, more than fifty English boroughs lost all of their seats, some lost half of them, and forty-two new boroughs were granted members of Parliament, some of them two members. The county electorate in England increased by about one-third and a uniform borough franchise was introduced based on ownership or occupation of a dwelling worth £10 in annual rent. The franchise as a whole grew only to a limited extent, from 3.2 per cent to 4.7 per cent of the total population, but more important was the new momentum behind liberal reformist interests.

Although the number of seats controlled by a single landed aristocrat fell from 276 to about 41 by 1840, it was not a simply a matter of owners of land being supplanted by owners of capital. Rather, the new Parliament better represented the 'rapid economic changes in the 1830s that

intensified landowner diversification into non-agricultural ventures'.[50]
The first election after the passing of the Act was held in
December 1832 and it gave Grey's government 483 of 658 seats and
a clearer mandate to support the interests of propertied electors in
finance, commerce and manufacture, alongside those with long-
standing interests in land.[51]

The new Parliament of 1832–3 was greatly energised, its pace of
legislation remarkable, and its reach far more global than is often appreciated. The parliamentary sessions of 1833 and 1834 were frantic, with
'Whigs and Tories rallying together against the threat from below' and
'groping towards the "Victorian Compromise" of moderate
Liberalism'.[52] The almost immediate passing of the Factory Act of
1833 limiting the working hours of children, the New Poor Law of 1834
providing workhouse relief for able bodied men, and the Municipal
Corporations Act of 1835 allowing borough councils to be elected by all
adult male rate payers, are well known to historians of Britain. It was the
weakening of the West India interest through the loss of the pocket
boroughs and the Anti-Slavery Society's support from around 200 of
the new MPs, securing the long-awaited passage of the Antislavery Act,
which is best known to historians of the Crown colonies.[53] At the same
time, as we will see in more detail below, the new Parliament renewed the
East India Company's charter at the price of terminating its commercial
activities. In Liverpool, the East India Association had supported free
trade candidates in 1830 and 1831, who continued to campaign for the
right of all British manufacturers to access Chinese markets in particular,
using whichever merchant companies they liked. Just as the raft of new
anti-slavery MPs in 1832 made the difference in finally passing the
Antislavery bill, these free trade supporters' accession to Parliament
swung the balance against the East India Company's remaining monopoly of East Asian trade.

The year 1833, then, was enormously significant for both Crown- and
company-administered spheres of the British Empire. Liberal reform was
required of Britain's imperial, just as much as it was of its domestic
governance, but in both cases reform was a prophylactic against more
revolutionary change. Within the Crown colonies, the Colonial Office
enforced the act which Stephen had drafted abolishing slavery, and at the
same time the East India Company's charter renewal ended its commercial operations entirely and turned it into the government of British India.
In both cases Britons with existing investments, in slaves in the West and
the Company in the East, were compensated as the empire was restructured. Even if most historians tend to have dealt with either one or the
other of these two major, simultaneous transformations, rather than both

together, there were common drivers and individuals behind them and their long-lasting effects were intricately connected. We will see how in Part I of this book.

Surveying the empire from his desk at the Colonial Office, James Stephen saw this as a time of flux and a time of opportunity. In the last months of 1837, as rebellion broke out in the Canadian colonies, he wrote of his frustration that, so far, the empire had been governed through 'the error of acting upon a policy which is purely occasional and transitional and which does not attempt the anticipation of events'. This, he noted, 'has been the source of our greatest national misfortunes. It lost us the United States. ... It has created slavery in the West Indies and has converted Australia into a den of thieves. To the same cause our Canada troubles may very well be ascribed and if they are now met by expedients which look no further than to the passing days those troubles will infallibly issue in national disaster and disgrace.' Now was the moment to plan ahead for the kind of empire that Providence had intended – one of which Britons could be justifiably proud.

Further Reading

Banton, M., *Administering the Empire, 1801–1968: A Guide to the Records of the Colonial Office in the National Archives of the UK*, Institute of Historical Research, 2015.

Bayly, C., *Imperial Meridian: The British Empire and the World 1780–1830*, Routledge, 1989.

Bowen, H. V., *The Business of Empire: The East India Company and Imperial Britain, 1756–1833*, Cambridge University Press, 2009.

Cell, J., *British Colonial Administration in the Mid-Nineteenth Century*, Yale University Press, 1970.

Darwin, J., *The Empire Project: The Rise and Fall of the British World System, 1830–1970*, Cambridge University Press, 2011.

Hall, C., K. McClelland, N. Draper, K. Donington and R. Lang, *Legacies of British Slave-ownership: Colonial Slavery and the Formation of Victorian Britain*, Cambridge University Press, 2014.

Laidlaw, Z., *Colonial Connections 1815–45: Patronage, the Information Revolution and Colonial Government*, Manchester University Press, 2005.

Part I

1838: The Year of Freedom

1   Setting the Scene for Emancipation

James Stephen spent much of his time in late 1837 preparing for a fundamental change in the constitution of the British Empire. Ever since the late seventeenth century, the production of lucrative tropical commodities, especially sugar, had been reliant on an enslaved workforce. Most, but not all, of Britain's slaves were located on Caribbean plantations where these commodities were produced. Parliament had ended chattel slavery in 1834, implementing the act that Stephen himself had drafted in 1833. But the act deferred the freedom of former slaves from their owners' control by 'apprenticing' them for at least a further four years. Now the year of emancipation was dawning. It was up to Stephen's Colonial Office to plan and manage some 800 000 formerly enslaved British subjects' transition to freedom.

Of all the kinds of freedom Britons believed they offered the colonised world, including the freedoms for settlers and traders that we will explore in the succeeding chapters, national pride would cohere most around freedom from slavery. In this and the next chapter, we will follow Stephen and his interlocutors around the empire as they sought to effect it. Colonial Office staff became increasingly aware during the course of the year that emancipation was a process that did far more than turn Caribbean slaves into free men, women and children. Beyond the chattel slavery of the West Indies plantations, a wide range of forced labour practices shaded into one another across the British Empire. Carrying into effect Parliament's mandate to free enslaved labour would be far more complex than it seemed. It would entail the consideration of bonded, Creole, indentured and convicted labourers in India, Ceylon, Southern and West Africa, Mauritius and Australia. During the course of the year, the Colonial Office had to decide who exactly was to be freed, and from what.

Slavery, Compensation and Apprenticeship, circa 1800–1838

In order to understand the magnitude of the transformation that the British Empire was about to undergo, we have first to acknowledge just how structurally significant slavery had been. Despite the groundbreaking work of the black historian and first prime minister of Trinidad and Tobago, Eric Williams, it is only recently that most British historians have appreciated how much of Britain's economy and society were invested in slavery overseas. Between 1600 and 1807 British registered ships embarked more than 3 million purchased captives on the west coast of Africa and disembarked around 2.5 million in the Caribbean and Americas. The remainder died on the horrendous two-to three-month 'middle passage' between continents.[1] The sheer scale of the Portuguese, British, Spanish, French, Dutch and American trade in African captives, amounting in all to some 12 million people by the late nineteenth century, rendered modern colonial slavery quite different from any historical antecedent. So too did the explicit linking of slavery to 'race' and the industrial-scale application of enslaved people's labour on plantations in the Americas. By the early nineteenth century the British had become the foremost exponents of this profitable modern slavery system.

British manufacturers and workers, shipping agents, rope and sail makers, insurance companies, banks, sailors, traders, merchants, retailers and consumers all had a stake in the eighteenth-century transatlantic slave trade. The economies of Liverpool, Bristol and London in particular were oriented around it. British manufactures were exchanged for captives bought from African intermediaries, whose polities came to specialise in meeting the European demand for captive labour by slave raiding in West Africa. The people captured were then shipped to the Caribbean and American colonies, and the commodities that they produced there were taken back for sale in Britain. Profits were made at each apex of this transatlantic trade triangle. British consumers used the sugar imported through this western trade circuit to sweeten the tea that was brought in through the East India Company's complementary eastern trade circuit, which linked opium and cotton grown in British India to tea purchased in China. We will come back to this eastern circuit in Chapter 5.

Many, perhaps most, Britons were direct or indirect beneficiaries of the transatlantic slave trade, but others had invested in slave ownership itself. One tends to imagine the typical slave owner as the occupant of a plantation mansion, issuing forth to instruct the paid overseers who drove his human 'assets' and occasionally inspecting his slave quarters personally. But there were plenty of absentee owners in Britain, a large proportion of whom would never see the people they owned. University College London's Legacies of British Slave Ownership project, led by Catherine Hall, has been tracking these owners at the point of slavery's demise in the 1830s. 'We know that in addition to the many absentee planters, bankers and financiers directly concerned with the business of sugar and slavery, there were many other types of [slave owners]: clergymen, for example, or the widows and single women, some of whom had been left property in the enslaved in trust. Slave ownership was spread across the British Isles, by no means confined to the old slaving ports, and included men and women of varied ages, ranging from the aristocracy and gentry to sections of the middle classes.'[2]

During the late eighteenth century, British evangelical Christian reformers and especially Quakers, had begun more vocally to question the morality of slavery. As their leading representative in Parliament, William Wilberforce faced seemingly insurmountable opposition. As soon as criticism of the system's brutality began to be aired consistently, those invested in it, known as the West India interest, mobilised in the House of Commons and the press. Obliged for the first time explicitly to defend and rationalise the capture and enslavement of other human beings, they popularised a coherent narrative of irredeemable racial difference between enslaved Africans and the white majority of owners. Edward Long, the absentee Jamaican slave owner and author of the popular *History of Jamaica*, was just one of the more influential planters arguing that Africans were more like animals than humans. In pro-slavery representations, enslaved people had primitive instincts with a disposition to irrational violence. As Africans, they were unable to work for their own improvement unless compelled. Granting them their freedom would be dangerous, both for the white people who had made the Caribbean and other colonies productive and for enslaved people themselves. In a free society, planters and their allies claimed, slaves of African descent would have only their primitive passions to guide them.

Nevertheless, anti-slavery activists successfully engendered sympathy for enslaved people in Britain. They did so with their own counter-narrative. In prints, pamphlets, speeches, petitions and sermons, missionaries, Quakers and their evangelical reformist allies vilified planters as inhumane and un-British. Their representations of enslaved people were also stereotypes. Africans and their descendants in the Caribbean were portrayed as compliant, inoffensive, almost infantile figures, just waiting to be led to the light of civilisation and Christianity by enlightened British benefactors. During the political ferment of the late eighteenth century, with fears aroused by the American and French Revolutions, and notably by the successful slave rebellion in Haiti and revolts in the British colonies too, such an image reassuringly down-played enslaved people's revolutionary potential. After much resistance from the West India interest in Parliament as well as competing appeals to the public, the transatlantic trade in slaves was finally abolished by the British government from 1807.

The focus of anti-slavery campaigners had since turned to abolition of the institution itself. This second anti-slavery campaign would continue for nearly thirty years and occupy much of James Stephen's attention as a young man in his twenties and early thirties, while he worked his way up the hierarchy of the Colonial Office. The campaign was bolstered by long term insecurities over the future profitability of the slave plantations once the trade was illegal, and by the resistance and activism of enslaved people themselves. When they rebelled in Barbados in 1816, Demerara in 1823 and especially Jamaica in 1831–2, enslaved people increased the costs of maintaining their subjection and provided more ammunition for anti-slavery activists, who pointed to the extreme violence that colonial gov-ernments were now obliged to use to maintain the institution. Given the ongoing strength of the West India interest in Britain and the persistence of slavery in rival European empires, however, it would take considerable compromise for Parliament to approve the end of British slavery.

When that approval was won with Stephen's Slavery Abolition Act of 1833, it was not the result solely of the strength of anti-slavery lobbying. The changes within Parliament brought about by the 1829 Catholic Emancipation Act and the 1832 Reform Act had altered the balance of political power. The West India interest was weakened by the loss of pocket boroughs, while the ranks of anti-slavery MPs, led by Wilberforce's successor, Thomas Fowell Buxton, were reinforced. MPs representing the East India Company investors were also mounting growing objections to trade preferences for Caribbean sugar over that grown in India. With a large majority in the newly convened Parliament of 1833, abolitionists finally secured support for the bill for which Wilberforce and then Buxton had fought so hard.

The abolition of slavery was not solely a Caribbean issue, however. The capture of new colonies during the Revolutionary and Napoleonic Wars meant that the British were now responsible for those held in slavery by the French, Dutch and Spanish, both in and beyond the Caribbean. Enslaved people from South and Southeast Asia and eastern Africa undertook the most arduous and lowest-status jobs in the recently acquired Cape Colony, Ceylon and Mauritius. India and Ceylon also had indigenous forms of slavery which the Company and Colonial Office respectively now administered. James Stephen would have the task of disentangling various kinds of enforced servitude in many, disparate places, to see whether they fitted with the primary emancipation project under way in the Caribbean.

When Stephen drafted the 1833 anti-slavery bill, he knew that a price would have to be paid for Parliament's assent, given how divisive the debates had been. That price was compensation, not for the formerly enslaved but for their owners. They would be paid for the confiscation of their property. The rate, set by commissioners in London, would vary according to the colony and the estimated productivity of each enslaved person. Enslaved people were worth the most in Honduras, where owners were paid £195 per slave, and least in Bahamas, were they were worth only £35. The amount required in total, for some 800 000 enslaved people, was vast. At £20 million, it equated to some 40 per cent of Treasury revenue – a sum equivalent to that which bailed out the UK banks during the 2008 financial crisis. Rather than increasing taxation to pay off the slave owners, the Treasury raised a loan through the issue of new government securities. In 1835 the new chancellor, Thomas Spring Rice, invited potential bidders for the contract to raise it. Baring Brothers & Co., Reid, Irving & Co. and Ricardo, Maubert and Melville all expressed interest but then withdrew from competition, leaving a syndicate led by Nathan Mayer Rothschild and Moses Montefiore (Jacob's cousin) as the sole bidder. Parliament agreed to a loan of £15 million for the Caribbean slave owners, with a further £5 million raised later for those in the Cape Colony and Mauritius. John Finlayson, the actuary of the national debt, expressed his gratitude to Rothschild for assisting the government 'on terms the very lowest that were consistent with his own [financial] safety'.[3] The British government finished paying off this loan only in 2015.

The abolition first of the slave trade in 1807 and then of slavery itself in the 1830s was undoubtedly a significant transition in world affairs. Patriotic British historians have celebrated that this was the first time an empire had voluntarily checked its own, still by and large profitable, trade in, and ownership of, enslaved people. It was the first time that anti-slavery became a popular moral and political cause capable of swaying governments and allowing women's public, political mobilisation. Some have claimed it as the first modern humanitarian movement, since it engendered sympathy for distant strangers and compelled ameliorative action on their behalf. Most would agree that Westminster Abbey is a suitable location for the commemoration of William Wilberforce, who campaigned tirelessly to bring the legislation about in Parliament until Buxton took over. Nevertheless, Stephen had to tread carefully as he framed the necessary legislation, passed by the House of Lords a month after Wilberforce's death.

Stephen may have rushed its drafting over a weekend, but the 1833 act was still a complex piece of legislation. It was the result of his decades of familiarity with the diverse legal codes of the various slaveholding colonies. It abolished the institution of slavery with effect on 1 August 1834 throughout the British Empire, with the exceptions of Ceylon and St Helena and the territories governed by the East India Company. Children below the age of six were freed from their owners' control immediately. On the advice of Evan John Murray MacGregor, a Scottish clan chief and the governor of Antigua, full emancipation for all came into immediate effect there and in Bermuda. Elsewhere, those freed from chattel slavery in 1834 were not allowed to leave their owners' estates. They remained bound to continue working for their employers, no longer as their property but as 'apprentices', for at least a further four years. If they abandoned their work or refused to comply with employers' instructions during this period, they would be punished by magistrates who were supposed to be independent of the employers. Three-quarters of the formerly enslaved workers' unpaid time was to be spent labouring for their former owners in return for food and clothing, with the remainder of their time their own. Stephen's under-secretary of state, George Grey, described apprenticeship as 'an intermediate system of modified coercion'.[4] If the former slaves were considered domestic labour working in households, they were to be freed from their apprenticeships and allowed to leave their employers on 1 August 1838. If they were classed as field labourers, however, their final emancipation would be delayed a further two years to 1 August 1840.

Stephen set this period of apprenticeship alongside the payment of compensation to owners as the inducement necessary to ensure the West India interest's compliance. He justified it with the belief that people held for much or all of their lives as chattel would require a period of instruction before they could become self-sufficient. A four- or six-year apprenticeship period would help prepare them for newfound responsibility. In practice, the measure was seen by most in the affected colonies as delaying transition on behalf of colonial elites, who feared the drastic repercussions of enslaved people abandoning the plantations en masse and seeking revenge on 1 August 1834.

Planter fears were especially acute in Jamaica, where, just two years before, around 60 000 of the 300 000 enslaved people on the island had sustained an eleven-day rebellion known as the Baptist War, killing fourteen white people. Five hundred enslaved people had been killed in the suppression of the revolt and judicial executions that followed. With the exception of MacGregor, Caribbean governors appreciated a four-year apprenticeship period in which to adopt measures for the prevention of such instability. In the longer term, plantation managers could use this period to secure future labour supplies. The slave system had enabled the scattering of families as husbands, wives and children were sold off to different owners. It was reasonable to expect that, once freed from their estates, many former slaves would prioritise familial reunion. In Jamaica, Maroon communities of escaped slaves had long subsisted independently in the mountainous central highlands, and planters correctly foresaw that the end of apprenticeship would bring desertion of their workforce as families sought smallholdings, free of planter control, among them. It might well take six years to find substitute labour for the sugar fields, even if domestic labour could be found within four.

In late 1837 Stephen was preparing the Colonial Office to manage the staggered end of apprenticeships. In August of the following year the first tranche of 'domestic' apprentices would be released and encouraged to retain employment in the homes of former owners-cum-employers. This would have to be handled alongside preparations for the final emancipation of all remaining former slaves in the Caribbean, Mauritius and the Cape Colony in 1840. As Stephen set about the task at the beginning of 1838, his imperative as an evangelical reformer was finding opportunities for freed slaves to join the ranks of a reformed, post-slaveholding, Christian society, ideally on the same terms as Britain's colonists. His aim as imperial administrator, however, was to oversee the empire's transition to free labour in as orderly a fashion as possible, with minimal disruption to established British interests and the imperial economy. Much of his time in this and the following years was devoted to managing the tensions between these aims.

Priorities for Emancipation

In the early months of 1838 Stephen, guided by Grey and Glenelg, developed three immediate objectives for emancipation. Each of them would have longer term outcomes for the nature of the British Empire. The first, and the focus of this chapter, was to distinguish exactly who was to be freed and from what kind of relationship. This was more complicated than it seemed. The fact that the British Parliament had agreed to emancipate slaves did not mean that it had embarked on a crusade against all kinds of coerced labour. Where slavery ended and free labour began was a moot point in a number of colonies. The second objective, examined in the next chapter, was to manage the inevitable trade-offs between morality, security and economy as the empire transitioned towards free labour. These trade-offs took on a different appearance in each colony.

The final objective was more forward-looking and it runs through both this and the next chapter. It was ultimately up to the Colonial Office to address the likelihood of severe shortages of labour on colonial plantations once the enslaved workforce was freed. Such shortages could threaten not only the individual interests of the plantation owners and investors, but the economy of Britain and the empire at large. The solution was already apparent. It would entail the redistribution of people across the empire, so as to match the supply of labour with demand. This would require intervening in debates about Britain's own population and forging new connections and flows between the populations of its colonies. Fulfilling this third objective imprinted upon the world a large-scale demographic shift, the legacies of which continue to shape national and international politics.

Investigating the Colonial Office's pursuit of these three objectives takes us around the early nineteenth-century empire, from Britain to North America, the Caribbean and the Mediterranean, to the Cape, Mauritius, Ceylon and India, to West Africa and Australia. It is as good a way as any to develop greater detail in our first snapshot of the British Empire, everywhere and all at once, in 1838.

The Colonial Office's instruction from Parliament seemed reasonably clear: bring an end to slavery and the apprenticeship system which had succeeded it. But during the course of the year, Stephen and his colleagues became entangled in the complexities of distinguishing slavery from other coercive labour relationships. Britain itself still had apprenticeship regulations and legal codes weighted heavily in favour of masters over servants and enforced by punitive magistrates. 'Free' labour, especially in agricultural regions was still protesting its subjugation to criminal punishment and incarceration, rather than just the withholding of wages, when employers found workers deficient. Such issues had recently fuelled the Swing Revolts of rural southern and eastern England. Both pro- and anti-slavery activists had highlighted perceived similarities between the conditions of enslaved and then apprenticed people in the Caribbean and those of the poorest workers in Britain and Ireland. Defenders of Caribbean slavery used the analogy to assert that charity should begin at home rather than on overseas plantations, while abolitionists drew attention to dire local working conditions as part of a broader reformist agenda.

Across the empire overseas there were many more varieties of forced labour. Transported British convicts were made to work without pay, either for the government or for respectable settlers in the Australian colonies. Indian, Ceylonese, Mauritian, Aboriginal, Khoisan and other convicts were serving sentences by labouring either within their own colonies or in exile in other parts of the empire. Even the African captives liberated from other nations' slave ships by the Royal Navy were assigned as unpaid apprentices, whether they liked it or not, for colonists in the Caribbean, Sierra Leone and St Helena. That was if they were not forcibly recruited into the West India or West Africa Regiments. As we will see, in late 1837, the East India Company's attention was drawn to the slave like conditions of its Indian subjects, recruited on contracts of labour indenture for Mauritius and the Caribbean. Of much greater numerical significance were those subjected to indigenous forms of slavery under Company rule in India itself. The British Empire of 1838 was sustained by many shades of labour relation in between Adam Smith's alternatives of wages and the whip.

The Act of 1833 had indicated that, within this varied palette of employer subjection, the chattel slaves of the Caribbean were the primary target of British benevolence. Those originally transported from West Africa to the West Indies and their descendants had been the focal point for the preceding decades of anti-slavery campaigning. These were the people to whom the British public and its government acknowledged a moral debt. They were represented by the propaganda image of the kneeling African man in chains pleading 'Am I not a man and a brother', reproduced on countless pamphlets, embroideries, posters, medallions and even Wedgewood China (Figure 1.1). In early 1838, James Stephen received an address that appeared to come from precisely this kind of idealised subject for emancipation. It was from apprentices in the Bahamas who wished to exclaim their delight at Queen Victoria's coronation. Glenelg replied on behalf of the monarch, assuring them that there 'is no class of persons whose welfare is more dear to Her Majesty … than those who during the reign of her late revered predecessor were raised … from the condition of slaves to free subjects of the British Crown'.[5] These were the kind of people – directly traded in and then owned by Britons, abused by British planters and now grateful and loyal members of British colonial society – whom Britons at home most wanted freed. It was in respect of them that Stephen's instructions were clearest.

The waters were muddied, however, by the inclusion in the 1833 Abolition Act of some further variants of slavery, and the exclusion of others, in different parts of the empire. The 1833 act also promised freedom to enslaved people in Mauritius and the Cape Colony, who had been traded and owned not by Britons, but by French and Dutch colonists. It explicitly excluded enslaved people in St Helena, India and Ceylon. We will consider the exclusions first.

India and Ceylon

On the mid South Atlantic island of St Helena, where Napoleon had died in exile in 1821, there were about 1200 slaves descended from captives

"AM I NOT A MAN AND A BROTHER ?"

Figure 1.1 'Am I not a man and a brother?' From *The Family Friend* published by S. W. Partridge & Co., London, 1875. An iconic anti-slavery illustration based upon the medallion produced by Josiah Wedgwood in 1787 as an important contribution to the movement for the Abolition of Slavery. Getty Images.

who had been brought initially from Africa and then from the East India Company's trade circuits in South-East Asia. They were being gradually emancipated by the Company administration even before the island was handed over to the Colonial Office in 1833, and so the island's inclusion in the act was seen as redundant. The most significant single omission from the abolition act was India. Long before the East India Company became the pre-eminent authority in the subcontinent, African, Southeast Asian and Indian people had been trafficked across the Indian Ocean. By the 1830s, an illegal trade supplied African chattel slaves to wealthy Indian families, but their households also contained Indian women and children who had been kidnapped or sold by destitute family members. People continued to be sold openly at slave markets in the Company supervised princely states. Beyond these practices, which the British might well identify as akin to Caribbean chattel slavery, there was a complex spectrum of labour bondage in the Indian countryside. Whole communities were tied hereditarily to the owner of the land they worked, their inferior status reinforced by caste distinctions. Landowners might not have bought and sold these peasants, but they inflicted physical punishment and limited their movement. Other Indians were obliged to serve those to whom they were indebted. Data on such practices are imprecise, but it has been estimated that between 1 million and 16 million in a population of more than 100 million people lived in some such kind of servitude under the Company's administration.

Proposals to use Company influence against slavery had been aired from the very beginning of the anti-slavery campaign in Britain and the Caribbean. Lord Cornwallis, the governor-general, had considered and then decided against abolition throughout the Company's dominions in 1789. The Company was already acting to stamp out the maritime trade in slaves into its territories but still benefitted from the rent extracted from slave owners in India itself. However, the British public's attitude to Indian slavery was more ambivalent than that towards Caribbean plantation slavery. In these early days of humanitarian campaigning it was not so much a case of compassion fatigue as compassion concentration.

In the 1790s and again in the 1820s, the British anti-slavery campaign had organised a boycott of slave-grown sugar in order to render Caribbean slavery unprofitable. Gleefully, the importers of East Indies sugar promoted it as the consumer's ethical alternative. Smith and Leaper of Bishopgate Street advertised 'East India Sugar made by Free People'. The Peckham Ladies' African and Anti-Slavery Association published *Reasons for Using East India Sugar* in 1828, claiming that buying Indian sugar undermined slavery in 'the safest, most easy, and effectual manner in which it can be done'. The West India interest furiously contested these claims, pointing out that the sugar imported from Company territories was itself grown by slaves. It was not just pro-slavery interests who identified abolitionist inconsistency. After reading the popular Indian travel narrative of Frances Buchanan, the radical writer William Cobbett complained that 'East India sugar is raised by slaves; by slaves who are property, by slaves who are bought and sold, by slaves who are mortgaged, by slaves who are let out like cattle'.[6]

In the same year that Stephen drew up the 1833 act, the East India Company's charter was up for renewal and revision. As we have seen, the president of the Board of Control at the time was none other than Charles Grant, later Lord Glenelg: Stephen's colonial secretary as emancipation dawned in 1838. As one might expect, the abolitionist Glenelg had raised the issue of slavery when discussing the terms of charter renewal. The Government of India Act that ensued placed Indian government more firmly into the hands of the governor-general in Bengal, stripped the Company of its commercial functions and of its monopoly on trade with China, and transferred the governance of St Helena to the Crown, but one thing it did not do was insist on abolishing slavery in Company territories. As the act for abolishing slavery in the Caribbean, Mauritius and the Cape was passed, all that the Company was enjoined to do was 'adopt measures to mitigate the state of slavery' at some point over its next twenty-year charter renewal period. The Company's directors had convinced Glenelg that the governance of India itself would be jeopardised if they pressed on with abolition against the wishes of slaveholding Indian elites.

As former slaves elsewhere in the empire were being emancipated from apprenticeship in 1838, Lushington and Jenkins at East India House and Hobhouse at the Board of Control were faced once again with the need to justify leaving Indian slavery intact. Although the British public's attention was still focused almost exclusively on the Caribbean, there were some dissenting voices still arguing for abolition in India, regardless of how impractical it may seem. Among them were missionaries in Travancore, backed by the London Missionary Society. They reported that there was no domestic slavery in the region since higher castes would consider themselves defiled by the proximity of slaves. Rather, 'the slaves were condemned to remain in the rice fields where they carried out the most arduous tasks, and when not required for labour they were left to starvation or to resort to theft'. One of the missionaries wrote home that 'those who reach maturity are doomed to work like beasts of burden, to live in wretched hovels, ... and to be treated as outcastes by their fellow-creatures. ... By few are they comforted, pitied or relieved; none seek to remove their distresses, and no man cares for their souls.'[7] William Adam, a former missionary who had worked with Ram Mohan Roy on the Bengali translation of the New Testament and now lived in the USA, was a particularly vocal enemy of British hypocrisy on the issue of slavery. In 1840 he would complain to Thomas Fowell Buxton that

The people of England have just paid twenty million sterling to emancipate eight hundred thousand slaves in the British West Indies; and while they are congratulating themselves that now at length every British subject is a free man, and insultingly reproaching republican America with her slavery, they are to be told that their congratulations are premature; that their reproaches may be retorted; that there are probably 800,000 slaves more, British subjects, in the East Indies.[8]

For all Adam's zeal though, as Stephen pinned down questions of who was actually to be freed, where and when, abolitionist campaigners' concern over Indian slaves receded once again.

Zachary Macaulay (the historian Thomas Babington's father) spoke for many when distinguishing between West and East Indian slaves' entitle-ment to freedom. As a teenager Macaulay had managed the books on a Jamaican sugar plantation, evincing little sympathy for its enslaved workforce. He developed evangelical sympathies after his return to Britain, where he befriended William Wilberforce. Once he became part of the inner circle of British abolitionists, Macaulay's horizons were further broadened when he visited the great abolitionist colonial experi-ment of Sierra Leone. He was appointed governor of this colony for emancipated slaves in 1794, seven years after it had first attracted 400 free black people from England. They had been joined subsequently by Jamaican Maroons and over a thousand African Americans, who had sided with the British in the American Revolutionary War and been settled initially in Nova Scotia.[9]

Macaulay had been a leading figure in the campaign to abolish the trans-Atlantic slave trade in 1807. Yet, in the 1820s he helped allay concern for the fate of India's slaves. Pointing out that Cobbett and others' information on slavery in India had been swayed by Buchanan's travel narrative, Macaulay insisted that Buchanan had travelled only in Mysore, from where little sugar was grown and none exported. The relative cheapness of Indian sugar compared to Jamaican could be attrib-uted, he argued, to better soils and the use of ploughs rather than hoes, not to an equally enslaved workforce. As emancipation became a practical project to be managed from London, Macaulay's thinking epitomised its concentration on western slavery and Britons' reluctance to extend it eastwards. 'There is a difference', he maintained, 'between the slavery of the East and West, that of the latter we ourselves are the sole authors, and are chargeable, therefore, with its whole guilt and turpitude. In the East whatever slavery exists we found there; we did not create it ourselves.'[10]

The Company was thus relieved again in 1838 from the necessity to intervene with any great urgency. Indian slave owners were to be left to their own devices. Indeed, up to late 1837 and again in the early 1840s, their bonded labour force was considered available for indentured service in other colonies as the 'free labour' alternative to enslaved labour. Indian slave owners would only lose their right to control bonded labourers

during the following decade and the East India Company would crimin-
alise slave holding only in 1862.

James Stephen was more worried about slavery in the Crown colony of
Ceylon, which, like St Helena and India, was also exempt from the 1833
act. The British had captured the island from the Dutch during the
Revolutionary War but unified it in 1818 with the defeat and incorporation of the kingdom of Kandy in the central highlands. The Dutch East
India Company had created an enslaved population in the Maritime
Provinces along the coastal belt by trading captives from South India
and what are now Malaysia and Indonesia to work tea, rubber, cinnamon
and sugar plantations. During the 1820s, British measures for the amelioration of slavery entailed the compulsory registration of these slaves. If
their owners did not register them, the penalty was their automatic
manumission. New born children were freed immediately, with
a modest payment of compensation to their would-be owners and
a small gift of cash and cloth from the colonial government to their
parents, to help launch them into the world as free subjects.

Ceylon was exempted from the 1833 act because this gradual process of
emancipation was already under way. In late 1837 the island's governor,
a former Colonial Office under-secretary and theorist of emigration,
Robert Wilmot-Horton, to whom we will return below, reassured
Stephen that the slavery system maintained by the Dutch had almost
disappeared.[11] At the same time he was ensuring that indentured Indian
immigrants were replacing their labour. More problematic was the indigenous system of slavery still practised in Kandy.

As in India, Ceylon's coercive labour relations had foundations long
predating British rule. The pattern was complex, with 'one servile status
overlapping into another'. Occupation-based caste distinctions further
complicated any neat distinction between slave and free. The Kandyan
kingdom's law code, for instance, preserved the caste dignity of those who
fell into slavery through destitution, prohibiting slaves being owned by
someone of inferior caste to themselves. A British commission reported in
1829 that 'Cruelty to a slave is scarcely known, and in general they are
treated more as adopted dependants of the family than as menials'.[12]
However, there were also Sinhalese-owned Tamil slaves labouring in the
hot and dry north of the island, whose ethnic difference marked them out
for a status more akin to the Caribbean chattel slaves of the abolitionist
imagination.

As in India, British governors approached Kandyan slavery cautiously.
Wilmot-Horton had appealed to the Kandyan chiefs to free their slaves
gradually in January 1832, suggesting that they adopt the system of
registration used in the Maritime Provinces. But the Kandyan aristocracy

proved uncompliant. They gave Wilmot-Horton a counter-proposal. They would free their slaves in sixty years' time, provided they received the same compensation that British slave owners were getting. When Wilmot-Horton responded by abolishing the traditional system of land tenure, Sinhalese aristocrats rebelled and Wilmot-Horton postponed his attempt at abolition.

As Stephen and Glenelg were trying to manage the imminent consequences of emancipation elsewhere, Wilmot-Horton was assuring them that he had made another cautious start in reconciling the Kandyan elite with abolition, passing a bill to develop an accurate slave register for the colony as a whole. What he did not tell them was that the bill was introduced without any sanction for a failure to register. But then Wilmot-Horton was hardly an ardent opponent of Kandyan slavery. He remarked, 'Slavery in Ceylon is the mildest possible condition of Slavery – and the Kandyan Slaves are not valued in consideration of the labour executed by them, but in some measure as appendages of rank, and for the performance of certain services which, being considered a badge of Slavery, cannot be obtained for hire'. Not only was local slavery 'mild', it was also amenable to decay without the need for vigorous intervention: 'it is highly probable that the prejudices ... will gradually disappear, when the objection to emancipation will cease, and Slaves become as they now are in the Maritime Provinces, nearly valueless. ... Slaves being of no value, the whole system ... will become obsolete and will have ceased'.[13] There was no need, then, for the Colonial Office to worry any further about emancipation in Ceylon. It would take care of itself. Glenelg would continue to push Wilmot-Horton's successor to abolish Kandyan slavery, but during the year of transition in 1838, Stephen accepted Wilmot-Horton's assurances with some relief. It would not be until 1844 that the government in Ceylon enforced the emancipation of unregistered slaves.

For varying reasons, then, enslaved people in St Helena, India and Ceylon had all been excluded from the liberation offered by the 1833 Abolition Act. While the Act was focused mainly on the Caribbean, however, it did include two other, relatively new, British colonies: the Cape Colony at the southern tip of Africa, and Mauritius in the Indian Ocean. Both had variants of slavery that were different in many respects from the West Indies system that conditioned the abolitionist imagination.

The Cape Colony and Mauritius

Stephen was relatively unconcerned about the process of emancipation in the Cape Colony. This was Britain's imperial crossroads, half way between Europe and the East India Company's Indian Ocean trade circuit. Cape Town had been established by the Dutch East India Company in 1652 as a supply and recuperation depot for its Southeast Asian trading fleets. It was now a port of call for British ships plying between Britain and India, and for those on the way to and from the Australian colonies. After initially capturing the port during the French Revolutionary War and returning it briefly to the Dutch Batavian Republic, Britain had seized the colony for a second time in 1806, to restrict Napoleon's maritime capacity. By this time colonists initially recruited by the Dutch East India Company, mainly from the European Low Countries, had already spread some 600 miles to the east and north of Cape Town, taking land from San hunter gatherers and Khoikhoi pastoralists known collectively as Khoisan and coercing them into providing labour. Their expansion to the east had stalled along a frontier contested with more densely settled, cattle-keeping, Xhosa chiefdoms.

In 1819, the Colonial Office had developed a subsidised emigration scheme to dupe 4000 British settlers into shoring up this war-torn eastern border zone. The governor, Lord Somerset, had called for settlers as a kind of frontier militia, but the Colonial Office had sponsored a scheme instead for Britons who had fallen on hard times, those who wanted to improve their station in life, and those who wished to maintain a declining status at home in a new land of opportunity. The office had conveniently forgotten to mention the governor's own incentive for welcoming these emigrants. Once located in territory from which amaXhosa had just been forcibly expelled, the poorer among them had quickly disregarded their contracts of indenture to wealthier emigrants and claimed land in their own right. The ensuing labour shortages were initially mitigated by laws inherited from the Dutch East India Company administration. These ensured that the Khoisan would be arrested if they did not work for white farmers. When convicted, their sentence was convict labour, for white farmers. To Stephen's relief, this particular settler privilege had been abolished by the time of the 1833 Abolition Act. In 1828, a new governor, the Anglo-Irish liberal, Richard Bourke, had passed Ordinance 50, freeing the Khoisan.

Bourke was born into the gentry in Dublin. He had served in the wars against France and, in 1799, was wounded with a shot through the jaw in the Netherlands. In the campaign against Napoleon he had commanded Wellesley's Spanish spy ring. After his military service Bourke had tried retiring as a gentleman farmer in Limerick, but with inadequate income to support his family on half pay, he sought out a colonial governorship. His previous service persuaded the Colonial Office that he was the right man to be sent to the Cape Colony's unstable eastern frontier as lieutenant governor in 1826. When Somerset, resigned, Bourke assumed control of the whole colony. He quickly gained a reputation as a reformer, starting off by freeing the local press of Somerset's restrictions. During a campaign led by the London Missionary Society director John Phillp, Bourke's Ordinance 50 freeing the Khoisan, pre-empted parliamentary action. Referred to in Britain as the 'Magna Carta of the Hottentots', it abolished the regulations tying Khoisan to colonial 'masters' and enabled them at least an element of choice among colonial employers on their former lands. A frequent interlocutor with Stephen and Glenelg, we will meet Richard Bourke again in the next chapter, when we come across him in 1838 in his next posting, New South Wales.

The enslaved people targeted by the 1833 Abolition Act in the Cape, then, were not the Khoisan whom Bourke had already liberated. The act applied instead to some 30 000 people owned as chattel slaves, mainly in the western half of the colony. The Indigenous Khoisan could never legally be owned outright, but the Dutch East India Company had been trading in these chattel slaves for the Cape's primarily Dutch-speaking colonists from what is now Malaysia and Indonesia since the late seventeenth century. They worked mainly in wheat and wine production. Their emancipation under the 1833 act would ultimately incite the mass emigration of Afrikaner colonists in the 'Great Trek', which would bring its own problems for the Colonial Office, but in early 1838 Stephen saw the process of ending their apprenticeship itself as relatively unproblematic, not least because of the promise of £3 million to the colony's slave owners.

In Mauritius too, enslaved people were included in the freedom offered by the 1833 act. Here, Stephen foresaw greater difficulty. French governments and settlers in the 'Isle de France' had traded in slaves from Africa and Madagascar long before the British seized the colony in 1810. These people, referred to as 'Creole', worked on the island's sugar plantations and now composed two-thirds of its population. The 1833 act abolished slavery in Mauritius with effect six months after its demise in the Caribbean, on 1 February 1835. Two million of the total £20 million raised by the British government as compensation to slave owners went to the island, in part intended to appease the French-speaking colonists, around a fifth of them free people of colour. Some of these were still threatening rebellion against continued British occupation. In early 1835 the formerly enslaved Creole workforce was apprenticed for three years to former owners. At the beginning of 1838, both James Stephen and the governor knew that they would face particular difficulty when these Creoles entered the island's free labour market later in the year.

From 1825, the Colonial Office had encouraged sugar production in Mauritius by granting tariff equality on the same favourable terms as West Indian sugar. By 1830, Mauritian acreage under sugar cane had doubled and slave prices had quadrupled. Even before they received their compensation money, slave owners were organising the recruitment of Indian migrant labourers on contracts of indenture, as the cheaper alternative. Over the last five years, the number of Indians brought to the island under indenture had increased from 8600 to 19 700 per annum. The trouble for the Creole apprentices was that even before they were freed, these Indian migrants had already undermined their position in the local labour market. Many Mauritian apprentices were being 'literally pushed off estates' to make way for the guaranteed, low-wage Indian workforce. James Stephen sympathised with them. He warned that the introduction of more indentured labourers from India could undermine the former slaves' ability to acquire profitable employment. He refuted the charge made by Mauritian employers that the Creole workforce had broken the terms of their apprenticeships by abandoning their plantations since 1833, insisting they had been forced to leave. However Stephen and his secretary of state were at odds on this issue. The patrician Glenelg believed that the fierce competition for paid employment with indentured migrants 'at this critical period' would have a 'most useful influence on the conduct of the apprenticed population'.[14]

Mauritius' governor William Nicolay felt that he had experience enough to compare the predicament of apprentices in the Caribbean and Mauritius. Having fought in the Artillery in India, helped capture St Lucia from the French, worked in intelligence in the Peninsular War and been one of the celebrated combatants at Waterloo, he had been appointed governor of Dominica from 1824 to 1831, and of St Kitts from 1832 to 1833. Four months before emancipation, he drew on this experience to agree with Glenelg. The apprentices, 'becoming accustomed to labour in the same fields with men in a state of entire freedom, will, on their final emancipation, betake themselves more willingly to their accustomed employments', he affirmed. In the same despatch, he could not contain his enthusiasm about the effect of the compensation payments to the 7000 former slave owners on the island:

The increase of Revenue in 1836, is stated at £31,308.4.6 ¼. The principal increase of Revenue has been ... the increased capital from the indemnity to Slaves. ... The Registration fees, in the Internal Revenue Department, have also afforded considerable augmentation in 1836: chiefly arising from the transfers of property, attributable also, in a great measure, to the altered circumstances of the

Colonial Society from the emancipation of the Slaves. . . . From the introduction of Indian labourers in 1836, the produce of the soil should show an augmentation in 1837.[15]

Stephen may have feared that the colonial government had failed to give Mauritius' apprentices sufficient support in their transition to free labour, but in the face of this boon to the colonial economy and the availability of cheap Indian labour, his disquiet was not enough to convince either the colonial secretary or the island's governor that they needed protection.

By the middle of 1838 Stephen's correspondence with governors around the world was allowing him to develop a mental map of emancipatory priorities. This was the map that would inform the imperial government's interventions in labour relations as slaves were freed. Stephen's primary concern was to ensure a smooth transition from apprenticeship to free labour in the Caribbean. This itself was much more difficult than it first seemed, but we will return to it in the next chapter. Despite his reservations about the fate of Creoles and news of the first Dutch-speaking trekkers to leave the Cape Colony, the alteration in status from apprentice to free labour seemed less problematic in Mauritius and the Cape Colony, both of which were included in the terms of the 1833 act. In the meantime, Britons could rest assured that the kind of chattel slavery that they had in mind had, to all intents and purposes, already been phased out in St Helena and Ceylon. In Ceylon, and more importantly in India, there were concerns about forms of indigenous slavery, which British administrations continued to tolerate if not condone. However, this consideration could be set to one side while still fulfilling the public and parliamentary mandate for emancipation.

Sierra Leone and Van Diemen's Land

Even if Stephen seemed assured of satisfying the British government and public that emancipation had been achieved in 1838, he harboured his own misgivings about two other forms of coerced labour, which shaded into one another in different colonies, and which were not a subject of any particular public concern. During the course of the year he engaged in correspondence with officials in Sierra Leone about the fate of those whom some describe as 'liberated Africans' and others as 'recaptives'. He also conversed with governors in the Australian colonies about the condition of convicts assigned to work for free settlers. At one point, he directly compared the situations of these two groups and considered whether reform on behalf of both was necessary in the light of emancipationist intent elsewhere.

Of all the groups benefitting from abolition, the British government had perhaps gone furthest out on a limb to assist Africans taken captive on board other nations' ships and freed by the Royal Navy. Britain's policing of the trans-Atlantic slave trade had begun with the searching of British registered ships in 1807. During the Napoleonic War, an extension of the Royal Navy's 'search and liberate' mandate to include the slave ships of enemies became both more feasible and strategically advantageous. By 1810, Portugal had agreed to let its ships be searched and at the Congress of Vienna, Viscount Castlereagh insisted on the abolition of the slave trade by all the European powers. The slaving crews captured by the Royal Navy from Portuguese, Spanish and Dutch ships thereafter were tried in Courts of Mixed Commission in Freetown, Sierra Leone, although the USA did not consent to British searches of its ships until the 1840s. Most of the captives freed by the Royal Navy's West Africa squadron were also resettled in Sierra Leone. The most well-known, if idiosyncratic, rendition of their experience comes from Ajayi, whose narrative was first published in Britain as emancipation approached in 1837.[16]

Ajayi was captured, along with other members of his family, by African Muslims raiding his hometown in what is now Nigeria in 1821. Held for three months in a household in Igboland, he was then moved to Lagos to await a slave ship. Fortunately for him, a British patrol intercepted the ship on the day that it sailed and took him and the other captives about 1200 miles up the coast to Freetown, where they were liberated. Ajayi found only a dozen people who spoke his Oyo dialect and, like most captives delivered there, was unable to reconnect with his kinship network or navigate his way home. To try the latter meant incurring the risk of being recaptured by slave raiding parties and embarked once again for the Caribbean or Americas. Settling in the colony that Zachary Macaulay had governed, Ajayi attended school, learned English and converted to Christianity. He became a 'liberated African' of celebrated accomplishment, studying in Britain thanks to a Church Missionary Society benefactor. He renamed himself Samuel Ajayi Crowther after his patron, was ordained as an Anglican priest, and finally became the first bishop on the Niger.

Ajayi's experience indicates how British abolitionist intent could transform individual Africans' fate, turning a potential slave into a bishop. Unfortunately his social mobility was by no means representative of the thousands of other 'liberated Africans'. For one thing, the slave ship holding Ajayi was intercepted by the West Africa patrol immediately after its departure, whereas other ships were captured by the West Indies fleet only once they had crossed the Atlantic. The men and boys freed from these ships were often impressed into the West India Regiment, although, as emancipation neared, Stephen condemned this extended form of servitude.[17] Colonial Office policy was that these 'liberated African' men and boys should, like the women and girls, join the free black population of the Caribbean colonies. Ajayi's trajectory was also quite exceptional among those who never crossed the Atlantic. Between 1808 and 1855 the Royal Navy rescued more than 40 000 Africans and brought them to Freetown. They came originally from all over West Africa and Central Africa. With the help of both white and black benefactors like Crowther, some prospered, joining the ranks of the free black settlers. Others tried to find their way home, risking the slave raiders plaguing the region. The majority, who stayed in Sierra Leone, did not fare as well as Ajayi.

Historians now tend to describe these 'liberated Africans' as 'recaptives'.[18] They were indeed fortunate to have been rescued from the middle passage and enslavement in the Americas and West Indies, but upon disembarkation they were thrown into an alien, polyglot environment far from home and lacking any kind of social ties, possession or wealth. Both black and white Sierra Leonian settlers benefitted from the Royal Navy's continual resupply and allocation of a bonded labour force. Stephen believed that the 'liberated' Africans in Sierra Leone should be treated similarly to those who had been enslaved in the Caribbean: freed from slavery but subject to enforced apprenticeships. Just like their West Indies counterparts, these destitute and dislocated people needed to be 'schooled' to re-acquire their freedom before they could be contracted through wages. A key difference was that Sierra Leone's 'recaptives' were not included in the date for emancipation from apprenticeships that had been set for the Caribbean, Cape and Mauritius.

While their Caribbean counterparts would all be thrown onto the free labour market on either 1 August 1838 or 1840, apprenticeships in Sierra Leone would continue, with most individuals being freed often only after fifteen years of servitude. Another difference was that in the Caribbean it was former owners who took on the responsibility for apprentices' 'schooling'. In Sierra Leone the colonial authorities registered new arrivals upon disembarkation and then ensured their 'disposal' either through enlistment in the West African Regiment or assignment to free settlers. These would be their new employers and guardians. An elaborate, and easily corruptible system had evolved through which government functionaries assigned apprentices to themselves, their families and friendly settlers.

The Colonial Office was aware that Sierra Leonean settlers, both white and black, often mistreated and exploited the 'liberated' Africans assigned to them. The colony's newspapers carried advertisements help-ing settlers track down runaway apprentices, which listed their physical descriptions, often including burns, cuts and even branding, adminis-tered by employers. Soon after the abolition of the slave trade in 1808, Sierra Leone's governor, the radical reformer Thomas Perronet Thompson, reported that 'recaptives' were bought and sold exactly like slaves. He considered 'the Inhabitants of this Colony to be brutal, violent, & inhuman towards all such unfortunate persons as are placed within their power'.[19] Soon afterwards, Thompson was sacked, with the approval of his friends Wilberforce and Zachary Macaulay, for alleging that British anti-slavery activists were consenting to a new system of slavery in their much-vaunted 'free' colony.

The more James Stephen considered the 'liberated' Africans some thirty years later, the more he appreciated what they had in common with another group of coerced workers: the convicted criminals that Britain had been sending out to its Australian colonies. In Van Diemen's Land (now Tasmania) in particular during the early 1830s, Governor George Arthur, fresh from imposing the amelioration of slavery on British Honduras' settlers, had set out the rationale for a system of private convict assignment, similar to Sierra Leone's 'disposal' system for liberated Africans. As the Australian colony experienced a mass influx of free settlers in the 1830s, Arthur was convinced that transported convicts should supply useful labour to their enterprise. He also believed that convicts' rehabilitation would be furthered by serving out their sentences working for free settlers, who would lead by example. For Stephen, this was a project very much akin to preparing Sierra Leone's 'liberated Africans' for integration into an entirely free, predominantly black society.

In late 1837 and early 1838, Stephen pondered whether both 'liberated Africans' and British convicts in Australia should be annexed to the project of emancipating the Caribbean's apprentices. His correspondence with George Maclean encouraged him to pause for further thought.

Maclean was agent to the African Committee, which had its origins in the African Company of Merchants, itself preceded by the Royal African Company. The Company was an association of slave-trading merchants from Liverpool, Bristol and London, managed by three members elected from each city. Before the 1807 abolition of the slave trade it had acquired coastal slave-trading forts and overseen the purchase of captives for the middle passage. Afterwards, it had morphed into a trading concern occupied mainly with the exportation of gold. In 1821, however, the British government abolished the company as a result of its failure to act against slavery and transferred its assets, including the Gold Coast slave-trading forts, to the government of Sierra Leone. By 1828 the governor there was keen to relinquish responsibility for the forts and so an African Committee was resurrected to administer them on behalf of the British merchants still trading along the coast. George Maclean, a former lieutenant in the Royal African Colonial Corps, had been appointed president of the committee. By 1837 he was acting on behalf of British traders in treaty negotiations with the surrounding African chiefdoms.

Maclean's official status was ambiguous. He was left to his own devices in conducting negotiations with both the Sierra Leonian colonial government and African authorities, but he could call upon assistance from Sierra Leone and the Colonial Office when required. By the late 1830s he had earned some influence along the Gold Coast by arbitrating among the Fante kingdoms and urging their cooperation against the powerful Ashanti to the north. On a visit to The Hague he had even advised the Dutch government, which held the slave-trading port of Elmina, on how it might procure soldiers for its colony in Java without complicity in the slave trade, by recruiting Sierra Leone's 'liberated Africans', prompting the Dutch to ask the Foreign Office for help in the matter. When consulted by his neighbour in Downing Street, Stephen ruled out the proposal.[20] Maclean continued to see the 'liberated Africans' as a useful resource, however, and became concerned that Stephen and the Colonial Office might, in some way, try to liberate them.

Possibly while in England getting married, Maclean became aware that Stephen was being influenced by Alexander Maconochie's *Report on the State of Prison Discipline in Van Diemen's Land*, which had been published in London earlier that year. He worried about the potential consequences for Sierra Leone.[21] Maconochie was a prolific writer who had served in the Royal Navy, promoted British commercial colonies in the Pacific, raised seven children with his wife Mary Hutton Browne (with what Lady Franklin called 'a certain outrageous liberality of principle'), and been appointed the first secretary to the Royal Geographical Society and the first Professor of Geography in Britain, at University College London. The fact that his lectures there were poorly attended did not deter him from instructing his fellow passengers on 'The natural history of man' when he sailed for Van Diemen's Land with its new governor, Sir John Franklin, as his private secretary in 1836.

Before leaving for Australia, the Society for the Improvement of Prison Discipline had asked Maconochie to report on the system of convict assignment established by Franklin's predecessor, George Arthur. Maconochie became a fierce critic of the system. Upon disembarkation, he reported, convicts in Van Diemen's Land were assigned by a public board to serve private free settlers for periods of four, six or eight years.

They were subject to 'all the discomforts and moral degradations' of slavery, with no incentive for good behaviour or rehabilitation.[22] They could be hauled before an obliging magistrate by their 'master' and subjected to severe and degrading punishments for minor offences. Such a system, Maconochie believed, did nothing to prepare them for the responsibilities of freedom.[23]

In early 1838, Stephen forwarded Maconochie's report on Van Diemen's Land to the Home Office, criticism of official policy and all, so that its lessons could be applied at home. He had also made no secret of the fact that he was struck by the parallels that the report contained with the critiques of 'liberated African assignment' in Sierra Leone. It was at this point that Maclean stepped in.

Worried that Stephen might apply Maconochie's criticism of Van Diemen's Land to Sierra Leone, Maclean, sought to persuade Stephen that Sierra Leone's 'liberated' Africans were not subjected to the same 'species of domestic slavery . . . injurious alike to the bond and free'. In Van Diemen's Land it might well be the case that convict assignment tended to 'deteriorate the character' of the assignee 'and unfit . . . him for resuming his place among freemen'. However, in Sierra Leone the system of private assignment still probably afforded 'the best school possible', and besides, no better system for integrating liberated Africans had been proposed. Maclean admitted that certain Sierra Leonean employers used an unacceptable degree of coercion, but insisted that the 'disposal' system for liberated Africans did not amount to slavery since 'the master' had 'no property in his assigned servant'. The 'liberated African', he assured the Colonial Office, has 'yet a legal and accessible remedy for any exercise of tyranny and oppression that may be exerted over him'.[24]

Even with Maclean's reassurance, Stephen retained some disquiet over the private assignment of both convicts in Australia and liberated Africans in Sierra Leone. Could the imperial government really be considered to have accomplished emancipation when British subjects, both convict and free, were farmed out to work for private individuals against their will and without any kind of freely contracted arrangement? The system of convict transportation and assignment, as Stephen well knew, was already being questioned by a committee chaired by William Molesworth, which we will come to later, but for now, Stephen called upon Franklin as the new governor of Van Diemen's Land to consider whether private assignment of convicts there should cease. Ought convicts' labour be reserved solely for public works under governmental authority, as part of their planned rehabilitation? Would not this accord better with the broader project of emancipation upon which the British nation had embarked? Could not 'the convicts in private service' in the colony be 'gradually displaced by free labourers'?[25]

In the early days of his lieutenant governorship, in late 1837, Franklin responded to Stephen's request.[26] Much as he agreed that ending the practice of private assignment would be desirable, he told Stephen that he was unable to oblige just yet. The main issue was the shortage of free labour with which to replace assignees. Franklin urged Stephen to consider his own colony in relation to the neighbouring ones: 'there is one material fact which should never be overlooked; – namely, that the immense extent of available territory still remaining open for sale in the colony of New South Wales creates a diversity in the condition of the two colonies which must be attended by a corresponding diversity in both their penal and their Immigration systems'.[27] With colonisation proceeding apace in the Port Phillip District (now Victoria) across the Bass Strait, Van Diemen's Land was struggling to retain its existing population, let alone attract a new free workforce.

Franklin told Stephen that his only solution was to use the convict labour supply to cut new roads on an East-West axis across Van Diemen's Land. With the main belt of British settlement running North-South connecting Launceston and Hobart through the island's centre, this government assigned labour force would open new pasture land for settlers. Assigning those settlers convict workers of their own would continue to be essential for the development of this pastureland until such time as sales of the newly accessible land could fund new emigrants from Britain to replace them. Only then would the phasing out of private assignment be compatible with the colony's much needed economic development.

By August 1838, when the apprentices of the Caribbean were freed, Stephen had accepted both Maclean's justification for continued assignment of 'liberated' Africans in Sierra Leone, and Franklin's defence of the convict assignment system in Van Diemen's Land. Although the Colonial Office had toyed with the idea of ending the forced assignment of these people, it was persuaded that they could not be seen as equivalent to the former slaves of the West Indies and their counterparts in the Cape and Mauritius. African 'recaptives' were left to the devices of their private masters and mistresses for at least a further decade but the system of private convict assignment in Van Diemen's Land would be phased out within three years, as the whole system of convict transportation was re-evaluated.

As emancipation dawned across the empire in the summer of 1838, one of the imperial government's major preoccupations during the first half of the year had been distinguishing who exactly was to be freed and from what kind of labour relation. Most certainly, the chattel slaves of the Caribbean sugar-producing colonies were the primary intended beneficiaries of British anti-slavery campaigners, and we shall discover more about their experiences of apprenticeship and emancipation in the next chapter. But there were other categories of forced labour whose entitlement to British benevolence was more uncertain. Here, Glenelg, Grey and Stephen had to exercise some discretion. On the one hand they were enjoined to administer a process of transition from bonded to free labour which would be loudly proclaimed as evidence of peculiarly British virtue, both at the time and ever since. On the other hand, they would be held accountable if the production of tropical commodities plummeted for want of affordable labour and if Britain's colonies collapsed into chaos through the overturning of their social order. The value accorded to emancipation had to be weighed in practice against that attached to security and prosperity. Free from the scrutiny that anti-slavery activists afforded to former slaves in the Caribbean, they allowed Indians, 'liberated Africans', Creoles, Tamils and convicts in other parts of the empire to persist in various states of coerced labour.

Further Reading

Allen, R. B., *Slaves, Freedmen and Indentured Laborers in Colonial Mauritius*, Cambridge University Press, 1999.

Anderson, C., 'Transnational Histories of Penal Transportation: Punishment, Labour and Governance in the British Imperial World, 1788–1939', *Australian Historical Studies*, 47, 2016, 381–97.

Blackburn, R., *The Overthrow of Colonial Slavery, 1776–1848*, Verso, 1998.

Brown, C. L., *Moral Capital: Foundations of British Abolitionism*, University of North Carolina Press, 2006.

Dooling, W., *Slavery, Emancipation and Colonial Rule in South Africa*, University of KwaZulu Natal Press, 2007.

Everill, B., *Abolition and Empire in Sierra Leone and Liberia*, Palgrave Macmillan, 2013.

Major, A., '"The Slavery of East and West": Abolitionists and "Unfree" Labour in India, 1820–1833', *Slavery and Abolition*, 31, 2010, 501–25.

Rupprecht, A., '"When He Gets among His Countrymen, They Tell Him That He Is Free": Slave Trade Abolition, Indentured Africans and a Royal Commission', *Slavery & Abolition*, 33, 2012, 435–56.

Sivasundaram, S., *Islanded: Britain, Sri Lanka, and the Bounds of an Indian Ocean Colony*, University of Chicago Press, 2013.

2 Managing Expectations

Satisfying Parliament and public opinion in Britain that emancipation had been achieved was a priority for Stephen, Grey and Glenelg during 1838, but so too was ensuring security and prosperity during the empire's transition to free labour. James Stephen's desire to see former slaves join the ranks of the Christian free was tempered by the need to reassure colonial elites that they were not about to be overthrown by newly assertive, liberated people of colour. In 1838, as the Colonial Office sought to turn emancipation from an imagined British ideal into a programme of real political, economic and social transition, the objective of freedom was ever more carefully balanced against those of stability and prosperity.

The way that the Colonial Office negotiated this trade off would ultimately propel vast British and Asian migrations, reshaping global demographics for centuries to come. In this chapter we focus on how the imperial government was working its way through the issues during the key year of transition, sowing the seeds of this global transformation.

Civil Rights in Jamaica and Mauritius

Emancipation was viewed with perhaps the greatest anxiety by the planters represented in Jamaica's Assembly. Since 1664 this body, elected on a restricted property franchise, had shared legislative responsibility with governors appointed from London. In December 1837, as governors in the other Caribbean colonies were preparing themselves for the apprentices' freedom, Jamaica's Assembly was still protesting the effects of the abolition of the slave trade thirty years ago. Governor Lionel Smith was obliged to pass on their memorial to Glenelg. Far from outlining the preparations being made for emancipation on the island, it reiterated their concern that rival nations were still profiting from a trade which Britain had perversely given up. The British government's sentimentality was causing 'the very great injury of all classes of Her Majesty's subjects in this colony'.[1] In a strained response, Stephen patiently asked Smith to remind his assembly 'that the entire suppression of the slave trade as carried on by

Foreign States is a subject to which the Queen attaches the very highest importance and which has occupied and will continue to engage H.M'.s most serious attention'.[2] If Jamaica's planters were agitated by their ongoing exclusion from slave trading, they were positively panicked by the looming prospect of more free black people on their island.

Their governor in 1838 was the son of the writer and feminist Charlotte Turner Smith. Lionel Smith's army career had begun with a posting to British North America, but during the Revolutionary War he had sailed back across the Atlantic to help repress an insurrection in Sierra Leone. In the Napoleonic War he had fought in both the West and East Indies, including against pirates in the Persian Gulf. He had taken part in the capture of Mauritius from the French, and after his posting to Jamaica he would return there as Nicolay's replacement. Part of the many familial networks through which the British Empire was governed, Smith had married the sister of Sir Henry Pottinger, the man who would shortly ensure the humiliation of the Qing Empire in the First Opium War (Chapter 6). With the fighting phase of his career over, Smith was appointed governor and commander-in-chief of the Windward and Leeward Islands, where he incurred the wrath of planters resisting the 1833 abolition act in Barbados. He had assumed the governorship of Jamaica in 1836, and was now finding its planters even more hostile.

Smith's predecessor in Jamaica, the Marquess of Sligo (Peter Howe Browne), had been a friend of Byron and Hobhouse in his radical youth, which included a spell in prison. As the inheritor of two plantations in Jamaica, the island's planters had expected the mature Sligo to be sympathetic when he was appointed their governor. However, he had objected vehemently to their cruelty and, after the 1833 act, made it clear that he wished Jamaica to be 'absolved forever from the reproach of Slavery'. Well aware of the abuses of the apprenticeship system, which we examine below, he sought out sixty special magistrates to ensure that the promised protections for former slaves would be enforced. Planters mocked him for giving 'a patient hearing to the poorest Negro which might carry his grievance to Government House'. Sligo admitted that the planters 'set out to make Jamaica too hot to hold me'.[3] They succeeded. The organised vilification of him in Britain, and the Legislative Assembly's vote to withhold his salary gave the colonial secretary no choice but to remove him from office in September 1836. For both Lionel Smith and James Stephen, the episode was a salutary lesson in the realpolitik of emancipation.

One of Stephen's greatest dilemmas in 1838 was the extent to which he could afford to mollify Jamaica's slave owners (whom he personally despised), without negating the benefits of emancipation for former slaves. Aside from trying to stop planters abusing apprenticeship, Sligo had earned their wrath by fostering a 'Coloured Party' for free black representatives within the Assembly, encouraging men of colour to run for membership as a counterweight to planter influence. In late 1837, as the end of apprenticeship and a drastic increase in the free black population neared, the last election to the Jamaican Assembly had returned five more 'Coloured Party' members and a corresponding reduction in the proportion of white representatives. Despite his liberal reputation, Smith was concerned that any further increase in black political representation would undermine the stability of the colony. He wrote to Glenelg privately with the sensitive suggestion that the franchise property qualification be raised upon emancipation so as to prevent even more 'Coloured' members being elected. 'Two more general elections', he wrote, 'would, I am persuaded, throw every white member out of the House under the present law'. Smith feared that free black people and especially former slaves 'are not yet qualified by education and property to command the respect of the country'. The consequence of allowing further black representation in these circumstances 'must be the rapid sale of property and abandonment of the Island by the few influential white Gentlemen who now reside in it'.[4]

Glenelg and Stephen conferred over Smith's covert strategy to maintain white political dominance. Although it might well buy the cooperation of Jamaica's planters, Stephen replied that such franchise manipulation would smack of explicit racial discrimination against those whom Britain wished emancipated. It could not be allowed. Normally such a discussion might have been kept between the governor and Colonial Office. Unfortunately for Smith, however, the correspondence that he had sought to keep secret leaked. The Assembly's black representatives came to hear of it from correspondents in Britain. An outraged Smith blamed a leak from within the Colonial Office, earning the haughty reply from Stephen that such indiscretion among his staff was inconceivable. By the time the apprentices were freed in August, Smith was mistrusted almost in equal measure by both the 'Coloured Party', for his covert attempt to undermine them, and by planters resisting his efforts to rein in their abuses of apprenticeship.

It was Smith's unpopularity with the majority of Assembly members which prompted the Bedchamber Crisis in Britain during May of the following year. In late 1838, the Jamaican Assembly simply refused to act on Smith's instruction to legislate on the island's prisons, causing a constitutional crisis in the colony. When the Whig majority government's bill to resolve the issue passed in the House of Commons by only five votes, it was tantamount to a vote of no confidence and Lord

Melbourne declared his intention to resign as prime minister. The nineteen-year-old Queen Victoria was distraught. Since her coronation two years previously, Melbourne had acted as her trusted mentor. Reluctantly, she invited the Conservative leader Robert Peel to form a government but he made it a condition that Victoria dismiss some of her Ladies of the Bedchamber, among them the wives or relatives of leading Whig politicians. When Victoria resisted, Peel refused to become prime minister, and Melbourne was reinstated. In Jamaica meanwhile, the Assembly reluctantly passed a modified prison bill, but too late for Smith who was recalled and sent on to Mauritius. Once there he would confront precisely that same issue that had caused his downfall in Jamaica: how far should the British obligation to former slaves extend beyond emancipation to include the same civil rights enjoyed by propertied white colonists?

In 1838, while Stephen was preventing Smith from limiting black representation in Jamaica's Assembly, he was simultaneously instructing Nicolay to open Mauritius' advisory Council of Government to the newly freed Creoles. Stephen was optimistic that free men of colour everywhere would ultimately prove themselves worthy to participate in representative institutions on the same terms (generally a property-based franchise) as white men. In reality, Governor Nicolay's plan for Mauritius was more modest. In March 1838 Stephen received a despatch that Nicolay had sent in September the previous year: 'Were I called upon to give an opinion as to when an extensive system of representative legislature could be safely introduced, founded on the consideration of the equality of legal rights which will be enjoyed by all classes on the expiration of the Apprenticeship, my answer must be that the period is far – very far – distant'. Rather, Nicolay would 'bring into effect the desire formerly expressed by His Majesty's Government, of granting to the inhabitants, a more free participation in the legislative affairs of the colony, by admitting a certain number (under various restrictions with regard to eligibility) into the Council of Government'.[5]

Whatever Stephen's long term ambition may have been, Glenelg noted that the management of post-emancipation transition required the cooperation of Mauritius' French-speaking elites, who were already expressing their discontent with the Anglicisation of their island's administration. Glenelg took Nicolay's warnings about rebellion seriously and agreed that the rights of Creole former slaves should be circumscribed as he saw fit. Disaffected British planters in Jamaica were one thing; a rebellion against British sovereignty itself was another. As ever in government, even in this celebrated year of freedom, security, economic and moral concerns were weighed against each other, with differing outcomes in different places.[6]

Timing Freedom in the Caribbean

The rights of future free black subjects was not the only prize that the Colonial Office traded off against other objectives as it managed emancipation. During the early months of 1838 Glenelg, Grey and Stephen faced a tricky calculation in determining the exact timing of release from apprenticeship. Ostensibly this should have been straightforward. The 1833 act had decreed that domestic slaves were to be freed after four years of apprenticeship on 1 August 1838 and field slaves exactly two years later. However, during the four years since the act was passed, things had become a lot more complicated as evidence mounted to show that apprenticeship was failing to deliver on the anti-slavery lobby's expectations.

Key to the rethinking of apprenticeship in Britain was the witness borne by a formerly enslaved Jamaican apprentice, James Williams. While working on the Pinehurst plantation in St Ann's Parish, the eighteen-year-old Williams had met Joseph Sturge, a British anti-slavery activist engaged, along with Elizabeth Heyrick, in a campaign to bring apprenticeship to an immediate end, regardless of what the 1833 act had promised. When Sturge met Williams, he saw an opportunity to bring the voice of a formerly enslaved Jamaican apprentice directly to the attention of the British public. Buying Williams out of his apprenticeship, Sturge brought him back to Britain to mobilise 'the battering ram of public opinion' against the abuses of apprenticeship. He helped Williams publish his *A Narrative of Events since the First of August, 1834.*[7]

Williams' account became to apprenticeship what Olaudah Equiano's narrative was to slavery. Republished in numerous editions and extracted in newspapers, it focused on the collusion between former slave owners and the supposedly independent magistrates entrusted with enforcing the apprenticeship codes. Both, Williams claimed, were doing 'all [they] can to hurt [apprentices] before the free come'. British readers found the account of apprenticed women sentenced to work semi-naked on mill house treadmills for minor offences particularly shocking (Figure 2.1). Williams also alerted his British audiences to the fact that former slave owners were threatening the expulsion of children under six, who were already free according to the terms of the 1833 act, if they refused to continue working alongside their apprenticed mothers.

Having received his own copy of Williams' book in September 1837, Stephen instructed Lionel Smith to appoint commissioners to investigate such abuses in Jamaica. During three weeks, special magistrate John Daughtrey and Justice George Gordon gathered evidence from more than 120 apprentices, largely verifying Williams' claims. As the MP Sir

Figure 2.1 House of correction for apprentices from James Williams'
A Narrative of Events since the 1st of August, 1834, London, 1838. British
Library.

George Strickland later put it, the 1833 Act might have 'declared, in
emphatic terms, that slavery should for ever be abolished', but in practice
that promise 'has been passed over, slurred, totally neglected'.[8]

Joseph Sturge, the man who had brought Williams to England, was
a Quaker pacifist farmer who had refused at the age of nineteen to serve in
the militia or to find a substitute, suffering as a consequence the confiscation of his livestock. A grain importer in later life, he left his business to his
brother in order to devote himself to philanthropic and political causes. In
the 1820s he had supported the anti-slavery campaign but grown impatient with the compromises being made to conciliate slave owners. He was
contemptuous of Wilberforce's and Buxton's emphasis on gradual emancipation, arguing for the much more radical project of entire and immediate emancipation for both domestic and field workers. After the furore
about apprenticeship that Williams and Sturge created, Buxton's campaign to reform apprenticeship, based on a rather apologetic parliamentary enquiry, was sidelined by Sturge's more radical activism. In
November 1837 Sturge's Central Negro Emancipation Committee
hosted a huge anti-apprenticeship convention at Exeter Hall, on the
Strand. The building's main hall held 3000 people and it was the

epicentre of evangelical reformism in early nineteenth-century Britain. In the following three months he held further public meetings pressurising MPs to 'do justice' to the apprentices. Lord Brougham used the campaign's petitions to support attacks against the apprenticeship system in Parliament and Grey and Glenelg were obliged to recognise that the staggered emancipation promised in 1833 may have to be revisited.[9]

Glenelg faced two ways though. Well aware of the growing momentum of political pressure in Britain, he needed also to know what the Caribbean governors thought about ending apprenticeship early for all categories of labour. In late 1837 he instructed Stephen to gather the opinions of all the West Indies governors about both the timing and 'the changes of the law which ought to accompany' the expiration of apprenticeship. Receiving the first of these reports from Governor Francis Cockburn in the Bahamas in February 1838, Grey warned his colleagues that 'the series will probably be rapidly increasing with the arrival of every mail; it appears necessary to determine how they should be disposed of, that is whether by appointing a Commissioner to examine into & report on the subject or by what other means'.[10] Predictably enough, Stephen himself proceeded to collate the reports and issue guidance as best as he could.

Cockburn, who had warned that a failure to enlist 'liberated Africans' in the West India Regiment would be resisted by Bahamas' settlers, felt that the differential timing of emancipation promised in the 1833 act should be observed. Delaying field apprentices' emancipation until August 1840 would pose no threat to stability and apprenticeship was business as usual in Bahamas, whatever domestic political campaigners might say. Not all of Cockburn's colleagues, however, were of the same mind. As we have mentioned, when the 1833 act was passed, the apprenticeship period had been skipped altogether in Antigua and Bermuda. The governor of Antigua, nineteenth Chief of Clan Gregor and second Baronet Evan John Murray MacGregor, had decided that apprenticeship was unnecessary and emancipated all enslaved people completely and immediately as of 1 August 1834. In early 1838, MacGregor was governor of Barbados and the Windward Islands. From Bridgetown he reminded Stephen that 'the measure of complete and simultaneous enfranchisement was happily accomplished' in Antigua 'without accident or inconvenience'.[11] It was actually staggered freedom, as promised in the 1833 act, that was the 'altogether untried experiment' rather than the immediate emancipation for all that many seemed to fear. Fully aware of the 'anti-apprenticeship meetings ... recently held in England', MacGregor recommended a full and total end to apprenticeship 'while the subject ... engages the attention of the public'. It may have been too late to free domestic apprentices before the promised date of 1 August but the risk of delaying field labourers' freedom for a further two years was prolonged agitation in Britain and unrest in the Caribbean.[12]

At first Stephen proved reluctant to alter the timetable for emancipation that he had set out in the 1833 act. His response to MacGregor's warning that field labourers would rebel if their emancipation was delayed while others were freed, was to focus on the 'natural' association that they must be making between agricultural work and the 'degradation' of slavery. It was not so much their desire to be free of their former owners' control that might lead to unrest, as the stigma of being categorised as 'merely' field labour. Stephen sought to assuage MacGregor that this stigma 'is one of those accidental prejudices which may reasonably be expected to yield to the influence of good, if not the pressure of want' during the two further years in which they remained apprenticed beyond their domestic counterparts. The immediate solution lay in persuading both employers and apprentices of the value and utility of agricultural work.[13] In the early months of 1838 Stephen stuck to his guns, refusing to admit that he may have been wrong to concede so much to the planters back in 1833. Immediate and full emancipation 'would have been at once a breach of National faith' to the planters, who had been promised a staggered cessation, he argued, 'and a sore evil to the object of their solicitude', the unprepared apprentices themselves.[14]

While he awaited Stephen's response to his alternative proposal, MacGregor continued to prepare for the staggered freedom anticipated in the 1833 act. He set about the task of categorising apprentices into field (or Praedial after Roman usage) and household (non-Praedial) workers during the second half of 1837. The initial categorisation was done by employers, but MacGregor was well aware of their incentive to retain forced labour for a further two years by categorising apprentices as field workers, regardless of what they actually did. He therefore constructed a system for apprentices to appeal their designation. Special Magistrates would give an opportunity 'to any individuals deeming themselves properly belonging to the [domestic] class, to substantiate their claims to freedom' in the coming August. The governor warned his magistrates that they could expect many dubious applications from field labourers seeking an early release, but explained that there was little alternative to such a system of judicial appraisal if staggered emancipation were to be effected fairly.

MacGregor may have predicted that employers would tend to inflate the proportion of field labourers, while apprentices themselves disproportionately claimed domestic status, but he had not foreseen just how difficult it would be for his special magistrates to apply the binary categories. Where, for instance, did skilled tradespeople fit? Their construction and mainten- ance work might be conducted either in the fields and agricultural buildings or in the home. As magistrates informed him of their difficulties, MacGregor supplied the Colonial Office with a case in point.[15] 'George' was an estate worker formerly owned by and now apprenticed to Joseph Evelyn, 'a respectable gentleman of this island'. 'George's' work consisted in supplying manual labour to skilled stonemasons and artisans who worked on the homes of the plantocracy. Since he was unskilled himself, Evelyn considered him a field labourer, but 'George' was appealing the classification and demanding that he be freed along with Evelyn's house- hold apprentices on 1 August. Where should the governor stand in relation to such disputes? Stephen responded only that the governor 'ought to advise his Magistrates as often as his opinion is solicited or whenever he thinks it desirable, leaving them to take the responsibility of acting'.[16] Using such local discretion, by February 1838 MacGregor informed the Colonial Office that 106 male and 165 female apprentices had been trans- ferred from the field to the domestic class upon appeal, and were hence awaiting their freedom in August.[17]

Even with MacGregor's insight into the complexities of staggered emancipation, in February 1838 the Colonial Office was persisting with the plan that Stephen had drawn up in 1833. When Sturge once again proposed immediate and full emancipation to the House of Lords in that month, the Colonial Office countered with an amendment to the 1833 legislation which would shore up the protections afforded to apprentices rather than free them. The reformist and anti-slavery Yorkshire MP George Strickland insisted on a parliamentary debate on this Abolition of Slavery Amendment Bill in March. Strickland began his speech by abhorring 'that strange species of legislation which consists in saying, that the [domestic] slaves shall be released in this year, but that the [field] slaves shall be retained in servitude for two years longer. ... Was there ever a piece of legislation which gave greater promise of dissatisfaction, irritation, and discontent?' Next, he directed Parliament's attention to the 'great experiment' that MacGregor had conducted in Antigua and Bermuda, where 'we see 45,000 ... at once set free without any inter- mediate state of apprenticeship'. Strickland's effort in the House of Commons was backed up by Sligo, Jamaica's former reforming governor, in the House of Lords. There, he announced that, whatever the outcome in the Commons, he would free all the apprentices on his own Jamaican estates on 1 August.

Speaking for the Colonial Office in the Commons, Grey sought to block full and immediate emancipation once again. He pointed out that 'a compact was made by the act of 1833 between Parliament and the West-India proprietors, with which we are not now justified in interfering'. He insisted that the period of apprenticeship was part of the compensation owed to slave owners alongside the £20 million. Combatting James Williams' evidence, Grey also quoted earlier despatches from a number of Jamaican magistrates as evidence that apprenticeship itself was working well, with abuses few and far between. He assured his fellow MPs that 'the most incorrect information has been circulated on the subject'.[18] Even with the support of the MPs successfully lobbied by Sturge's campaign group, Strickland lost the debate and the Colonial Office's moderate bill for the reform rather than termination of apprenticeship was passed.

Yet within the next month both parliamentary and Colonial Office opposition to immediate emancipation for all apprentices would collapse. Most historians credit Sturge's campaign with the victory. But the domestic campaign directed at Parliament was reinforced by the influence of MacGregor's continuing advocacy from Barbados. In a despatch of February 1838, received and read by Stephen around the same time that Grey was stalling in the March parliamentary debate, MacGregor forced an acknowledgement of the risks of delaying the majority of apprentices' emancipation. He included reports from his lieutenant governors in the Windward Islands: Grenada, St Vincent and Tobago. All raised concerns about the response that could be expected from those retained as apprentices when others were freed. MacGregor supplemented these with new intelligence from Barbados' special magistrates. Certain apprentices had always sought to escape coerced labour by running away, but the magistrates were now warning that wholesale desertion could be expected after 1 August, when field apprentices could seek refuge 'among their numerous liberated relations, and friends' classed as domestic.[19]

Furthermore, the details of staggered freedom promised back in 1833 were not necessarily understood by all apprentices. 'Having visited every Estate in the District last month', one special magistrate reported, 'and in communication with the [field] apprenticed labourers, I found several under the impression that all classes were to be liberated next August ... and, when that period arrives, much discontent, in my opinion, will exist with the [field] Class; and their services to their employers for the two years ensuing, will be given with much reluctance'. Despite one magistrate's confidence that 'the crisis' of a staggered emancipation 'will ... pass off favourably – provided the injudicious interference of Persons at Home does not produce a contrary result', Stephen admitted the force of MacGregor's argument. For the first time, during March 1838, he reconsidered his solution of 1833. Minuting that MacGregor's latest despatch 'should be laid before Sir G. Grey & Lord Glenelg', he wrote that 'they will find that the dispatch & its enclosure have a material bearing on the questions now pending before Parliament'. Stephen conceded that 'there is some cause for anxiety as to the effect of the partial liberation on the 1st August next, and good reason for the proposed interference of Parliament on the subject of the classification lists'.[20]

Just three days after the rejection of Strickland's motion in the House of Commons, Glenelg sent a circular to the Caribbean governors. While still maintaining that Parliament needed to respect the compromise made with planters in 1833, it urged colonial legislatures themselves to abolish apprenticeship for all classes of labour on 1 August.[21] Glenelg cited as his reasons both 'the force of public opinion' in Britain and the difficulty of maintaining 'tranquillity in the Colonies'.[22] As governors were considering and consulting on Glenelg's plea, the president of the Central Negro Emancipation Committee and Conservative MP, John Eardley Wilmot, brought a new resolution to Parliament. It would prove successful in May but by then the colonial legislatures were already acting upon Glenelg's recommendation to take the initiative in the face of the inevitable. The Caribbean planters gave up the struggle against full and immediate emancipation and all apprentices in the Caribbean were freed on 1 August, with their counterparts in the Cape and Mauritius to follow.

Redistributing People: The British and Indian Diasporas

By the 1830s the slave trade had partially depopulated West Africa and brought millions of Africans and their descendants to the Americas and the Caribbean. As slavery in its own colonies came to an end, the future labour force of much of the British Empire came into question and the imperial government began to orchestrate two other kinds of global demographic redistribution. The first was the emigration of millions of Britons to North America, Australasia and southern Africa. Britain's settler colonies, later dominions, were the result. The second propelled Britain's Indian subjects to its plantation colonies in the Indian, Atlantic and Pacific Oceans. Both of these redistributions had been under way before emancipation and both would continue afterwards, but in 1838 the imperial government intervened to shape them decisively.

Concurrent with the anti-slavery campaign, the Rev. Thomas Malthus had been warning of British overpopulation for the last forty years. Famously, he had argued in his 1798 Essay on the Principle of Population that population growth tends to outpace its means of subsistence. Checks on growth through disease, famine, war or birth control were only partial remedies. Malthus' concerns became more pressing in the wake of victory in the Napoleonic War, which threw former service-men onto an oversupplied labour market and fuelled agrarian unrest, culminating in the Swing Revolt of 1830. Malthus' musings placed Britain within its imperial context. While believing himself that it would be unjust for Europeans to exterminate Indigenous peoples, it was easy to make an association between an overabundance of people in Britain and the acquisition of vast new territories overseas. By the late 1830s, in the midst of widespread foreboding about labour short-ages in the post-emancipation plantation colonies, there was yet more reason to link the oversupply of labour in British Isles with the needs of the empire overseas.

During the 1820s Malthusianism had influenced a number of government-backed colonial emigration schemes. One of their early progenitors was Robert Wilmot-Horton, whom we met above as the governor of Ceylon in 1838. Aside from his notoriety as the man who had protected Byron's reputation by destroying his memoirs, Wilmot-Horton was known, more prosaically in his pre-gubernatorial life, for experimenting with new agricultural techniques at his Catton Hall estate (ironically helping to fuel the rural unrest that Malthusians attributed to overpopulation, by replacing workers with machines). Once he had taken an interest in something, Wilmot-Horton tended to pursue it obses-sively. In 1821 he became Stephen's predecessor as permanent under-secretary for war and the colonies, a post which he retained until 1828. He was the man who had promoted Stephen within the office. A frequent interlocutor with Malthus, he combined imperial adminis-tration with shaping public debate over population and emigration. His *Outline of a Plan of Emigration to Upper Canada*, published in 1823, had proposed government-assisted emigration in order to ease the pressure of domestic population.

Wilmot-Horton's idea was that parishes, burdened with poor relief in England and even more so in Ireland, could mortgage their poor rates in order to raise loans from central government. These would fund indigent parishioners' emigration to Canada. With his customary energy he secured Cabinet support for two experiments in government funded emigration from Ireland to Canada, in 1823 and 1825. The government became concerned about the cost and encouraged joint-stock companies such as the Canada Land Company to develop private business models for emigration instead, but Wilmot-Horton was undeterred. He estab-lished and chaired emigration committees of the House of Commons in 1826 and 1827, insisting that government-backed emigration would provide 'a safety-valve' by which excess population could be redistributed across the British Empire, with 'millions added to those who speak the English language, and carry with them ... the sympathies of their native country'.[23] Malthus told Wilmot-Horton of his concern that the character of such people might not be conducive to the building of new societies, and his schemes would never be implemented in full, but they did influence the 1834 Poor Law Act, which encouraged ratepayers to fund emigration of the local poor.

In the late 1820s Wilmot-Horton had admitted that his relentless focus on emigration schemes was damaging his health and preventing him from indulging his pastimes of riding and walking. He may have seen his proposals as a neat way of fixing social problems both at home and in the colonies, but pamphlets and newspapers were by now satirising him as fanatically 'shovelling out paupers'. Disillusioned and in need of respite, he withdrew from the Colonial Office in 1828. After some time spent pamphleteering in favour of Catholic emancipation, he accepted the governorship of Ceylon in early 1831, reporting to his previous mentee, Stephen. There, as we have seen, he would progressively undermine the system of slavery established by the Dutch in the Maritime Provinces, while approaching Kandyan forms of slavery with kid gloves. By encouraging indentured labour migration from India, he would also acquire the power to effect demographic redistribution – albeit of a different kind – that he had lacked in the first phase of his career in Britain.

By the time Wilmot-Horton was governing Ceylon, his ideas for emigration schemes had been superseded back home. In the early 1830s British reformers saw the repeal of the Corn Laws, which protected British landowners by maintaining high domestic food prices, and to which we will return in Chapter 5, as the solution to domestic pauperism. When it came to emigration Edward Gibbon Wakefield, who described Wilmot-Horton as 'an ignorant and meddling pretender in political economy', was taking the limelight.[24]

Born into a Quaker farming family, Wakefield seems to have rejected the faith's pacifism early in life. After his expulsion from three schools for fighting he gained employment with the British envoy at Turin. While in London in 1816 he met Eliza Pattle, a ward of chancery whose father had been a merchant in the opium trading port of Canton. Seeing an opportunity to advance himself, Wakefield persuaded Pattle to elope with him and the couple got married in Edinburgh. Much to Wakefield's disappointment, Pattle died just before she could inherit the £30 000 due to her on her twenty-first birthday. Five years later the ambitious Wakefield saw a second opportunity. He abducted Ellen Turner, the fifteen-year-old heiress of a wealthy manufacturer, from her boarding school in Liverpool. Telling her that her father was seriously ill, he bundled

Turner into a coach and drove her to Gretna Green, where he insisted that her father's fortune depended on their marriage. The wedded couple were caught by Turner's concerned relatives in Calais as they made their way to Paris. The court case attracted considerable attention, and Wakefield was sentenced to three years in jail. When Wakefield first recorded his thoughts on emigration in 1829, he did so from his cell in Newgate Prison, publishing them anonymously in instalments of the *Morning Chronicle*. Wakefield claimed authorship only after his release. His notoriety as an abductor of heiresses made his proposals all the more enticing to the British elite.

Despite languishing in Newgate, Wakefield wrote his book, *A Letter from Sydney*, from the perspective of an imaginary settler in Australia. The preface made his intent clear:

No pains should be spared to teach the labouring classes to regard the colonies as the land of promise, which it should be their highest ambition to be able to reach. Nor does this matter concern the poorer orders among us alone. . . . It is unfortunate that these establishments should so long have been regarded as fit only for the residence of convicts, labourers, mechanics, and desperate or needy men. . . . Hitherto, at least, our population has been increasing at the rate of between 300,000 and 400,000 annually, while those removed to our colonies, including convicts and emigrants, have not exceeded the rate of 7,000 or 8,000 at the utmost. We may, however, expect the ratio of emigration to rise considerably above this, and we ought to use all our efforts with that view.[25]

Wakefield may not have acknowledged it, but it seems that much of his thought about a better form of British colonialism may have been influenced by his grandmother, the Quaker writer Priscilla Wakefield. Not only had she chided Adam Smith for ignoring women's 'proportion of usefulness' in his writings on political economy; she had also lamented the degeneration of Britons in North America. Their dispersal across the wilderness, rather than concentration into well-planned settlements had led them to be 'unrestrained by law or good manners'.[26] Her grandson's imaginary Sydney-based narrator went on to ventriloquise three key principles to guide emigration policies. The first was that land in Australia should be sold for a 'sufficient price'. This was to prevent those who emigrated with little money from being able to purchase it. If they could not become land-owners in their own right, they would be forced to supply their labour to wealthier, landowning emigrants. If wealthier settlers could not rely on British workers, Wakefield's letter writer warned, they would be obliged to resort once again to imported slave labour. This was just the kind of shocking prospect to catch a proud abolitionist public's attention.

The lesson that the majority of colonial emigrants should be priced out of the land market was apparently being learned anew even as Wakefield was writing his *Letter*. In 1827, Captain James Stirling had pressed for a survey of the Swan River in Western Australia as a potential site for colonisation. He and the wealthy speculator Thomas Peel gained permission from the Colonial Office to establish the Swan River Colony (now the city of Perth), on the Nyoongar people's land in 1829. It would be Australia's first non-convict colony. The Colonial Office had stipulated that settlers should be granted land in proportion to the assets and labour that they brought with them. Provided they improved that land, the emigrants would secure full title to it. The proposers of the scheme envisaged that indentured British labourers would continue to work the wealthier settlers' land for contracted periods of three, five or seven years. But as Wakefield proclaimed in 1834, 'Those who went out as labourers, no sooner reached the colony than they were tempted, by the superabundance of good land, to become land-owners. One of the founders of the colony, Mr. Peel, who, it is said, took out a capital of £50,000, and 300 persons of the labouring class, – men, women, and children, – has been left without a servant to make his bed, or to fetch him water from the river'.[27] With the Nyoongar still resisting colonisation and settlers, at this point, for the most part unable to see their potential economic value as workers, Wakefield pinned the failure of the colony to provide for its own subsistence on the neglect of his 'sufficient price' maxim.[28] Never mind that, as the Swan River colonists themselves pointed out, it was the quality of the land that was actually the more significant limitation.

Wakefield's next principle was that the proceeds of the sale of Aboriginal land 'at sufficient price' would fund the transportation of further, poorer, emigrant labourers to the colonies, thus freeing British rate payers of the cost. Finally, he urged, the transplanted microcosms of British society resulting from the first two principles should govern themselves at the earliest opportunity, under an imperial viceroy. Put all the principles together and you had 'systematic colonization'.

In May 1830, newly out of prison, Wakefield began to campaign for public and government support for his programme by forming the National Colonisation Society. He networked vigorously. Among the early members of the society were Robert Rintoul, the editor of the *Spectator*, and the liberal political economist and philosopher John Stuart Mill, who was soon to be promoted to the East India Company's Political Department. Mill's mentor and the most famous political philosopher of the day, Jeremy Bentham, also offered Wakefield his advice. Lord Howick, son of Prime Minister Lord Grey, persuaded the Colonial Office to pass the Ripon regulations in January 1831, ordering the governor of New South Wales to cease distributing land for free and start selling it at not less than 5s. per acre.

By 1834, Wakefield was pressing ahead with plans for the new colony in South Australia and the following year he chaired the first meeting of the New Zealand Association, which would later become the New Zealand Company. The parliamentary bill that Wakefield drafted following the meeting, seeking government permission to colonise New Zealand under the auspices of the association, proved unpopular with both the Colonial Office and the Church Missionary Society (CMS), which had missionaries among the Māori. They baulked at the 'unlimited power' that Wakefield's directors proposed to wield in New Zealand, just as the Colonial Office had done in the case of South Australia. The CMS in particular was also concerned for the bill's implications for the Māori. Again Wakefield was undeterred and the association engaged in a bout of intensive lobbying and rebranding, which was still under way in 1838.

Wakefield's relations with the Colonial Office were tense. Stephen in particular never seemed to bow to Wakefield's bidding, no matter how hard he lobbied. Nevertheless Glenelg recognised that the Cabinet would have to act upon the suggestions for more organised emigration. He appointed Thomas Elliot, whom we met in the introduction, as the first agent general for emigration in 1837. Ellliot's task was to create a new department within the Colonial Office to oversee the selection of emigrants for the colonies and to advise the secretary of state.[29] Elliot came from a well-connected Scottish family and had spent six years in India following his father's appointment as governor of Madras in 1814. He believed that growing up with a father who had extensive experience in both the West and East Indies had taught him 'liberality'. He found employment as a junior clerk in the Colonial Office from 1825 and was promoted to précis writer in 1827. James Stephen had advocated his responsibility for emigration schemes to Australia in 1834. Elliot returned from secondment to a commission of inquiry into Canadian affairs, which we will come onto in the next chapter, to take up Glenelg's newly created role.

Elliott's position enabled him to become a prominent figure not just in political but also in literary circles. He was friends with John Stuart Mill and William Makepeace Thackeray, the author of *Vanity Fair*, who described Elliot's house in London as his favourite place. Elliot was also close to the increasingly celebrated literary figure, Thomas Carlyle, organising the series of lectures in 1837, in which Carlyle outlined his principle 'that great men should rule and that others should revere them'. By then Elliott himself was confronting issues which seemed to require someone of greatness to resolve: not just apparent British population 'overspill', manifest in rural and urban unrest, but also the threat of labour shortages following emancipation in the former slaveholding colonies. His work behind the scenes for Stephen and Glenelg during the months leading up to emancipation focused on the means by which government could promote migration of the 'right kind' to address each colony's needs.[30]

Elliott realised that in principle, both domestic and colonial demographic problems could be solved by directing the British 'overspill' to fill the labour gaps created by the emancipation of plantation slaves. One of Elliott's first suggestions, in March 1838, bore some of the hallmarks of Wilmot-Horton's prior pauper emigration scheme for Canada, only directed at the Cape Colony. As with British planters in Jamaica, Dutch/Afrikaans-speaking colonists in the Cape feared that their slaves would revert to subsistence living on marginal land as soon as they were freed by the British, leaving farms and vineyards bereft of labour. By 1838 thousands of slave owners were already taking their slaves with them across the colony's border, partly in anticipation of emancipation, by-passing the amaXhosa along the eastern frontier, and heading north and east onto the lands of the BaTswana, BaSotho and amaZulu. Their escape would later be dignified and mythologised with the title 'The Great Trek'.

Early in 1838, Elliott's first proposal was that a commission should be formed in the Cape Colony to conduct a new system of emigration from Britain to remedy the colony's anticipated labour shortfall. Indigent British boys between the ages of ten and fourteen would be sent out to work for farmers in the colony. Mainly orphans and workhouse inmates, they would remain apprenticed to their Afrikaans and British employers until the age of twenty-one. Their welfare would be overseen by the local Clerks of the Peace, who were still mainly Afrikaners. Elliot estimated that 15 000 to 20 000 British boys could, in this way, be kept constantly under indenture in the colony. The scheme blended Wilmot-Horton's emphasis on pauper emigration to solve Britain's 'overpopulation', with Wakefield's insistence on the maintenance of a permanent white labouring class in the colonies. At the same time it promised a way of replacing the labour of freed slaves, with potential applicability elsewhere.

Stephen's response was less than enthusiastic. He dismissed the idea even before it could be passed on to Bourke's successor in the Cape, Benjamin D'Urban. As well as being concerned about the effects of the distance and the conditions of employment on the British boys' welfare, Stephen alluded to the failure of a prior proposal to import labour to the Cape Colony. This too would have brought people on conditions of indenture, only from Mauritius rather than Britain. Aside from the Creole slaves owned by French planters, Governor Nicolay in Mauritius had inherited enslaved and now apprenticed people formerly belonging to Napoleon's colonial government. It was these 'Government Blacks' whom Nicolay had proposed as a suitable labour supply for the Cape. Stephen noted that colonists in the Cape had rejected Nicolay's offer because they 'did not feel equal to [the workers'] remuneration', even under contracts of indenture. If the Cape's colonists were not willing to pay formerly enslaved Mauritians enough, how likely was it that they would remunerate British children sufficiently? Stephen saw in Elliott's proposal the hint of a new system of white slavery.[31]

Nicolay's and Elliott's were not the only proposals for the redistribution of British subjects to come before Stephen. In the Caribbean colonies planters were particularly vocal in agitating for a labour supply to replace the soon-to-be liberated apprentices. In late 1837, Stephen considered plundering the Mediterranean island of Malta in response. The Maltese proposal came via Jamaica's governor Lionel Smith, whose suggestion of limiting 'Coloured' representation in the Assembly was being considered at the same time. Smith got the idea of conciliating Jamaica's planters with imported Maltese labour from the commissioners he had appointed to enquire into the apprenticeship system, after the publication of James Williams' book.

Having assisted the Maltese to overthrow French occupation in 1800, Malta had become a strategically valuable naval possession and a vital nodal point in the transmission of communications between Britain and India. From their vantage point in Jamaica, it seemed to Smith's apprenticeship commissioners, Daughtery and Gordon, that Malta might also provide a solution to the impending labour crisis on the sugar plantations. The commissioners suggested that 'Europeans [were] physically unfit for toil beneath a tropical sun and that only the natives of Malta were fit to fill the void soon to be left by the emancipated negroes, [who] could not be depended on'. As far as the *Jamaica Standard* was concerned, this was 'the most important, and ... feasible, proposition which we have for some time seen. ... Emigrants indeed we must have, if we would wish to make anything like crops after 1840; and the sooner we set seriously to work the better'.[32]

Clearly the 'natives of Malta' were considered more capable of working in hot and humid conditions than fairer northern Europeans. It was by no means a new idea that different 'races' were suited to conditions of work in different climates, but as the threats and opportunities of emancipation loomed and as the British government grappled with an apparent surplus of population at home, the imperial government was putting such ideas to the test more directly in 1838. Stephen, Grey and Glenelg rejected the proposals that we have considered so far, for labour flows between Britain or Mauritius and the Cape, and also from Malta to Jamaica. But at the same time, they were managing two other redistribution schemes which indicated an emerging policy based very largely on race.

'Surplus' white Britons would be sent to the temperate settler colonies where they would supplant Indigenous peoples from the land and, initially at least, supply labour to other white settlers. Colonial subjects of colour, mainly Asian, would substitute for enslaved labour by moving from colonies of labour surfeit to subtropical plantation colonies of deficit. For all of Stephen's professed non-racialism when it came to civil rights, the Colonial Office would become the managerial centre of this racialised global redistribution of people and their labour.

The government-backed schemes which best indicate this emerging policy orientation in 1838 involved the settler colony of New South Wales and the plantation colony of Ceylon. New South Wales' governor in late 1837 was the same liberal Richard Bourke who had produced the Khoisan 'Magna Carta' in the Cape. Bourke had arrived in Sydney in late 1831, when the population of New South Wales was around 51 000. With routes through the Blue Mountains to the west opened for colonisation over the last twenty years and further prospects for settlers in the Port Phillip District around Melbourne from 1836, the colony's frontiers were expanding rapidly. By 1838, the settler population had increased to 97 000, including former convicts and their free descendants. The New South Wales that Bourke sought to govern was a very different entity from the small penal colony of the late eighteenth century.

One immediate problem that Bourke faced was the same as that which had confronted governors of the Cape Colony: although many more free migrants were arriving from Britain, business opportunities and the easy availability of land had enabled the Ripon regulations on relatively expensive land sales to be bypassed. Employers were still struggling to find sufficient labour. The Aboriginal population within the colony's limits had been drastically reduced by disease and violence, and although some settlers relied upon Aboriginal people's employment, as far as most were concerned, there were still too many opportunities for Indigenous survivors to evade working for the British invaders.

In March 1837 Stephen sent Bourke a further proposal from Elliott, for 'a more efficient and systematic scheme of emigration to the Australian colonies'. Elliott suggested the importation of both white and Asian labour. For white sources, he drew upon Wakefield's ideas. Two-thirds of the Crown land sales fund – money raised from the government sale of appropriated Aboriginal land to settlers – should be paid as bounties to emigrants, or recruiters of emigrants from Britain. Glenelg agreed with Elliott that this would help remedy New South Wales' labour shortages and Bourke was willing to adopt this aspect of the proposal, although still unhappy about its financial implications. Given the violence involved in overcoming Aboriginal resistance, he needed to use the Crown land sales fund for a more effective police force. His most emphatic concerns, however, were in response to Elliott's suggestion of complementary Asian immigration, drawing upon the precedent being set in Mauritius.

If Mauritius could continue to attract sufficient labour from India, Elliott wondered, why could not New South Wales? What Elliot did not know was that as he was preparing his proposal, accounts of disease, death and overcrowding among the Indian workers recruited for Mauritius were being brought to the attention of the East India Company government in Calcutta, and then of the British Parliament. A police superintendent would shortly be appointed to check the engagements of the labourers and conditions on board their ships. In the same year, John Gladstone, West Indian slave owner and father of the future prime minister William Ewart, was planning to recruit indentured Indian labourers for the South American colony of British Guiana. Faced with evidence of wholesale entrapment through fraud, violence and degrading conditions, the government of India was compelled to ban all indentured labour recruitment for other colonies. It would not be until 1842 that indentured Indian labourers were recruited for Mauritius again, this time regulated by a Protector of Immigrants.

In the meantime, Elliot's proposal for Indian labourers to be imported to New South Wales coincided with a more local initiative of the same kind. In 1836–7 the entrepreneurs John Mackay, formerly a trader in India, and J. R. Mayo from Mauritius, also drew upon their knowledge of the Mauritian precedent. Elliot was unaware that Bourke had already established a committee to investigate their proposal for a scheme to import Indians to New South Wales. The governor had decided to reject its recommendation that Indians be recruited with certain protections, and he now rejected Elliot and the Colonial Office's suggestion too. 'Upon the subject of Indian labourers', Bourke wrote, 'the attempt would, I fear, prove a sacrifice of permanent advantage to temporary expediency'.[33]

While New South Wales' settlers might well secure their immediate labour needs from imported Indian indentured workers, Bourke's fear was that the price would be intractable long term demographic problems. His explanation anticipated the concerns of other governors in colonies where British emigrants were settling en masse. What was most important in these colonies of settlement was the racial profile of the imported labour force. Colonised people of colour were fine if the governor's task was to maintain a colonial economy dominated by a 'plantocracy' in need of cheap, exploitable workers. Some parts of the settler colonies resembled plantation societies, and in the following decades sugar production in both Queensland in Australia and Natal in southern Africa, would come to rely on indentured Pacific Islander and Indian workers respectively. Chinese indentured labourers would be employed in the Australian, southern African and North American colonies once gold was discovered and large quantities of cheap labour were needed to extract it. Even in 1838, Charles Prinsep, whose family had investments with the Company in India as well as Van Diemen's Land, independently sent an overseer to recruit one Chinese and thirty-seven 'Lascar' Indian workers for his estate on the Leschenault Estuary near Perth, described by one visitor as a 'droll sort of East India establishment'.[34]

But in the temperate settler colonies during this moment of emancipation British governors interpreted their task differently. Rather than securing workers for the most unpleasant conditions cheaply, their primary task was the reception of British emigrants and the building of neo-Britons. Despite some support for an indentured Indian labour scheme among pastoralists in New South Wales, many of whom were already employing Aboriginal workers, Bourke insisted that any new government scheme for labour importation be restricted to Britons only.[35]

At the same time that Bourke was determining the racial profile of imported labour in Australia (a policy with considerable longevity), the former emigration theorist Robert Wilmot-Horton was back at the centre of innovation around migration in Ceylon. Unlike his counterpart in New South Wales, Wilmot-Horton had become an enthusiastic proponent of migrant Indian workers. He saw them, under suitable contracts of indenture, as the remedy for impending labour shortages on the coastal belt plantations. In the lead up to emancipation, he wrote as energetically as ever, in support of a large-scale Indian-Ceylon indentured labour circuit. Ceylonese planters, he explained, were now emulating their counterparts in Mauritius, tapping into the same indigenous systems of agricultural bondage in southern India which had formerly supplied the island with slaves, to recruit indentured labourers instead. In early 1838, he told James Stephen that he was keen to deploy the East India Company's new steam ships (which we will come onto in Chapter 6), to move these contracted workers more regularly and reliably across the thirty- to fifty-mile-wide Palk Strait.

While Bourke was cautioning the Colonial Office to restrict Australian immigration to Britons alone (and requesting at the same time that Wilmot-Horton himself cease sending Ceylonese convicts to his colony), Wilmot-Horton was advocating flows of Indian workers for all the plantation colonies. During the months leading up to emancipation in August, these two governors' correspondence with Stephen contributed to the imperial government's emerging policy of racialised population redistribution – perhaps the largest scale government-orchestrated migration policy in history.

At the moment that it emancipated enslaved people, the British government saw investment in the emigration of Britons as being worthwhile, so long as they were bound for the temperate settler colonies, where they might work for established or immigrant employers in the construction of neo-Britons. Some 20 million of them emigrated during the course of the century, the largest single group to the USA beyond Colonial Office control, but the rest largely to the British settler colonies of North America, Australasia and southern Africa. Certain kinds of inter-colonial labour flows to address post-emancipation shortages elsewhere, such as those from Mauritius to the Cape or from Malta to Jamaica, were considered impractical. However, indentured migrants from Company controlled India were seen as suitable substitutes for freed slaves. It was their labour, rather than that of Britain's population 'surplus', which would ensure the continued productivity of the empire's plantations. An Indian diaspora of more than half a million would be transported to the Caribbean, Mauritius, Ceylon and Fiji as indentured labour between the late 1830s and 1917.

Together, these twin diasporas, of white Britons to the settler colonies and of Indians to the plantation colonies, would allow Stephen, Grey and Glenelg to fulfil the British promise of emancipation in 1838. Simultaneously, they eased Britain's perceived demographic crisis and guaranteed the imperial economy's labour supply. Britain could have its cake as the nation that emancipated its colonial slaves, and eat it by colonising other peoples' lands for its 'overspill', while securing cheap Asian labour to produce its tropical commodities.

Further Reading

Banivanua Mar, T., *Violence and Colonial Dialogue: Australia-Pacific Indentured Labor Trade*, University of Hawai'i Press, 2007.

Bashford, A., and J. Chaplin, *The New Worlds of Thomas Robert Malthus: Rereading the Principle of Population*, Princeton University Press, 2016.

Hall, C., *Civilising Subjects: Metropole and Colony in the English Imagination 1830–1867*, Verso, 2002.

Huzzey, R., *Freedom Burning: Anti-Slavery and Empire in Victorian Britain*, Cornell University Press, 2012.

Kumar, A., *Coolies of the Empire: Indentured Indians in the Sugar Colonies, 1830–1920*, Cambridge University Press, 2017.

Twaddle, M., ed., *The Wages of Slavery: From Chattel Slavery to Wage Labor in Africa, the Caribbean and England*, Frank Cass, 1993.

3   Political Freedom

Given the complexities of emancipation during the first half of 1838, one might have forgiven James Stephen for putting other issues on the back burner.[1] However, during the first months of 1838 and indeed throughout the year, the Colonial Office was simultaneously confronting an imperial crisis in British North America. At the same time that he was seeking to manage the advent of enslaved people's freedom, Stephen had to deal with the far reaching implications of colonists demanding the freedom to govern themselves.[2]

Both Glenelg and Stephen feared that allowing emigrant settlers self-government might have two catastrophic consequences. First, it could set in train a process of concession leading the Canadian, Australian and southern African settlers down the path that colonists in the USA had adopted – towards complete independence from Britain. This could spell the humiliating end of the British Empire in its current form. Secondly, granting settlers control over their own policies would in all likelihood have devastating consequences for the empire's Indigenous peoples. The evangelical Stephen and Glenelg wished to redeem, reclaim and 'civilise' the prior inhabitants of settler lands, even as they encouraged British emigrants to dispossess them. By and large the majority of settler emigrants were more interested in Indigenous peoples' lands and potentially their labour, than they were in their eternal souls or their material welfare. Greater liberty for settlers would undoubtedly have to be traded off against reduced liberty for Indigenous peoples.

In this chapter we see how Stephen, Grey and Glenelg sought to manage the crisis in North America and what it meant for settlers and First Nations. In the next, we turn to the repercussions in Australia and southern Africa. In each of these vast regions, the freedoms of settlers and the ever greater restrictions placed on Indigenous peoples were inextricably connected. Taking the two chapters together, we ask how far Stephen, Glenelg and the Colonial Office would go to resolve the tension between settler and Indigenous freedoms in 1838, and indicate the longer term consequences of the compromises they made in that year.

Rebellion in the Canadas

The most gripping correspondence that Stephen received in 1838 was written in British North America in November–December 1837. The very first despatch that Stephen read, on 1 January, was sent from Lower Canada by Archibald Acheson, second Earl of Gosford, governor-general of British North America and lieutenant governor of the colony. Written on 30 November 1837, one of the Colonial Office clerks précised it breathlessly for Stephen's benefit: 'Detailed report of occurrences at St. Denis, St. Charles, and other points on the Richelieu – price set on the heads of Papineau & others. Proclamation calling on the rebels to return to their Allegiance – anticipation of necessity of placing disturbed districts under martial law – Volunteer corps raised for the defence of Quebec'. Over the next two days, as Stephen read the details behind these events, he appreciated that 'the very framework of state power was in danger of collapse'.[3]

Despite Gosford lacking the military background of most colonial governors, Glenelg's predecessor had appointed him to British North America, which comprised the six colonies of Upper Canada, Lower Canada, New Brunswick, Newfoundland, Prince Edward Island and Nova Scotia, in 1835. Gosford had formerly been Lord Lieutenant of Armagh in Ireland and the colonial secretary thought that the sympathy he had displayed there for Catholics would fit him for the delicate task of appeasing Lower Canada's French Catholic majority. As governor-general, Gosford would also oversee the lieutenant governor of the adjoining colony of Upper Canada. Between them, these two British North American colonies contained the bulk of overseas settlers for whom the Colonial Office was responsible.

In Lower Canada, French-speaking colonists inherited by the British Empire after James Wolfe's conquest in 1759, predominated among a settler population of some 500 000. In Upper Canada government-sponsored emigration had seen the largely Anglophone settler population increase to 400 000 by 1838. Numbers of First Nations people remain imprecise but in the 1870s it is thought that around 100 000 lived in the whole of British North America, with the largest nations each numbering about 9000. Their much greater numbers in the 1830s were already overwhelmed by an overall settler population of around 1.2 million in the six colonies taken together. By comparison, only about 58 000 Britons had emigrated to all of the Australian colonies since 1815.

Glenelg told Gosford to take commissioners with him, who would help him conduct a 'mission of peace and conciliation' with the French-speaking settlers. Gosford appointed Charles Grey, a former Company judge from India, and George Gipps, a military engineer who had been devising schemes for the employment of apprentices on construction projects in Demerara, in anticipation of their emancipation. Gipps was soon to become Bourke's controversial successor as governor in New South Wales, and we will catch up with him in the following chapter. Thomas Elliott had sailed with Gosford, Grey and Gipps as the commission's secretary, immediately prior to taking up his role as agent general for emigration in London.

These men's most urgent task was to negotiate a way through a stalemate in Lower Canada's governance. On one side was the lieutenant governor and his appointed Legislative Council, which composed the government executive. On the other was the House of Assembly. In both Upper and Lower Canada, the lieutenant governor could nominate a body of men to govern in concert with him. This executive would pass legislation and appoint the officials to effect it. Normally governors would appoint their executive from among the local settler elite, adding one or two trusted colleagues from previous postings to fill roles such as attorney general or colonial secretary. Governors would often arrive in a new colony accompanied by a minor retinue of such men alongside their family and retainers. The House of Assembly was a concession to the broader mass of propertied settlers in each colony, enabling their representatives to propose and vote on legislation. However, they were mainly advisory, their powers generally more limited than their counterparts in the former slaveholding colonies. In the Canadas, the legislation that they proposed could be vetoed by the Legislative Council and they lacked the ability to make appointments. Nevertheless, they could hold up everyday governance, since the executive could be stymied by non-cooperation if it failed to secure their assent before implementing legislation.

Louis-Joseph Papineau had come to speak for the *Patriote* party representing the French-speaking majority in Lower Canada's Assembly. His was quite a distinctive political position, not necessarily reflective of the bulk of the French-speaking colonists, or *Canadiens*. Since the late seventeenth century, Lower Canada had been colonised using a semi-feudal seigneurial system. Seigneurs were granted land by the French monarchy, which they would subdivide and allocate to other emigrants. Tenants paid the seigneurs in cash and kind for the land itself and for services such as milling and transport, while also paying tithes to the Catholic Church. Even under British rule in the 1830s, some 75 per cent of the settler population lived on land owned by about 200 seigneurs. Papineau's father had become a seigneur by purchasing land from the seminary of Quebec and he sought to preserve the status and influence of the seigneurial elite against Anglophone and Anglican influence. His was by no means a revolutionary agenda on behalf of poorer tenant farmers.

By the late 1820s British immigrants were assuming positions of authority and influence traditionally monopolised by the seigneurs. Papineau complained 'the resources of the country are devoured by the newcomers. And although I have had the pleasure of meeting among them educated and estimable men, who are glad to see me, the thought that my compatriots are unjustly excluded from sharing in the same advantages saddens me when I am at their gatherings'. Trained as a lawyer, Papineau's political career began as the Assembly's representative for the county of Kent, a district whose very name symbolised the Anglicisation of the colony. In 1835 Elliott reflected, 'I have never seen anyone who appeared more skilled than this Canadian speaker in the contrivances . . . by means of which a single man dominates the minds of a large number. . . . One look from Papineau would subdue all his Canadian flock'.[4]

Papineau did not have it all his own way among the *Patriotes*. He was a conservative *Canadien* nationalist, but the party was also an umbrella for more revolutionary activists. They sought the recreation of Quebec as a new republic, threatening to do away with the seigneurs' privileges as well as the governing British clique. When Gosford arrived in the colony and Grey, Gipps and Elliott began their work, the *Patriotes* were nevertheless agreed on one thing. They would use what limited powers the House of Assembly had to frustrate British investment in the timber trade, transport infrastructure and banks, all of which were wresting economic power from rural seignures and tenants while consolidating an urban Anglophone elite. Gosford arrived to find the executive and Assembly routinely resisting each other's initiatives and government grinding to a halt. In 1836, for example, all funding for elementary schools had abruptly ceased because neither body could agree on its distribution.

At this point, Papineau would have been happy with the Colonial Office granting the *Canadiens* a large degree of autonomy within the empire, along, he hoped, with Anglophone settlers in Upper Canada and the Catholics of Ireland: 'A local, responsible, and national government for each part of the Empire, as regards settlement of its local interests, with supervisory authority held by the imperial government, to decide on peace and war and commercial relations with foreign countries: that is what Ireland and British America ask for; and that is what within a very few years they will be strong enough to take, if there is not enough justice to give it to them'.[5] He organised the Assembly to produce ninety-two somewhat rambling and disjointed resolutions detailing *Patriote* demands. They included the election of legislative councillors with control of government revenue, which would diminish greatly the power of governors and their appointed executives.

Gosford and the commissioners advised the British government that some reform was necessary to get the colonial government functioning again, but the Colonial Office's hands were tied by very clear guidance from both the King and the Cabinet that no real political concessions should be made. Their fear was that reform in Lower Canada would set a precedent for more assertive demands from the other colonies of large-scale British settlement. At this point, even the model of an appointed executive and elected Assembly was being withheld in the new colony of South Australia, at least until such time as the settler population reached 50 000. Until then, the governor reigned supreme. Caught in a difficult political bind, Gosford sought to string out the concessions he *could* make. He appointed a few moderate *Patriotes* to the Executive Council, while prevaricating on the more substantive demands for governmental restructuring. Unfortunately for Gosford, in March 1836, Papineau and the Assembly were made aware of his covert instructions from London to limit concessions. This was thanks in part to a second key agitator, in some ways Papineau's Anglophone counterpart across the Ottawa River in Upper Canada, William Lyon Mackenzie.

Although Upper Canada lacked the French-British dimension of Lower Canadian politics, it shared tensions between an established settler population and a narrow governing clique. These tensions had been exacerbated by the recent flood of immigrants from Britain. In the late 1820s, up to 80 per cent of Upper Canadian settlers had been born in the USA, many of them loyalists escaping the American Revolution. Yet Upper Canada's lieutenant governors tended to exclude such 'ordinary' people from their appointed Legislative Council, just as *Canadiens* were excluded in Lower Canada, preferring both established and more recent British aristocratic arrivals instead. Everyday government in Upper Canada proceeded through the patronage of a confined group of Anglican Tories, known as the 'Family Compact'. By the late 1820s, the emigrant Scottish newspaper editor William Lyon Mackenzie had become the leader of the Reformers who took them on in Upper Canada's House of Assembly.

Known as a diminutive, combative and uncompromising character (often stereotyped as a 'fiery Scot'), Mackenzie edited the *Colonial Advocate* in York (a settlement soon to be recognised with town status as Toronto). He used the newspaper to advocate reform of the Tory establishment, often urging American constitutional precedents. In 1826 a group of fifteen young Tories had dressed themselves as Native Americans to raid his office, smashing the press and throwing his type into the bay. Thanks to the activities of this colonial style Bullingdon club, Mackenzie not only gained enhanced motivation but also £625 in damages with which to take on the colony's establishment.

Although the Colonial Office prompted incremental reform, Mackenzie sustained his sometimes hyperbolic attacks until a Tory majority expelled him from the Assembly in 1831. 'The Tories' short-sighted action helped recreate his image as a martyr and raised him to a key position at the very time the system they represented was being changed by local moderates and a new attitude in England'.[6] When Mackenzie was re-elected the following year, he marked his return with a sleigh procession through the streets of Toronto, accompanied by bagpipes and hundreds of supporters. Expelled, re-elected again and beaten up by Irish Catholics who supported the government, Mackenzie departed for London to agitate in person. There he met Joseph Hume, the radical Scottish MP, former East India Company surgeon, and friend of John Cam Hobhouse. He also published his grievances as *Sketches of Canada and the United States* (1833) under the pseudonym Patrick Swift.

In May 1834 Mackenzie published a private letter from Joseph Hume encouraging him in his struggle against the lieutenant governor and the Family Compact. Hume wrote that Mackenzie's treatment must 'hasten that crisis which is fast approaching in the affairs of the Canadas, and which will terminate in independence and freedom from that baneful domination of the mother country, and the tyrannical conduct of a small and despicable faction in the colony'. Hume was warning of precisely what the King and Colonial Office most feared – a repeat of the American Revolution, and the fragmentation of the British Empire. 'The proceedings between 1772 and 1782 in America ought not to be forgotten', he advised; 'and to the honour of the Americans and for the interests of the civilized world, let their conduct and the result be ever in view'. Hume also reminded Mackenzie and his allies in Upper Canada that they were not alone in North America. His postscript read 'The people in Lower Canada are taking the means of forcing their affairs on the government, and will, I hope, Succeed'.[7] Predictably, the lieutenant governor, the Tory establishment and the Colonial Office were all out-raged at Mackenzie's publication of Hume's letter.

By November 1834 an Assembly now dominated by reformers allowed Mackenzie to author its *Seventh Report on Grievances*, mirroring Papineau's ninety-two resolutions in the neighbouring colony. While Gosford played for time in Lower Canada, Glenelg instructed the newly appointed lieutenant governor of Upper Canada, Frances Bond Head similarly: to appease without making substantive concessions. Early in 1836, Bond Head, who was referred to by some colonists as Bone Head, informed Upper Canada's Assembly of his and Gosford's instructions. Mackenzie promptly shared them with Papineau.

Once the strictures on reform from the Colonial Office were leaked, more moderate reformers in both colonies found it much harder to contain their more militant allies. By 1836 Mackenzie, voted out of the Assembly again, was prepared to advocate the use of force for constitutional change. In both colonies events then came in swift and, for Stephen and the Colonial Office at least, bewildering succession. In Lower Canada, Papineau planned for an armed revolt to begin in December 1837 but the government faced insurrection beforehand as local officials and magistrates refused to govern in the countryside. Gosford outlawed 'seditious assemblies' and dismissed eighteen magistrates and thirty-five militia officers. By October, there were revolutionary local 'governments' across Montreal including the dismissed officials. As the 2400 regular British troops in the two colonies were marched to Montreal, Papineau and the revolutionary leaders organised a great Assembly at Saint-Charles. There a statement of the Rights of Man, tantamount to a declaration of independence, was drafted. When Gosford ordered the arrest of the ringleaders, Papineau and the other 'refugees' fled to Saint-Denis. Realising the scale of the threat on 10 November 1837, Stephen wrote to his wife, 'The state of things in this office at this moment would make a good farce or tragedy ... such a paralysis ... I never before say or imagined, much less partook of ... I see nobody, I hear of nobody – I have nothing to do, to say, or to think of, but Canada'. A few weeks later, he despaired, 'Oh Canada, what wrongs have I done thee that thou thus pursuest me in my house & my office, my walks & my dreams?'[8]

The Battle of Saint-Denis had been fought on 23 November 1837, a week before Gosford wrote the despatch that Stephen read on the first day of 1838 (see Figure 3.1). Some 800 rebels, half armed with guns, had prepared for the arrival of the British troops by barricading themselves in and around a formidable stone coach house. The rebels proved successful in repelling British troops, all but one of whose cannon rounds bounced off the thick walls. By then Papineau had already fled the scene and he played little further part in the rebellion. After receiving the disturbing news of the army's failure to stem the rebellion at the first opportunity, Stephen and his clerks anxiously awaited the next instalment in a frantic stream of despatches. On 5 January they read, with some relief, of the Battle of Saint-Charles, fought on 25 November 1837 at the second of the rebels' rallying points. Gosford told Glenelg, 'The slaughter among the insurgents was very great: An individual who left St. Charles on Monday the 27th, two days after the engagement, states that he saw upwards of 152 bodies interred and that there remained many more besides a great number killed in the buildings and burnt with them. It is

Figure 3.1 The Battle of Saint-Denis. The History Collection/Alamy.

supposed that their wounded amounted to about 300'.[9] The British soldiers suffered three killed and eighteen wounded.

On 1 February 1838, the Colonial Office celebrated the news that the rebellion in Lower Canada had apparently ended on 14 December 1837, with the defeat of the remaining 200 rebels barricaded in the village of Saint-Eustache. Gosford exulted, 'the measures adopted for putting down this reckless revolt been crowned with entire success. ... It will, however, still be incumbent on the executive government to maintain for some time longer a guarded and vigilant attitude'.[10] Despite having now received 'loyal addresses from the French and the Clergy' and secured 'tranquillity' in Lower Canada, Gosford had decided that he should resign, with the recommendation that his successor be given powers of martial law.

What Stephen could not have anticipated in February 1838 was that those rebels who had fled across the border to the USA would return with American allies in November 1838 to take on the British forces again. Although they would be defeated in a series of battles, the repressive techniques employed to put down this second phase of revolt in Lower Canada – burning, looting and executing surrendering rebels and American supporters on the spot – would leave a lasting legacy of resentment among many neutral settlers. That legacy would not be quite so

bitter in Upper Canada, but the implications for future imperial governance were just as great.

While *Canadiens* initiated rural insurrection in the summer of 1837,
Mackenzie was organising committees of vigilance and political unions in
Upper Canada. When all of Gosford's troops were sent to Montreal in
October 1837, Mackenzie seized his chance. He planned to lead his
supporters into Toronto, seize the armoury and government buildings,
and overthrow the government. He promised that Lower Canadian rebels
were ready to join them, spreading the resistance across both colonies,
and that his provisional government would confiscate and distribute 300
acres of Tory land to each participant in the assault. In the interlude
between the battles of St-Charles and St-Eustache he wrote
a 'Declaration of Independence', which would be printed over the weekend and distributed immediately before marching on Toronto. However,
on the day of the march Mackenzie decided to attack local Tories' homes
first. By the time he led his men into Toronto, a well-armed loyal militia
was lying in wait for them. Mackenzie's marchers quickly dispersed and
those who were not captured fled, along with Mackenzie himself, across
the border to the USA.

Immediately before his attempted rebellion, Mackenzie had published
a request for support in an American newspaper based in Buffalo. When
he reached the town he gave public addresses claiming that his compatriots wished to emulate their American kin and free themselves of British
tyranny. His appeals fell on many a sympathetic ear. When first confronted
by the need to fight, Papineau too had tried to mobilise Americans from
across the border but his insistence on maintaining the French seigneurial
system had militated against revolutionary support. It was only from
November 1838 that significant numbers of Americans, styling themselves
'Patriots', would come to the aid of the Lower Canadians. Mackenzie's
more revolutionary rhetoric appealed to them more immediately.

In December, Ogden Creighton, Justice of the Peace for the Upper
Canadian District of Niagara, wrote to the British consul in New York,
James Buchanan, to complain that

Under the eye of the American authorities, on the night of the 13th and 14th
December, an armed body of 200 men or more marched from Buffalo to Black
Rock with music and two field pieces and paraded in view of our militia at that
time guarding our Frontier. A portion of this armed force on the 15th day of
December crossed over in American Boats from the American shore to Navy
Island above the Falls of Niagara, an island ceded by Treaty to Great Britain and
there remain at the present moment. Their numbers are variously stated to be
600, 800, or more. They have thrown up entrenchments and are commanded by
an American of the name of Van Rensslaer. On the 17th December we sent a Row

Boat with a Magistrate and a few volunteers to examine their position. This boat whilst in our own waters passing to a British Island was fired upon by a field piece from Navy Island, the ball from which fell ahead of the Boat, and my informant states that Van Rensslaer, an American Subject, pointed the gun.

James Stephen read Ogden's despatch to Buchnanan on 29 January 1838, commenting that 'Treason and Rebellion have been crushed in both provinces, and happily in this without the aid of a single soldier [not quite true], but I confess we were unprepared for the sudden invasion of the whole American People, although we have spirit sufficient left to say in the language of our respected Governor, "Let them come if they dare"'.[11]

The journals and letters of those American Patriots subsequently captured by the British indicate that most were motivated by republicanism. As one of their historians notes, 'the capacity of other peoples for self-government could be doubted by Americans, but never its desirability or their desire for it'. These Patriots were inspired by a rising tide of revolutionary success on either side of the Atlantic: Bolivar's liberation of most of Spanish America in the 1820s, popular uprisings in Italy, France and Poland in the 1820s and 1830s and, above all, the multinational struggle for the liberation of Greece from the Ottomans, which Byron had done so much to publicise. As one of the captured Americans explained, 'When Greece tore the crescent [of Ottoman rule] from her standard, a Bozzaris and a Byron were ready to yield up their lives in her defence'. He and the other Patriots were obliged to do the same when their neighbours sought to overthrow imperial oppression. Other Americans' motivations were perhaps more prosaic. 'Desperation and idleness induced by the economic collapse of the late 1830s, Jacksonian democratic chauvinism, and pervasive anti-British sentiment influenced many'.[12]

In late 1837 Mackenzie was able to recruit enough Americans to resume the struggle against the Upper Canadian government. In December, as we have seen, he led them in occupation of Navy Island near Niagara Falls, which he declared the base of his provisional government. He and his followers were supplied by an American steamer, the *Caroline*, and when that was destroyed in a daring loyalist Canadian militia raid with the loss of an American crewman, more Americans were spurred to revenge by supporting the rebels. In early January a group of them attempted to establish a base at Bois Blanc Island, from which to attack the British garrison at Fort Malden. Several were captured before the remainder fled back to the USA. As raids continued through 1838, secret societies of 'Hunter Patriots' recruited up to 200 000 American sympathisers, although far fewer actually crossed the border to fight against the British and Canadian loyalist militia. They were ultimately disappointed in their hope that thousands of Upper

Canadian rebels would rally to their side, and by the American government's refusal to aid them.[13]

The man who had to decide upon the fate of the captured rebels and their American allies in Upper Canada was George Arthur, whom we met briefly in the last chapter, when he was lieutenant governor in Van Diemen's Land. Arthur was no stranger to conflict. His long and varied career as an imperial governor means that he crops up repeatedly in this book. He is best known as the official who presided over the genocide of Van Diemen's Land's Aborigines in the early 1830s, which we will come to shortly, immediately before his posting to Upper Canada. He arrived in Toronto while Mackenzie was instigating the cross-border Patriot raids in March 1838. Stephen had written to Arthur privately, deploring his predecessor, Bond Head's misgovernment: 'such putting off, such dawdlings, such panics ... such a paralysis ... I never before saw or imagined, much less partook of'. Arthur, he hoped, would turn things around. 'A resolute stand by a resolute man a few weeks ago would have subdued this violence. . . . Even yet there is time to stem the torrent by opposing a stern and uncompromising front to the Agitators'.[14]

Like most of his peers, Arthur had served during the Napoleonic War. Recognised for his bravery in a number or battles, he seemed to have the backbone that Glenelg and Stephen required. Also like most of his counterparts, and indeed most of the British elite, his experience of warfare against the French conditioned him to despise any revolutionary notion of democratic rights. While serving as a young man in Jamaica, Arthur had declared himself 'a perfect Wilberforce as to slavery', and as superintendent of British Honduras in the 1820s he had prosecuted British slave owners, freed slaves captured illegally along the Mosquito Coast and attempted to improve the conditions of enslaved timber cutters. But nothing in these anti-slavery measures indicated a sympathy for the 'Rights of Man'. Arthur believed in the rights of subjects rather than of citizens. To confer the responsibility of government to the masses would be to instil a state of chaos and violence as bad as the ungodly oppressions of slavery on the one hand and French Revolutionary Terror on the other. To compound matters, revolutionary Americans were now fermenting rebellion in a colony with which he had been personally entrusted. As he assessed the situation in Toronto, Arthur wrote that the British 'Canadas must always be hateful to the view of persons so enthusiastically attached to democratic institutions as are the Americans. ... When the Americans ... find a good opportunity they will attack us ... they feel their inferiority to England in civilization, it hurts their vanity, and they will turn upon us when we are in distress'.[15]

As the cross-border Patriot raids continued, Arthur told Stephen, 'I have caused 17 of the Ruffians who invaded the province to be executed which has damped the courage of the Patriots. ... They are the most Vain people in the world, and certainly believed that we did not dare to hang an American citizen'.[16] In addition, two of the Canadian rebel leaders, Samuel Lount and Peter Matthews, had already received capital sentences from Bond Head. Despite appeals from many settlers and the personal pleading of their wives, Arthur had them both hanged. His harshness was supported by thousands of settlers who had resettled from the USA to escape one revolution and, alienated by Mackenzie's radicalism, joined the local militia to prevent another.

It is easy to overstate the support that the rebels enjoyed in each colony, and especially in Upper Canada, in 1838. However, there were also a great many in the colony, including relatively recent immigrants from Britain, who agreed with their demand for governmental reform, even if they rejected their revolutionary ideology and violent tactics. Some of the British elite, including those upon whom Arthur would rely for everyday governance, were calling for clemency. As the rebellion fizzled out later in the year, Arthur told Stephen that his next steps would be a compromise between the demands of the divided factions. He would transport the other convicted rebels and Patriots back the way he had just come to Van Diemen's Land. In all, twenty-five American Patriots were executed, and eighty-one were transported. Mackenzie remained safely in New York until such time as he felt able to petition for a pardon and return to Canada. Papineau too received his pardon and returned from exile in France in 1845.

By the time the two rebel instigators had returned, the governance of British North America was being transformed, with tremendous implications for both settlers and Indigenous peoples around the empire. Before we turn to this transformation, though, it is worth pausing to consider where Canada's First Nations stood in relation to the rebellions. Their exclusion from the post-rebellion political settlement also introduces a much broader story concerning the relative freedoms of different kinds of imperial subject in the British Empire.

The Settler Rebellions and First Nations

Arthur clearly arrived in Upper Canada full of anti-democratic conviction and intent on stamping out rebellion. But he was also somewhat chastened from his experience of governing over Indigenous peoples seeking to defend their lands and societies. Arthur had been appointed lieutenant governor of Van Diemen's Land in 1823 in part because the Colonial Office considered that his humane actions on behalf of enslaved people in British Honduras would translate into a more sympathetic approach to Tasmanian Aborigines. At the same time that he developed the system of assignment to rehabilitate the penal colony's convicts, he had tried to reconcile the influx of free settlers with a show of 'humanity' to the island's prior inhabitants. He had failed utterly. Despite his public protestations that a solution had been found, he knew it.

The year before Arthur had arrived in Van Diemen's Land, one of the new immigrants, Samuel Guy, noted that a new settler 'will now have some difficulty in obtaining good land except he gets into the infrequent parts of the colony – among the wild natives'.[17] Although only 132 500 acres had been awarded to former convicts and free settlers between 1804 and 1822, within seven years of his arrival, Arthur had overseen the allocation of a further 1 899 332 acres. The central Aboriginal peoples had sought to defend their country by initiating a guerrilla war. Arthur responded by licensing settler retaliatory parties while employing a former builder from the East End of London, Gorge Augusts Robinson, to negotiate the surviving Tasmanian Aborigines' surrender and relocation. Despite Arthur's assurances that he would punish the unwarranted killing of Aboriginal people in exactly the same ways as those of white settlers, the *Colonial Times* insisted that Aborigines 'will be hunted down like wild beasts and destroyed'. By the mid 1830s the Black War, as the attempted settler extermination of Tasmania's Aboriginal people became known, combined with the introduction of new diseases, had claimed the lives of all but 200 of the main island's Aboriginal people. Estimates of the population prior to colonisation vary from around 3000 to 15 000.[18]

Accompanied by Aboriginal guides and intermediaries, Robinson had sought out these survivors from various Aboriginal groups on his 'conciliatory mission' and persuaded them to live in exile on the barren and neglected Flinders Island some sixty miles off the north-east coast of the main island. There they were subjected to a regime of schooling and agricultural training intended to 'civilise' them, but without adequate sanitation or nutrition. The forty-eight of them who survived that regime were finally allowed to return to Oyster Bay on the main island in 1847. Their deaths soon after meant that Tasmania's Aboriginal population today is descended primarily from Aboriginal women who had been forced or chose to live with white sealers in the islands of the Bass Strait.

Despite this genocidal outcome of his tenure in Van Diemen's Land, Arthur was by no means a murderous imperial autocrat. A committed, somewhat Calvinist evangelical, whose fight against slavery in British Honduras had been in earnest, he was deeply affected by the outcome of the Black War, writing to the Colonial secretary that the violence 'wholly engrosses and fills my mind with painful anxiety'.[19] He returned to Plymouth in March 1837 and between then and December, when he departed for Upper Canada, his state of 'afflicted mind' compelled him to talk directly with both Glenelg and Britain's leading humanitarian campaigner, Thomas Fowell Buxton, about the measures needed to protect Indigenous peoples undergoing colonisation at the hands of emigrant Britons.[20] His timing could not have been better and we will return to the effect that he had on imperial policy while in London in the next chapter.

More immediately, Arthur's tenure in Upper Canada was short-lived and he was so preoccupied with putting down the rebellion and deciding the fate of the captured Patriots that he had little time to effect any reforms of the colony's 'Indian policy'. The British government, however, was grateful that some of the first Patriots to launch incursions from the USA were rounded up by Mohawk. They were acting in accordance with deep rooted alliances. Since 1754, the British military in North America had relied upon its Indian Department to secure Native Americans' allegiance against the French. In the 1812 war against the USA, First Nations warriors had helped the British and Canadians. The treaties that secured this assistance had effectively recognised their sovereignty.

By the time of the rebellions though, Britain's strategic need for Indigenous allies had diminished. Glenelg's predecessor, George Murray, noted that 'the course which has hitherto been taken in dealing with these people has had reference to the advantages which might be derived from their friendship in times of war, rather than to any settled purpose of gradually reclaiming them from a state of barbarism and of introducing among them the industrious and peaceful habits of civilised life'.[21] The latter aims would entail rendering Canada's First Nations subjects of the colonial government rather than independent allies. This would also be more compatible with the settlement of hundreds of thousands of British emigrants on their land. In pursuing the aims of 'industry' and 'civilisation' among formerly independent allies, British authorities were interfering in every aspect of First Nation peoples' lives well before the settler rebellions broke out.

In late 1837, the Department for Native Affairs (civil successor to the military's Indian Department) was cutting back on the commitments made during wartime. These included what the British construed as 'presents', and what First Nations saw as reciprocation for military aid and payment for land occupation. More portentously, Bond Head, Arthur's predecessor, was planning the mass removal of Upper

Canada's Anishinaabe nations from their traditional lands. In November 1837, he had sent a despatch to Stephen rationalising the 'Indian' policy that he had begun to adopt the preceding year. It was based upon local settlers' assertion that the attempt to make 'farmers of the Red Men has been, generally speaking, a complete failure'.[22] They had proved themselves incapable of 'civilisation' while living among settlers. In fact, as we will see, there were small but proliferating examples of First Nations communities in both colonies, who were adapting to encroaching settler colonialism by farming their own reserve land and selling their produce to colonists. Such communities could not win: they were resented by settler farmers, who saw them as competitors with the 'unfair' advantage of access to communal land and community resources.[23]

Bond Head was persuaded that 'congregating' First Nations on mission stations and reserves, while settlers filled in the gaps between them, 'has implanted many more vices than it has eradicated' and that 'the greatest kindness that we can perform towards these intelligent, simple minded people is to remove and fortify them as much as possible from all communication with the Whites'.[24] The lieutenant governor's plan was to remove the Anishinaabe nations from southern Ontario to Manitoulin Island in Lake Huron. This was a place well known to many of them since it was here that the colonial government's 'presents' were distributed annually among treaty partners. By the end of 1836, as tensions between the executives and assemblies of each colony mounted, some Odawa and Ojibwa bands were moving to the island voluntarily, but others saw in it a betrayal of promises made. As settlers in the two colonies prepared for rebellion, an Anishinaabe representative travelled to London to protest.

Kahkewaquonaby (Sacred Feathers) was also known as Peter Jones. His background prepared him well to mediate between the broader Anishinaabeg and the Colonial Office. He was born in 1802 to an Ojibwa mother, Tuhbenahneequay, the daughter of a Mississauga chief, and Augustus Jones, a retired colonial surveyor whose grandfather was Welsh, and who had moved to Canada with the loyalists during the American Revolution. With his polygamous father already married into an Iroquois family, Peter was raised by his mother as Mississauga Ojibwa. When his largely absent father discovered that a Mississauga band at the western end of Lake Ontario was breaking up, with poor harvests, diminishing game and rising alcoholism, he sent Kahkewaquonaby to a school at Stoney Creek. There he became known as Peter Jones and learned English. When he was fifteen he learned to farm on his father's land at the Grand River among the Iroquois. Initially baptised so that, as he put it, 'I might be entitled to all the privileges of the white inhabitants', he became a more sincere Christian convert after a Methodist camp meeting in 1823. At the end of the meeting the Reverend William Case cried out: 'Glory to God, there stands a son of Augustus Jones of the Grand River, amongst the converts; now is the door opened for the work of conversion among his nation!'[25] Thereafter Jones progressively rallied his family and many of his childhood community around the converted chief Thomas Davis' home and chapel, teaching Sunday school. In 1826, he attracted government support for a village for the Credit River converts in what is now Mississauga.[26]

Jones' mother and her community's willingness to become Methodist converts on mission land becomes more explicable when one appreciates that, within a single generation, their population had been halved and they had lost access to virtually all of their hunting and fishing grounds, thanks to the encroachment of British settlers and their diseases. There seemed little option other than to adapt as a community of farmers, demonstrating their willingness to engage with the particular kinds of 'industry' and 'civilisation' that the invaders of their land vaunted. At the Credit River mission Jones and his brother John could mediate with both the missionaries and the Indian Department in attempts to secure their future. In 1829 Peter was elected one of three chiefs there. Over the following decade, he and his supporters intervened with the government repeatedly on the community's behalf, requesting that settlers be prevented from fishing out all the salmon in the Credit River and insisting that the Indian Department continue to pay the band what, in 1818, they had promised in return for their original land. He also toured white communities raising contributions, especially among Methodists, for educational materials and equipment. By 1827 each family in the village was farming its own small plot and sharing in the cultivation of a 30-acre field. The acreage under crops increased, until their removal was threatened once again by Bond Head's plan for the relocation of the Anishinaabeg.

The trip to London that Bond Head's plan prompted was not Jones' first. He had taken part in a Methodist tour of Britain in 1831, writing to his brother, 'When my Indian name, Kahkewaquonaby, is announced to attend any public meetings, so great is the curiosity, the place is sure to be filled'. Wearing his Ojibwe clothing he spoke at over 150 venues, including at the anniversary meeting of the London Missionary Society at Exeter Hall. Having hosted the largest anti-slavery meetings, the building was now becoming the hub of a new campaign on behalf of Indigenous peoples in the settler colonies. Kahkewaquonaby's speech attracted an overspill of up to 5000 delegates.[27] When he fell ill in London, he was treated by James Cowles Prichard, the ethnologist who would soon launch a campaign to gather as much knowledge as possible about Indigenous peoples before, as most Britons 'regretfully' anticipated, they inevitably became extinct. He also met Eliza Field, his future wife, and petitioned the Colonial Office, securing a private audience with the King.

As a result of this eventful 1831 visit, by 1836, Jones had useful contacts in London willing to help him represent the Ojibwa's opposition to Bond Head's plan. Just as importantly, they would help him refute the lieutenant governor's pretext: that First Nations were incapable of adapting to life among the settlers. The most prominent among Jones' allies in London was Dr Thomas Hodgkin. Raised a Quaker and trained as a doctor at Edinburgh, Hodgkin had specialised in pathology in Paris before introducing the stethoscope to Guy's Hospital. As lecturer there, he gave the first comprehensive talks on morbid anatomy in England, but he has become best known in medical circles for his analysis of the disorder of the lymph glands and spleen, which was later named Hodgkin's disease. At the same time that he was carrying out his pioneering medical research, Hodgkin carved out his place at the centre of the colonial philanthropic networks that were emerging in London. He was on the British and Foreign School Society, supported freed black people's colonisation of Africa from Liberia and Sierra Leone as the solution to slavery, and extended his youthful interest in Native Americans into agitation on behalf of all of Indigenous peoples. In 1838 he would found the Aborigines Protection Society to safeguard what he saw as their interests across the empire.

When Jones met him again in 1836, Hodgkin, dressed as usual in Quaker clothing and using antiquated Quaker speech, was trying to gain promotion at Guy's in the face of a hospital treasurer who was also deputy chairman of the Hudson's Bay Company. The outspoken and principled Hodgkin had publicly criticised the HBC for its poor treatment of First Nations. His application failed. In the meantime, Jones informed Hodgkin, along with Buxton and his reformist allies, that most of Manitoulin Island was too rocky to farm. If Bond Head's plan were to be carried through, the Mississaugas would have to revert to hunting, abandoning their adoption of Britain's civilisation. By the time Jones got the chance to speak directly with Glenelg and Stephen in the spring of 1838, in between their frantic dealings with Parliament over the date of emancipation, the rebellions and the occurrences in Australia and southern Africa that we come to in the next chapter, they had already disallowed Bond Head's proposal, thanks in part to the agitation from Jones, Hodgkin and Buxton. Glenelg nevertheless ensured that Jones had a short audience with Queen Victoria before his return to Upper Canada.

Jones presented the young monarch with a petition, along with wampum, and requested title deeds to Credit River settlement on behalf of his community in order to safeguard against their future dispossession. Although the Queen gave her assent, it would not be enough. When he returned to Upper Canada, Bond Head's successor, Arthur, claimed no knowledge of the Queen's promise. By 1847, the 200 farmers at the Credit River mission had to move again in the face of the pressure of surrounding white settlement, the scarcity of wood and a government scheme to concentrate their settlement with other bands. They took up an offer of land from the Six Nations in the Grand River reserve, who wished to repay a debt incurred when the Mississauga had helped them move from the USA into Canada. They called their settlement New Credit, and their title to it remains today.[28]

As the rebellions broke out in late 1837, Jones was still in London protesting Bond Head's removal plan. Given the resentment that was simmering among affected nations, a few among the rebels reached out, albeit briefly, for such Indigenous allies. However, as the Mohawk's handover of captured US Patriots indicates, they had little success. Arthur told Stephen that Upper Canada's First Nations had 'turned out with alacrity and joined their brethren in the militia in defence of the country'.[29] They helped retain the integrity of the British Empire during its greatest crisis of the century so far.

This is not to say that the majority of loyal settlers were particularly grateful. Even as they set about recruiting First Nations men into the militia, settler magistrates expressed their deep reservations. The Anglican priest of London, Upper Canada, Richard Flood, acknowledged that it was only fear of loyal 'Indians' that prevented more rebels taking up arms in his parish. But he was still mightily relieved that the local loyalists had not in the end resorted to Anishinaabe communities for help. Flood was not alone in fearing that the 'Indians would probably have resorted to all those horrid barbarities of scalping and burning', had they been set lose upon the rebels.[30] For similar reasons, most of the rebels too, were afraid of the consequences of involving First Nations. Even in the midst of warfare between loyalist and rebel settlers, the bonds that distinguished them both from First Nations remained intact. Some among the *Patriotes* particularly hated the bands who had aligned themselves with the British during the conquest of Quebec. Upper Canadian rebels resented those like the Mississauga who had converted to Christianity and were successfully farming the mission and reserve land that they craved. In both colonies, self-government appealed to rebels not only as alternative to a Tory oligarchy, but also as a means of eliminating Indigenous claimants to land that would be required by the next generation of settlers.

In 1838 Glenelg and Stephen's unease about the way in which Bond Head was swayed by settlers' demands was transparent, even before they heard about it first-hand from Peter Jones. If the kind of locally responsible government demanded by rebels included settler representatives assuming responsibility for 'Indian' policy, they foresaw disastrous consequences for First Nations. As Glenelg's predecessor, Murray, had warned in the early 1830s, 'there is a proneness in the new occupants of America to regard the natives as an irreclaimable race, and as inconvenient neighbours whom it was desirable ultimately to remove'.[31] At the very moment that Britons were proudly proclaiming their virtue as the nation that had freed its slaves, the nation might well become tainted again by the annihilation of whole races of Indigenous peoples. George Arthur himself opposed the ceding of greater powers to settler assemblies not only due to his entrenched antipathy to democracy, but also, in the light of his experience in Van Diemen's Land. Yet precisely such a transfer of responsibility occurred in the wake of the Canadian rebellions. In order to understand how this happened, even with Stephen and Glenelg's opposition, we need to examine the broader British government's response to the Canadian rebellions.

The Durham Report and Self-Governance

In early 1838, as the significance of the Canadian rebellions sank in, Glenelg and the Cabinet sent a former radical MP to investigate how the settlers could be appeased. The man that they chose for the task was John Lambton, later Earl of Durham and widely known at the time by his nickname 'Radical Jack'. Durham had a tremendously wealthy background with an income derived from coal mines in County Durham. His childhood home, Lambton Castle, was one of the first houses in Britain to be lit by gas. An observer noted in 1832 that Durham's 'haughty and disdainful demeanour as well as petulant and ungovernable temper' made him 'generally unpopular'. He was known for personalising disagreements and readily taking offence.[32]

Durham had gained his political reputation as a radical after his denunciation of the Peterloo massacre in 1819. In the months that followed he proposed extensive parliamentary reform including a wide franchise. When his father-in-law, Earl Grey, became prime minister, he was commissioned to write the bill that would ultimately lead to the 1832 Reform Act. Some manoeuvring was required to bring the King to Parliament in time to prevent opponents from delaying the bill, so Durham went early one morning to Lord Albemarle, the master of the King's horses, to demand that he summon the King's carriage immediately. When

Albermarle asked 'Is there revolution?' Durham had replied, 'There will be if you stay to finish your breakfast'.[33] It would not be the last time that he saw reform as the counter to rebellion. Believing that he was the man to help conciliate the Canadian settlers, Melbourne's government asked Durham to become the new governor-general of British North America with powers to reform the governments of both Upper and Lower Canada.

Durham delayed his departure until April 1838, prodigiously spending government funds on preparation and equipment. The inclusion of enough musical instruments for an orchestra prompted Sydney Smith to quip that he was planning 'to make overtures to the Canadian people'.[34] Unperturbed, Durham added two particularly controversial figures to his entourage. Both of them had been involved in sexual scandals, and both alarmed Stephen and Glenelg. One of the new 'commissioners' was Thomas Turton, an old friend of Durham's from Eton public school, who had helped draft the reform bill and been employed since by the East India Company. He had left his wife Louisa Browne after having a child with her younger sister in Calcutta. Browne had become only the second woman in the British Empire to sue her husband successfully for divorce. As the scandal of Turton's inclusion in Durham's mission spread in the press, Melbourne would deny that this 'man of flagrant immorality', as he was labelled in the *Times*, had any official capacity. Durham himself insisted that Turton was his legal adviser.[35] The second controversial appointee was none other than the notorious emigration theorist and serial heiress abductor, Edward Gibbon Wakefield. Durham was a friend of Wakefield's and a proponent of his National Colonisation Society. As an adviser in Canada, Wakefield saw a new opportunity to secure the kind of settler self-government he envisaged under 'systematic colonisation' in Australia.

Wakefield was not the only recruit with an interest in Australian colonisation. Charles Buller, a third appointee whom Durham enrolled as chief secretary, was another. The author of the satirical portrait of the Colonial Office extracted in our introduction, he would become particularly influential in the spread of settler self-government around the empire. Buller had been born in Calcutta, the son of an East India Company civil servant. He was part of Wakefield's social and political circle, a friend of Thackeray and John Stuart Mill and a former pupil of Carlyle, who described him as 'a great tower of a fellow, six feet three in height, a yard in breadth'. Carlyle worried about Buller's 'lack of serious application', but nevertheless thought him 'a fine honest fellow' and 'the genialest radical I have ever met'.[36] By the time of his trip to Canada with Durham, Buller was a politician known for his parliamentary wit, and a gifted journalist.

Charles Dickens not only used his scathing description of the Colonial Office 'Sighing room' as the model for his 'Circumlocution Office' in *Little Dorrit*; he was also inspired by Buller to introduce a number of other veiled attacks on James Stephen and his family.

Buller had become an ally of Durham when he published the pamphlet 'On the Necessity of a Radical Reform' in 1831. Buller's neighbour in Cornwall was Sir William Molesworth, who, as we will see in the next chapter, chaired a committee on transportation to Australia just before Buller left for Canada. Buller gave evidence to this committee, opposing transportation and advocating Wakefieldian settlement as the alternative. Just before he left for Canada, he became the paid agent in London for the Australian Patriotic Association, founded by William Wentworth, the son of a convict woman and the publisher of the *Australian* newspaper, to campaign for representative government with a broad franchise in New South Wales: a project mirroring Papineau's and Mackenzie's in the Canadas.[37]

With Turton, Wakefield and Buller, Durham could not have picked a group of colleagues more enthusiastically and vocally committed to governmental reform and British settler colonisation. Stephen remained diplomatic, but he was clearly unhappy with the team that Glenelg had allowed the Cabinet to appoint in order to determine future policy for the Canadas. Along with his friend Arthur in Upper Canada, he feared that a 'terrible democracy' seemed inevitable. He would later write to Arthur, 'All those things must float to the surface of Society which one would wish to keep out of sight. . . . Canada is . . . a theatre for selfish conflicts under the specious pretext of Public Spirit. . . . Mere democracy must triumph there, and the ultimate catastrophe is not difficult to foretell'.[38]

Stephen's own preferred solution, however, did concede a much greater degree of self-governance than he had previously countenanced. Carefully apologising for 'deviating into topics which nothing but the magnitude of the occasion would have tempted me to enter upon at all', he suggested that, rather than Durham and his accomplices playing fast and loose with their own radical democratic notions, a federation should be formed of elected representatives from the British North American colonies to propose measures which would prevent the unrest in Lower and Upper Canada spreading. 'I therefore propose to conquer the Lower Canada Assembly by the creation and not the suspension of popular franchises', he wrote. Stephen was overruled, although his idea of a federation of Canadian colonies would become highly influential, as we will see in Part III.[39]

Possibly to Stephen's private relief, things did not go well for Durham and his entourage. Arriving in Lower Canada on 28 May 1838, Durham resigned and was back in England again within five months. The issue prompting his departure was the same that Arthur had faced in Upper Canada: what to do with captured rebels. Durham feared that a trial of Lower Canada's *Canadien* rebels might threaten public order and that it would be impossible to secure impartial juries. Taking Turton's dubious legal advice, he decided to banish eight of the rebel leaders to Bermuda. Since the loss of ports on the eastern seaboard of the USA, Halifax in Nova Scotia had become the Royal Navy's main harbour in North America, but the fleet spent each winter in Bermuda, and there were close ties between it and the Canadian colonies. The radical Durham disagreed with Arthur that the rebels should be transported as convicts to the Australian colonies. As political exiles they were deserving of more lenient treatment. Turton advised that Bermuda was the most suitable location for banishment, prompting the comment from one observer in Britain that 'Turton's law is not a jot better than his morals'.[40] Once a copy of Durham's ordinance reached the Colonial Office, Stephen, perhaps with some private satisfaction, reminded Glenelg that Durham may have had oversight of all the North American colonies, but he had no jurisdiction in Bermuda, the governor of which had given no assent. The rebels had already been taken there by the time Durham learned that his ordinance was disallowed and there they would have to be released.

As the freed rebels departed Bermuda for Louisiana to join the Francophone American community, Durham resigned on principle at this check to his authority. He had returned home even before the second phase of the rebellion broke out in November. Wakefield and Buller tidied up some of the investigations that Durham had delegated to them and returned shortly afterwards. It was not, then, these reformers' short-lived presence in Canada itself which would transform imperial governance during the ensuing years. Far more significant was the impact of the report that Durham belatedly submitted, and above all, its popularisation by Buller, in 1838–9. Wakefield ensured that Durham's *Report on the Affairs of British North America* was published serially in the *Times*, beginning on 8 February 1839, without authorisation from the government. Only afterwards was it produced in *Parliamentary Papers*. Durham's rival as leader of the Radicals in the Commons, Lord Brougham, summed up many contemporaries' understanding of its provenance: 'Wakefield thought it, Buller wrote it, Durham signed it'. Its most immediate recommendation, duly effected, was the unification of Upper and Lower Canada, largely in order to swamp the *Canadiens* within an Anglophone majority. As for British settlers in the two former colonies, Durham warned that 'if the mother country forgets what is due to the loyal and enterprising men of her own race, they must protect themselves'.[41]

Historians tend to have focused mainly on Durham's official report, but Buller's *Responsible Government for Colonies* was perhaps more influential. He wrote it from December 1838 to support Durham in the face of criticism from those, like Stephen, who doubted the wisdom of conceding to the rebels' key demands. Durham was urging that responsible or representative government (the two terms were used interchangeably at this point but would come to refer to different degrees of settler colonial autonomy over the next few decades) was essential. Far from threatening the disintegration of imperial governance, Durham argued that responsible government was the only concession which would prevent it. Buller was in some sense to Durham what Huxley was to Darwin. He popularised Durham's recommendations and mocked his critics, especially Stephen and the Colonial Office, in pugnacious style. 'A large portion' of British settler communities', he wrote, 'are ruled in the silence and obscurity of an essentially arbitrary form of government: and their policy is determined, without reference to public opinion, in the secret deliberations either of the Colonial Office at home, or of close councils in the Colonies composed of the nominees of the Governor'.

Despite acceptance of the need for political reform in Britain, Buller complained, 'we have got into a habit of considering the privation of free institutions as a necessary incident of the infancy of colonies'. Responsible government, he argued, was not 'about rebels, and Mackenzie, and Joseph Hume'. Nor was it that kind of government 'which prevails in the various States of the American Union, where every officer of government is appointed either by the direct vote of the people, or by that of the representative bodies of the State'. Rather, Durham was calling for a fast-forward version of the moderate political process that had benefitted England itself since the seventeenth century. Such reform was the antidote rather than the spur to revolution: 'The increased independence of the colony would rivet its connexion with Great Britain, by removing those numerous causes of collision that constantly arise in the practical working of the present system'.

Buller dedicated an entire section of *Responsible Government* to 'Mr Mothercountry's Faults'. There was no mention of James Stephen by name but it was not hard to discern who its central character was. He began with the office rather than the man: 'In nine cases out of ten', Buller wrote, 'parliament does not concern itself with colonial affairs'. It 'merely registers the edicts of the Colonial Office ... at the end of that cul-de-sac so well known by the name of Downing Street ... the appeal to the Mother Country is in fact an appeal to "the office"'. Buller then narrowed his sights: 'even this does not sufficiently concentrate the Mother Country. It may indeed at first sight be supposed that the power of 'the

Office' must be wielded by its head [Glenelg]; ... But this is a very erroneous supposition. ... Perplexed with the vast variety of subjects presented to him ... every Secretary of State is obliged at the outset to rely on the aid of some better informed member of his office. ... We do not pretend to say which of these persons it is that in fact directs the Colonial policy of Britain. It may be, as a great many persons think, the permanent Under Secretary'. While denying any personal criticism in his conclusion, Buller then drove the attack on Stephen home:

Probably married at an early age, he has to support and educate a large family out of his scanty though sure income[42] ... he has a modest home in the outskirts of London, with an equally modest establishment: and the colonist who is on his road to 'the Office', little imagines that it is the real ruler of the Colonies that he sees walking over one of the bridges, or driving his one-horse chay, or riding cheek by jowl with him on the top of the short coach as he goes into town of a morning. ... By day and by night, at office or at home, his labour is constant. No pile of despatches, with their multifarious enclosures, no red-taped heap of Colonial grievances or squabbles, can scare his practised eye. He handles with unfaltering hand the papers at which his superiors quail: and ere they have waded through one half of them, he suggests the course, which the previous measures – dictated by himself – compel the Government to adopt.

Buller had nothing to say about governance of the empire's Indigenous peoples or newly freed slaves, but when it came to British colonists, 'the system of intrusting ... power (for such it is) to one wholly irresponsible ... has all the faults of an essentially arbitrary government, in the hands of persons who have little personal interest in the welfare of those over whom they rule; who reside at a distance from them – who never have ocular experience of their condition'.[43]

Durham and Buller concluded that the Colonial Office should retain control of foreign policy, external trade and grants of Crown land, but that all other affairs (presumably, although this was never stated, including the government's relations with Indigenous peoples) should be left to elected colonial legislatures. These legislatures should also be responsible for the appointment of representatives on the executive who would implement their decisions.

Buller's conclusions were portentous for the empire as a whole. 'Were other [settler] colonies to be investigated by an inquiry as enlightened and as laborious as that instituted by Lord Durham', he declared, 'we should discover that' they too 'have suffered from the same causes quite as much as the Canadas'.[44] At the same time that he was writing *Responsible Government*, Buller was drafting a constitution on behalf of the Australian Patriotic Association in New South Wales. He would go on during the following year to write the charter of the New Zealand

Company and argue with Stephen and the Colonial Office on its behalf in the run up to the colonisation of New Zealand.[45] Stephen was quite right to fear that conceding to settlers in the Canadas would open a Pandora's Box of settler agitation for self-governance across the empire. In the next chapter we examine what impacts settlers' calls for the freedom to govern themselves had in the southern hemisphere.

Further Reading

Burroughs, P., *The Canadian Crisis and British Colonial Policy*, Hodder & Stoughton, 1972.

Greer, A., *The Patriots and the People: The Rebellion of 1837 in Rural Lower Canada*, University of Toronto Press, 2003.

Martin, G., *The Durham Report and British Policy*, Cambridge University Press, 1972.

Shaw, A. G. L., *Sir George Arthur 1784–1854 – Superintendent of British Honduras, Lieutenant-Governor of Van Diemen's Land and of Upper Canada Governor of the Bombay Presidency*, Melbourne University Press, 1980.

Smith, D. B., *Sacred Feathers: The Reverend Peter Jones (Kahkewaquonaby) & the Mississauga Indians*, University of Toronto Press, 1987.

4   Settler Liberties

Throughout most of 1838, as Stephen and the Colonial Office struggled to contain settlers' demands for self-governance within the rebellious Canadian colonies, settler communities elsewhere made similar demands with ever greater vehemence. Once Durham, Wakefield and Buller had released the genie of responsible government, it proved impossible for the Colonial Office to put it back in its bottle. At the same time that he corresponded frantically with the governors in North America, Stephen's office sent 343 despatches to New South Wales, 215 to Van Diemen's Land and around 50 to South Australia and Western Australia, many of them dealing with the balance between settler and Indigenous rights and freedoms.

Some of the key figures in and around imperial governance whom we have already met, including Thomas Fowell Buxton, Thomas Hodgkin and George Arthur, had transferred their earlier anxiety over the fate of Van Diemen's Land's Aboriginal people to the Khoisan and Xhosa peoples of southern Africa and the Aboriginal people of New South Wales. By the middle of the year, thanks to theirs and others' lobbying, a new office of colonial government was opened specifically to protect Aboriginal people from British settlers in what became Victoria. At the same time, the trial of white men accused of massacre in New South Wales prompted a concerted backlash, which rendered settlers even more resolutely determined to govern their own affairs.

Stephen was forced to acknowledge that the emancipation of former slaves was spurring increasing numbers of Dutch-speaking Afrikaner colonists to vacate the Cape Colony altogether. What had been a trickle of emigrants in the mid 1830s had become an organised incursion into neighbouring African chiefdoms by the time the emigrant 'voortrekkers' confronted the amaZulu at the Battle of Blood River in December. Afrikaner colonists' occupation of vast areas of the southern African Highveld to the north and north-east of the Cape Colony not only set an example of self-government for the Britons left behind; it ultimately created the geographical template of what is now South Africa. More immediately, the Colonial Office was concerned with the need to reign in British settlers' land lust, which was provoking the amaXhosa to war on the Cape Colony's eastern frontier, while at the same time, quite contradictorily, encouraging the emigration of more Britons there.

In this chapter we focus on how, in the wake of the Canadian rebellions, New South Wales and the Cape Colony moved towards their own forms of responsible government. We also develop a sense of just how committed Stephen, Grey and Glenelg proved to be, in practice, to the clashing 'natural rights' and liberties of the empire's Indigenous peoples. In 1838, both the promise of a new paternalistic, governmental concern and the incipient surrender of that promise were revealed.

The Eastern Cape Frontier and the Aborigines Committee

We will begin on the eastern frontier of the Cape Colony. The year 1838 was the year of peak lobbying by those sympathetic to Indigenous peoples' loss of land and livelihood, and the Colonial Office seemed more receptive to their concerns than ever. For a while during the British summer it even looked as if Stephen and Glenelg might actually threaten further British settler expansion in the southern hemisphere on behalf of the people of colour being devastated by it. But in order to understand where this humanitarian inclination came from, we have to examine events on the eastern frontier of the Cape Colony in the years immediately preceding.

The 4000 British settlers who had emigrated under false pretences to the eastern margins of the Cape Colony in 1820 had joined their Dutch-speaking counterparts in a struggle for grazing land with Xhosa chiefdoms. Chief Maqoma in particular was organising fragmented amaXhosa resistance to further colonial encroachment. His father Ngqika had attempted to repel colonists from the strip of land between the Fish and Keiskamma Rivers by attacking the colonial garrison at Graham's Town in 1819. After the beleaguered British soldiers were rescued by mounted Khoisan troops, Ngqika was forced to cede the land to the colony. The British authorities declared the ceded territory a neutral zone, to be left vacant as a buffer between colonists and amaXhosa. However successive governors had then acceded to colonists' demands to graze their stock there. The enraged Maqoma moved back in, re-establishing his chiefdom in the Kat River valley in 1822 and either turning a blind eye or encouraging his followers' raiding the settlers' sheep and cattle. Amid considerable tension, Maqoma was expelled again in 1829, to make way for a London Missionary Society-led settlement for dispossessed Khoisan

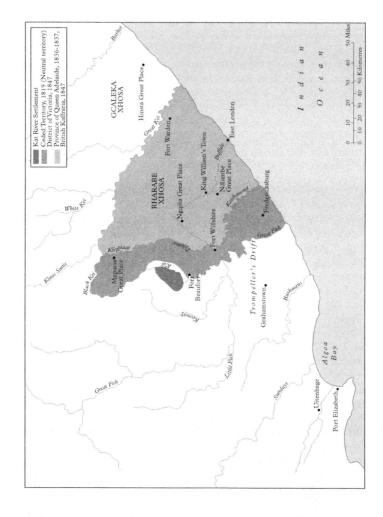

Map 4.1 The Eastern Cape frontier, 1838–57.

Kat River Settlement
Ceded Territory, 1819 (Neutral territory)
District of Victoria, 1847
Province of Queen Adelaide, 1836–1837,
British Kaffraria, 1847

GCALEKA
XHOSA

RHARABE
XHOSA

Hintsa Great Place

Fort Warden

Ngqika Great Place

King William's Town

Ndlambe
Great Place

Keiskamma

Fort Wiltshire

Fredericksburg

Maqoma
Great Place

Klipplaat

Fort
Beaufort

Grahamstown

Uitenhage

Port Elizabeth

East London

Indian
Ocean

Algoa
Bay

Trompetter's Drift

Great Fish

Buffalo

Kat

Black Kei

White Kei

Great Kei

Bashee

Klaas Smits

Kei

Koonap

Little Fish

Great Fish

Sundays

Tyumie

Buffalo

Keiskamma

0   10   20   30   40   50 Miles
0 10 20 30 40 50 Kilometres

Christian converts, who developed a successful agricultural community, the Kat River settlement (Map 4.1).

In the meantime, British settlers were consolidating themselves in the formerly 'neutral territory' and agitating for further eastward expansion. Their farms were occasionally raided by Xhosa warriors, their livestock taken or killed, fuelling their notion that the amaXhosa whose land they coveted were 'irreclaimable' savages and inveterate thieves.[1] The colonial authorities formalised the well established Afrikaner system of commandos – impromptu mounted militia – which had served in the dispossession of the Khoisan during the first century and a half of Dutch colonial expansion, to track the 'spoor' or trail of raided cattle to the nearest Xhosa kraal. There, British troops aided in their retribution, regardless of the particular homestead's culpability. Xhosa raiders soon learned to lead the vengeful commandos to innocent kraals just across the frontier before diverting back to their own homesteads.

When, in December 1834, a commando including British soldiers killed a high-ranking chief protesting his homestead's innocence, Maqoma and his half-brother mobilised a force of 10 000 warriors from an alliance of frontier chiefdoms to attack the colony. Twenty-four British settlers were killed and the Khoisan mission settlers were driven from the houses and farms they had built in Maqoma's former Kat River valley. As Afrikaner colonists mobilised swiftly to engage Maqoma's forces in the Winterberg Mountains to the north, British troops from Cape Town disembarked at Algoa Bay in the south. They were led by Colonel Harry Smith, who surely has to be one of the most bombastic characters in the record of British imperial governance.

Harry Smith had fought in many of the key battles in South America and Iberia during the Napoleonic War. In the midst of the carnage at the Battle of Badajoz he had taken a fourteen-year-old Spanish girl into his protection, and the couple married shortly afterwards. Juana Maria de los Dolores de Leon became a famously exotic member of Regency society and was the inspiration for Georgette Heyer's novel, *The Spanish Bride*. She accompanied Smith as he participated in the Battles of Salamanca, Vitoria and Toulouse. Smith next took part in the capture of Washington and burning of the White House during the War of 1812. Unaware that a peace treaty had already been signed in London, he negotiated the truce after the failed British attack on New Orleans. Somewhat more illustriously, he fought at Waterloo, and it was this which elevated him and Juana into the ranks of London society. As we will see in Part II, Smith would delight in his opportunity to humiliate the Xhosa chiefs in future years, with an interlude acquiring fame as the vanquisher of the Sikhs in the Punjab.[2] Right now, upon news of Maqoma's attack reaching Cape Town in December 1835, he rode 700 miles in six days to take command of the troops on the frontier. There he determined not just to punish Maqoma and the allied chiefdoms who had attacked the colonists, but to press home his advantage among the passive amaXhosa chiefdoms well to the east of the frontier.[3]

To the delight of most British settlers in Graham's Town, Smith led his forces across the Kei River into the territory of Hintsa, paramount chief of the separate branch of Gcaleka Xhosa. In May 1836, he took Hintsa hostage until such time as he could compel his people to raise an enormous indemnity of 25 000 cattle and 500 horses, to compensate the British settlers for the losses sustained in Maqoma's attack. Hinsta's protestations that, whatever moral and material support they may have lent their kinfolk to the west, his people were innocent of any attack upon the colony, were all in vain.

Taking Hintsa with him, Smith led a column of troops and settler guides through Hintsa's lands, seizing cattle wherever they could. When the mounted Hintsa, sensing an opportunity, tried to escape over the top of a rise, Smith himself chased after him. He tried to fire his pistol twice at the fleeing chief but finding it jammed, threw it instead. Missing him, Smith caught up and reached across at full gallop, pulling Hintsa from his saddle. By the time Smith had reigned in his careering horse Hintsa had picked himself up from the ground and, although hurt, was running towards the cover of a nearby stream bed. Before he could reach it the chasing settler guides and soldiers shot and wounded him. Hintsa made it to the stream bed and sought somewhere to hide. George Southey, a British settler and member of the Corps of Guides, was the first to discover him hiding behind a large rock. Realising that he had no escape, Hintsa called out for mercy but Southey immediately shot him through the head. Southey and others then cut off the dead chief's ears and dug out his teeth as trophies.[4]

Both the commando system, with its targeting of innocent amaXhosa homesteads, and the murder of Hintsa, would shortly become well-known symbols of colonial aggression in London, and problems of imperial governance for Stephen and Glenelg. This was largely because of the efforts of Dr John Philip. The London Missionary Society (of which James Stephen was a director) was well represented in the Cape, with up to twenty-five missionaries, and John Philip was its superintendent in the colony.

A Fife weaver's son and former manager of a spinning mill in Dundee, Philip had left the industry in disgust at its use of child labour and trained as a Congregational minister. He quickly established a reputation is a charismatic preacher. He and his wife Jane Ross, arrived with their seven children in Cape Town in 1819, just before the group of 4000 British emigrants reached the frontier.[5] Philip would remain there until his retirement, apart from three eventful visits to England 'Heavily influenced both by the political economists of the Enlightenment in Scotland, and successors such as David Ricardo and Sir William Blackstone, [Philip] believed that the colonial system of southern Africa in the early nineteenth century did not allow converts to lead Christian lives'.[6] Philip's first visit home was in 1827, to agitate for the reforms to the coercive labour laws which, as we saw in Chapter 1, bonded Khoisan to colonial masters. It was Philip's agitation which culminated in Governor Richard Bourke's Ordinance 50, the 'Hottentot magna carta' the following year.

On this first visit, Philip also wrote *Researches in South Africa*. Read widely in mission and evangelical circles, and, uneasily, by James Stephen, it was a narrative of systematic colonial mismanagement. On this visit Philip also established an enduring friendship with Thomas Fowell Buxton, engaged at the time in securing the abolition of slavery in Parliament. Philip helped persuade Buxton that philanthropic reform needed to reach beyond the institution of slavery and the colonies of the Caribbean. Deeply unpopular with the Cape's settlers as a result of this stirring in London, when Philip returned to the Cape Colony, he found himself convicted for libel against a local magistrate. His evangelical friends in Britain paid his substantial fine.

In 1835, as Smith was still trying to subdue Maqoma's forces and extend British rule over their lands, Philip travelled to Britain once more. This time he took with him James Read, the veteran missionary among the Khoisan converts in the Kat River settlement, and two Indigenous men from the Cape frontier, Andries Stoeffels, a Khoikhoi, and Jan (Dyani) Tzatzoe, a Xhosa chief. Philip hoped that both these men would testify in person to the reforms required if Africans were to enjoy the potential blessings of Christian British influence. Philip stayed in Britain for three years, and the party from the Cape became central figures in the growing campaign on behalf of Indigenous peoples during 1838.

This campaign was centred upon a remarkable extended family. Thomas Fowell Buxton's sister Sarah Maria; his daughter Priscilla, who had organised the largest anti-slavery petition ever presented to Parliament (signed exclusively by women), and her husband Andrew Johnston, were all involved. Perhaps most significant of all, however, was Thomas Fowell's cousin and Sarah Maria's 'partner', Anna Gurney (Figure 4.1).[7] Gurney came from a well-known Quaker business and anti-slavery family, into which Buxton had married. Disabled by polio

Figure 4.1 Anna Gurney by John Linnell, 15 February 1824. The Picture Art Collection/Alamy.

in her childhood, Anna was a wheelchair user best known today either as a pioneering scholar and translator of Anglo-Saxon English, or as the organiser of shipwrecked mariners' rescue.

Gurney was described by her friend Elizabeth Whately as possessing 'an actual hunger and thirst for knowledge of all kinds, which knew no pause, and could never be satisfied'. A speaker of Arabic, Danish, Dutch, French, German, ancient and modern Greek, Hebrew, Icelandic, Italian, Old English, Old Norse, Russian and Swedish, she published the first translation of the *Anglo-Saxon Chronicle* into modern English in 1819, aged just twenty-one. All this while 'striving to avoid the display of talents that might render her subject to the imputation of vanity or conceit' as a female author. Because of her gender, Gurney's publications in the journal of the Society of Antiquaries were anonymous until 1852.

Among those who are not scholars of Old English, Gurney is better known for her dedication to the rescue of shipwrecked sailors. Not only did she privately purchase a Manby Life Saving Rocket which could be carried along the Norfolk shore to fire lifelines to distressed ships; she would ask to be carried down to the beach to direct rescue operations on the dangerous stretch of coast near the Northrepps estate, and offer shelter and food to shipwrecked sailors. She was generally able to converse with the foreigners among them in their own languages.[8] Anna Gurney was one of those who hosted the 'liberated African' from Sierra Leone, Samuel Ajayi Crowther, whom we met in Chapter 2, when he was in England. Of course, when he visited Northrepps to preach at nearby Overstrand church, she learned Yoruba from him. She would go on to collaborate on a grammar of the Hausa language and work with the visiting African Baptist Augustus William Hanson on a translation of the scriptures into Accra.[9]

Upon meeting Philip, Stoeffels and Tzatzoe in 1835, Gurney joined Priscilla Buxton working behind the scenes to sustain Thomas Fowell Buxton's public and parliamentary campaign on behalf of Indigenous peoples. Over the next two years the group assembled and managed a network of missionary, philanthropic, governmental and settler correspondents which stretched around the world. Through these contacts they solicited and gathered information on the damage that British intrusion was doing to Native American, Khoisan, Xhosa, Aboriginal, Pacific Islander and Māori societies. With his evangelical connections, James Stephen was a family friend of the Buxtons and Gurneys, and he agreed to assist Priscilla Buxton's and Gurney's enquiries by granting them access to the Colonial Office files of official correspondence.

In 1835–6, Gurney spoke at length with Philip about the commando system and the murder of Hintsa, the two developments that were most symbolic of British injustice to the amaXhosa. She drew up a pamphlet to be signed by Buxton and submitted for the Colonial Office's consideration. Buxton secured swift passage through the 'Sighing Room' to meet in person with Stephen and Glenelg. He wrote to Gurney: 'You remember how cold used to be my reception at the Colonial Office when I talked about South Africa, Kaffirs, aborigines. ... I went there yesterday, saw Glenelg and Stephen. ... I found the atmosphere changed to blood, almost to fever heat. They talked of Hintza, Southey, Philip ... with absolute familiarity, intimated that they would ... acknowledge error and national disgrace. ... Stephen said ... "I am lost in astonishment, indignation, shame, and repentance"'.[10]

Stephen and Glenelg's concern over Hintsa's death was no doubt magnified by the fact that the story of his dramatic demise had featured in the British press. Thanks to Philip, the London Missionary Society's influential *Missionary Chronicle* decried that Britons should have 'mutilated and mangled the corpses of their enemies'. The *Chronicle* feared that 'the British name' would be handed 'down to posterity like that of the Spanish loaded with the execrations of all Nations'. The Whig *Edinburgh Review* lamented that although the 'Hottentots [Khoisan]' serving with the column 'heard [Hintsa's] prayer [for mercy] and spared him ... a British officer, climbing the rock above him, shot the unfortunate chief'. Even the Tory journal *John Bull* mocked Smith's official the version of events, which we will come to shortly.[11] Glenelg was prompted to write caustically to the Cape's governor, Benjamin D'Urban, informing him that he was well aware that Hintsa's fertile country offered the local settlers 'a far more tempting prospect of indemnity, or of gain', than the lands of the frontier chiefs who had actually invaded the colony, but that this was no pretext for killing him. D'Urban was obliged to hold a military court of inquiry in 1836 to determine how Hintsa came to be killed and then 'basely and inhumanly mutilated'.[12]

D'Urban was another governor who had served with distinction in the Peninsular War. In 1820 he was given the governorship of Antigua and he had stayed in the West Indies to combine the settlements of Demerara and Essequibo with Berbice, forming British Guiana in 1831. He had been appointed the Cape Colony's governor in 1833, but his relationship with Stephen and then Glenelg was never cordial. He tended to write infrequently and Stephen grew frustrated that he had continually to prompt the governor for information. D'Urban assumed, rather complacently, that his friends in high places at Horse Guards and the royal court, would adequately represent him and his interests at the Colonial Office. This became a more pressing problem for him when John Philip was busy supplying Buxton, Gurney and Stephen with his own version of events in the Cape.

In 1836, Smith and D'Urban managed to survive the immediate consequences of Hintsa's killing. Smith ensured that the court of inquiry was conducted on home ground in Fort Willshire, from where he commanded the British troops on the frontier. As well as testifying as a witness in his own right, Smith demanded that he be allowed to examine the other witnesses, all of them his military subordinates. The Khoisan soldier Nicolas had been the first witness to tell James Read that Hintsa had been trying to hide, and that he had called for mercy just before Southey shot him. He was also the first to bear the brunt of Smith's cross-examination. 'You say [Hintsa] turned his head when he stood up [upon being discovered by Southey]. Did he do so as a Kaffir does when he is about to throw an assegai?' It may come as no surprise that Nicolas answered his commanding officer's somewhat leading question with a simple 'yes'.[13]

Never one to hold back, Smith overreached himself in his attempts at exoneration. Taking the witness stand himself, he testified that far from fleeing his captors, Hintsa was trying to spring a well-planned ambush. To the surprise of all the other witnesses Smith suddenly declared that there had been an overwhelming force of Xhosa warriors hidden among the rocks of the river bed. They were awaiting their chief's escape before launching their attack on the gallant but vulnerable British column. The presiding officers seem to have been embarrassed by this unexpected addition to the story. Tentatively, they asked their superior why, in that case, the troops had not only been left unmolested after Hintsa's killing, but were able to advance a further fifty miles the next day without any sign of opposition. Clearly disbelieving Smith's supposition that the Xhosa' force was immediately demoralised, they felt obliged to state in their summing up that there was 'no satisfactory proof of [Hintsa] having ... meditated an attack upon, or any other act of treachery towards, the British force'. Nevertheless, both Smith and Southey got away with it. Southey was found to have 'fired ... from the impulse of the moment and very possibly from a sense of personal danger also'. The court expressed its 'pain and indignation' that the mutilation of Hintsa's body could have been 'perpetrated by any person or persons calling themselves Englishmen', but concluded that, 'in the midst of so much conflicting and contradictory Evidence', they were 'unable to fix this foul act on any person in particular'.[14]

Smith's career was not dented in the slightest, but D'Urban proved unable to evade the longer term consequences of Hintsa's death. Lacking any explanation from the governor, Stephen and Glenelg conflated Hintsa's murder with D'Urban's decision to annex a further 7000 square miles of Xhosa territory beyond the former 'neutral zone' as punishment for Maqoma's attack on the colony. He intended to grant the new tract, which he named Queen Adelaide Province, to the appreciative British settlers, who had long complained about being penned in behind the frontier. The plan was for Smith to round up Maqoma's forces, who had not yet surrendered, and expel them onto the late Hintsa's lands. While Philip and his companions were supplying Gurney and Buxton with the evidence they needed to lobby the Colonial Office on behalf of the amaXhosa in 1836, D'Urban placed the province under Smith's authority so that he could clear out its Xhosa inhabitants. However, Smith's troops proved unable to flush the remaining Xhosa fighters out of the rugged and dense bush of the Amatola Mountains. The amaXhosa surrendered only when guaranteed a return to their lands and what herds remained to them after Smith's scorched earth tactics. The British settlers were denied their eagerly anticipated land grab for a while longer.

For about a year, D'Urban still failed to communicate with Glenelg and Stephen while Smith sought to govern the unvanquished Xhosa chiefdoms in Queen Adelaide Province. Meanwhile, Buxton told Philip, 'It will be of great importance to get the ear of the ministers before they shall have time to form an opinion on the Governor's Despatches on this subject, and one word from you in the present state of England will be enough to prevent them taking the wrong course'.[15] Anna Gurney continued to cultivate other correspondents willing to undermine D'Urban, among them the poet, journalist and anti-slavery activist, Thomas Pringle, who had emigrated to the Cape Colony with the 1820 British settlers and returned to become treasurer of the Anti-Slavery Society.

With the evidence amassed by Priscilla Buxton and Anna Gurney, Buxton had already accumulated enough damning material by July 1835 to persuade Parliament of the need for an inquiry. He was able to chair a House of Commons Select Committee on Aborigines (British Settlements). The Aborigines Committee, as it became known, sat for some eighteen months summoning witnesses with experience not just of the Cape Colony, but of each of the territories where British emigrants were settling in large numbers. These witnesses, many of them missionaries, would answer a series of penetrating questions from Buxton and the other Committee members. These included Thomas Hodgkin, members of the Gurney family, and others with greater or lesser affiliations with the Clapham Sect and Buxton's philanthropic circle. The exceptions were William Ewart Gladstone, the future Liberal prime minister who was at this time a conservative and anti-abolitionist MP (and whose father had recently claimed compensation for the loss of his slaves on a plantation in British Guiana while planning, as we have mentioned, to import Indian indentured workers there); Sir Rufane Donkin, who had been acting governor of the Cape Colony when the British settlers had arrived on the frontier in 1820, and Colonel Wade, D'Urban's predecessor as acting governor. Gladstone and Wade in particular consistently tried to undermine Buxton's line of questioning, insisting on giving the few colonial settlers who testified the chance to raise objections to the philanthropic premises of their questions.

In the winter of 1836–7, the Buxton family, Gurney and John Philip ensconced themselves at Northrepps to write up the committee's findings, largely ignoring the interventions of Gladstone and Wade. Gurney wrote the first draft of what would become the Aborigines Committee's official report. It was a scathing condemnation of the brutal dispossession of Indigenous peoples on behalf of British settlers. James Stephen was awkwardly positioned as both a friend of the evangelical philanthropists, and the target of their campaign. When D'Urban finally wrote to Glenelg from the Cape, Stephen insisted that Gurney and Buxton at least consider his belated exculpations along with a mass of other official correspondence which might add nuance to their polemical narrative. The effect was to tone down Gurney's most strident condemnation of Colonial Office policy. Buxton himself then had further to edit down the draft at the last minute, because Parliament would dissolve upon King William IV's death in late 1837, and would have time to consider only a brief report. Buxton told Gurney that he had no option but to remove 'all your wit – & your wisdom – & your sarcasm – & your point'. Even after this butchering, though, he was convinced that the Aborigines Committee's Report, which the family referred to as 'Aunt Anna [Gurney]'s report', was a document 'of vast importance to millions of mankind – and to the interests of the missionary cause'.[16]

The formal Report of the Aborigines Committee has been much studied by historians of late because of its reverberations around the British Empire. In some ways it defined why many Britons thought of that empire as a potentially benevolent entity. It was also a document which, from today's perspective, seems hugely constrained by its early Victorian evangelical sensibilities. In the testimony that he gave in person, John Philip, for instance, had the opportunity to voice Maqoma's outrage at the remorseless advance of British settlement, the persecution of his people and the denial of their self-determination, since he brought with him a letter transcribed from the Xhosa chief, appealing for the restoration of his land. Yet for Philip the letter's significance lay not so much in its record of violent invasion, but more in its 'beautiful simplicity . . . touching pathos . . . confiding magnanimity . . . [and] dignified remonstrance' of expression. This all hinted at the all-important prospect of the African chief's Christian conversion.[17] Upon hearing the letter read aloud, the Committee descended into an argument between Gladstone, Wade and Donkin on the one hand, who maintained that the illiterate Maqoma must have been ventriloquised by Philip's missionaries, and the Clapham Sect evangelicals on the other, who insisted that the chief's sentiment and expression were genuine. Both parties lost sight of the substance of Maqoma's grievance.

The two Indigenous men who had accompanied Philip from the Cape in 1835, Andries Stoeffels and Dyani Tzatzoe, fared little better. Stoeffels had been raised as a servant on a white farm under the pre–Ordinance 50 labour bondage laws, and was compelled as a youth to join his master on commando raids against the amaXhosa. He had converted to Christianity in 1809, and afterwards lived at James Read's London Missionary Society mission at Bethelsdorp. 'Believing that Christianity could revitalize black communities in Africa', he had travelled extensively, seeking to convert

other Africans.[18] In 1829, he and other Bethelsdorp converts had petitioned the Cape's governor for the official return of all the land in the
colony that had not yet been allocated to settlers. They were unsuccessful.
After 1829, Stoeffels was one of the Khoisan converts to be awarded
Maqoma's former land at the Kat River settlement. Tzatzoe was the son
of a relatively minor Xhosa chief who, sensing the likely effects of colonial
encroachment, had asked Read to educate him at Bethelsdorp. He had
been acting for some time as a cultural and political intermediary and
translator between British officials and missionaries and Xhosa
chiefdoms.[19]

Even before they gave their testimony to Buxton's committee, the
Africans' reception in Britain was conditioned by their evangelical allies'
expectations. They were represented on the frontispiece of the *Evangelical
Magazine*, where Tzatzoe 'was shown posing with a regal air in Western
military garb and Stoeffels was portrayed in more rustic guise as "the
honest worker"'.[20] Tellingly, when Philip presented them before the
thousands assembled for the annual meeting of the LMS at Exeter Hall,
he 'proclaimed that the goal of missionaries was not to colonize the land
but to "colonize the mind"' of such people.[21] When Stoeffels and Tzatzoe
finally got their chance to testify in person before the Aborigines
Committee, Tzatzoe took the lead, calling for Britain to disown the
emigrants who had fought the amaXhosa. He stated 'they are South
Africans – they are not Englishmen', the implication being that the
British government should cease supplying them with the troops and
finance that enabled them to occupy Xhosa lands. He next tried to
represent Maqoma's imperatives more effectively than Philip had done.
Describing how Philip had urged upon Maqoma the necessity of having
his children educated in a missionary school, he reported the chief's
response as 'Yes, all that you have said is very good, but I am shot
every day, my huts are set fire to, and I can only sleep with one eye open
and the other shut. I do not know where my place is, and how can I get my
children to be instructed'.[22] One can only guess at Tzatzoe's frustration
when Colonel Wade responded to his evidence by asking whether he
really was literate, and how much of the Bible he actually understood.
When Buxton concluded Stoeffels and Tzatzoe's examination by asking
whether the spread of Christianity would be some recompense for 'the
injuries which Europeans have done to the natives of Africa', Tzatzoe
replied only, 'I come here to complain'.[23]

The Committee saw New Zealand as the place having perhaps the
greatest potential for a more Christian form of British influence.
Although there were hundreds of Britons, like Joseph Barrow
Monefiore, engaged in whaling and trade there, large-scale British

settlement had not yet taken place. Thankfully though, some of the Māori around the Bay of Islands had encouraged a significant community of missionaries to settle. One story from New Zealand that the committee considered in gruesome detail demonstrated perfectly the danger of allowing this nascent missionary influence to be corrupted by more avaricious Britons. This was the tale of the trading brig *Elizabeth*.

The Church Missionary Society (CMS) director Samuel Marsden, who had first established the mission in New Zealand in 1814, told the committee what he had learned from the Ngati Toa chief, Te Rauparaha, about the incident back in 1830. Te Rauparaha had employed the *Elizabeth*'s captain, William Stewart, to transport himself and his warriors from Kapiti, an island between the North and South Islands, to Akaroa on the South Island. Their mission was to take revenge on their old enemy, the Ngai Tahu chief, Tama-i-hara-nui. Pretending to be engaged solely in the trade of flax, Stewart had lured the unsuspecting Tama-i-hara-nui on board the *Elizabeth*, where Te Rauparaha's warriors were able to capture him, together with his brother, two daughters, his wife and her two sisters. Marsden told the Committee that one of the daughters was killed when the ship's crew prised her away from her father and threw her against the side of the cabin. The sailors then joined in with the killing of all those who had accompanied Tama-i-hara-nui in their own canoes. On the voyage back to Kapiti, Te Rauparaha had Tama-i-hara-nui suspended by a hook through his chin, before finally executing him along with his wife in front of the assembled Ngati Toa.

Appalled by this story, the Aborigines Committee compared such violence, condoned and colluded in by British traders, with the humane and 'civilising' influence of Marsden and the missionaries.[24] Although the Colonial Office and British government as a whole was under considerable pressure from Wakefield's New Zealand Company to permit colonisation, the Committee concluded that this would only encourage further undesirable elements like Captain Stewart. It advised against settlement so that the missionaries could be left to their improving work among the Māori undisturbed.[25]

Outside New Zealand, in the settler colonies that had already attracted large numbers of Britons, the best formula for a humane empire that the members of the Aborigines Committee could come up with was essentially: Christianity and access to British civilisation in exchange for dispossession and cultural genocide. If, as even the most philanthropic of Britons tended to believe, British settlers were entitled to make a productive living on Indigenous people's lands, then at least Britain should offer the salvation of their souls and the material blessings of 'civilisation' in return. Missionaries should be in the vanguard. Those who formerly occupied the 'wastelands' now cultivated by settlers should be converted into black and brown Christian Britons, living most immediately on their own reserves but ultimately among the British settlers who had usurped their lands. In the Buxton family circle's ideal settler empire, Indigenous peoples' 'civilisation' would proceed hand in hand with their Christian conversion, enabling them to become full members of British colonial societies.

Kahkewaquonaby/Peter Jones' visit to London, which we described in the last chapter, occurred while the Aborigines Committee was in progress. It made its mark upon Buxton and Gurney, since the Report upheld his Credit River community as the model of what could be achieved in this ideal British Empire. 'About ten years ago', Gurney wrote, the people there 'had no houses, no fields nor horses, no cattle, no pigs, and no poultry. . . . They are now occupying about 40 comfortable houses containing furniture, crockery and cutlery. Some have clocks and watches'. Furthermore, there had been a 'great amelioration of the condition of the women, who have been raised from the drudgery of beasts of burthen, and are now treated with consideration by their husbands'. Surely this must have been God's intention in granting Britain such power and reach: 'it is our office to carry civilization and humanity, peace and good government, and, above all, the knowledge of the true God, to the uttermost ends of the earth'.[26]

'Aunt Anna's' humanitarian template for empire took on different forms as it was reprinted, adapted and disseminated around the empire by both the Aborigines Protection Society and the Quakers.[27] Its rhetoric of Christianity, civilisation and commerce, manifested in various guises thereafter, may well have persuaded later generations of Britons that their empire had benevolent intent and beneficial effect. At the time it was both feared and deeply resented by many Britons in the colonies. Even as it continued to gather evidence, the committee occasioned the most dramatic intervention that Glenelg made as secretary of state. On Boxing Day of 1835, he sent probably the most forthright and impassioned despatch that he (or perhaps his amanuensis Stephen) ever wrote, chastising Governor D'Urban and ordering him to relinquish Queen Adelaide Province. Buxton credited Gurney with this triumphant and almost unprecedented reversal of colonial expansion: 'It is nothing short of this ... the hand of the proud oppressor in Africa, has been under Providence, arrested by Miss Gurney of North Repps Cottage – and ... a whole Nation doomed ... to ruin, exile and death has been delivered and restored'.[28]

D'Urban was angered and also quite surprised when he received Glenelg's directive in early 1836. He had failed to appreciate that, with

Melbourne in government, his Tory supporters in London were on the wrong side of the political fence. They were also simply outclassed by the Buxton-Gurney's network's campaigning acumen. Glenelg dismissed the governor in May 1837, after which official communication with the Cape almost ceased until April 1838.

Some of the British settlers on the Cape frontier were quicker than D'Urban to grasp the importance of cultivating support in London. From Graham's Town, they launched a propaganda campaign as soon as they read of the Aborigines Committee's hostility to their expansion. Robert Godlonton, a former London printer who edited the settlers' main paper, the *Graham's Town Journal*, was their spokesman. In 1836 he sent printed copies of *A Narrative of the Irruption of the Kafir Hordes* to be distributed in his former home city. Its purpose was to convince Britons that their compatriots in the wilds of the Cape frontier had first been attacked by 'irreclaimable savages', and then stabbed in the back by their own compatriots. John Philip, the Buxtons, and the majority of witnesses before the Aborigines Committee were 'canting hypocrites', 'wretched and degraded calumniators', whose sentimental sympathy for a 'coloured race' was 'arresting sympathy for our sufferings' in the heart of empire.[29]

Direct appeals from settlers like Godlonton would increasingly influence British public opinion during the years to come, but in 1836–7 the British settlers in southern Africa, along with their governor, were losing the battle for influence at the Colonial Office. Stephen's support for the evangelicals was well known, given that he was one of the LMS's directors, but there was another significant motivation for Glenelg's abrupt recall of D'Urban, and for handing 'Queen Adelaide Province' back to the amaXhosa. The secretary of state was under pressure from the Treasury to cut expenditure on colonial administration in accordance with Melbourne's policy of retrenchment. The last thing Melbourne wanted in 1836 was to take on a new territory occupied by fiercely resistant chiefdoms on the premise that sooner or later it would be farmed by a few thousand land grabbing British settlers. D'Urban's protestations that restoring the province to the amaXhosa would allow them to 'penetrate' into the colony, 'especially as the country is in rapid process of abandonment by the invaluable race of [Afrikaner] Colonial Farmers', were all in vain.[30]

By the beginning of 1838, 'Queen Adelaide Province' was no more. Maqoma's and the other chiefdoms had rid themselves of Smith and signed treaties with a very different new lieutenant governor of the Eastern Cape. This was Andries Stockenström, an Afrikaner frontiersman whose father had been killed by amaXhosa resisting expulsion from the Zuurveld in 1812. He had fought alongside the British in the war of

1819, and would do so again in subsequent frontier wars against amaXhosa, but he was also a friend of Philip. He had supported the campaign to free the Khoisan in 1828, helped establish the Kat River settlement, and testified to colonial provocation of the amaXhosa before the Aborigines Committee. Stockenström's evidence had informed Stephen and Glenelg of the Commando system's role in provoking Maqoma's attack. Given his deep acquaintance with all the characters of the frontier – British, Khoisan and amaXhosa – and his ability to empathise with them all at least to a certain extent, Glenelg appointed Stockenström lieutenant governor even before he recalled D'Urban. He proved an inspired choice.

From late 1836, Stockenström was able to negotiate treaties with the Xhosa chiefs which promised to halt further British settler expansion onto their lands and recognised their sovereignty in return for their recognition of settlers' right to lands already seized. British resident agents living alongside the chiefs would control amaXhosa entry to the colony for trade and employment, and colonists' egress to trade with the amaXhosa. The chiefs would prevent their followers from raiding colonial farms. The new treaties regulated relations between the British Empire and Xhosa chiefdoms successfully for a decade. They were finally undermined by Godlonton and the British settlers' remorseless campaign against them and their progenitor in the 1840s. Digging up accounts of a lethal fight with Khoisan in the earlier days of Afrikaner settlement, Godlonton and his allies accused Stockenström of murder. They must have found the irony of expressing their moral outrage against the philanthropist who was preventing them from further colonial expansion delicious. Although Stockenström was acquitted, his ability to govern was fatally impaired and he was dismissed by D'Urban's successor.

In 1844 the Cape Colony would receive a new governor. Sir Peregrine Maitland had led the Guards when they repelled the French Imperial Guard's final assault at Waterloo, supported the Tory Family Compact as lieutenant governor of Upper Canada and devised the notorious system of residential schools for First Nations children there. In 1846, after intensive lobbying from Godlonton and the settlers, who sent him inflated tallies of stock supposedly lost to amaXhosa raids every week, he reneged on Stockenström's treaties and imposed a new system, which once again treated the chiefs as recalcitrant British subjects. With severe drought biting, the chiefs proved uncompliant in restraining their followers from raiding colonial farms. When a Khoisan military escort was killed by friends of the Xhosa man they were taking to trial for the theft of an axe, Maitland saw an opportunity to accede to the settlers' demands and reconquer the amaXhosa. After his ultimatum for the handover of the culprits was ignored he launched the Seventh Frontier War. The ensuing defeat of the amaXhosa gave the returning hero of Aliwal, Harry Smith, his second opportunity to reign over them as the former Queen Adelaide Province was re-annexed and called British Kaffraria.

To return to 1838, though, after all the agitation that the 1834–5 war had caused, Stephen and Glenelg felt that Stockenström's treaties were at last providing the right structure and personnel to govern the troublesome Cape frontier inexpensively, effectively and humanely. Unfortunately for them, New South Wales was a very different matter. The Cape Colony had triggered the Aborigines Committee and 'Aunt Anna's' report in late 1837, but in 1838 its effects were most marked in Australia. The limits of the imperial government's new benevolence towards its Indigenous subjects were also tested most immediately there.

Protection and Massacre in Australia

Directly after leaving Gosford's commission in Lower Canada, the former Royal Engineer George Gipps arrived to govern New South Wales in February 1838. He was in the unenviable position of having been instructed by Stephen to facilitate the mass settlement of British emigrants on the one hand, while on the other hand, governing the Aboriginal peoples they were displacing according to 'Aunt Anna's' philanthropic precepts.

Gipps had been wounded at the siege of Badajoz in 1812, and fought throughout the Peninsular Campaign, but missed Waterloo because he was preparing fortifications in the Netherlands. After the war he was sent to the West Indies where he devised a programme of employment on public works for formerly enslaved apprentices. James Stephen greatly admired Gipps' philanthropic intent and the scheme's apparent effectiveness in preparing apprentices for emancipation. It was this which led Gipps to join Gosford's commission in Lower Canada. There he developed some sympathy with the *Canadiens*, arguing that the Crown should retain control of land on behalf of all colonial subjects rather than allowing narrow colonial cliques to do so. It was a position which would make Gipps unpopular with the more exclusive landowners and squatters of New South Wales.

Once he got to Sydney, Gipps realised just how many challenges he had inherited from his liberal predecessor, Richard Bourke. Aboriginal people were meeting the increase in immigration from Britain and the expansion of settler pastoralism with intense resistance, rendering some resolution of their legal status urgent. Fundamentally, the British authorities had yet to decide whether Australia's Indigenous peoples should be seen as members of independent nations or subject to the British authority which had been assumed over their lands. They had never been wartime allies like Canada's First Nations and, aside from a private deal in Melbourne, which Bourke disallowed in 1836, no treaties had ever been signed with them. Around 600 Aboriginal nations' rights to a landmass which they had tended for some 50 000 years prior to Cook's 'discovery', had simply gone unrecognised by British officialdom.

When Gipps arrived, the British Crown was assuming the right to dispose of land to settlers as their private property, while at the same time expressing its disapproval of Aboriginal peoples' dispossession. Despite Stephen bemoaning 'the hatred with which the white man regards the black', Gipps was left to resolve the contradiction pretty much alone. Visiting London en route from Canada to Australia, Stephen briefed him on the rising influence of Buxton's philanthropic campaign as well as the government's desire to continue promoting emigration to its colonies. Thereafter, with the Colonial Office preoccupied with both looming emancipation and the Canadian rebellions, Stephen's guidance was limited, time lagged and distinctly lacking in clarity.

Gipps felt unable to prevent the intrusion of settlers onto Aboriginal land, even had the emigration policy not compelled it. He despaired that 'as well might it be attempted to confine the Arabs of the Desert within a circle, traced upon the sands, as to confine the Graziers or Woolgrowers of New South Wales within any bounds that can possibly be assigned to them'.[31] Gipps himself was a vocal advocate of free immigration and, the following year, would enhance funding to the bounty agents who recruited settlers from Britain. Between 1838 and 1846 the population of New South Wales would almost double to more than 190 000. The new governor decided that his immediate imperative must be to bring at least some order to the free-for-all land grab that inevitably ensued.

For all of Bourke's attempts to constrain them, pastoralists known as 'squatters', some well established in the colony and others recent immigrants with capital, were using the convict labour assigned to them and employing time-served former convicts as well as British newcomers, to claim and 'clear' land beyond the existing limits of settlement. This entailed not only destroying the fauna and flora which sustained Aboriginal people, so that livestock could graze, but also frequently, the forcible removal of the people themselves. Some settlers were willing to use more lethal means than others. In general Gipps found that his immediate measures, including taxes on livestock to pay for a border police force, did little to deflect or ameliorate an intrinsically violent process of frontier extension. Nor did they resolve the question of how to deal legally with Aboriginal people fighting to defend their country. In practice, they were still being treated on occasion as enemy combatants and at other times as rebellious subjects.

In early 1838 squatters were expanding the limits of the colony in three main directions. To the south was the Port Phillip settlement around Melbourne (later Victoria), upon which settlers were converging mainly from Van Diemen's Land to the south and overland from Sydney. The ease with which these settlers were able to establish themselves on Aboriginal land is indicated in the Colonial Office's response to a suggestion received from Governor Bourke in February 1838. Bourke had received a memorial from 'a considerable number of persons who removing from Van Diemen's Land have placed themselves with their flocks and herds upon the Western Shore of the waters of Port Phillip'. These new settlers in Geelong were now requesting that the colonial government of New South Wales effectively follow on behind them so as to 'prevent any collision between their scattered population and the Aboriginal Natives who frequent in rather large numbers the fertile districts in which the memorialists are seated'. Bourke wrote that 'They evince a very laudable anxiety to prevent ... any aggression upon the natives and seem willing to make considerable sacrifices to establish an amicable intercourse with them'. Given their pacific intent in seizing the land of the 'natives', Bourke 'thought it right to appoint a Police Magistrate for Geelong with a small constabulary, ... relying upon the good disposition of the settlers to provide the Magistrate with such a force as ... to preserve peace between them and the Aborigines. ... I have appointed Captain Fyans late of the 4th Regiment to this Magistracy and place the greatest reliance on his activity, humanity, good temper, and considerate disposition'. James Stephen minuted, simply that 'These appointments should be recommended to the Treasury for confirmation'.[32] Unbeknown to him, Foster Fyans, the magistrate whom Bourke appointed, had already earned the nickname Flogger Fyans for his treatment of convicts on Norfolk Island. In the Western District of Port Phillip, he would go on to acquit the Henty brothers of the mass killing of Aboriginal people and appoint them to the magistracy, condone a series of massacres, and write that 'in my opinion, the only plan to bring [Aboriginal people] to a fit and proper state is to insist on the gentlemen in the country to protect their property, and to deal with such useless savages on the spot'.[33]

To the more immediate west and south-west of Sydney pastoralists were seizing and claiming land along the Murrumbidgee River, while to the north-west the most immediate conflicts were taking place on the Liverpool Plains. Along the Gwydir River in particular the Kamilaraay people were engaged in a last ditch attempt to drive out settlers from their hunting and grazing grounds. During the interval between Bourke's departure and Gipps' arrival, in December 1837, the acting governor, Kenneth Snodgrass, a pastoralist himself, had sent Major Nunn and his mounted police into the district to restore order. Far from deterring the advancing squatters, on 26 January 1838, Nunn's force killed between forty and fifty Kaamilaraay men, women and children at a place called Waterloo Creek, the name lending the massacre some semblance of a more even sided battle.[34]

In March, Gipps tabled two papers for the consideration of his Executive Council which neatly summed up his precarious position between conflicting Colonial Office imperatives. The first was Nunn's report on the Waterloo Creek massacre. To Gipps' obvious discomfort, and despite Nunn's evasions, it encapsulated a stark logic: if the empire was to include colonies of settlement for emigrant Britons, like it or not, those who refused to give up their lands to the incomers and abandon their former lifeways would have to be eliminated. The second report was more in line with Gipps' own conflicted disposition. It was the Report of the Aborigines Committee, which Stephen had now sent to all the settler colonial governors, along with the Colonial Office's endorsement. Considering Nunn's and 'Aunt Anna's' reports in quick succession, this meeting of the New South Wales governing elite could not have encapsulated more neatly the juxtaposition between British emigrants' actions on the frontiers of empire and what many Britons back home fondly imagined their empire could and should be.

In the aftermath of the Executive Council meeting in March, Gipps issued a public notice declaring 'that each succeeding dispatch from the Secretary of State marks in an increasing degree the importance which Her Majesty's Government, and no less Parliament and the people of Great Britain, attach to the just and humane treatment of the aborigines'.[35] Privately, he wondered how on earth to implement its recommendations while encouraging British settlement. Drawing on the precedent of Protectors of Slaves, employed to oversee the amelioration of slavery in the West Indies, the Colonial Office had already insisted that Wakefield's South Australian venture and the colony in Western Australia include officials whose role was explicitly to protect and safeguard Aboriginal people. The Aborigines Committee now gave further impetus to the 'protection' of Australia's Aboriginal people as a key function of government. Its rhetoric was converted into action by George Arthur. The conscience stricken former governor of Van Diemen's Land was back in Britain as Gipps consulted his Legislative Council in March 1837, awaiting his posting to Upper Canada. Before he left to deal with the rebels and US Patriots there, he met with Stephen and Glenelg as they considered how best to implement the Aborigines Committee's recommendations. Arthur was determined to bring the lessons he had learned from overseeing the genocide in Tasmania to bear on mainland Australia before it was too late.

Anna Gurney had included a quote from one of Arthur's despatches in the Aborigines Committee's report: 'being reduced to the necessity of driving a simple, but warlike, and ... noble minded race from their native hunting grounds, is a measure ... so distressing, that I am willing to make almost any prudent sacrifice that may tend to compensate for the injuries that the Government is unwillingly and unavoidably ... inflicting'.[36] The report had concluded that such 'was the unfortunate nature of our policy' in Tasmania, 'that no better expedient could be devised than the catching and extirpating of the whole of the native population ... the adoption of any line of conduct, having for its avowed or secret object the extinction of the native race, could not fail to leave an indelible stain upon the British Government'.[37] Within a few weeks of the report's publication in July 1837, Arthur had persuaded Stephen and Glenelg that George Augustus Robinson, the 'conciliator' who had brought the survivors from Van Diemen's Land to Flinders Island, be appointed to the new role of Chief Protector of Aborigines in the Port Phillip District. Here 'fewer difficulties would oppose themselves to the successful establishment of the untried scheme, than would have to be encountered in the older portion of [New South Wales] where the native tribes had long been in pernicious contact with the prison population'.[38]

By December Arthur himself had interviewed and selected three assistants for Robinson, on behalf of the Colonial Office in London. Edward Stone Parker and William Thomas both ran private schools in the city, while James Dredge had resorted to teaching after being declined as a Wesleyan missionary. These three Methodists would be supplemented by Charles Wightman Sievwright, a gambling-indebted army officer recently returned to England from Malta, where, for now, he had left his family. He was awarded the position of assistant protector more by virtue of his contacts at Horse Guards than his philanthropic credentials. The new Protectorate of Aborigines, staffed by these men, would be one of two ways that Gipps tried, during the remainder of the year, to reconcile the two reports that he asked his executive to consider in March. The Protectors of Aborigines were charged with protecting Aboriginal people 'from cruelty, oppression and injustice' and 'from encroachments upon their property'.[39] The Colonial Office instructed Gipps to grant them magisterial powers to prosecute settlers for excessive violence. At least in the Port Phillip District, Gipps hoped they would be able to exercise a firmer grip on the kind of atrocity described in Nunn's report.

Gipps discovered a second way in which he could try to square the circle of philanthropic dispossession before the new protectors had even arrived in Sydney. From June, reports of another massacre of Aboriginal people, at Myall Creek, gave him an opportunity to demonstrate resolve in the punishment of those who killed to 'clear' the land. On 10 June 1838, twenty-eight Wirrayaraay women, children and elderly men were preparing their camp for the night in northern New South Wales while the younger men were away cutting bark for a neighbouring settler. They were on their traditional lands, now claimed as a cattle station by Henry Dangar. Charles Kilmeister, the man over-seeing the station in Dangar's absence, was accustomed to their presence. Late that afternoon, however, a party of twelve armed white strangers arrived on the station. Anticipating trouble, the Wirrayaraay band sought Kilmeister's protection and he let them into his hut. The visitors were eleven convict and former convict stockmen led by a free settler named John Henry Fleming, a landowner who, it seems likely, had participated in previous massacres on the Gwydir River. They told Kilmeister that they had come to eradicate the Wirrayaraay from Dangar's land and that he was either with them or against them. Kilmeister later testified that, reluctantly, he helped the men tie up the Aboriginal people and force them to walk out of sight of the huts. Fleming and the others then fired at them with pistols and a fowling piece before hacking and bludgeoning them with swords and cutlasses. They set fire to the bodies and left after instructing Kilmeister to continue burning them until all evidence was removed.[40]

Besides Kilmeister, there were two, non-complicit, witnesses. George Anderson, the other resident stockman employed by Dangar, had locked himself in a hut. After seeing a Wirrayaraay elder and a boy crying as they were roped together, he heard the ensuing gunshots. Yintayintin was one of the two Aboriginal workers employed on the run, and promised silence in return for one of the Wirrayaraay women. It was Yintayintin who guided the overseers of two neighbouring runs, William Hobbs and John Foster, to the site where Kilmeister had burnt the bodies. Recognising the victims and knowing them to be innocent of any stock thefts or retaliatory attacks, Hobbs and Foster resolved on risking their standing among other settlers by reporting the atrocity to the authorities. They wrote a letter to the colonial secretary in Sydney that would ultimately result in the arrest of eleven of the twelve murderers and the conviction and hanging of seven of them.

The only 'respectable' settler, John Henry Fleming, however, was not named in Hobbs and Foster's letter. Even when an arrest warrant was issued after others had named him, he continued to be protected by local landowners. Despite false stories of his having fled the colony, Fleming would later return to public life, marrying Charlotte Dunstan, perversely in a settlement named Wilberforce, on the Hawkesbury River, where he remained a respected landowner. 'What made Myall Creek unique in Australian History was that white witnesses', including Kilmeister and Anderson, 'were prepared to testify, enabling officials to pursue justice through the court'.[41] Even then it took two trials to convict the seven stockmen, after a sympathetic settler jury dismissed the evidence against all of them the first time around. One of the original jurors was overheard saying 'I knew well they were guilty of the murder but I for one would never see a white man suffer for shooting a black'.[42]

It was due to the persistence of the idiosyncratic Justice William Burton and Gipps' own firmness that the case was seen through to its conclusion, with the execution of the convicted men. The response from much of the settler community, first to the trials and then to the executions, would have lasting repercussions. Their anger was stirred not just because white Britons (and one Briton of colour, a former convict from Liverpool) were being executed for killing Aboriginal people; it was also because the long drawn out process of the arrests and trials coincided with the arrival of the new Protectors of Aborigines. Robinson and his assistants were assembling in Sydney, with much publicity, from September 1838, shortly before the second trial, and when the colony's newspapers were taking sides on the story's implications for the colonisation of Australia.

The Protectorate of Aborigines' beginnings were far from auspicious. Even before the assistant protectors arrived, two of them had almost come to blows on the voyage out, when the Methodist school head Parker had accused the former army officer Sievwright of attempting to seduce his wife. Despite the frosty relations among them, which would never really thaw, the presence of the five protectorate staff in Sydney during the Australian winter of 1838 swelled the town's incipient and somewhat besieged humanitarian lobby, even if only briefly. On 19 October, a few weeks after they had received copies of the Aborigines' Protection Society version of 'Aunt Anna's' report, local philanthropists launched the town's counterpart to Hodgkin's British Aborigines' Protection Society. As Chief Protector, Robinson gave one of the opening addresses.[43] As it turned out this would be both the first and the penultimate meeting of the Australian APS. The assistant protectors were shocked by their instant unpopularity in the colony. Dredge reported a 'chilling reception' with all the protectors encountering 'an amount of obloquy which could not well have been exceeded had we been expatriated for notorious offences'.[44]

The *Sydney Herald*, whose editor was Ward Stephens, the owner of large runs seized from Aboriginal people to the north-west, greeted the protectors with mingled dismay and ridicule. Surely no decent settler would ever assist such 'useless officials'.[45] As Robinson, Sievwright, Parker, Thomas and Dredge were trying to establish the principle of a more philanthropic form of governance in the town, its main paper was warning that 'in every Colony where such vermin have introduced themselves, they have been the wholesale traducers of the settlers – as witness their proceedings at the Cape'.[46] When Robinson and his assistants left Sydney for Melbourne in November, the few Sydneysiders who had enthusiastically mobilised the Australian APS were beleaguered.

Robinson would have had a much better understanding of the Port Phillip District than his assistants from London. It had been inhabited by at least 1600 generations of Aboriginal people before the first British squatters had arrived to set up stock runs two years beforehand.[47] Although the assistant protectors had been recruited on the understanding that they would try to learn 'the language' of their new Aboriginal charges, they found that they had in fact to engage with around thirty different cultural-language groups and hundreds of clans distributed across an area larger than England. They arrived amidst a 'frenzied decade of settlement', as settlers followed the overland route literally carved into the drought-afflicted ground by Major Mitchell's exploratory journey in 1836.[48] The drought was persuading yet more overlanders to arrive from Sydney, joining the growing throng from Van Diemen's Land, and a stream of emigrants from Scotland, where Elliott's emigration office was more concertedly promoting Australia as an alternative to rebellious Canada. The fact that the 'opening' of the district followed the payment of compensation to former West Indian slave owners was also propelling colonisation, as beneficiaries like Celia Scott, 'pioneer female squatter' at Buninyong, turned their investments from slaves in one part of the empire to land and stock in another.[49]

Well before Robinson and the protectors arrived, the Aboriginal people of the region had become all too aware of what this influx foretold. There were long established seal hunting communities along the coast worked by local Aboriginal people as well as those from Van Diemen's Land, Māori and Pacific Islanders. From them, they would have learned not just of the Black War in Van Diemen's Land, but of the encroachments of Britons on Indigenous societies across the Pacific.[50] Furthermore, they had already contracted the settlers' smallpox via overland trade routes, and many bands had been devastated by it. When Robinson and his team turned up in Melbourne, most of the people they were charged with protecting were familiar enough with colonists to appreciate the difference between the protectors and the potentially murderous squatters and stockmen. They readily approached the new officials and sought to utilise whatever influence they had. By and large, the small band of protectors tried to live up to their promise, doing their best to stem the tide of dispossession, disease and murder that accompanied the British invasion. Aboriginal depopulation continued nonetheless, with a decline of up to 90 per cent during the ensuing decade.[51]

From late 1838 into the early 1840s, each of the assistant protectors and their families was guided by Aboriginal people in their own local struggles to survive the settler onslaught. In Melbourne itself the Wurundjeri tried to use William Thomas as an ally against ejection from their traditional camping grounds along the Yarra River. The settler townsfolk insisted that Thomas would best perform his duties by removing them from the town as if they were pests. When the new superintendent of the district, Charles La Trobe, arrived in 1839, even he complained that 'a number of the Blacks has again made their appearance in the streets of the town and [I am] requesting that you take measures to induce them to remove'.[52] In 1840 he would get his wish when the entire body of Wurundjeri, along with visiting Aboriginal people from inland, were rounded up and forcibly expelled. An elder who tried to resist and a number of their hunting dogs were shot in the process. Thomas proved powerless to prevent it and then sought to use the opportunity to proselytise among those forced onto his new protectorate station.

Assigned to the north-east of Melbourne, James Dredge was outraged by the verdict of 'not guilty' in the first Myall Creek trial when he, his wife Sarah and their four children arrived among the Daungwurrung people. Rapidly made to appreciate Aboriginal people's struggle for basic survival as they were squeezed between invading squatters, he was the most vocal of the assistant protectors, quickly denouncing the protectorate experiment's 'imbecility and failure' in the face of contradictory imperial policies. Robinson noted that 'three [squatter] individuals have 280 miles of country between them. And they think it a hardship if a native appears upon their run, imagining that a £10 licence gives them a legal right to expel the blacks'.[53] Dredge was the first assistant protector to resign, with the declaration that 'I do hope, even against hope, that justice will at length be rendered to this plundered and injured race of men'.[54] He would later tell the British Methodist leader Jabez Bunting that, whatever the protectors may have done, the other elements of the New South Wales government continued to treat Aboriginal people merely as 'a grievous annoyance, and an irksome expense'. Aboriginal populations were being decimated 'while we are subjecting them to our Godless political experiments. . . . If the people of England imagine that the Government is befriending these outcasts they are greatly mistaken. The Government is deriving immense revenues from the sale of their lands but they are giving them nothing in return. . . . What an awful reckoning awaits these destroyers of mankind and the Government which suffers such things'.[55]

Charles Wightman Sievwright was sent to the Western part of the district near Geelong, where, as we have seen, Bourke had appointed 'flogging' Foster Fyans as police magistrate. There, the Wathawurrung people spurred the former soldier into efforts on their behalf, which came at a tremendous personal cost. Sievwright had been born in Edinburgh, the son of a solicitor. Aside from enraging Parker by flirting with his wife on the voyage out, he also stood out among the other protectors because of his lack of evangelical or educational connections. He had purchased a commission as ensign in a Scottish infantry regiment at the age of fifteen and served for twenty years without ever being involved in combat. In 1822 he had married Christina Watt, but was obliged to sell his commission in 1837 to pay off gambling debts accrued while serving in Malta. When Sievwright arrived in the Port Phillip District with Christina, their four daughters and three sons, he too was immediately appalled by the viciousness of British colonisation.

The Wathawurrung's country extended over more than half the size of Scotland and Sievwright was the only official with any responsibility to see to their welfare as their food resources were destroyed by British pastoralists. Wathawurrung elders told Sievwright that their hunger was fuelling conflict not only with the invading settlers, but also with other Aboriginal groups onto whose country they were being forced. They also impressed upon him the fact that they were being killed as a result of avenging the stockmen's practice of raping Aboriginal women, either by direct assault or by offering the starving food only in return for sex. The land grabbing squatters, who were mostly 'respectable' men of property, considered themselves removed from such violence and exploitation. John Henry Fleming was the exception in being implicated directly in a massacre. As Robinson noted, most of them preferred to employ emancipated convicts like those involved alongside Fleming in the Myall Creek massacre, because the 'conscience' of such men is 'seared, and they will meet [the squatters'] wishes in destroying blacks'.[56]

By August 1839, Sievwright was writing that the Wathawurrung's 'wants, their grievances, their protracted sufferings, and lingering death, have been reiterated for months, and I am still in the midst of the same scenes, and have not . . . an ounce of food to save them from starvation. I am surrounded by them in the bush, where my family are hourly importuned for the pittance we have it not in our power to grant'.[57] Since he could not offer the means of survival on his station, Sievwright threw his energies into investigating the murders that the Wathawurrung reported. In his first year he rode more than 9000 miles, visiting the stations of forty-five different squatters, attempting to collate evidence for prosecutions. In every case he failed. Local magistrates refused to prosecute or settler juries acquitted the suspects. When Sievwright appealed to the colony's attorney general, his response was surprise that the assistant protector could have expected anything else, especially when the settler community was so inflamed by the Myall Creek trials. The *Port Phillip Gazette* mocked his attempt to bring 'gentleness or religion to beings who have scarce a sense beyond the brute' as bringing 'pearls to swine''. One of the most prominent squatters described Sievwright as 'the most unpopular man that ever breathed'.[58]

A few months after the family's arrival, Sievwright was away investigating a stock theft when his wife Christina and their eldest daughter, seventeen-year-old Frances, abandoned the station, borrowed money from one of their convict servants and travelled by mail coach to Melbourne. After staying at an inn for a few days, the pair were offered accommodation by the police magistrate, Captain William Lonsdale. Lonsdale was soon telling other officials what Christina had confided in him: that Sievwright had indeed not only attempted to seduce Parker's wife on the voyage out from England, but that he had also attempted to seduce his own daughter, Frances. She and Christina had 'eloped' to Melbourne for Frances' protection.[59] By the time Christina and Frances returned to Geelong a few days later to meet with Sievwright, accompanied by a solicitor who had volunteered to mediate, the rumours had been passed to Superintendent La Trobe. When Sievwright requested a meeting with him, La Trobe declined to meet a man who possessed only 'the outward manners and demeanour of a gentleman'.[60] The brother of a squatter whom Sievwright had tried to prosecute for murder gleefully told the story to Gipps in Sydney and Sievwright was dismissed.[61] Sievwright would fight to clear his name over the next decade, and Christina and Frances would both testify in his favour, renouncing the story that they had allegedly told to Lonsdale.

In the meantime, Sievwright's successor, Dr Watton, effectively summed up the next phase of governmental policy towards the Wathawurrung, and indeed Aboriginal people in the whole of the Port Phillip District. He reported in 1845 that 'Their wandering habits, their natural indolence, their thievish propensities, their innate pugnacious disposition, being in my opinion only to be kept in check by force, I fear that nothing short of a system of absolute coercion can effect any change worthy of the name of civilization'.[62]

As for what Aboriginal people themselves made of the protectors among them from 1838, the records of Edward Stone Parker, Sievwright's adversary on the voyage from England, leave some useful clues. Parker had intended to become a Methodist missionary, but had ruled himself out by marrying Mary Cook Woolmer in 1828. He turned to teaching, and by 1838 he was headmaster of a Methodist day school.[63] He seems to have been motivated to become an assistant protector on the other side of the world as a result of reading one of the versions of 'Aunt Anna's' report in the mission press. Parker was assigned to the region north of Melbourne tended mainly by the Dja dja wurrung, but took nearly a year to leave Melbourne and establish his station because Mary was about to give birth to their seventh child. He too would endeavour 'to represent the wants, wishes and grievances of the Aborigines' to the best of his ability.[64] Parker's district covered a 2500-square-mile area which, by the early 1850s, would become the centre of the Victorian gold rush. In a census that he conducted in 1840, he enumerated 282 Dja dja wurrung individuals, smallpox having already reduced the population significantly from around 1500 by the time he arrived.

The area around Parker's first station may later have been called Parker's Plains, but it was Neereman to the Aboriginal people, who accompanied him there. Appropriately enough it meant 'hide here'.[65] Neereman became a space of refuge for the Dja dja wurrung, a depot for supplies provided with protectorate funds and a place at which Aboriginal groups could leave the sick and aged in relative safety. Within ten days, fifty-five Aboriginal people had assembled. They provided the labour to set up the station as a collection of rudimentary buildings, some cultivable land and a flock of sheep, and within a month, 170 people were living on the station most of the time.[66] Eleven months on, however, one of the elders, Yeenebulluk, persuaded Parker to relocate, largely, it seems in order to try to use the protectorate to secure more valued land now threatened by squatters. Parker's attempt to secure the site were thwarted, but the Dja dja wurrung hoisted Parker's sons on their shoulders and set off ahead of his cumbersome drays to lead him to another place twenty-three miles away, which they called Lalgambook (and which Parker would call Mount Franklin), a traditional camping and ceremonial site.

Parker was successful this time in using the protectorate's limited influence to defend the 30 000-acre site (about the same size as one average squatter run) from an outraged squatter named Henry Monro, who was already in the process of stocking it. For the next twenty years, even after the protectorate was terminated in 1850, the Dja daja wurrung and Parker together were able to defend it, hunt upon it and cultivate it, despite Monro's persistent attempts to eject them. Monro had led a party of stockmen in an attack on Dja dja wurrung men in 1839, killing two and wounding several more. It was only Parker's intervention which saved the lives of others. One of them was Munangabum, who went on to become a particular friend of the Parker family and the protectorate's envoy among Aboriginal people inland. Monro would regularly complain through the 1840s, to anyone who would listen, that 'the blacks are still lurking about the creeks – that they seem determined to act as lords of the soil'.[67]

Like Indigenous people in other colonies, the Dja dja wurrung used the assistance provided by well-meaning British allies strategically. They left young children, the sick, or older people on the station while they sought work among the encroaching settlers but most continued to resist Parker's attempts to proselytise and convert. One elder, Parker wrote, 'complained in his anger that the white fellows had stolen their country, and that I was stealing their children by taking them away to live in huts, and work, and 'read in book' like whitefellows'.[68] Parker came to believe that early intervention to isolate Aboriginal children from the influence of their parents was the best means of helping Australia's Aboriginal population to adapt within a colonial society. Such an idea would have a long and especially destructive history in modern Australia.

Even though they engaged with Parker on their own terms, the Dja dja wurrung developed a close bond with him and his family. When Mary died, her son Joseph Parker reported that 'the lamentations of the blacks were something to be remembered – the men cut their head with tomahawks, and the women scarred their breasts with fire sticks, and scratched the flesh off their cheeks with their fingernails, all refused food, and kept up a wailing for forty-eight hours'.[69] In reciprocation, and much to the annoyance of the local settlers, Parker had Mary buried among the Dja dja wurrrung's own dead.[70]

Despite the small scale achievements of the British men and women who came closest to engaging with Aboriginal people in Victoria, the Protectorate of Aborigines as a whole was undermined as soon as it began. In the lead up to 1838, Buxton's family circle including Anna Gurney and John Philip had succeeded in holding the Cape Colony's governor accountable for the effects of the British invasion of Xhosa people's land. They had also sustained and extended the reformist momentum of the anti-slavery campaign to produce a blueprint for the British Empire's 'civilizing mission'. But in 1838, the attempt to translate paternalistic concern for Indigenous peoples, first to Sydney and then to the Port Philip frontier, failed even before it got going in earnest. Colonial governors like Gipps simply could not govern effectively if the bulk of settlers refused to cooperate with them. At the same time, the Colonial Office itself was hamstrung by the twin imperatives of keeping the settler colonies within the empire and promoting continued emigration to them. Gipps' efforts to ensure that the Myall Creek murderers were punished served simply to inflame settlers' opposition to 'naïve' and 'sentimental' philanthropic intervention in the business of colonisation: a business with which the British government itself had entrusted them.

It was not only emigrant British settlers who opposed the evangelicals' efforts. Aboriginal people in the Port Philip District were willing to engage with the protectorate to secure remnants of their land and to obtain physical protection and supplies, but most resented and resisted proselytisation. As New South Wales' Archbishop Broughton complained in his testimony to the Aborigines Committee, 'they have no wants; you find it impossible to excite any want in them which you can gratify, and therefore they have no inducement to remain under a state of restraint, nor are they willing to leave their children'.[71]

The imperial government's experiment in reconciling evangelical philanthropy with settler colonisation would be terminated by 1850. For all his efforts to navigate a middle ground between Nunn's and 'Aunt Anna's' reports, Gipps came to appreciate that both the protectorate and the Myall Creek trials were fatally undermining his relationship with the British settlers. From Port Phillip, Superintendent La Trobe warned him that the protectorate was provoking 'a spirit in the European residents which it is the most anxious desire of the government to remove'.[72] While settlers who killed Aboriginal people learned to cover their tracks with a code of silence, and occasionally adopted alternative methods such as poisoning the food distributed to Aboriginal people, Robinson and the protectors became simply an irritating thorn in the governor's side. From 1839, Gipps and La Trobe developed a close friendship. The Chief Protector's pomposity, and the tiresome length and detail of his appeals on behalf of Aboriginal people, became a running joke among them. Far from lending the government department that was supposed to ensure humane colonisation their continued support, La Trobe complained about the protectorate's 'prodigal waste of stationary' and Gipps of being 'bombarded' with its useless reports.[73]

As for the Colonial Office, despite its endorsement of 'Aunt Anna's' report in early 1838, the more immediate problems of imperial governance took precedence. Even by the end of that year, Robinson and his assistants had been relegated to the peripheries of Stephen's correspondence with Gipps. By the early 1840s, the dominant motif was Australian settlers' ever more assertive demands for self-government, including greater control over land distribution. James Stephen, the architect of emancipation and friend of the evangelical philanthropists, turned out to be far more sanguine about the fate of Australia's Aboriginal peoples than one might have expected at the beginning of 1838. When he belatedly received Gipps' bland report on the Waterloo Creek massacre, he wrote privately to Glenelg, 'The cause & the consequences of this state of things are alike clear and irremediable; nor do I suppose it is possible to discover any method by which the impending Catastrophe, namely the extermination of the Black Race can long be avoided'.[74] It seems that even as he publicly endorsed it, he anticipated the failure of the protectorate.

Self-Government in the Southern Colonies

Robinson's Protectorate of Aborigines, Gipps' trials of the Myall Creek murderers and the abandonment of Queen Adelaide Province *had* achieved something by the end of 1838, albeit quite unintentionally. They had significantly helped unite previously disparate settler factions in Australia and southern Africa around calls for self-government. Much to Gipps' and Stephen's concern, prosperous former convicts known as Emancipists, and the free settler elite known as Exclusivists, previously divided on most issues of governance in New South Wales, now at least agreed on the need to take more affairs into their own hands. Both wished to be free of the Colonial Office's philanthropic interference. In the Cape, D'Urban's recall and the Colonial Office's rejection of his plans for a land grab persuaded the British settlers of the eastern frontier to ally with Cape Town liberals, whom they otherwise despised, in more vocal demands for responsible governance. In both places, Stephen and Glenelg's interventions on behalf of Indigenous subjects, however limited they were in practice during 1838, fuelled settlers' determination to govern in their own preferred ways.

In New South Wales the *Sydney Herald* screamed during the Myall Creek trials that Aboriginal people were 'savage and murderous cannibals', the 'very lowest scale of human degradation', who could apparently now 'inhumanly and treacherously' murder 'with impunity'. Ward Stephens, its editor and proprietor, had arrived in Sydney a free settler in 1829, establishing the newspaper two years later. He rapidly developed it as a mouthpiece of the Exclusivists, who sought to dilute the colony's taint of convictism by barring Emancipists (former convicts) from status and office. One of his first campaigns had been against governor Bourke for his leniency towards convicts, both serving and emancipated. The *Sydney Herald* was supported mainly by magistrates who were wealthy landholders and squatters. During the Myall Creek trials, though, Ward Stephens found a sudden sympathy with those convict assignees 'placed, AND NOT FROM CHOICE, at their mercy, and far, far in the lonely forests', where 'seldom a day passes but [the blacks] kill and spear cattle of the graziers'.[75] Settlers of all kinds, emancipist and freeborn, needed now to unite, Ward Stephens maintained, to shed the 'double burden' that Gipps and the distant Colonial Office had imposed upon them. Not only was the government raising its revenue from their hard work through the lease and sale of Crown land; it was using that revenue to pay for the trials of the men who sought to protect them from Aboriginal 'marauders'. The arrival of Robinson and the assistant protectors in Sydney added insult to injury. These 'useless officials' were wasting 'their time about our towns, indulging in all of the luxuries of life, in idleness, meetings, speechifying, and many other useless matters', while being funded out of 'the hard earnings of the Colonists'.[76]

Spurred on by Ward Stephen's strident tones, land owning Exclusives and Emancipists joined with stock keepers and shepherds to raise money for the legal defence of the Myall Creek accused. With greater success in the long run, they also began to combine more effectively to agitate for self-governance. As early as 1833 the Emancipist elite, represented by Wentworth's Australian Patriotic Association, had, as we have mentioned, employed Charles Buller to press in London for responsible government. Bourke had contemplated appeasing them with a half elected Legislative Council, but had been overruled by the Colonial Office. Now these Emancipist campaigners and Exclusivists like Ward Stephens joined in alliance against the imperial government's philanthropic disposition, and for self-governance. Echoing the refrain of Robert Godlonton and the settlers of the Eastern Cape frontier, Ward Stephens promised that with responsible government, all the Australian Britons would be able to rid themselves of that 'whining crew who infest the colony', these 'hypocritical libellers' and their 'bewildered fanatics'. The *Sydney Herald* was far from alone. Confronting the protectorate on its doorstep directly, and Sievwright in particular, the *Geelong Advertiser* warned:

Let the matter [of the protectorate] be taken up vigorously by the local press, backed by the settlers, and the subject will ultimately be forced upon the notice of our rulers, and the influential part of the British public, through a thousand channels. We are not without advocates at home, and a hint dropped in the colonies may be picked up in England, and made use of in the promotion of colonial reform and the substitution of some sounder system of policy.[77]

Although Emancipist and Exclusivist factions within New South Wales would continue to fight, especially over the distribution of land, the Colonial Office's philanthropic interventions of 1838 helped steer them on a course of combined activism which would have lasting political repercussions. Stephen's and Glenelg's waning enthusiasm for the protection of Indigenous subjects is explained at least in part by this combination.

The Colonial Office may have been able to resist Australian calls for responsible government for longer by retreating from a vigorous commitment to Indigenous subjects' welfare, if it were not for simultaneous agitation over the British penal system. As Ward Stephens was building bridges with the Emancipists, Charles Buller's Cornish neighbour, William Molesworth, was calling for an end to convict transportation to the Australian colonies. The effect would be to add weight to the settlers' desire for self-government.

Molesworth was a combative character. As a student in Cambridge he had challenged his tutor, Henry Barnard, to a duel after a gambling dispute. Thrown out of the university he and Barnard settled with a harmless exchange of shots in Calais. Molesworth was encouraged by Buller to stand for Parliament as a radical during the debates over parliamentary reform. Although Molesworth vocally declared his 'hatred of all instituted authorities', Richard Cobden responded 'let him *say* what he pleases, there is nothing about him that is democratic in principle'. In 1835 Molesworth had funded John Stuart Mill to launch the *London Review* (later *Westminster Review*) and the following year he helped to found the Reform Club, his intent to destroy the alliance between philosophically pure radicals like Wakefield, Durham and Buller, and the 'loathsome' Whigs. Along with Buller, he backed Wakefield's campaign for systematic colonisation, joining both the South Australian Association and the New Zealand Association. Molesworth's open support for the rebels in Lower Canada in 1838 prompted 'very general execration', not least from Glenelg, but he responded 'I don't care a dam [*sic*]'.[78]

In March 1838, Molesworth moved a vote of censure on Glenelg in the House of Commons, accusing him of 'indecision and supineness' and describing his office as 'Government by the misinformed with responsibility to the ignorant'.[79] Although he did not secure the vote then, he had a second chance to stick the boot into the secretary of state when he chaired a parliamentary select committee to investigate the transportation and treatment of convicts in Australia. His committee, which met immediately after the Aborigines Committee in 1837–8, amassed the most salacious and condemnatory evidence it could to assert that transportation had created 'moral dunghills' in both Van Diemen's Land and New

South Wales. Molesworth's report would be but one contribution to the gradual and staggered phasing out of transportation. In New South Wales, it ended effectively from 1840, although a brief resumption at the end of the decade meant that the last convict arrived in 1850. Transportation to labour-starved Western Australia was revived in 1850, as it was ending in Van Diemen's Land, but would cease there too, in 1868. Molesworth's more immediate effect was to bolster Australian settlers' demands to be free of Colonial Office policy in its entirety.

In the Cape too, it would be an immediate crisis occasioned by the transportation of convicts which brought the demands for self-government to a head. When a convict ship was diverted there because of Tasmanian settlers' opposition to continued transportation in 1849, Cape Town's British inhabitants refused to cooperate with the governor, our old friend Harry Smith. Combined with the agitation from the Eastern Cape, where renewed frontier war broke out in 1850, the stand-off would trigger the concession of self-government in 1854. Thanks to the threat posed by the Kat River Khoisan, who had defected to the amaXhosa during the war, the Cape Colony emerged with a non-racial franchise which included propertied people of colour as well as the vast majority of white settlers. In the meantime, Molesworth's proposed solutions to the moral corruption caused by transportation in Australia included granting free emigrant settlers the ability to govern their own affairs. His committee's report complemented Buller's attack on the Colonial Office and Durham's prescriptions for British North America. Together, these were tributaries which conjoined in 1838–9 to produce a powerful current for settlers' self-government, even before the ink on 'Aunt Anna's' plea to protect Indigenous peoples from those same settlers was dry.

Those like Arthur, Stephen and Glenelg, who were suspicious both of democracy and of settlers' intentions towards Indigenous peoples, found it ever more difficult to resist the logic of responsible government through the second half of 1838. During the 1840s Hodgkin's Aborigines Protection Society would continue to insist that it was the British government's duty to protect the rights of Indigenous British subjects, rather than licence their dispossession and eradication at the hands of self-governing settlers, but their lobbying was in vain. The momentum generated by the rebels of Lower and Upper Canada in 1837–8 had been sustained by their counterparts across the British settler diaspora. Durham's response to Canada's settlers in 1838 unleashed unstoppable demands for self-government in the years to come, whether Stephen, Glenelg and the imperial government, and whether the empire's

Indigenous subjects, liked it or not. The Colonial Office's retention of responsibility for 'Native affairs' proved nominal and short-lived once overall governmental responsibility had been transferred to elected settler assemblies.

Having now examined selective freedom from slavery and the uneven freedom to govern oneself in 1838, in the next chapter we turn to Britons' growing belief in a third kind of freedom: one that would only reinforce the logic of settler self-governance. This was the idea of free trade, and it was seen by most Britons as compatible with both emancipation and responsible settler government.

Further Reading

Arkley, L., *The Hated Protector: The Story of Charles Wightman Sievwright, Protector of Aborigines 1839–42*, Orbit Press, 2000.

Brock, P., *Outback Ghettos: A History of Aboriginal Institutionalisation and Survival*, Cambridge University Press, 1993.

Curthoys, A., and J. Mitchell, *Taking Liberty: Indigenous Rights and Settler Self-Government in Colonial Australia, 1830–1890*, Cambridge University Press, 2018.

Elbourne, E., *Blood Ground: Colonialism, Missions, and the Contest for Christianity in the Cape Colony and Britain, 1799–1853*, McGill-Queen's University Press, 1991

Evans, J., P. Grimshaw, D. Philips and S. Swain, *Equal Subjects, Unequal Rights: Indigenous Peoples in British Settler Colonies, 1830s-1910*, Manchester University Press, 2003.

Keegan, T., *Dr Philip's Empire: One Man's Struggle for Justice in Nineteenth-Century South Africa*, Zebra Press, 2016.

Lester, A. and F. Dussart, *Colonization and the Origins of Humanitarian Governance: Protecting Aborigines Across the Nineteenth Century British Empire*, Cambridge University Press, 2014.

Mostert, N., *Frontiers: The Epic of South Africa's Creation and the Tragedy of the Xhosa People*, Alfred Knopf, 1977.

Nettelbeck, A., *Indigenous Rights and Colonial Subjecthood: Protection and Reform in the Nineteenth-Century British Empire*, Cambridge University Press, 2019.

5   Free Trade, Famine and Invasion

Even while Stephen and the Colonial Office resisted it, British settlers' clamour to govern themselves was amplified in 1838 by the increasingly influential idea of free trade. The vocal colonial reformers around Wakefield, Durham and Buller wanted imports and exports to flow unrestricted between the newly fashioned colonies of settlement and their British motherland. An imperial economy inherited from the eighteenth century, based on Caribbean and Indian tropical commodities and slavery, and hidebound by tariffs and preferences, should, in their view, be succeeded by a modernised nineteenth-century one, based on wool, meat and other temperate products freely traded from self-reliant British communities in North America and Australasia. The colonial reformers were a vocal, brash lobby, quietly resented by Stephen and Glenelg. But the notion of mitigating, if not removing, trade restrictions and tariffs between Britain and its colonies, was already taken seriously within the Colonial Office and other government departments.

In 1838, widespread agitation against the Corn Laws joined the calls for the removal of restrictions on colonial trade, setting the scene for Victorian Britain's adherence to free trade doctrine during the following decade. Implementation of that doctrine would bring the states recently independent of Spanish and Portuguese rule in Latin America into Britain's informal sphere, administered by the Foreign Office, as well as lending settlers' bid for responsible governance added momentum. However, in this chapter we turn away from the Colonial and Foreign Offices' domains to examine the effects of freer trade primarily in the eastern portion of the empire administered by the East India Company.

The Idea of Free Trade

William Huskisson may be most famous today for becoming the first person ever to die as a result of a train accident, when he was run over by Stephenson's *Rocket* in 1830. However, his greater contribution to

British and imperial history occurred during the decade preceding the opening of the Liverpool and Manchester steam railway. It was to nudge Britain and its empire away from a labyrinthine system of tariffs and preferences and towards freer trade. Huskisson achieved this as president of the Board of Trade, or more properly the Lords of the Committee of the Privy Council Appointed for the Consideration of all Matters Relating to Trade and Foreign Plantations.

Educated by his mother's uncle in Paris, Huskisson was introduced to the French *philosophes*, as well as Franklin and Jefferson as a boy. He was in the French capital during the Revolution and witnessed first-hand the fall of the Bastille. During the panic occasioned by the ensuing Terror, Huskisson, who had returned across the Channel, felt obliged to insist 'that his ideas had been formed in England' rather than France.[1] His first governmental appointment entailed the reception of French émigrés, and he helped to set up a new British secret service to conduct the Revolutionary War. Aged just twenty-four he became under-secretary at the Admiralty and then an MP. He also became intimate with the affairs of the newly captured colonies, as agent first to the Cape Colony and then Ceylon. Throughout Huskisson's meteoric rise within government, he was driven 'to secure stability and prosperity for Britain at a time of revolutionary political and economic change'.[2]

In 1814 Huskisson secured the trivial sounding post of First Commissioner of the Woods and Forests. In fact the position enabled him to play a major role in the rebuilding of late Georgian London, advising the Cabinet under Lord Liverpool. He was especially influential in directing government retrenchment after the Napoleonic War, which included the substantial cuts to the royal family's budget that had made Glenelg so unpopular with the monarch. In 1821 he co-authored a report with David Ricardo which laid the intellectual groundwork for scrapping the Corn Laws, which protected British landowners from cheaper foreign grain imports. Freer trade in basic foodstuffs, he anticipated, would enable Europe to feed industrialising Britain's growing population more effectively than could its own landed aristocracy. Huskisson really wanted his next position to be head of the Board of Control of the East India Company, but he was denied that and, in 1823, accepted that of president of the Board of Trade instead.

First established in the seventeenth century to advise on the exchange of commodities between England and its plantations in the Caribbean, the Board of Trade had become a significant government department. It determined who could trade with the British at home and overseas, in what, and with what tariffs and customs requirements. It was the body which oversaw policies tying the expanding American colonies into trade dependency with Britain by precluding their commerce with rival powers. Abolished for a brief period after its policies had played their part in the loss of those colonies, it was revived in 1783 and its significance enhanced as it advised on commercial strategy against France. In the aftermath of the defeat of Napoleon and the seizure of new colonies, Huskisson's gift was to appreciate that a more liberal trading regime, cast widely across the world, would suit a Britain rapidly transitioning into an industrial power-house. This realisation was prompted in part by his and Ricardo's con-sideration of the Corn Laws at home, but also by the role that he had played as agent for the Cape and Ceylon. The latter's coastal plantations, he wrote, could well become a 'small spearhead of the imperial economy', supplying primary produce that British manufacturers could turn into profitable exports if only 'our ancient colonial system' of trade regulations could be reformed. Despite his friendship with the slave owning John Gladstone, he also appreciated that the preferential tariffs benefitting Caribbean slave owners would have to be reformed as Britain moved towards emancipation.

It certainly did Huskisson no harm that his views on freer trade accorded with the Clapham Sect's conviction that Providence should be left to determine the economic order, untrammelled by governmental interference.[3] Huskisson remained a pragmatist though. Free trade for him was no doctrinaire ideal but rather a pragmatic strategy to be applied only where favourable to Britons. For instance he retained imperial preference for Canadian timber and corn imports so as to boost Anglophone settler entrepreneurialism – which, as we have seen, would later prompt the *Patriotes* to rebel. This preference was removed only in 1843. Nevertheless, through the 1820s Huskisson's Board of Trade repealed more than 1000 separate customs acts. It also began to mitigate the Navigation Acts, which had prevented direct trade between different British colonies and barred them from trading with foreign nations' merchant ships.[4] Under Huskisson, treaties offering equality of duties on goods and shipping were offered to any country willing to reciprocate. As his biographer concludes, 'Huskisson was *par excellence* an "imperial statesman" with a vision of Britain as the dynamic centre of an expanding colonial horizon, with empire offering tangible economic and political resources to the British state'.[5]

Huskisson failed to jump out of the *Rocket*'s way well before free trade became the dominant motif of Victorian economic policy.[6] He was suc-ceeded as president of the Board of Trade by Charles Grant, later our colonial secretary of 1838, Lord Glenelg. In that year, the remaining Navigation Acts still ensured that two-fifths of British tonnage was engaged in trade reserved only for British ships. Despite Huskisson's pruning, a bewildering range of prohibitions and tariffs on commodities traded between Britain and its colonies persisted, with a general tendency for preference for British colonial sugar, timber and coffee. Just as the Corn Laws favoured the landed domestic classes, these favoured emigrant colonists at the cost of domestic consumers.

Two successors at the Board, however, were continuing Huskisson's legacy by chipping away at these rules. James Deacon Hume (no relation of Joseph Hume whose letter to Mackenzie had helped ignite the Canadian rebellions) was the son of a customs official, and had followed in his father's footsteps. In 1822 he had asked Huskisson if he could take on the ambitious project of consolidating Britain's customs law. After three years' effort he had condensed 1500 acts dating back to King Edward I into ten bills. At the Colonial Office, the grateful James Stephen celebrated Hume's 'masterpiece of legislative skill. . . . He succeeded in the invention of a legal style, so clear . . . that everyone seized his meaning'. Hume became the Board of Trade's joint secretary in 1828, after Huskisson had left, and it was he who would propose a select committee on import duties in 1840, which declared a further thousand customs regulations 'vexatious and expendable'. Taking aim particularly at the Corn Laws, Hume summed up the appeal of freer trade in a debate at London's Political Economy Club in 1834: 'Gentlemen land-owners, you have your landed estates, they are secured to you by law, you may fence them round and exclude all intruders, why are you not content with the possession of your property, why do you attempt to invade the property of the labourer by interfering with his right to exchange the produce of his own toil for the produce of other lands?'[7]

Hume was supported at the Board of Trade in 1838 by John MacGregor, who had been raised a British North American settler himself, on Prince Edward Island. After returning to England in 1827 he became known as a writer on the maritime colonies before being recommended by Hume because of the enquiries he had made on behalf of his own potential business into trade with France. In 1836 it was MacGregor who visited the German states on behalf of the Board, to investigate the implications of the *Zollverein*, the first full economic union of independent states without a political federation, and a prototype of the European Union. Having been unsuccessful in negotiations on tariff agreement there because of Prussian objections to Britain's protective Corn Laws, MacGregor was engaged in 1838 on a commercial treaty with Austria. In 1840, he would succeed Hume as joint secretary of the Board, but even beforehand he had acquired a reputation as a dogmatic free trade advocate.[8] In 1838, his and Hume's preference for freer trade within government was loudly reinforced by the new Manchester Anti-Corn

Law Association (from 1839 the Anti-Corn Law League), the body mainly credited with bringing about the repeal of the Corn Laws in 1846.

If the Board of Trade and the Colonial Office were manoeuvring towards freer trade by 1838, so too was the East India Company. Led by Chair Sir James Lushington and Deputy Chair Sir Richard Jenkins, its directors had already seen the progressive erasure of their two centuries' old grasp of trade relationships between Britain and India. The most momentous changes had occurred on the last two occasions that the Company's charter had come up for renewal, in 1813 and 1833.

In Chapter 1 we glimpsed the depth of British society's investment in the West Indian system of slavery, just prior to emancipation. Britons' stake in the East India Company also ran deep. As with slavery, the Company's distant activity was taken for granted by most Britons unless and until parliamentary scrutiny was applied. During the debates around charter renewal in 1813 though, Thomas Plummer noted that a 'large portion of the community are directly or indirectly interested, by themselves or their connections, in the prosperity of the East India Company'.[9] This community in Britain exceeded the numbers that the Company employed in India, where, in 1830, there were 895 civil servants, 745 medical officers and around 20 000 Company-paid soldiers. In Britain, the Company employed 3490 staff in its London offices and warehouses alone, with at least another 30 000 in trades servicing its fleets. The Board of Control's solicitor was tasked with estimating the Company's significance for London when is charter came up for renewal in 1813. He complained, 'It would be almost impossible to enumerate the tradesmen, artificers, and others, who, by the means of this regular, and as it were, fixed trade, earn and obtain honest livelihoods in building, rigging, and careening of ships, and furnishing guns, anchors, timber, iron, cordage, and various other sorts of implements and tackle used therein'.[10]

Beyond those engaged in direct servicing of the Company, Britons with a stake in it ranged from its stockholders, through the merchants and ship owners contracted by it, to the manufacturers, miners and farmers who bought and sold the commodities in which it traded. Its orders are thought to have prolonged the existence of otherwise hard-pressed textile manufacturers in the West Country and East Anglia, and the tin miners of Cornwall. When the Company held sales of Indian imports, merchants and retailers would disperse them by employing transporters throughout the British Isles and beyond, especially with the re-export of the tea it brought in from its India-China trade in opium and cotton. The Company's outgoings were around a quarter of annual government expenditure. 'Company wages, salaries, dividends and interest payments, together with a variety of private profits, all contributed to the making of

East Indian fortunes, great and small', in much the same way that investments in slaves and their products from the West Indies also underpinned
British economic activity. Equally far removed from the effects of
Company activities in India as slave owners were from the brutal relations
of the plantation, Company shareholders received around £790 000 per
annum in dividends and bond interest.[11]

By the 1810s, the Company's directors were already being criticised for
confining the opportunities available to British merchants and manufacturers. Scandalously, Company ships were said to be sailing to India full
of ballast to bring Company-bought commodities home, when they could
have been transporting British manufacturers to the staggeringly large
market of 100 million Indians. It was no surprise that the renewal of the
Company's charter in 1813 was conditional upon the end of its monopoly
of trade with India. An element of free trade had in fact already developed
under the Company's aegis. From the late eighteenth century its employees in India had been able to repatriate their generous salaries through
London-based agency houses. These agencies had then established associated agencies in India itself, which invested employees' savings in
private ventures such as indigo and cotton production. The produce
would be sold to the Company for import to Britain. These London
and Indian agency houses had also developed an illicit trade with
China, effectively on behalf of the Company. As we will see in the next
chapter, using both their own and Company ships they bought and
smuggled opium, grown under Company direction in India, into China,
flouting the Qing emperors' prohibition on the trade. This enabled the
Company to earn local currency with which to buy Chinese tea, legally,
for importation to Britain. Alongside the extraction of rent from Indian
subjects, this had become the Company's most lucrative revenue stream.

When the charter renewal of 1813 threw open the trade with India
there was a spell of great economic volatility, as both the London-based
East India agency houses and a range of new entrants sought to strike
deals with manufacturers wishing to access the Indian market.
Established agencies like John Palmer and Co. competed with merchants like Huskisson's friend John Gladstone, who had redirected
investments to the newly opened Indian textile trade even before he
was foiled in his attempts to import Indian indentured workers to
British Guyana. In 1812 the Company had exported cotton goods
worth £107 306 to India. By 1829, seventeen times that value was
being sent by independent traders, doubling the total value of British
exports to India.[12] While this new integration between British and
Indian economies ultimately stimulated British-dominated Chambers
of Commerce in Calcutta, Bombay, Canton, Penang and Singapore, it

simultaneously threw Bengali textile manufacturers out of work and ended the Company's export of finished Indian cotton to Britain. The 1813 charter pushed the Company decisively away from being a commercial entity and towards being more a governmental one, although for now it still retained a nominal monopoly on the trade between India and China.[13] Even that would be discarded when the charter was next renewed, in 1833.

1833 was a momentous year for the British Empire, decisively propelling both its broad reorientation from west to east and its economic transition. We have seen already that the year was a turning point for owners of enslaved people in the West Indies, as their slaves were converted into apprentices by Stephen's Abolition of Slavery Act. But it was also a decisive year for the directors and investors of the East India Company. With Glenelg (still known as Charles Grant) president of the Board of Control in 1833, the renewal of the Company's charter came at the cost of ending its commercial activities altogether. Most immediately this meant that the Company's directors had to repay long term loans and award compensation and pensions to former employees within its trading arm. The Company's wealthier creditors as well as many of its labourers, ship commanders and clerical staff were able to access liquid capital for investment elsewhere at the same time that former slave owners were receiving their compensation. Their activities have not yet been traced, but some of them may well have invested in settler colonisation projects in the same way that emancipation compensation beneficiaries like the Montefiore brothers and Celia Scott invested in Australia.

The fact that the British government was already so preoccupied with arranging compensation for slave owners in 1833 was one of the key reasons why the Company was not dissolved entirely, but rather mutated to become the proxy British government of India. In many respects this was a bizarre outcome. During the parliamentary debate on the 1833 charter, James Silk Buckingham, former editor of the *Calcutta Journal* and a long-standing critic of the company, complained that 'the idea of consigning over to a Joint-Stock Association ... the political administration of an empire peopled with a hundred millions of souls, was so preposterous, that if it were now for the first time to be proposed, it would be deemed not merely an absurdity, but an insult'. Buckingham pleaded for a delay to charter renewal until such time as a proper branch of imperial government for India could be established. However, even he had to admit that, tied up as the government was with the abolition of slavery as well as the raft of domestic legislation following the 1832 Reform Act, he could envisage no better alternative for governing the subcontinent at present.[14]

The man who conducted the Board of Control's negotiations with the Company's directors on Glenelg's behalf as the charter renewal date loomed, was its secretary, Thomas Babington Macaulay. Soon to become England's most famous historian, Thomas Babington had been raised among his father Zachary Macaulay's circle of evangelical reformers. His and Glenelg's fathers were close friends. Apparently a precocious boy who was reading by the age of three, he developed a love of erudite and eloquent argumentation, derived in large part from his veneration of the Bible. Macaulay was already well known for his writings on history and political economy before he entered Parliament and lent his support to the 1832 Reform Act. He was appointed to the Board of Control in the same year, probably due to Glenelg's patronage.

In late 1832, Macaulay was promoted as the Board's secretary and became its spokesman in the House of Commons during the 1833 charter debates. Thinking about both the Company's charter and the abolition of slavery act at the same time, in May 1833, prompted him to write to his sister:

> The N*****s in one hemisphere
> The Brahmins in the other
> Disturb my dinner and my sleep
> With 'Ain't I a man and a brother'?[15]

Macaulay explained to the House of Commons why the Company was being allowed to govern India after it had ceased to be a trading concern. Following Buckingham, he too pointed to the lack of any better alternative at a time when Parliament was so busy and the Colonial Office in particular was so focused on emancipation. There simply was not enough time on the parliamentary calendar, nor Commons expertise on India, to establish a new branch of government in the foreseeable future. Reverting to the Company infrastructure, which had already insinuated itself over and alongside India's other polities, was the only option. Besides, barring the Company from its governing and rent-raising function as well as its commerce, would mean winding it up altogether, and this would be infinitely more fraught than it might first appear.

It was one thing to compensate creditors and employees of the Company's former trading branch, but disentangling the accrued investments behind the entire company edifice would be almost impossible. So 'entangled together in inextricable complication' were the Company's 'mercantile and political transactions', Macaulay cautioned, that his predecessor as board secretary, Thomas Hyde Villers had been brought to an early death by the prolonged strain of trying to distinguish them. 'The existence of such a body as this gigantic corporation – this political monster of two natures – subject in one hemisphere, sovereign in another – had never been contemplated by the Legislators or Judges of former ages'. Winding up such a behemoth with justice to its stock-holders, directors and employees would be enough 'to exercise all the ingenuity of all the lawyers in the kingdom for twenty years'.

As for Lushington, Jenkins, the other directors and the shareholders in Britain, any opposition they may have mounted to the Company's transi-tion was deflected by Macaulay's promise that they would continue to receive an annual dividend of 10.5 per cent. This was 'precisely the same dividend which they have been receiving for forty years, and which they have expected to receive permanently'. Rather than being derived in part from trade, the shareholders' returns would from now on be extracted exclusively from the rent paid by the Company's Indian subjects in return for the privilege of being governed by it. Despite Buckinghan's objection that 'confiding the political Administration of our East-India possessions, with the interests of 100,000,000 of people, to the direction of a Joint Stock Company, and taxing the natives of those countries for the payment of the dividends ... [to] the constantly varying holders of East-India Stock, is a question involving too many important considerations to be hastily decided on, more especially for so long a term as twenty years', the Company's stockholders returns were indeed enshrined for the next twenty-year charter duration.[16]

Free labour, with the abolition of slavery, and free trade, with the end of the East India Company's commercial functions, both heralded an imperial economy that was more attuned to the needs of Britain's rising commercial, financial and manufacturing classes in 1833. But by the end of the year the British government had made it clear that those whose existing investments in slave ownership or East India Company stock were threatened by the transition, would be taken care of. Former slave owners would be compensated for the loss of their property and guaran-teed free, apprenticed, labour for a further four or six years, while Company shareholders would continue to receive their dividends just as if the Company was still a profitable trading enterprise.

Macaulay explained that it was actually a privilege for Indians to be governed by the Company, and for the rent that they paid to be remitted to its shareholders in Britain. After all, it was Company rule which had seen 'the horrors of war' in late Mughal India mitigated by the 'chivalrous and Christian spirit of Europe'. He was confident that 'though few of' the shareholders 'have ever seen or may ever see the people whom they rule – they will have a great stake in the happiness of their subjects'. 'We are trying', Macaulay assured his parliamentary colleagues, 'to give a good government to a people to whom we cannot give a free government'.

Whereas 'In Europe' and, as we have seen, increasingly in the British settler colonies, 'the people are ... perfectly competent to hold some share ... of political power', 'In India, you cannot have representative institutions. Of all the innumerable speculators who have offered their suggestions on Indian politics, not a single one, as far as I know, however democratical his opinions may be, has ever maintained the possibility of giving, at the present time, such institutions to India'.

Macaulay turned to James Mill, the East India Company clerk who had never visited India, but whose *History of British India* was apparently 'the greatest historical work which has appeared in our language since that of Gibbon', for affirmation that representative government was suitable for Britons but not for Indians: Mill 'has written strongly – far too strongly, I think, in favour of pure democracy. ... But when he was asked ... whether he thought representative government practicable in India, his answer was – "utterly out of the question"'.[17] The British Parliament was thereby assured that the political and organisational backwardness of the Indians themselves demanded government by the Company's Directors in London and its appointed governors in Madras, Bombay and Calcutta.[18]

This dismissal of Indian abilities in the early 1830s was somewhat ironic given that the very restructuring of the Company that the British government had overseen since 1813 was being exploited by prominent Indian political leaders and entrepreneurs like Dwarkanath Tagore, who were willing to work with, and indeed financially bail out, their British commercial partners. From a large extended family belonging to the subcaste of Brahmans known as Pirali, who were considered 'ritually impure' by other Bengali Brahmins, Tagore had attended Mr Sherbourne's English school for upper-class Indian boys in Calcutta. He soon became a legal adviser to *zamindars* or large landowners in Bengal, while acquiring land himself. Tagore backed Rammohun Roy's campaign to work with British reformers to outlaw suttee (the self-immolation of a woman on her husband's funeral pyre) and extend freedom of the press. From 1828 to 1834, he had held the important post of *diwan* of the board of customs, which included regulation of opium, and begun his business career in overseas trade, indigo and sugar production and moneylending, including to Company servants. In 1829 he led a group of British and Indian merchants in establishing the Union Bank of Calcutta. When most of the British-run agency houses collapsed in the economic crisis following trade liberalisation in the 1820s–30s, Tagore's businesses survived. While Macaulay was declaring Indians' inability to govern themselves, and while London agency houses were shunning former Indian business partners, Tagore was using his commercial advantage to partner with William Carr and William Prinsep, forming Carr, Tagore & Co. The company acted as managing agent for joint-stock companies investing in the new steam technology, including the Bengal Coal Company, the Calcutta Steam Tug Association, the India General Steam Navigation Company, and the Steam Ferry Bridge Company. Tagore put much of his own proceeds from these investments in Indian infrastructure into hospitals, medical education and charitable funding for the poor and the blind in Calcutta, while Prinsep invested in the colonisation of Western Australia.[19]

Elite Indians like Tagore and Roy were beginning to advocate a British–Indian partnership for the governance and reform of India at the very moment that Macaulay was persuading Parliament of their inability. 'It is true, that the power of the Company is an anomaly in politics', admitted Macaulay, but 'what constitution can we give to our Indian Empire which shall not be strange – which shall not be anomalous' in 'a territory, inhabited by men, differing from us in race, colour, language, manners, morals, religion. ... It is the strangest of all Governments: but it is designed for the strangest of all Empires'.[20] Under Macaulay's charter renewal act, a new supreme council was created to oversee the Company's administration in Calcutta, with a post for a 'law member', which Macaulay took for himself. He calculated on saving half his salary of £10 000 so as to return to England in a few years 'with a competence honestly earned'. He would proceed to write his famous *Minute on Indian Education* in 1835, arguing for the instruction of Indians in English so that they could be led to greater civilisation by a more advanced culture.[21] By 1838, then, 'the East India Company's business was ... government, and government was its business'.[22]

The Governance of India

The men directing the East India Company from London had plentiful experience in the region they governed. Both the chair of the Board of Company Directors, Sir James Lushington, and his deputy, Sir Richard Jenkins, had played prominent roles in establishing Britain's predominance on the subcontinent over the previous four decades, the former with violence and the latter with persuasive force predicated upon it. Lushington had fought at the siege of Seringapatam which ended Tipu Sultan's reign in Mysore, and in the suppression of the Maharajah of Travancore's rebellion, when he had tried to renegotiate the terms of his own subordination as a princely ruler.[23] The high point of Lushington's military career had been leading the relief charge at the Battle of Maheidpoor during the final defeat of the western Indian Maratha

Empire.[24] Jenkins had arrived in Bombay in 1801 to begin a career as a translator, having been awarded prizes for his Arabic, Hindustani and Persian at the Company's Fort William College in Calcutta. His experience in Company employment was as one of the Resident Agents, appointed to oversee the governance of the subordinated princely states. He articulated the policy of indirect rule, which he helped to establish, in 1821: 'our general plan in all things has been to avoid innovation, and to regulate the old machinery and restore it where deficient'.[25]

In the 1830s, Lushington and Jenkins reluctantly accepted the end of the Company's commercial activities in return for guaranteed shareholder returns and the preservation of its governing functions in the eastern half of the British Empire. Just as Stephen and Glenelg did not have things all their own way at the Colonial Office, Lushington and Jenkins were constrained by a number of factors in their governance of India. The most significant, of course, was the time lag involved in their correspondence with the governors of the three presidencies, who necessarily acted largely autonomously of the directors in London. We will return to their communications infrastructure, in transition to steam technology at the time, in the next chapter. Besides the problem of geography, however, the Board of Directors was constrained by its accountability in two directions, to its own stockholders and to the government's Board of Control.

The Company was governed internally by three distinct types of Court. At the Public Court, anyone holding a certain amount of stock could participate in what were often rambunctious and quasi-parliamentary debates over Company policy. The directors' Court featured only the handful of directors who managed the Company, and were usually called only for the election of new members. Finally, the Court of Proprietors, which we will refer to as the Court from now on, was convened at least once every week and often more, and was where the real business of executive governance took place. Most meetings began at around eleven in the morning, and carried on until well after dinner time. These meetings were highly structured affairs. Correspondence was read out and sorted between three committees dealing with Political and Military, Revenue and Judicial and Financial and Home affairs. The Court would adjourn for a few hours while the committees conferred and, upon their return, considered their replies, decisions and draft paragraphs for inclusion in despatches to the presidency governors in India. The drafts of this correspondence were either voted upon or laid by for a week or two so that all members of the Company could see them. Once voted on, they were despatched from Company House to the Board of Control in Westminster, which either approved them or suggested amendments. Drafts could pass back and forth for weeks, to the frustration of both Court and Board, with the Board always holding the power of veto.

Some of the issues causing the most voluminous relays of paper between Leadenhall Street and Cannon Row in early 1838 were the extent to which the Board could determine the appointment of professors to the East India Company's College at Haileybury, the oversight of judicial appointees in Indian courts, and the Company's latitude to grant pensions to ex-employees. While the Court remained preoccupied in 1838 with the minutiae of coal depots en route to India, the regularity of Mediterranean packet voyages, and Chelsea Pensioners' prize money from the Deccan wars, Lushington and Jenkins bore the brunt of the more significant negotiations over the limits of the Company's authority with Hobhouse at the Board of Control. The scope of the Company's authority in India was defined by the remit that these men hammered out between them in London. Governance itself, however, was conducted primarily by the Government of India in Calcutta and its presidencies in Madras and Bombay.

In Madras, John, thirteenth Lord Elphinstone and first Baron Elphinstone, presided in 1838. His uncle, Mountstuart Elphinstone had become a great friend of Jenkins during the wars of the 1810s and would go on to play a major role in the 'Great Game' against Russian influence on India's northern frontier. John had been appointed governor one year ago, after serving in the Horse Guards and acting as lord-in-waiting to King William IV. The rumour was that Prime Minister Melbourne had sent him to India to avoid the scandal of the young Queen Victoria falling in love with him. Demonstrating how governance of the British Empire was a family business, Colonial Secretary Glenelg's younger brother, Robert Grant, was governor of the Bombay presidency in 1838. Like Glenelg, he had been born in Bengal and educated privately among the evangelical Clapham Sect by John Venn. The dilettante diarist Charles Greville described both Glenelg and his brother as 'forgetful and unpunctual', declaring that 'if you asked Charles to dine with you at six on Monday, you were very likely to have Robert at seven on Tuesday'.[26] During the debates over charter renewal in 1813, Robert had published a history of the Company which defended its trading monopoly. When his brother became president of the Board of Control in 1830, Grant was appointed one of the board's commissioners. Glenelg's continued nepotism had seen him appointed governor of Bombay in 1834, and by 1838, he was promoting a number of 'improving' projects including a regular steam ship service to Britain, a department for the construction of roads and experimental agricultural gardens. After a short and unexpected illness, Robert Grant died in July 1838, leaving his mourning brother to arrange for the publication of the hymns that he had written as a lasting tribute.

Both Elphinstone and Robert Grant were outranked by the governor of Bengal and governor-general of India, George Eden, a barrister who had turned to politics when his elder brother drowned in the Thames in 1810. Eden took his seat in the House of Commons and became a Whig MP, striking up a close friendship with Melbourne, Hobhouse and the later foreign secretary, Viscount Palmerston. In 1814, when his father died, he moved to the House of Lords, from then on being known as the second Baron Auckland. Auckland was known to be shy, modest and anxious of public speaking. He was also inseparable from his two sisters, Emily and Fanny. With Melbourne's government, he succeeded Huskisson and Glenelg to become president of the Board of Trade and then, briefly, First Lord of the Admiralty. He was criticised in this role for his 'unpopular manners, his want of talent for public speaking and of distinction as a public man'. Auckland admitted 'I have no turn for great elevation and am not very confident of myself', and yet he was the man who, in 1838, most directly governed Britain's hundred million subjects in India. He accepted the responsibility mainly so that he could guarantee financial support for his sisters.[27]

Auckland had arrived in India in March 1836 inspired by Thomas Babington Macualay's recent call to instruct Indians in English, and with a programme of cautious reform in mind. At the dinner organised in London by the Company's Court of Directors to send him on his way, he declared that he 'looked with exultation to the new prospects ... of doing good to his fellow creatures, of promoting education and knowledge, and of extending the blessings of good government and happiness to millions in India'.[28] He had begun his tenure with a leisurely fact-finding tour of northern India accompanied by his sister Emily, who generated a colourful account of the tour in her subsequently published letters and journals.[29]

The Agra Famine

On 1 January 1838 Auckland was diverted from his and Emily's tour, and indeed from any long term planning for the improvement of India, by the need to visit the Company's newly annexed North-Western Provinces. These had been set to become the new Presidency of Agra, but the planning was interrupted by reports of a severe famine, concentrated in the Doab between the Ganges and Yamuna rivers. Company servants had reported previous periods of scarcity in the region, but their concern had always been for Company revenue rather than Indian lives. Losses were reckoned 'in terms of balances, suspensions and remissions, and little attention was paid to recording mortalities'.[30] What has come to be known as the Agra famine of 1837–8 was of a different order. It affected 8 million Indian subjects of the Company across an area of 25 000 square miles. Auckland felt obliged to intervene.

As scholars of famine are well aware, what at first sight appears to be the main cause – an environmental change causing crop failure – is actually just the trigger which plunges a population already brought to a precarious position to the point of starvation. People die not because their own means of producing food fails *per se*, but because they have no other means of securing food. The economic volatility brought by the end of the Company's monopoly over the last five years had contributed to economic depression and extreme poverty in the Agra region. Those reliant on cotton production and export to Britain and China had been undercut by imported British textiles, while the region's previously flourishing indigo export trade had also been undermined. El Niño weather events causing the failure of the 1837 summer monsoon rains then ensured that the poorest people, even those employed to grow opium on the Company's behalf for export to China, were unable to afford scarcer food supplies.

The demands for revenue placed upon Indian farmers, so as to supply the shareholders' 10.5 per cent dividend in Britain, did not help. The costs of this rent were passed down through Indian society, with little of the revenue being spent within India itself. Lushington and Jenkins assured the Board and the British public that considerable investment was taking place in canal building and cultivation improvements, but the sums remained small in comparison to the investments traditionally expected of ruling authorities, until a surge of investment in government and infrastructure followed the Uprising of 1857 (see Part II). The Company's continual 'revenue demand also acted to keep areas under perpetual cropping', leading to soil infertility. Paradoxically, even the lull in the Company's succession of conquests between the end of the Napoleonic War and the 1830s had an effect, since fewer Indians had been able to gain employment in its armies. By the time the harvest failed in 1837, 'the authority of the Indian [princely] states was reduced and their resources widely dissipated', meaning that market centres in the smaller towns had already 'dwindled or stagnated'.[31] After Auckland arrived in the region, the winter monsoon rains failed too, and no spring harvest was expected.

In February 1838 Auckland reported to Hobhouse the 'harrowing accounts of famine and distress' that were 'pour[ing] in from Calpee, Agra, Etawah and Mynpoorie':

Not only has the khareef crop [the main subsistence summer crop] in these districts entirely failed but the grass and fodder were also lost. This has led to extensive mortality amongst the cattle, and in some districts nearly all those which have not perished on the spot, have been driven off to other parts of the country in order that they might be saved. It has thus happened that great difficulty has been experienced in irrigating the land for the ... crops, and much land which would otherwise have been cultivated has lain waste from this want of means of irrigation.

Auckland appealed to the Company directors for funds. The 'largest expenditure' was required 'in order to palliate the evil, and prevent the total depopulation of the country by starvation and emigration'. By the end of the year around 800 000 people had died of starvation.

The Company directors' response was conditioned by the zealotry of their newfound belief in free trade.[32] While Lushington agreed a sum of Rs 2 million of Company funds to be spent on immediate relief of the able bodied who could work for it, 'all interference in the price or sale of grain on the part of the officers of the government was strictly prohibited', so as to afford 'the greatest possible facilities for free and unrestricted commerce'. Those who could labour on the roads and police stations, which, incidentally, would help cement Company authority in the region, were given ration tickets which they took to Indian grain merchants and exchanged for food. The Company then paid the merchants the cost of their grain plus some profit. Until that was, Auckland learned that some of the merchants were adulterating the grain with sand or powdered bones. From April, he ensured that the Company distributed food directly to those who worked for it.

Neither Lushington and Jenkins in London, nor Auckland himself, believed that it was up to the Company to offer charity for those already too sick to work. This was for Indians to organise among themselves. As the Deputy-Collector of Cawnpore, the man whose job it was to secure Company shareholders' dividends, observed in February 1838, 'the relief afforded, in its present state, is inadequate to the wants of the people, but it must not on that account be considered valueless. Thousands have by it been saved from death by starvation, and the flood of emigration has been checked. The aid afforded ... will ... evince to the people that the Government are anxious to relieve their present unparalleled suffering, and the example thus set forth has ... been an inducement to hundreds [of wealthier Indians] to bestir themselves, on behalf of the starving poor, who never before thought of lending their aid in relieving the distress'. As the famine claimed more lives during the course of the year, and as more children and especially girls were sold into slavery and prostitution by desperate parents, Auckland noted, 'The subject that most demanded attention ... was the crowded state of the criminal jails', rather than the death rate. Company magistrates and commissioners complained that 'neither the stores of merchants nor the grain in transit was safe from attack. ... The starving people forgot all rights of possession, and violently laid their hands on their neighbours' supplies'.[33] Desperate, often village-organised, attempts to raid food supplies meant that, 'for a short period the foundations of the Raj in Hindustan trembled'. However, 'as yet there was no defection from the military or police such as was to occur twenty years later'.[34]

In pre-Company controlled Indian famines, in urban areas at least, Mughal and other Indian authorities had forced merchants to open grain stores, intervened in the market to fix prices, and distributed cash directly: all measures that the Company was loath to undertake. During the Chalisa famine of 1783, the Nawab of Awadh, for instance, had given out Rs 5000–10 000 to the starving every day and employed 40 000 people in the construction of the great Imambara. In the provinces, even under Company administration, it was still largely up to local notables to provide food, and many *zamindars* attempted to do so during 1838. The targets for most of the 'crime' reported by Company officials tended neither to be the Company itself nor local *zamindars*, but rather Indians who had profited by seizing opportunities to work with the Company, while failing to live up to their obligations to the poor. These merchants, moneylenders and transporters included the salt merchants who now switched to grain to 'make a killing' while prices were high, and the hoarders of grain who adulterated the supplies that the Company paid them to provide. These were 'the nouveaux riches of indigenous society', who 'were not willing to be new patrons'.[35] In this, they were supported by the Company's insistence on the irresponsibility of providing charity or fixing food prices.

In Delhi, where rioting broke out on 5 October 1837, it was both the Company and profiteering merchants who were targeted. The commissioner, T. T. Metcalfe refused to follow the Mughal precedent of forcing grain dealers to bring down their prices. Refugees who had travelled to Delhi expecting to find food, attacked grain merchants' boats, which were moored on the river en route to Gwalior, where there was even greater scarcity and where the merchants therefore expected to attain even higher prices. The refugees were soon joined by local wage labourers and other citizens who felt that Metcalfe had failed in the most fundamental duty of a just ruler. When, the following year, the Delhi magistrate John Bell, sought to learn the lesson and tried to persuade grain merchants to lower their prices, they knew full well that, whatever Bell's protestations, Auckland would not force them to do so as Mughal rulers once had, and so they forced him to back down.

The First Afghan War

Even before the next monsoon rains finally assisted in bringing the Agra famine to an end, Auckland had become embroiled in the second major crisis of Indian governance in 1838. His reputation emerged unscathed from the famine, since he had done all that the Company Directors and Board of Control expected of him, but the new crisis would ultimately lead to his governorship ending in disgrace.

During the winter of 1838, Auckland travelled to meet Ranjit Singh, the powerful Sikh Maharaja of the Punjab, to discuss the problems of the north-west frontier. His friends Hobhouse at the Board of Control, and Palmerston at the Foreign Office, had primed him for the meeting, while Lushington and the Company's directors merely looked on from the side lines. The British government had long been paranoid about Russian intentions to invade India through Central Asia and Afghanistan, and before Auckland had left England, Hobhouse and Palmerston made it clear that he should use the Company's power on the British government's behalf against Russian influence. The Punjab was seen as a potentially important strategic ally in what would come to be called this 'Great Game'.[36] Ranjit Singh was promising to help Auckland secure Afghanistan as a buffer against Russian advance.

In late 1836, Auckland had sent Alexander Burnes as an envoy for the Company, to form an alliance with Afghanistan's Amir, Dost Mohammad. Like Lushington, Burnes had joined the Company's army as a cadet aged sixteen, and like Jenkins, he had rapidly learned Hindustani and Persian, becoming a Bombay army interpreter. He had been singled out for espionage and, in 1831, set out on a mission to gather intelligence beyond the Company's north-west frontier. His pretext was the delivery of a gift of five dray horses from King William IV to Ranjit Singh. Claiming that the horses might be weakened by travel over land, he sailed with them up the Indus to Lahore, charting the river and gathering information on the independent states of the Sind as he went. Despite the region's amirs knowing full well what he was up to and repeatedly delaying his progress, Burnes then set off on a more ambitious covert expedition to tease out Russian capabilities and intentions across Central Asia. Together with a Company surgeon, an Indian surveyor and a Kashmiri secretary, he reached the Caspian Sea before returning via Tehran, where the Persian rulers were allied with Russia. In 1833 he received a hero's welcome in England and his book, *Travels into Bokhara*, sold out in multiple editions.[37]

When Auckland sent Burnes to Kabul, Dost Mohammad had welcomed him, together with the British support that he appeared to be offering against the Amir's two main enemies: Persia, which threatened his hold on Herat and was backed by Russia, and Ranjit Singh himself, who had captured his second capital, Peshawar. In particular, the Afghan ruler hoped that Burnes and the Company would help him reclaim Peshawar from the Sikhs. Burnes concurred, advising Auckland in 1838 that an alliance with Dost Mohammad was the Company's best strategy against Russian incursion. However, Burnes was not the only adviser seeking to bring Auckland's attention away from Agra and the famine in order to concentrate on Afghanistan.

William Hay Macnaghten was Burnes' more successful rival for Auckland's ear. The son of a Madras Supreme Court judge, Macnaghten had been schooled in England but returned as a cavalry cadet in the Company's Madras army. He too learned Persian and Hindi, supplementing them with Tamil, Telugu, Kanarese and Marathi. Like Jenkins, he distinguished himself at Fort William College, winning every linguistic prize. He was, apparently, not quite so modest about his linguistic attainments as his contemporary Anna Gurney.[38] Macnaghten next embarked on a legal career, playing a major role in codifying Muslim and Hindu laws so that they could be bent to fit British precedents. He toured the north-west as Governor-General Bentinck's secretary before he was elevated to the role of secretary of the Company's Political and Secret Department. This was the department for which John Stuart Mill worked in London, responsible for corresponding with Lushington and Hobhouse on policy towards the princely states as well as those neighbouring British India. Together with the reports from Palmerston's spies in Central Asia, it informed British strategy in the 'Great Game'.

Significantly for the fate of Afghanistan, and of Auckland, Macnaghten's position gave him the ability to filter Burnes' messages from Kabul before Auckland read them in Calcutta or Simla. When Auckland left Calcutta to visit the famine districts in 1838, Macnaghten went with him, editing the Arabic text of *A Thousand and One Nights* and warning him of Burnes' ambition and untrustworthiness on the way. Despite Burnes' advice to support Dost Mohammed, Macnaghten was convinced that the Company should ally with his enemy, Ranjit Singh, instead. This was partly because, compared to the seemingly fractious tribal levies commanded by the Afghan Amir, the Punjab had a powerful standing army. But it was mainly because Ranjit Singh was harbouring a former Amir in exile, who had the potential to become the Company's puppet ruler of Afghanistan, a far more compliant ally than the independent-minded Dost Mohammed.

Despite an attempt some thirty years ago to ally with the Company in order to shore up his rule, this former Amir, Shah Shuja, had been overthrown after failing to unite the major familial factions in Afghanistan. Nevertheless the Company continued to pay him a pension, enabling his lavish lifestyle in Ludhiana, just in case he might prove useful. Ranjit Singh had combined with him in 1833 to seize Peshawar from Dost Mohammad, but their joint invasion had stalled before Shah Shuja could re-enter Kabul.[39] In 1837, Burnes had warned Auckland that there was very little appetite among the most influential Afghans for Shah Shuja's attempts to return. Dost Mohammad had far more legitimacy among the main tribal leaders. Indeed he was seen as a relatively successful Amir. He certainly had less of a reputation for personal cruelty than the Company-backed alternative. But Macnaghten was convinced that Shah Shuja would ultimately be accepted by the majority of Afghans. He used his influence with both Auckland and Hobhouse, and his ability to mediate Burnes' intelligence from Kabul, to make his case.

The intelligence that prompted Palmerston and Hobhouse to urge Auckland into action was Burnes' report that an envoy from Russia, Yan Vitkevich, had reached Kabul in late 1837 to cultivate a rival alliance with Dost Mohammad. Burnes had apparently 'abandoned himself to despair' at the news, 'bound his head with wet towels and handkerchiefs and took to the smelling bottle'. Afghan sources indicate that Dost Mohammad intended to use Vitkevich only as leverage to obtain the British support that he really wanted.[40] However, within the 'Great Game's' atmosphere of suspicion, rumour and miscalculation, Hobhouse and Palmerston's panic that Russia had gained a foothold on British India's doorstep was conveyed to Auckland, unaccompanied by any clear guidelines on how he should respond. Recovering from his initial despair, Burnes insisted that Dost Mohammad could be persuaded to dismiss Russian overtures, if only the Indian government became more proactive in cultivating him as its ally, but Macnaghten dismissed his arguments. The sense of urgency was compounded by the Persian siege of Herat, supported by Russia, which seemed to amplify the Russian threat and diminish Dost Mohammad's utility as an ally in any case.

Fearing that he would become known as the governor-general who unwittingly fulfilled the British government's worst fear of a Russian takeover on the border of India, Auckland grasped at Macnaghten's assurances. The restoration of Shah Shuja, he hoped, would turn the tide. In early 1838, while he was calling for Company help with the famine, Auckland also sent an ultimatum for Burnes to deliver to Dost Mohammad: 'You must desist from all correspondence with Russia. You must never receive agents from them, or have aught to do with them without our sanction; you must dismiss Captain Viktevitch with courtesy; you must surrender all claims to Peshawar'. Burnes considered the governor-general's response 'so dictatorial and supercilious as to indicate the writer's intention that it should give offense'. He was right. Dost Mohammad expelled Burnes in April 1838. From July, while he deliberated with advisers in Simla, leaving his council in Calcutta in the dark, Auckland allowed Macnaghten to negotiate terms with Ranjit Singh, initially for a predominantly Sikh invasion of Afghanistan, led by Company officers, with the aim of reinstating Shah Shuja.

By October 1838, Afghan defenders had repulsed the Persian siege of Herat and Palmerston had persuaded the Russians to back away from potential conflict by ordering Viktevich home, where he would later commit suicide. Fatally though, Auckland was already committed. On 1 October, he issued the Simla Declaration, which accused Dost Mohammed of making 'an unprovoked attack ... on our ancient ally, Maharaja Ranjit Singh', declared Shah Shuja the legitimate and 'popular ruler of Afghanistan', and pledged that he would return the former Amir to his realm 'surrounded by his own troops and ... supported against foreign interference and factious opposition by the British Army'. Furthermore, Auckland had taken Macnaghten's advice that the invasion should be undertaken by British and Indian Company troops, rather than Punjabi Sikhs, to demonstrate British capabilities and settle the issue of the north-west frontier once and for all. As his sister Emily wrote, 'poor, dear peaceful George had gone to war. Rather an inconsistency in his character'.[41]

The invasion would be launched in March 1839, with Hobhouse privately taking responsibility in London and exonerating Lushington and the Company Directors of any misfortune that might befall. With the successful occupation of Kabul in July 1839 and then the surrender and exile of Dost Mohammad, Auckland seemed for a while to have neatly replicated in Afghanistan the kind of control that the Company had forged over India's own princely states. 'Regime change' was accomplished and Hobhouse ensured that Auckland was rewarded with his earldom.[42] But it did not necessarily take the benefit of hindsight to see the disaster portending. There were good political, geographical and military reasons why the Mughal rulers of India had simply paid off

Afghanistan's chiefdoms in times of tension. When Hobhouse had approvingly reported Auckland's decision to invade to Parliament, Mountstuart Elphinstone, uncle of the governor in Madras and active player in the 'Great Game', warned that 'if 27,000 men were sent up the Bolan pass to Kandahar, and we could feed them, there was no doubt that we might take Kabul, and set up Shah Shuja; but it was hopeless to maintain him in a poor, cold, strong and remote country, among a turbulent people like the Afghans'. Auckland's predecessor, Bentinck, described the idea as 'an act of incredible folly' and the Duke of Wellington, Lushington's former commander at Seringapatam, decried its astonishing naivety. Affirming that the army would encounter little resistance taking Kabul, he warned that the real 'stupidity' of the invasion plan would be revealed thereafter. Afghanistan's tribal fighters would begin a guerrilla campaign, cutting off the occupying force from supplies and reinforcements through the Hindu Kush's narrow mountain passes to India.[43]

It was more Auckland's lack of political insight than poor military or geographical understanding which proved the occupation's downfall. Macnaghten's wishful thinking alone could not make Shah Shuja acceptable to Afghanistan's tribal heads. He and Auckland underestimated the Afghan elite's ability to perceive that the former Amir was back merely as a Company puppet. Macnaghten insisted that the Afghans would eventually come to see the British as their friends, but had to admit that British forces would be necessary to prop him up longer than originally expected while their 'hearts and minds', as later generations of occupiers would put it, were won over. Over the next three years, as Macnaghten spent £8 million of Company funds sustaining Shah Shuja in Kabul, the British garrison underpinning his authority came to be ever more deeply resented. Many Afghans saw both British officers and their largely Indian subalterns as infidels who flouted their religion, customs and etiquette.

In November 1841, Burnes and all in his household were killed by Afghan men outraged by his lasciviousness with Afghan women. Open rebellion broke out in Kabul. Cut off exactly as Wellington had predicted, the Indian and British troops could now do little but defend themselves and their exposed cantonment from incessant attacks, awaiting the exhaustion of their ammunition and food stocks. While the garrison suffered from a lack of leadership and direction, Dost Mohammad's son, Akbar Khan, organised an alliance of tribal leaders to finish off the occupation. The following month, as Macnaghten tried desperately to negotiate a way out for the beleaguered garrison, Akbar Kahn lured him into a trap and killed him with the pistol that Macnagthen himself had gifted him.

By the end of 1841 Auckland finally admitted that it was 'too hazardous and costly in money and in life for us to continue to wrestle against the universal opinion, national and religious, which has been so suddenly and so strongly brought in array against us'.[44] In London, Hobhouse, who had insisted that Auckland do something about the Russian threat in 1838 and failed to call him off when that threat had diminished, now urged him either to secure control of Afghanistan with more troops (his favoured option) or abandon it. This time taking the advice of his council in Calcutta, in January 1842, Auckland finally ordered the recall of the Kabul garrison. Akbar Kahn persuaded the 4500 British and Indian troops and 12 000 camp followers to leave the cantonment with a promise of safe passage to the Company fort at Jalalabad some ninety miles away. He then either allowed, or directly ordered them to be harried all the way, as they endured freezing conditions on the march. Stragglers were killed, and then almost all the survivors in the column were massacred as they tried to negotiate the narrow and steep sided Khurd Kabul pass. The soldiers of the 44th Regiment of Foot, who had tried to force a passage through, were killed by Akbar Kahn's forces when they ran out of ammunition at the village of Gandamak. The only Briton from the retreating column who made it to the nearest British garrison at Jalalabad was the Company surgeon William Brydon, immortalised in Elizabeth's Butler's paining, *Remnants of an Army* (see Figure 5.1). The few Indian *sepoys* or Company infantry and camp followers who also made it to Jalalabad in the days following the massacre went largely unremarked in Britain.

In February 1842 Auckland wrote that 'the plans of public good and public security upon which I had staked so much' were 'all broken down under circumstances of horror and disaster of which history has few parallels'.[45] For Hobhouse too, the disaster was personal, since his nephew John Byron Hobhouse had been one of those killed on the retreat. His own reputation was damaged once it got out that he had probably doctored Burnes' and other intelligence from India to burnish the Board of Control's argument for replacing Dost Mohammad. When Melbourne resigned in September 1841, Hobhouse went with him. Despite Auckland's partial recovery of pride when he ordered an Army of Retribution to re-enter Kabul, destroy the central bazaar and recover prisoners before returning swiftly to India, Britain's first occupation of Afghanistan left his reputation and his health in tatters.[46] Remarkably though, the First Anglo-Afghan War was just one of two major wars that the East India Company's governing men, including the seemingly timid Auckland, helped to precipitate in 1838. In order to understand the second, we will need, in the next chapter, to return to the effect that free trade was having on the Company's activities.

Figure 5.1 Arrival of Dr Brydon at Jalalabad, 13 January 1842, 1900, after Elizabeth's Butler's *Remnants of an Army*. Photo by The Print Collector via Getty Images.

Further Reading

Bayly, C. A., *Rulers, Townsmen and Bazaars: North Indian Society in the Age of British Expansion, 1770–1870*, Oxford University Press, 1998.

Bowen, H. V., *The Business of Empire: The East India Company and Imperial Britain, 1756–1833*, Cambridge University Press, 2009.

Burton, A., ed., *The First Anglo-Afghan Wars: A Reader*, Duke University Press, 2014.

Dalrymple, W., *Return of a King: The Battle for Afghanistan*, Bloomsbury, 2012.

Hall, C., *Macaulay and Son: Architects of Imperial Britain*, Yale University Press, 2012.

Sen, S., *Empire of Free Trade: The East India Company and the Making of the Colonial Marketplace*, University of Pennsylvania Press, 1998.

Webster, A., *The Twilight of the East India Company: The Evolution of Anglo-Asian Commerce and Politics 1790–1860*, The Boydell Press, 2009.

6 Steam and Opium

The Auckland administration's second war, brewing in 1838, involved the trade between India and China. Before we come to the Opium War and its disastrous outcome for China's Qing Dynasty, though, we need to pause in order to consider the technological revolution that was being wrought by new applications of steam power. In our snapshot year, this wide ranging technological shift, initiating a period of unprecedented anthropogenic climate change, was altering the established China trade and transforming British imperial communications.

Steam Power

As Auckland's ill-timed invasion of Afghanistan demonstrated, delays in communications between the governor-general in India and the offices of imperial governance in London, in this case the Foreign Office, considerably hampered Indian governance. Reports from Macnaghten's Political and Secret department for the first quarter of 1837 were carried by sail around the Cape of Good Hope to be read in London only in February 1838. Had Auckland been appraised sooner of Palmerston's and Hobhouse's revised thinking in London, the invasion may have been cancelled. More routinely, accounts dating back five years or more piled up with every package of presidency despatches from Madras, Bombay and Calcutta received at the East India Company headquarters in Leadenhall Street. The South-West Monsoon in particular severely limited travel from the Bay of Bengal and the Arabian Sea towards Europe, enforcing a seasonal rhythm to the Company's communications. Adding in the work of bureaucracy and implementation at either end, the cycle of administration, from making policy in London to applying that policy in India was rarely shorter than a year. During the course of 1838, it was no wonder that the Company was getting serious about utilising steam to speed things up.

Steamships, with their ability to make way against prevailing winds (up to a certain point, at least), promised a year-round, faster and far more predictable service. The first commercially successful steamship had begun operating in the USA in 1807, more than twenty years before Huskisson was killed by the first steam rail engine.[1] By 1837, steam technology of the kind that Tagore and other Indian and British entrepreneurs were helping to fund had been benefitting the Company's administration within India for over a decade. The directors in London had arranged for two steam engines to be built and shipped to India to navigate the Brahmaputra, conveying troops and supplies to Assam in 1825. Auckland's predecessor, William Bentinck had them diverted to the Ganges, so that they could carry Company personnel in greater comfort between Calcutta and Upper India. However, enabling steamships to ply the route between India and Britain required investment of a different order, and it was only in the late 1830s that the challenges began to be resolved.

James Henry Johnston had played an especially important role in developing the Company's steam capabilities. Joining the Royal Navy aged sixteen in 1803, Johnston fought in Nelson's fleet at Trafalgar before heading to India at the conclusion of the Napoleonic War. As a Company naval captain, he made two return voyages to England which, by the early 1820s, persuaded him that two combined innovations were necessary. The first was regular use of the shorter Mediterranean and Red Sea route between Britain and India, rather than the route around the Cape of Good Hope. The second was necessitated by the first. Since sail ships were regularly becalmed in the Red Sea, steamship technology would have to be developed to enable exploitation of this more direct route. Johnston sailed to England to draw up a proposal. He found that he was not the only person interested in the potential for larger-scale mercantile steam shipping. Having attended a meeting convened in London to establish a General Steam Navigation Association in 1822, Johnston joined its committee and returned the following year to India to present his plans for ten annual return voyages. The governor-general considered them premature.

At this time the Company was deterred by the many difficulties of establishing the Red Sea route. Not only was there the issue of the investment required in coaling stations along the way; there was also the matter of the extensive diplomacy, and possibly warfare, that would have to be undertaken to construct them on territory belonging to other powers. Most significantly, there was the major inconvenience of the seventy-five-mile-wide block of land lying in between the Mediterranean and the Red Sea, the Isthmus of Suez. Steamships might sail relatively easily from Bombay or Karachi to the Red Sea port of Suez, but then their freight and passengers would have to be offloaded onto carts or camels for overland transport to the Mediterranean port of Alexandria, where they could be embarked by sea again to Britain. Until the Suez Canal was constructed some forty years later, this overland passage of people, despatches and commodities was logistically complex, but more importantly, it would have to be negotiated with the Egyptian Pasha, who was himself subordinate to the Ottoman Empire. These practical and diplomatic obstacles meant that even the General Steam Navigation Association opposed the Suez route, and so Johnston cut his ties with it.

Although he was not permitted to develop the Red Sea route in the 1820s, Johnston was able to secure funds from East India merchants, Indian agency houses and the Company itself to test the viability of a steam-driven voyage around the Cape to Calcutta. His intention was to use the publicity of his triumphal arrival there to drum up investors for a new Steam Company plying between India and Suez. This company would undertake to link passengers across the isthmus with the steamers belonging to an allied English company plying between Alexandria and England. However, Johnston's voyage around the Cape was not quite the success he had anticipated. It was fortunate that the vessel Johnston had built for it, the *Enterprise*, had three masts and sails as back up for its steam power. Given that the ship could access only one coaling depot in Cape Town along the 12 000-mile route, the few passengers who joined the ship found every nook and cranny filled with coal. They complained of the great heat and coal dust throughout the 114-day voyage. At least they did not faint as regularly as the firemen who had to feed the boiler with fuel carried from the furthest reaches of the ship. The sails were deployed after coal stored on top of the boilers caught fire, nearly destroying the ship before it reached Cape Town.

Once the *Enterprise* had finally made it to Calcutta, Johnston's shareholders were all too relieved to sell it to the East India Company, which employed it to ferry troops and supplies to Rangoon for its latest war in Burma. The ship proved its worth within Indian waters at least by steaming news of the treaty which ended the war back to Calcutta before fresh supplies and reinforcements were sent. Johnston was granted a reward from Bengal subscribers in recognition of his work in promoting steam navigation between England and India and employed by the Company as superintendent of steam vessels in Bengal.[2] In that role he organised the development of the Company's steamships as tugs, towing freight and passenger barges along India's major waterways.

By the late 1830s the Company was paying Johnston to engineer adapted steam vessels and oversee the building of coaling stations across its territories with more than just freight transport in mind. Anticipating 'increased benefit from the extension of their Sphere of Employment' the Court, with its fingers on the pulse of technological change in London, wanted him to send steamboats up the Ganges past Allahabad, and eastward up the Brahmaputra into Assam. This was not only to project force and enhance the military control of territory, useful as that was in the subordination of princely states; it was also because the directors calculated a saving of Rs 12 000 per annum by discontinuing military escorts for boats carrying treasure. They proposed six more iron-hulled, shallow-draft river steamers, four new accommodation boats for soldiers, and some provision for training so that the Company could use six *sepoys* and the river-gunboat's own firepower to do the job of a much larger escort.[3]

The small, flat bottomed, iron ships that Johnston developed in India were by no means sufficient to communicate with England. Greater promise lay in the Company's investment in a steam warship, built in Bombay in 1830. That year the *Hugh Lindsay* made the first of four voyages to Suez. Its captain, J. H. Wilson, was able to bring news from London that was only fifty-one days old, despite having made no prior arrangements for linking with steamers on the other side of the isthmus. This success revived the idea of a regular route for Company business via the Mediterranean.[4] Wilson repeated the voyage, escorting Company officials to and from Suez and despatching mails which Bedouin were paid to transport by camel to Alexandria for onward shipping to London. Encouraged by this, in 1837 Bentinck, now an MP in the House of Commons, headed a select committee to enquire into the Company's use of steam and the modernisation of its fleets. He recommended that the Company's Indian Navy be reconstituted as the Indian Flotilla, comprising entirely steam vessels, and brought under the supervision of the Admiralty. Hobhouse was concerned by French and Russian progress in steamship technology and so the Board of Control was also enthusiastic about a rapid modernisation of the Company's fleet, although it conceded that the Company could retain control of its fleet independently of the Royal Navy. By early 1838 Lushington and the Court of Directors were investing in steamships and determined to tackle the technical and logistical challenges of the Suez route, just as Johnston had first advised.[5]

During the first three months of 1838, Lushington tasked the Company's agent in Alexandria, Colonel Patrick Campbell, with negotiating access to coaling depots at Ottoman and Arabic controlled Mediterranean and Red Sea ports. Fuelling depots at Mocha and

Cosseir (Al-Qusayr) on the Red Sea supplemented stations at Madeira, Alexandria and Suez. Campbell was also arranging the protection of armed Egyptian Janissaries for despatches conveyed over the isthmus.[6] In the absence of any large-scale coal mining in India, Lushington was meanwhile contracting British merchants to carry coals from Llanelli and Newcastle to Bombay.[7] In February, he issued a circular to all the Company's agencies: 'It being desirable that our correspondence with the several governments in India upon Marine subjects or on Matters in any wise connected with Steam Vessels and their Establishment and Engines ... should be conducted separately ... we direct that all such subjects be addressed to us in future in the [Marine] "Department"'.[8] Alongside its Military, Judicial, Revenue, Home, Ecclesiastical and Secret and Political Committees, the Company now had a Marine Department focused specifically on the application of steam technology for its governance of India.

Immediately, the department was deluged with correspondence. In its first couple of months it received a petition from a group of concerned citizens of Madras requesting that the project of regular steam navigation through the Red Sea be carried forward as a matter of urgency; twelve copies of a pamphlet 'On Steam Communication to India by the Cape of Good Hope', from the chairman of the India Steam Ship Company; an offer from a Glasgow shipbuilder to build and refit Company steamers; a proposal from an employee at Alexandria for a system of horse-drawn cars for rapid transit across the isthmus, and a letter from a Mr C. Barwell Coles, informing the Company that he had a patent pending on a revolutionary new means for propelling ships, without steam and in all weathers, by means of a large pendulum.[9] In the meantime a new system of communication was taking shape. The directors' outward correspondence was being steamed from London to Marseilles. From there, French steamers carried it to Malta, and then a mail steamer continued its passage from Malta to Alexandria. The janissaries arranged by Campbell took it overland across the isthmus to Suez, where it was collected by one of the Company's two new steamers, the *Atalanta* or the *Berenice*. One of these paddle wheel, hybrid Company craft, with sails and gunports, would take the despatches and passengers down the Red Sea and onward to India, refuelling at one of the depots arranged by Campbell. Through this means, the despatches from Leadenhall Street dated 7 March 1838 reached Bombay via the *Atalanta* in a record forty-one days, and Calcutta in fifty-four.

Throughout 1838, as Auckland and Hobhouse sought to communicate about Afghanistan, the Egyptian ports of Alexandria and Suez were still critical bottlenecks, where freight, letters and passengers had to be disembarked to cross the isthmus and then re-embarked. Around this time a theme began to emerge in British travel literature, which would persist until the construction of the Suez Canal: the ennui endured by passengers on either side of the isthmus awaiting the arrival of the next steamship to continue their journey. Visits to the pyramids became popular among the travellers as they waited. Throughout 1838, Campbell himself was travelling constantly between Cairo, Alexandria and Suez, reporting on the arrival and departure of the Malta steamer, arranging for the janissaries to escort the mails over the isthmus, and answering the Company's often rather plaintive enquiries as to how the transit could be further accelerated.

The Alexandria-based Company agent also played a significant role in what would today be called technology transfer. In late 1837, the *Berenice* was laid up in Suez with a broken paddle wheel shaft. It remained there for the first three months of 1838 while the shaft was sent back to Glasgow, where it had been manufactured, and then transported, along with senior engineers, out to Egypt for fitting. Campbell persuaded Lushington and the Company Directors to the have the mould of the engine parts duplicated in Egypt, and the copies sent out to Bombay, so that future repairs might be dealt with there.[10] The episode prompted the directors to consider the rapid rate at which steam technology was advancing. The Royal Navy was already experimenting with screw-propeller rather than paddle wheel – driven ships, so Lushington instructed Auckland to be cautious about repairing the Company's existing steamships in future.[11] New, updated vessels might be more appropriate and cost effective.[12]

In 1838, then, the East India Company was in the midst of adapting to a disruptive technology. Its use of paddle steamers on Indian waterways was now accompanied by the ability to employ ocean going steamships in service of considerably more rapid communications with shareholders' representatives and the Board of Control in London. This maritime steam technology had other applications too, however. The Company's adaptation to steam power would shortly have fearsome consequences for the Manchu Qing dynasty's sovereignty over the Chinese empire.

The First Opium War

The East India Company had not pioneered the cultivation of opium in India – it had been a staple crop since Arab traders had introduced it to western India in the eighth century, and Dutch traders had exported it from Bihar and Bengal to Canton – but the Company had developed its industrial-scale production for export to China. After its conquest of Bengal, British officials had been able to take control of opium production and sale from a syndicate of Indian merchants based in Patna, which had formerly extended credit to producers and sold the drug on to Dutch, British and French traders. Warren Hastings, governor-general of Bengal, had first declared a Company monopoly on opium production and sale in 1772, letting out contracts to its employees for purchase, process and export. After twenty years of abuse by employees who bought up opium farms and then demanded peasant producers hand over their product at less than cost price, the Company appointed two senior officers as Opium Agents to reform the process from offices in Patna and Benares.

In 1838 the system overseen by these Opium Agents was still in operation. All private cultivation was banned. Indian peasant farmers, concentrated mainly the north-west territories affected by the famine and in Bengal along the Ganges River, were allocated a specific plot of land on which to grow poppies. In 1828 cultivation had taken place on 79 488 acres, but by 1838, 176 745 acres was incorporated. By then, the rival independent cultivation and export of what was known as Malwa opium from western India had also been brought effectively within the Company's remit, since conquest of the Maratha Empire had enabled control of its export through Bombay, with the Company taking a slice of the profit in transport charges. In the north-west territories and Bengal, where the Company itself controlled production, the Agents paid peasant producers an initial advance in return for delivering their entire crop to the Company at its fixed price. The Agents preferred to contract peasants from castes they considered to have hereditary market-gardening skills, and those with access to the most fertile soils and irrigation. The 'Kachhis and Koiris came to form a virtually hereditary pool of licensees accustomed and prepared to grow poppies of the highest quality'.[13] This meant that Company-produced opium was of a higher quality than Malwa opium, as well as that which other countries sought to import to China, or that which was grown in China itself. Accordingly it demanded a higher price.

The production of opium from the poppies was an extremely labour intensive process. The Agents supervised it in Company-owned factories, receiving a small percentage of the profits as their salary. Each individual poppy seed was lanced to extract its raw opium gum. The gum was then collated, set and dried in trays (Figure 6.1). Finally it was pressed into cakes, coated in crushed, dried poppy stems and leaves, and packed in mango wood chests for transport to Calcutta. The 'Patna' or 'Benares' brand stamped on the 15 000 or so opium chests that the Company produced each year was a mark of quality, guaranteeing that the drug inside was either 70 or 77 per cent pure. This 'state controlled system'

Figure 6.1 The stacking room, an opium factory at Patna, India.
Illustration from *The Graphic* XXV, no 656 (24 June 1882). Getty
Images.

enabled British India to become the greatest producer of opium in the
world and the main supplier to China.

Both the Company's own, and a large part of the British economy was
surprisingly reliant on this narcotic trade. As well as keeping India's
northern borders secure from Russian threat, Auckland's fundamental
remit as a governor-general, accountable to both Company directors and
the British government, included its maintenance. Over the last fifty
years, an eastern triangular trade had developed to complement that in
enslaved people across the Atlantic. Around £12 million worth of textiles
and manufactures flowed from Britain to India and £20 million worth of
tea flowed in the other direction, from China. The British Exchequer
obtained up to one tenth of its total revenue from taxation on this tea.
Together with the sugar imported from the West India trade, with which
it was combined to create the national drink, it was the most heavily taxed
item. The British-China trade deficit that it created was counterbalanced

only by the Company's export of opium and cotton to China. Whereas Company-ruled India imported some £10 million worth of silver, sugar and silk from China, it exported around £21 million worth there. Between 1795 and 1840, opium accounted for 64 per cent of Calcutta's exports to China, with cotton making up 28 per cent. The return of the Company's profits to Britain 'made it unnecessary to export British silver to China to foot a part of the tea bill'.[14] This in itself was significant because Latin American independence had caused a global shortage of silver bullion over the last decade or so. By the 1830s the £2–3 million overall surplus on trade between Britain-India and China can be said to have composed 'the annual Indian tribute to Britain'.[15]

The opium trade supported the British economy and especially its tea consumption, but it was also important for the Company's own revenues. Exchanging opium for Chinese silver meant that the Company had currency with which to run its government of India.[16] Between 1834 and 1839, opium proceeds accounted for Rs 6.8 million or 6 per cent of the Company's total income. Without opium the Company's Indian subjects would have been pressed to raise even more revenue for the British shareholders' guaranteed dividends. As the economic historian Tan Chung puts it, 'we see the equilibrium in the trade triangle under review, namely: Indian opium for the Chinese, Chinese tea for the Britons, and British Raj for the Indians!'[17]

The problem for the Company, and the British government, was that, despite its being the main staple in the Chinese empire's foreign trade (which would remain the case until the late nineteenth century), the Qing imperial authorities had banned the import of opium. The deleterious effects of large-scale opium addiction were very well known in both China and Britain, and the Company Directors and Board of Control had long had to make at least some effort to justify its production and trade, especially in the light of Britain's own suppression of inward opium smuggling. They did so effectively by shrugging their shoulders and pointing out its necessity for the national benefit. In 1817 the directors explained that 'Were it possible to prevent the use of the drug altogether except for the purpose of medicine, we would gladly do it in compassion to mankind', but of course the advantages that opium brought for the good governance of India and for the wealth of Britain necessarily out-weighed such considerations.[18] Even so, the Company was wary of openly flouting the Qing Empire's prohibition on opium imports, so it had developed an elaborate system to facilitate its smuggling through Canton, the only port opened by the Qing Empire to foreign trade.

Private traders would purchase the Company-produced opium in Calcutta and sign a bond obliging them to remit the proceeds of its sale to the Company's representatives in Canton. They were paid by Chinese wholesalers in silver, which the Company could then use to buy Chinese tea for export to Britain. In return for the silver, the Company agents gave the private opium smugglers bills which they could take to the Company's office at Leadenhall Street in London and exchange for cash. Before the ending of the Company monopoly on the Chinese trade in 1833, these private traders had been licensed by the Company to engage in legitimate trade to disguise their real purpose. For example, in 1828, the Company issued licences to the ships *Hercules*, owned by Mackintosh and Co., *Louisa*, owned by William Clifton, and *Jane Eliza*, owned by Crattenden, Mackillop and Co., to import saltpetre. All three ships were actually clippers built specifically for the opium trade. After 1833, there was no need for a Company licence but the Company had already created the mechanism for the private smugglers of its Indian product to take over. Its Canton office had invested in good relations with the guild of Chinese hong merchants, who monopolised the Canton trade and supplied the tea. These Cantonese merchants in turn bribed the Manchu customs officials appointed from Beijing, so that they would disregard the authorities' periodic protests about industrial-scale smuggling.[19]

Even bribed officials would not tolerate opium clippers openly unloading their illicit freight in Canton. Each year, during the defined trading season from September to January, British, American, Danish, French and other opium traders came to live in factories outside Canton's walls, buying certificates to trade from the hong merchants and wholesalers. The clippers themselves would anchor near Linton island, between Hong Kong and Canton. The hong merchants would organise Chinese smuggling craft, rowed by twenty to seventy armed men, to bring the certificates purchased by the traders and exchange them for opium on board the clippers. Covering the drug with legally purchased items such as clothes, they would disperse into the inlets around Canton, distributing the opium through other Chinese inter-mediaries, each taking their cut. All 'along the south coast's threadwork of narrow waterways' a massive narcotic operation took place for five months each year while officials looked the other way. When the Company ceased to be the key intermediary in this trade in 1833, companies like Jardine, Matheson & Co., founded when the loss of the East India Company's monopoly on the trade was on the cards in 1832, were able to continue the arrangements it had made with the hong. A Jardine Matheson Associate in Calcutta joked in the late 1830s, 'Only think of the Chinese going to smuggle tea on the coast of England in a junk!'[20]

After 1833, with the trade 'deregularised', the British government appointed commissioners to superintend it in Canton. Charles Elliot (no relation to the Colonial Office's Thomas Elliot), a former naval officer and latterly Protector of Slaves in British Guiana, was sent to Canton, initially as a secretary to the new office. By 1836 he had become chief superintendent and plenipotentiary representing the British traders. Like Auckland in Calcutta, Elliott was well aware that the production and the private importation of the Company's narcotic to Canton was a mainstay of both the governance of India and the British Exchequer. As Auckland was responding to the Agra famine and then organising the invasion of Afghanistan, Elliott was becoming increasingly concerned that the Qing Emperor, Daoguang, was finally mobilising more determinedly against the opium trade.

Opium use was widespread in China, including among high-ranking officials. Daoguang's own son had died of an overdose. Its geographical spread to all provinces and its more extensive use up and down the social hierarchy during the 1830s was leading the Qing authorities to see it less as a convenient, if occasionally irritating, way of engaging in trade with the outside world, and more 'as the culprit for a rich repertoire of late-Qing ills: economic stagnation, environmental exhaustion ... decline of the army and general standards of public order'.[21] The Manchu Qing dynasty was coming to see Cantonese participation in an illicit trade with foreigners as symbolic of the much deeper challenges to its order. In 1838, as Elliot feared, Emperor Daoguang decided to appoint Lin Zexu Imperial commissioner to Canton, with instructions to stamp out opium smuggling and consumption once and for all.

Lin made a start by writing an open letter to Queen Victoria, published in Canton, urging her to help him end the trade. He pointed out that while China was sending Britain its tea, porcelain, spices and silk, Britain insisted on sending only 'poison' in return. He continued, 'I have heard that you strictly prohibit opium in your own country, indicating unmistakably that you know how harmful opium is. You do not wish opium to harm your own country, but you choose to bring that harm to other countries such as China. Why?' Lin's hope that the Queen would act 'in accordance with decent feeling' and support his punishment of British opium smugglers in Canton, while turning the fields of India to 'food crops' instead of poppies, proved somewhat naïve.[22] Queen Victoria never replied and so Lin set about arresting Chinese opium dealers and confiscating consumers' opium pipes.

Given what was at stake for the Company and the British government, Elliot anticipated serious conflict. In November 1837 he had written to Foreign Secretary Palmerston advising that a special commission be sent out to negotiate an agreement which might allow the trade to continue with Chinese imperial sanction. He was ignored. As Auckland was being entrusted to safeguard British geopolitical interests on India's northern frontier without any clear guidance, Elliott was expected to perpetuate opium smuggling without precise instructions on how to deal with the ban. In December 1838, finding the British authorities uncooperative, Lin threatened violence against the traders in Canton and their clippers from India unless all the opium on the coast was handed over. Afraid of a massacre, Elliot ordered the traders to comply. In June 1839 Lin oversaw the destruction of over £4 million worth of opium, a task on which 500 workers were employed for twenty-three days, mixing the opium with lime and salt and throwing it in the sea. When a Chinese civilian was killed in a fight with British sailors, the stakes were raised yet higher. The British refused to hand over the suspects and Lin forbade Chinese merchants from bringing supplies to the foreign traders in Canton, enforcing their isolation with a naval blockade. Elliott responded by ordering a Royal Navy frigate to disperse the Chinese war junks and in the meantime British parliamentarians and the Cabinet debated the rationale for war.

As they were with Afghanistan, Lushington and the Company Directors were more spectators than participants in the discussions in London. Far more active was William Jardine of Jardine Matheson, the foremost British opium trader. In December 1838, as Lin enforced the prohibition on further Chinese opium sales, Jardine lamented that 'Not an opium pipe [was] to be seen, not a retail vendor ... not a single enquiry after the drug'. On 1 January 1839, he instructed his Bombay agents to leave further opium supplies in the hands of the East India Company in Calcutta, but he and the other British traders already had 20 000 unsold chests off Canton, which would soon be destroyed, and another 32 000 awaiting shipment at Bombay and Calcutta. In September 1839, after Lin's confiscation, Jardine was back in London bending the ear of Palmerston. In a long private session he briefed, or rather lobbied, the foreign secretary with maps and charts before a crucial Cabinet meeting.[23]

It was not just Jardine and the other clamorous traders who persuaded Palmerston to war. Both the government's free trade doctrine and the transition to steam power played critical roles. While Huskisson was working to free up Britain's trade in the mid 1820s, the barrister and law reformer James Mackintosh was already advocating the protection of private financial interests as a potential *casus belli*. He sought to persuade the government that if the newly independent South American states, which had borrowed heavily from private British financiers, defaulted on their repayments, Britain's government should go to war with them, since 'the mass of private interest engaged in our trade with Spanish America, is so great as to render it a large part of the national interest'. At this point the Tory government rejected the argument, asserting that British financiers and traders 'ought not to carry with them the force and influence of the British government, in order to compel foreign states to fulfil their contracts'.[24] By 1838, however, the Whig government had become far more receptive to the principle of Mackintosh's argument.

This was due in part to the colonial reformers around Wakefield, pressing for settler colonial expansion and free trade with self-governing Britons abroad. In the House of Commons both Charles Buller, the architect of responsible government, and Joseph Hume, the radical MP whose letter to Mackenzie helped spark the Canadian rebellions, pushed for war on China. Buller portrayed Emperor Daoguang as an unpopular and outdated impediment to free trade. War against the Qing dynasty was as an opportunity 'to place the trade on an entirely new, secure, and progressive footing', so that 'a really free intercourse' might be established between England and 'China's three hundred millions', just as it was between Britons at home and in the settler colonies.[25] Hume backed him up, arguing that 'from the moment British subjects at Canton were placed in prison [confined to their enclave in Canton] to the danger of their lives the Chinese became the aggressors', and that Britain was now obliged to wage war. The parliamentary debate split along party lines with Whigs in favour of free trade, even in opium, and Tories against. While Whigs like Stephen Lushington, one of the 'Saints' who had long campaigned against slavery and supported the rights of Indigenous peoples against settler aggression, argued for war, the Tories mainly condemned it. Even Gladstone, the man who had defended settlers on the Aborigines Committee, and profited from his father's slavery business and the flooding of India with British textiles, declared 'I do not know, and I have not read of a more unjust and iniquitous war'.[26]

The Board of Control, represented by Hobhouse, unsurprisingly, saw merit in defending the opium trade: 'England was not pursuing purely selfish trade ambitions; rather she was fighting for the opening of trade for all nations', he declared.[27] With Manchester industrialists fearing that the end of the opium trade might undermine Indian purchasing power for their cotton too, Melbourne's Cabinet concluded that there was a satisfactory case for military action. Rather than sending British gunboats to enforce legal contracts, as Macintosh had first urged in the case of Latin America, they would be sent to enforce Britons' entitlement to engage in illegal drug smuggling. 'While openly preaching free trade in poison', wrote Karl Marx some twenty years later, when the next Opium

War was looming, 'it secretly defends the monopoly of its manufacture [in India]. Whenever we look closely into the nature of British free trade, monopoly is pretty generally found to lie at the bottom of its "freedom"'.[28]

When twelve Royal Navy ships and four of the East India Company's new steam warships arrived off Canton in June 1840, they turned the balance of power decisively. Britain's main 'weapon of mass destruction' during the First Opium War was the *Nemesis*, a paddle wheel–driven steamship commissioned by the East India Company's new Marine Department as part of the modernisation of the fleet. As the *Times* reported, 'for the purpose of smuggling opium she is admirably adapted'.[29] Finished as preparations for war were under way, the *Nemesis* was provided with an Admiralty letter of marque so that the Royal Navy could have a welcome opportunity to test the design in action against the Chinese fleet. It offered an entirely new way of projecting force. Steam power alone gave it and the Company's other steamships greater facility to point whichever way their captains wanted, and manoeuvrability up and down rivers. When that steam power was combined with an iron hull capable of supporting *Nemesis*' heavy guns, the military advantage proved to be overwhelming, even if the metal hull rendered its compass unreliable.

During the first hour and a half of fighting in earnest on 7 January 1841, British forces landed along the river by the Company's steamers assaulted the Chinese forts while the *Nemesis* attacked fifteen Chinese junks offshore. The Qing forces suffered 280 dead and 462 wounded, while eleven of the ships attacked by the *Nemesis* were totally destroyed. In return the British land forces sustained thirty-eight wounded and the *Nemesis*' paddle box was damaged. Following this initial encounter, the unevenness of which was unanticipated even by the British, the ship's shallow draught allowed it to travel along inland waterways to attack poorly defended forts at will. Chinese defenders named it the 'devil ship'. In March 1841, it enabled the capture of Canton.

Elliott was dismissed in 1841 after negotiating a treaty to end hostilities which fell short of Palmerston's demands. The British government had resolved not only that the traders' lost opium be compensated and the trade in Canton resumed, but that China's northern ports should also be opened to the opium trade and China should cede an island to the British for a local base. Elliott had achieved the cession of Hong Kong but conceded the other objectives. His replacement, Sir Henry Pottinger (whose nephew was captured and spared by Akbar Kahn in the retreat from Kabul), resumed the war. British forces spearheaded by the *Nemesis*, captured Amoy (Xiamen), Chushan, Chintu (Chengdu) and Ningpo

(Ningbo). Emperor Daoguang learned the truth of the Qing's successive military defeats only when the British fleet entered the Yangtze River, preparatory to capturing Nanking (Nanjing). At the Treaty of Nanking the British inflicted humiliating terms on the emperor. China would pay an indemnity of 21 million silver dollars, Hong Kong was ceded to Britain with Pottinger as governor and would remain in British hands until 1997, and five 'treaty ports', Canton itself, Amoy, Foochow (Fuzhou), Ningpo and Shanghai, were opened to British traders, represented by British consuls. China's 'century of humiliation' at the hands of the West had begun, and much of its foreign policy and approach to Hong Kong today is still marked by the experience.[30]

Further Reading

Chung, T., 'The Britain-China-India Trade Triangle (1771–1840)', *Indian Economic History Review*, XI, 1974, 426–7.

Lovell, J., *The Opium War: Drugs, Dreams, and the Making of Modern China*, Picador, 2011.

Mao, H., *The Qing Empire and the Opium War: The Collapse of the Heavenly Dynasty*, Cambridge University Press, 2005.

Richards, J. F., 'The Indian Empire and Peasant Production of Opium in the Nineteenth Century', *Modern Asian Studies*, 15, 1, 1981, 59–82.

Semmel, B., *The Rise of Free Trade Imperialism: Classical Political Economy the Empire of Free Trade and Imperialism, 1750–1850*, Cambridge University Press, 1970.

Conclusion to Part I: An Empire of Freedom?

The British Empire of 1838 was transitioning in many ways all at once. The basis of its economy was shifting, from slave-produced tropical commodities towards emigrant-produced temperate products, although opium remained a constant; its geography was shifting, from twin circuits of trade in the West and East Indies towards new centres of gravity in the vast terrains of the southern hemisphere and North America; and its mode of governance was shifting from the autocratic military elite which had violently seized new colonies from Britain's enemies towards a bureaucracy more accountable to settlers overseas and reformers at home.

These multiple transitions were all connected to an imperial political economy increasingly attuned to the needs of Britain's rising and newly enfranchised commercial, financial and manufacturing classes. The task of the men governing the Empire was to manage the transformation with due regard to those who had invested heavily in the empire's earlier form. By the end of 1838, Britons who had owned slaves in the Caribbean had been compensated for their emancipation and assured of continued labour supply through indenture, while those who had bought East India Company stock had been assured of continued dividends as the Company became exclusively the government of India and continued as a monopolistic producer of opium. Imperial government was an ongoing negotiation between different offices, agendas and personalities, with family and social connections still enormously influential in governing, and compensating for, transition.

Certain individuals were prominent across a range of geographically dispersed events that historians tend to examine discretely. Wakefield and his circle's influence on colonisation in Australia and New Zealand, the promotion of self-government, free trade and the Opium War is relatively well known, as is James Stephen's influence at the Colonial Office. Glenelg's sustained influence on imperial governance is noted less often. In recent years historians have accorded him prominence as the humanitarian-inclined secretary of state for the colonies who attempted to respond to the Aborigines Committee's critique of settler brutality. We should also appreciate that he pursued free trade as president of the Board of Trade and negotiated East India Company shareholders' entitlement to continuing dividends as president of the Board of Control, just a few years beforehand. Better known to literary scholars as Byron's friend, Hobhouse is another figure who lurks in the background of imperial history, but whose social connections and policy interventions were critical to the restructuring of the Company, the invasion of Afghanistan and the First Opium War.

The men who governed the British Empire at this moment of transition were very often preoccupied with the theme of freedom. Through the course of the year 1838 alone, we see how they allocated that divisive virtue differentially in respect of different kinds of imperial subject. Stephen and his office had been tasked with the abolition of slavery, which meant ending apprenticeships for African captives and their descendants in the Caribbean. Most Britons now considered that Africans were entitled to freedom from captivity and enslavement; this much was clear. But when exactly, and how exactly, that freedom was to be achieved, and how, in the longer term, captive labour was to be replaced, were all undecided by the 1833 Abolition Act. As the date initially set for the emancipation of domestic apprentices neared in the early months of 1838, one of the Colonial Office's major tasks was to distinguish who was to be freed and from what kind of labour relation. The promise of empire-wide emancipation had to be weighed against colonists' need for security and prosperity.

Fortunately for British planters in Ceylon, Mauritius, the Caribbean and the Pacific, the East India Company's governance of India provided a means to persuade Indian peasants to leave their homes and work for them under indenture. Not entirely, but almost free from the scrutiny that anti-slavery activists afforded to those enslaved in the Caribbean, the Colonial Office itself could allow 'liberated Africans', Creoles, Tamils and convicts in other parts of the empire to persist in various states of coerced labour for some time to come. Stephen and Thomas Elliott considered the use of British emigrants' labour to plug the gaps left by emancipation, but their correspondence with governors during the course of the year affirmed that 'race' was critical to the empire's division of labour.

The men governing the empire overseas made it clear that only people of colour were suitable for work formerly conducted by slaves, at low wages on tropical plantations. Only with great reluctance would they be considered suitable for labour needs in the temperate settler colonies. Here, the growing British emigrant population should be augmented by other Britons. Poorer Britons were surplus to economic requirement at home and valued as settlers in North America, southern Africa and Australasia, but they were not to be considered a suitable alternative to slave labour elsewhere.

At the same time that freedom from coerced labour was being redefined, the freedom to govern oneself was being debated in 1838. Macaulay made it quite clear that this was not the moment to allow Indians a role in government of their own country. Even if the East India Company had run its course as a viable commercial entity, the Board of Control would rather see it re-purposed as the British government of India than trust Indians with the slightest degree of self-governance. The post-emancipation granting of civil rights to people of colour elsewhere was also a cause for concern. Stephen was committed to non-racialism as a principle but tended to concede to an inherited racial order when governors expressed concern about colonists' resistance. British emigrants demanding civil rights was a different matter. Although Stephen and Glenelg retained a conservative suspicion of settler democracy, the group around Wakefield, Buller and Durham had powerful supporters, while the Canadian rebellions provided a convincing case that responsible government would be taken by force if it was not ceded by the Colonial Office.

Permission for British settlers to govern themselves did not just contrast with the reluctance in respect of Indians and people of colour elsewhere. It also had dire consequences for the Indigenous peoples on whose lands Britons had settled. 1838 was a high-water mark in the campaign by British philanthropists such as Buxton, Gurney and Hodgkin, and by governing men like the guilt-ridden Arthur, to consider Indigenous peoples' natural rights and freedoms alongside those of settlers. Stephen and Glenelg circulated the Aborigines Committee's report of the year before, along with the injunction to governors to act upon its guidance. Even within the report, though, the freedom of Indigenous peoples to live in their own fashion was circumscribed. Just as Indians should be grateful enough for the stability offered by the Company government to pay rent to its share-holders, so Māori, Aboriginal people, amaXhosa, Khoisan and First Nations should gratefully receive Christianity and 'civilisation' in return for handing their land over to British settlers and abandoning millennia old cultural practices and beliefs.

As Robinson, Dredge, Sievwright, Parker and Thomas were establishing a new office to protect Aboriginal people in Australia from the liberties accorded to settlers while they performed this cultural transition, the trial of white men accused of massacre prompted a concerted backlash. Whether Stephen and Glenelg liked it or not, British settlers around the empire became ever more resolutely determined to govern their own affairs, excluding Indigenous peoples from their newfound freedom. The realpolitik of running an empire meant that settlers were granted liberties at the expense of Indigenous peoples.

Finally, in 1838, the empire's governing men considered the freedom to trade. Bound up with settlers' liberty to flourish on Indigenous peoples' land by trading wool, meat and wine with Britain, free trade reinforced the commercial transition of the empire as a whole. It led to the loss of the East India Company's monopolies (other than in opium production) and its role exclusively as the governance of India. It also became a *casus belli* when the Qing Empire challenged British traders' entitlement to smuggle Company-produced opium. What Britons, other Europeans and Americans were entitled to do in China, no one was entitled to do in Britain, since opium trading was banned there. But again national interests were paramount. The realpolitik of maintaining an imperial nation that was heavily dependent for its finance on narcotic smuggling meant that uncomfortable decisions had to be made. The freedom of British traders to engage in commercial activity otherwise considered illicit overrode the freedom of other sovereign powers to set the terms of their own trade. The pioneering of new steam technology at just the same time enabled a projection of violence on traders' behalf that had been inconceivable just a few years beforehand.

Our snapshot of the British Empire in 1838 reveals connections between transformative processes that are more often understood in isolation, and throws up some revealing paradoxes. Britons' abolition of slavery in the Caribbean was linked to their colonisation of Australia as some of the compensation for the loss of slaves was reinvested in settler pastoralism; the same British men who complained of the injustice meted out by settlers to Indigenous peoples simultaneously supported a war on behalf of drug runners; settlers were accorded greater self-determination while a puppet ruler was disastrously placed on the throne in Afghanistan against the will of the majority of its people, and new technology enabled Indian produce to be shipped across the world at speed while hundreds of thousands of those from whence it came starved to death. There was quite some irony in a comment of Macaulay's during the 1833 charter renewal debate, which set the scene for so many of the events of 1838. He was rejecting the idea that Britons living in India should be able contribute to the legislation imposed by the Company administration there, as they could in the settler colonies. He said, 'No man loves political freedom more than I. But a privilege enjoyed by a few individuals in the midst of a vast population who do not enjoy it, ought not to be called freedom. It is tyranny'.[1]

Part II

1857: The Year of Civilisation

7 Setting the Scene: Hubris and Crisis

The year 1857 opened with imperial crises under way in southern Africa and China (again). Primarily afflicting Xhosa and Cantonese people respectively, these were accompanied from May by a third crisis – one that was of unprecedented significance for British imperial governance – in India. Each of these crises had its own dynamic and its own set of local conditions and actors, but they shared a root cause in imperial men's assertive promotion of British civilisation around the world. The three crises had become connected by the summer of 1857, most immediately by the trans-imperial movement of British military forces. In the longer term, their combined effect was to bring about a major revision of imperial governmental attitudes and structures.

The year 1838 had been a year of transition. As we saw in Part I, a balance of relative freedoms was being established, in Britain and its empire, somewhat tentatively, so as not to undermine the essential productivity of colonies, after the tumult and expansion of the Revolutionary and Napoleonic Wars. The multiple crises of 1857 followed two decades of governmental consolidation in the colonies seized in those wars, as well as further expansion, particularly in New Zealand, southern Africa and India. Each of these crises was conditioned by a greater self-confidence among the men who governed; by their propensity to reach beyond the insertion of British sovereignty in order to deliberately undermine the viability of other polities and cultures. In 1838, these men had been preoccupied with the kinds of freedom that should be offered to different and novel classes of British subject. By 1857 their overriding preoccupation was the extent to which they could, and should, impose what seemed to them the self-evident advantages of British civilisation.

Men like Herman Merivale and Henry Labouchere at the Colonial Office, Lord Canning in India and Lord Clarendon at the Foreign Office, together with governors like George Grey in the Cape Colony and John Bowring in Hong Kong, all of whom we will meet in Part II, tended to display a greater self-confidence and a more nationalistic chauvinism than their counterparts in 1838.[1] Overseeing an established empire of unprecedented reach, theirs was a sense of entitlement, not only to rule the wider world, but also proactively to restructure it for its own good. A combination of intergenerational changes, post-emancipation thinking on racial difference and technological mastery all underpinned this change. We will come on to understandings of race and the technologies of the mid-nineteenth-century empire as we recount the story of each crisis in turn, but we begin with the experiences that had conditioned these men differently from their predecessors.

A New Breed: Governing the British Empire in 1857

Fewer colonial governors in 1857 had direct experience of fighting and killing for what appeared to be Britain's survival on the globally distributed battlefields of the Revolutionary and Napoleonic Wars. Rather than having risked their own lives and taken others to carve out a larger British imperial sphere, they had inherited one. Their scope for autocracy had also receded, especially in the settler colonies which were now, by and large, self-governing. Governors were esteemed for their scholarly acuity and bureaucratic efficiency, for their articulation and rationalisation of British power, as much as for their military valour and decisiveness. Figures like George Grey and John Bowring had reputations as men of intellectual pursuit and distinction rather than as courageous and capable battlefield commanders.

The emerging generation of East India Company officials, too, lacked the personal experience of military conquest and politicking among Indian allies that Company men like Lushington and Jenkins had shared. They took it for granted that British supremacy had been established in the subcontinent, especially after the annexations of Sind and the Punjab during the 1840s. Trained at Haileybury, they arrived in India with Macaulay's confident expectation that they would be the vehicle of its progressive 'civilisation'. Their role was to bestow upon India the benefits of Britain's superior way of doing things. They had far less intention of learning about, let alone adapting to, its own political, social and military systems. What these imperial men, in the governments of both halves of the British Empire of 1857, shared, was a diminished sense of self-doubt, a greater personal distancing from the intimate violence of conquest, and from the necessity for negotiation and compromise to achieve it. They manifested a belief in their providential duty to govern others by virtue simply of being British.

In this first chapter of Part II we focus on the men who provoked the two crises that were under way quite discretely, in the Cape Colony and in

China, as 1857 began. Subsequently we consider the causes of the Indian Uprising before identifying the connections that emerged between all three crises during the summer and autumn of 1857 as the imperial men of London sought to respond, everywhere and all at once.

George Grey and the Great Xhosa Cattle Killing

In April 1856, Nongqawuse, a fifteen-year-old Xhosa girl, went out into the fields around her homestead, just beyond the Cape Colony's frontier, to scare birds away from her family's crops. When she returned, she told her uncle Mhlakaza of a vision that she had experienced while standing by a river. Two men had appeared before her and identified themselves as ancestors who had died long ago. They instructed Nonqawuse to return to her people with this important message:

Tell them that the whole nation will rise from the dead if all the living cattle are slaughtered because these have been reared with defiled hands, since there are people about who have been practising witchcraft. There should be no cultivation. Great new corn pits must be dug and new houses built. Lay out great big cattle-folds, cut out new milk-sacks, and weave doors from buka roots, many of them.[2]

Should their instruction be followed, the unearthly visitors explained, the ancestors would arise in great numbers to drive the British away from Xhosaland. The new corn pits, cattle folds and milk sacks were preparations for a new golden age since, with the colonisers gone, the amaXhosa's cattle and corn would be restored in abundance.

In order to contextualise Nongqawuse's vision, we have to return to the recent history of the Eastern Cape frontier, which we last visited in Chapter 4. When Harry Smith's troops had killed Hintsa as he sought to escape from the invading column during the 1834–5 war, his son Sarhili had become paramount chief of the Gcaleka Xhosa, to whom Nongqawuse belonged. Although still living just beyond the reach of the British colonial authorities, which now extended right up to the Kei River (see Map 4.1), Nongqawuse and her fellow Gcaleka were continuing to suffer from the effects of colonial dispossession. Successive waves of their Rharabe Xhosa kin to the west had been expelled from the encroaching colonial regime, and were now overstocking their grazing land and sharing their water. Successive colonial governors, subject to intense and prolonged British settler lobbying for more land, had progressively undermined the treaties that Andries Stockenström had carefully negotiated, recognising Rharabe Xhosa sovereignty, in 1838.

The Seventh Frontier War, or War of the Axe, in 1847 had enabled the bombastic Harry Smith to return to the colony, fresh from assuming the title 'hero of Aliwal' during the conquest of former Sikh allies in the Punjab, as the Cape's new governor. He was now able to embark upon the re-annexation of the former Queen Adelaide Province – the territory that Glenelg had restored to the Rharabe Xhosa. The annexed region extending to the Kei River was renamed British Kaffraria and Smith spent the late 1840s attempting to corral its inhabitants into new, confined settlements, subject to British military oversight. He lacked the soldiers completely to displace the Xhosa occupants and allocate their land to settlers, so, like the Sikhs of the Punjab, he sought to govern them through their own chiefs and headmen. The differences were his far greater interference in the Xhosa chiefs' ability to fine and punish their subjects, and far less interest in recruiting Xhosa subjects into his army. His intention was to undermine the chiefs' authority as far as possible by awarding their former powers to British magistrates.[3]

Inspired in part by the war doctor Mlanjeni, who prophesied that British bullets would turn to water before striking their targets, Rharabe Xhosa had risen in rebellion once more in 1850. They were joined by many of the converted Khoisan settlers of the Kat River settlement, who were now also being progressively pushed out by British settlers and magistrates. Maqoma, who had led the resistance to Smith in 1834–5, had been sidelined by alcoholism during the War of the Axe, but he sobered up in 1850 to act, once again, as the amaXhosa's most effective resistance leader. The Eighth Frontier War of 1850–2 saw Maqoma frustrating his old adversary Smith with guerrilla attacks and evasion in the natural fortress of the Amatola Mountains.[4]

While Smith had provoked this most destructive Frontier war yet, his bluster failed to convince the colonial secretary that he was winning it. Smith was replaced by George Cathcart, a former Aide de Camp to Wellington at Waterloo. Cathcart led the suppression of Maqoma's and the other rebellious chiefs' immediate resistance through scorched earth tactics and raids to capture them. After his surrender, Maqoma and his 3000 followers were evicted from the Amatola Mountains and allotted the southernmost portion of a new 'location' under the close supervision of British troops at King William's Town. They were confined to a strip of land five miles wide by thirty miles long, shared with 2000 other rebellious amaXhosa evicted from lands across British Kaffraria, which were finally allocated to British and Afrikaner settlers.

By the time Nongawuse told her uncle Mhlakaza of her vision, her kin to the west had either been driven into confined locations or crossed the Kei onto Sarhili's lands as refugees. Their most powerful chiefs had been defeated in three desperate attempts to keep British settlers and their government at bay over the last twenty years. Even the chiefs' ability to govern within the permitted locations had been undermined by British magistrates' usurpation of their ability to distribute cattle. Sarhili's own father Hintsa had been killed by British colonial troops and his lands had been invaded by British soldiers again during the latest war. Environmental stress was evident with the overstocking of more densely populated land on both sides of the colonial frontier. In 1855, Maqoma, by now released and reduced to being the recipient of a colonial government pension, had appealed to the governor: 'The Gaikas [Ngqika] say they have no country, they pray that their former country be given to them. ... The inheritance of a chief is not cattle, it is lands and men. ... I pray to you my father to whom I have been given. I have no other word, I ask alone for land'.[5]

The amaXhosa's situation was dire enough in 1856, but by the time Nonqawuse encountered her ghostly ancestors, yet another calamity was stalking the land. Over the last eighteen months, a disease which the colonists called lungsickness had been afflicting the amaXhosa's cattle on both sides of the Kei River frontier. Bovine pleuropneumonia had first appeared in Europe during the seventeenth century. A Dutch ship importing Friesian bulls had brought it to the colony in 1853 and colonists had then spread it through ox wagon routes to the Cape frontier. The British settlers at Grahamstown described its 'fearful ravages' in July 1854:

First the affected cattle began to cough, then they gasped for air, breathing faster and more urgently. Yellowish fluid crept over their lungs which stuck to their ribs, and as the disease spread, the cattle putrefied from the inside out, becoming first constipated and then diarrhoeic. In their final agony, the beasts were unable to move or lie down at all. Their nostrils dilated for lack of air and their muzzles frothed with saliva until, unable to eat, they wasted away and died mere skeletons.[6]

By February 1855 the sickness had spread to the Xhosa's herds including those of Mhlakaza, Nonqawuse and her people. The complete reliance of amaXhosa society on cattle rendered its effects far more devastating than it was among the more diversified settlers. In British Kaffraria Chief Phatho lost 2400 out of 2500 cattle, his brother Kobe lost 130 out of 150 and his brother-in-law Stokwe saw all of his die. Many among the amaXhosa were pre-emptively killing their cattle to save them from an agonising death.

As catastrophe followed catastrophe, it was clear to Xhosa diviners that the predatory British and the devastating lungsickness could only have been occasioned by the living amaXhosa's disregard of their ancestors' injunctions. The practice of witchcraft in particular, traditionally ascribed as the cause of misfortune within Xhosa society, must be checked. New sources of hope, however, were being identified. News of the British being at war in the Crimea had infiltrated Xhosaland and some were claiming that the Russians were black people, formerly Xhosa warriors who had died fighting the British, but were now resurrected to resume the struggle. The fact that the former governor and victor of the Eighth Frontier War, Cathcart, was killed in the Crimea shortly after leaving the Cape, reinforced the association.

Prophets like Mlanjeni, the war doctor of the 1850–2 war, had adapted tenets of the Christianity taught by British missionaries, including the possibility of resurrection. Mlanjeni himself, it was said, had been resurrected, and would join those bringing the cattle back to life and driving the British away if only the amaXhosa would renounce witchcraft. Mhlakaza, Nonqawuse's uncle, conveyed news of her encounter to the Gcaleka Xhosa paramount, Sarhili. The leading historian of the Cattle Killing, Jeff Peires, believes Mhlakaza to have been the same Wilhelm Goliat who had formerly been employed as servant and companion by the Archdeacon of Grahamstown, Nathaniel Merriman. Goliat/Mhlakaza's understanding of Christian theology and particularly of resurrection possibly informed and lent further credibility to the dissemination of his niece's message.[7] Sarhili summoned his councillors to deliberate.

In their calamitous circumstances, the Xhosa chiefs were split. Some saw the prophecy as wishful thinking and warned of its potential for self-immolation.[8] Others, especially those in the districts hardest hit by lung-sickness, placed a desperate hope in Nongqawuse and Mhlakaza. Most, including Maqoma, ultimately fell into line with the prophetic call to action for a number of reasons: because their followers wished to conform and they risked losing the remnants of their legitimacy if they opposed; because their cattle were enduring an agonising death from lungsickness anyway and so they may as well sacrifice them quickly and as painlessly as possible, and perhaps because they saw adherence as a way of pressurising the more sympathetic British officials on the frontier to restore some of their land and authority.[9] Sarhili visited Mhlakaza's kraal in July 1856, after which the Gcaleka paramount gave his sanction for the sacrifice of cattle and destruction of crops. Over the months that followed, until May 1857, 'about 85 per cent of all Xhosa adult men killed their cattle and destroyed their corn in obedience to Nongqawuse's prophecies. Around 400 000 cattle were slaughtered and 40 000 amaXhosa died of starvation. At least another 40 000 left their homes in search of food'.[10]

While some of the British officials and missionaries in the region sought to persuade the amaXhosa not to partake in this mass destruction, the colonial government's response was crafted by one of the most intriguing of the new men governing the British Empire, George Grey. For him, the Great Xhosa Cattle Killing was a tragedy that could be turned to very useful ends.

George Grey is something of an enigma. His most diligent biographer complained that 'he has been denounced as an autocrat and a Conservative and hailed as a great Liberal and a radical reformer'; portrayed as both 'an ambitious self-seeker who humbugged the author-ities by professions of philanthropy' and 'a genuine humanitarian pursu-ing high ideals by dubious methods which exposed him to misinterpretation'.[11] It is easy to see him as a Jekyll and Hyde figure: 'The humane, reserved, intellectual gentleman co-existed with a racialist and imperialist zealot'.[12] Part of the difficulty lies in the loss of his personal correspondence in a fire in Wellington. Historians are reduced to sketching his character using largely his official correspondence and in this, at least for most of his illustrious career, Grey proved a masterful self-publicist.

Grey was born in Lisbon in 1812, just eight days after his father, a lieutenant colonel, had been killed in the storming of Napoleon's fortress at Badajoz. His mother was Elizabeth Anne Vignoles, a member of the Anglo-Irish gentry in County Westmeath. His self-invention began with his service as a young army officer in Ireland. Despite returning to Sandhurst for military training for a further two or three years, Grey later held that he had left Ireland bound immediately for Australia, selflessly determined to solve the problem of Irish poverty by finding new land for settlement.[13] In late 1836, the young lieutenant applied to the Royal Geographical Society (RGS) for endorsement of an exploratory survey of Australia's west. At the same time, Grey drew upon his friendship with Glenelg's brother, the later governor of Madras, to meet the colonial secretary and solicit Colonial Office support.

The RGS proved less compliant than Grey had hoped. Although keen to sponsor the exploration of Australia, they worried about Grey's lack of any kind of relevant qualifications whatsoever. The RGS secretary and naval officer John Washington, advised that he 'gain some experience of the mode of "living in the bush" and of conciliating the natives – of making acquaintance with their manners and customs' before heading off to explore their territory. The impatient Grey ignored the advice and bypassed the RGS instead, obtaining Glenelg's permission for a more reckless and self-glorifying plan.[14] Hitching passage to Western Australia on Darwin's former ship the *Beagle*, Grey and his small party entered the Kimberley region from Hanover Bay December 1837. He soon learned that proceeding beyond the colonised parts of Australia without an Indigenous guide, and without any understanding of Aboriginal diplomatic protocol, was dangerous. When he failed to negotiate passage through new country appropriately, Grey was speared in the leg by an Aboriginal warrior, whom he in turn shot dead. The injury would affect Grey for the rest of his life and he was forced to retreat from his intended exploratory feat. The *Beagle* rescued the party from the shore, Grey having explored very little of the interior.

Undaunted, Grey took passage to Mauritius to let his wound heal, but swiftly decided to try again. This time he made his way to the Swan River Colony near Perth, determined to explore Yamatji country to the north. He did recruit a guide from the Swan River area whom he called 'Kaiber', and this time prepared by employing Kaiber and others to send gifts ahead to the people whose lands he intended to cross. However, the expedition turned out just as disastrously as the first. After losing their boats and most of their provisions, Grey's party was forced to make its way back on foot to Perth, one of the men dying of starvation on the way while others survived only with the help of Aboriginal people.

The Australian colonists were unimpressed by Grey's exploratory attempts. The *Sydney Herald* credited him with the invention of a new tool for explorers – the 'circumbendibus', a 'geometrical instrument which allowed its user to travel in circles'.[15] On his second expedition, he had recorded his discovery of a natural harbour surrounded by lush terrain. The Colonial Office's favourite cartographer, John Arrowsmith represented the find as 'Port Grey' on a map that was consulted by British investors signing up to a new Western Australian colonisation scheme. Unfortunately, when the *Beagle* went to investigate, Port Grey appeared not to exist.[16] The *South Australian Register* told the story in an acrostic:

> Pray! tell me, can we really boast
> Of Port Grey on the Western Coast –
> Report says it is all a sham,
> The offspring of a wily man.
> Good Heavens! what will they say at home
> Receiving news – Port Grey is gone!
> E'en parts explor'd, with skill profound,
> Yet nowhere by the *Beagle* found.[17]

By 1848 the *Geelong Advertiser* was describing 'the fashion to treat the results of Captain Grey's discoveries, with a degree of superciliousness' in the Australian colonies.[18] In the meantime, however, Grey had managed to establish a very different reputation in Britain. Not only was he regarded as a fearless explorer; he was also seen as a precociously talented colonial governor and a leading scholar of Indigenous peoples, or ethnographer.

Grey's career had been advanced in Britain by the publication of his exploration narratives, 'modelled on the style of Fenimore Cooper, his favourite novelist'. In them, Grey 'cast himself in the role of an antipodean Deerslayer to emerge as a great explorer-hero'.[19] His fame was further propelled by his assiduous circulation of an accompanying pamphlet, *Report on the Best Means of Promoting the Civilization of the Aboriginal Inhabitants of Australia*. It outlined a scheme for the humane governance of Aboriginal people, arguing that they would be far better off freed from the primitive constraints of their own society and subjected to British legal systems and employment by British settlers.

Australia's Aboriginal people, Grey argued, were 'as apt and intelligent as any other race of men', but as long as their code of laws prevailed, it would be impossible for them ever to 'emerge from a Savage state'. A system of proper schooling for Aboriginal children in order to inculcate the habits of skilled labour, together with rewards for settlers who paid Aboriginal people to work, would benefit all 'by rendering one who was before a useless and dangerous being, a serviceable member of the community'.[20] Aboriginal men who had demonstrated their capacity and perseverance by working for three years, should, Grey suggested, be allocated land and capital with which to establish themselves as self-reliant members of colonial society. By this means their amalgamation would be attained. As would the total annihilation of a distinct Aboriginal culture.

Grey promoted his *Report* assiduously via James Stephen, who enclosed it with the instructions sent to Hobson for his first lieutenant governorship of New Zealand, together with the suggestion that he consider it in relation to the Māori. It was published in *Parliamentary Papers* and republished in periodicals in Britain and the Australian colonies. The colonial secretary in 1840, John Russell, believed Grey was 'a man destined to reclaim an aboriginal race and amalgamate them with civilization'.[21] Stephen's successor as Permanent Under-secretary at the Colonial Office, Herman Merivale, with whom Grey cultivated a lively correspondence, thought of him as possessing 'the rare faculty of entering into the savage mind, and becoming . . . intelligible to it'.[22]

Merivale would become a key ally of Grey's. The two men shared a disposition that was characteristic of those governing the empire in 1857. A precocious scholar and, briefly, a lawyer, Herman Merivale was more self-assured in his understanding of the colonies than James Stephen had been and more pugnacious in defending his decisions.[23] Whereas Stephen was driven to advise on behalf of colonised peoples by his earnest Christian evangelicalism, Merivale's sense of entitlement to govern was based upon a more secular understanding. It was Britons' hard earned advantages in reason, political economy and social organisation that gave them the right to decide what was best for those who were less advanced. Stephen had painstakingly revised draft despatches in an effort to persuade and cajole, but Merivale was blunter, believing that 'a changed dispatch was a bad dispatch'. His intellectual reputation and robustness meant that he was infrequently challenged. A subsequent secretary of state, Edward Bulwer Lytton compared Merivale 'to no other of less calibre than Macaulay'.[24] Like Stephen, Merivale kept much of the business of Colonial Office to himself, writing for instance on the matter of Canadian railway building, 'There is much written & printed correspondence on this subject. I do not, however, inundate Mr. Labouchere [the colonial secretary] with it for it would occupy much of his valuable time to peruse it, & would require a short time only for me to furnish him *viva voce* with the information he might require on the subject'.[25]

In 1838 Merivale had been Professor of Political Economy at Oxford, where he was about to deliver an influential course of lectures outlining the 'principles of the art of colonization'. His lectures were extremely well received when first published in 1841. They included a critique of Stephen's humanitarian protectorate policy for Indigenous peoples in the settler colonies. Merivale believed that the protectorates, such as those established by Dredge, Parker, Thomas and Sievwright in Port Phillip, and a new protectorate which assisted Māori with the negotiation of land purchases in New Zealand, fostered useless and precarious 'nurseries' for Indigenous people. Regardless of the good intent behind them, he argued, protectorate stations would soon be 'overrun' by self-governing settlers, leading to the utter extinction of their intended beneficiaries. The only hope for these 'unfortunate people' was to be 'amalgamated' within the emigrant British population that now claimed their lands. With Merivale orchestrating Colonial Office policy in the 1850s, assimilation was the intended 'euthanasia for savage peoples', although its implementation was now to be effected by self-governing settler legislatures rather than from London. By 1857, the Colonial Office thoroughly approved of George Grey's intention to 'change by degrees our present unconquered and apparently irreclaimable foes into friends who may have common interests with ourselves' through 'amalgamation'.[26]

Grey's and Merivale's amalgamation programme shared Gurney, Buxton and Stephen's former goal of Christianising and 'civilising' Indigenous peoples in the settler colonies, so their ideas could be supported by Britons who considered themselves humane in their treatment of 'Aborigines'. But the new generation shared a very different immediate emphasis. Far from protecting Indigenous individuals from the destruction of their culture and society, and from violence at the hands of settlers on reserved lands in the meantime, Grey in particular was all for immediate intervention to undermine their grip on the land and the sovereignty that went along with it. Indigenous peoples' conversion to new ways of being in the world should happen sooner rather than later, using violence if absolutely necessary. Of course, Grey maintained, it was only in their own interests, since they were otherwise doomed to extinction. The rationale took on new force as Grey joined the ranks of scholars like James Cowles Prichard who were influenced by the pseudo-Darwinian idea of human races engaged in an evolutionary contest. These men felt compelled to conduct a 'salvage ethnography' of Indigenous peoples, before, regretfully, they disappeared in the wake of a more advanced Anglo-Saxon race.[27]

Grey saw his *Report* as a blueprint for action in each of the colonies that he came to govern. He started on his new career in 1841 as the youngest British colonial governor, aged twenty-eight, in South Australia. Despite the local settlers' scepticism about his exploratory claims, he helped rescue the fledgling colony from insolvency and earned their gratitude as well as the glowing approval of the Colonial Office. It was during Grey's brief tenure in South Australia, however, that he blamed the death of his five month old son on his young wife, Eliza Lucy Spencer. He would never forgive her, and it was an incident concerning his relationship with Eliza in later life that revealed more about his character than any of his official correspondence.

In a remarkable maiden voyage in 1860, the steam frigate HMS *Forte* would carry Grey and Eliza from Plymouth to Cape Town via Rio de Janeiro. Also on board were Rear-Admiral Sir Henry Keppel, hero of the Opium Wars and the Crimean War, en route to assume naval command at the Cape, and J. H. Speke and J. A. Grant, launching their expedition to discover the source of the Nile. On the third day out from Rio, Grey intercepted a note from Keppel intended for Eliza, which sympathised with her grievances against her husband. The supportive letter convinced Grey that his wife was conducting an on-board romance with the illustrious admiral. Despite his own reputation for numerous affairs and Eliza's allegation that he routinely slept with another woman in their house, Grey threatened either to kill Eliza or commit suicide if the ship continued. After insisting that the *Forte* turn about, he abandoned Eliza at the dockside in Rio, making arrangements for her to be taken back to England by the next mail ship. The couple would live on opposite sides of the globe for thirty-six years before a reunion in the last few years of their lives.[28]

While governing South Australia, the imperious Grey also began writing the ethnographic studies of 'disappearing' Indigenous peoples which would continue throughout his career in New Zealand and the Cape Colony. He would send his findings on both the people and the plants of the regions that he governed to the most famous luminaries of the day, including Charles Darwin, Charles Lyell, Queen Victoria, Florence Nightingale and of course Merivale at the Colonial Office. He made a consistent case for Indigenous subjects' amalgamation, while also emphasising his unique ability to bring it about.[29] Grey became a particular friend and acolyte of Thomas Carlyle, sharing his belief in the demonstrable excellence of Anglo-Saxon culture, embodied in Great Men.

After South Australia, Grey was promoted to the governorship of New Zealand, where he claimed the credit for finishing a war with Māori in the Bay of Islands. Grey also closed down the Protectorate of Aborigines, which had sought to negotiate the Crown's purchases of Māori land under the Treaty of Waitangi in 1840. He produced studies of Māori culture with the help of the Arawa historian and a man who seems to have become a genuine friend, Wiremu Maihi Te Rangikaheke, and donated a collection of Māori artefacts to the British Museum. It was Grey who had the Ngati Toa chief Te Rauparaha, whom we met in the story of the brig *Elizabeth* in Part I, apprehended. 'Caught naked and unarmed in his house, the old chief struggled desperately until a sailor seized him by the testicles, so symbolizing both the ethics and the effectiveness of Grey's tactics'.[30]

The next move in Grey's remarkable career saw him arrive in the Cape Colony at the end of 1854. Never one to hide his light under a bushel, he set about founding Grey College in Bloemfontein and Grey High School in Port Elizabeth, while planning the wholesale awakening of the amaXhosa to the benefits of Western medicine with a hospital at King William's Town in British Kaffraria, also named after himself. Having stalled progress towards settler self-government in New Zealand, believing the settlers there not yet ready to assume his own powers, he steered the fractious representatives of Afrikaans and British settlers in the Western and Eastern Cape towards a form of responsible government which included certain 'amalgamated' Africans.

Faced with the devastation that the Cattle Killing movement was generating among the amaXhosa as his hospital was being built in late 1856, Grey saw an opportunity to crush their dogged resistance to his programme of amalgamation once and for all. The hospital, run by Dr John Patrick Fitzgerald, saved the lives of many starving amaXhosa in the early months of the Cattle Killing, until Grey ordered that survivors must work for their relief. In accordance with the blueprint of his original *Report*, the amaXhosa, like Australia's Aboriginal people, would be educated in English schools, build public works under British supervision, spend their wages on British clothes and houses, and become black British subjects among the settlers who occupied their former lands. By employing them, these settlers would also act as their guides towards civilisation.

Grey told Merivale that the amaXhosa had been stirred into a belief in Nongqawuse's prophecies by a conspiracy among their chiefs, including Maqoma. AmaXhosa men were apparently being encouraged to rid themselves of their cattle so that they could prepare for war. As the Xhosa oral historian of the tragedy, William Wellington Gqoba later wrote, 'If cattle were but slain for war to be waged, then oxen alone would have been killed, and shields strengthened, and weapons forged in earnest in all this land of amaXhosa, and blades fixed to shafts. There would have been [wardoctors], to put men in the right state to fight a war. If it were a war scheme, why were those things absent?'[31] Far from being a despairing resort to spiritual assistance, Grey warned Merivale that this was the latest manifestation of the formidable threat that the amaXhosa still posed to British settlers, even after eight frontier wars. He would need the full support of the Colonial Office if he were to meet it with the same success that he had enjoyed among the Aboriginal people of South Australia and the Māori in New Zealand.

Merivale's political boss at the Colonial Office in 1857 was Henry Labouchere.[32] Labouchere had come to prominence as chief secretary of Ireland during the Great Famine of the middle to late 1840s. When the staple potato crop had disastrously failed, pushing an Irish Catholic population already rendered precarious by land reform over the precipice into mass starvation, he had adopted the same response as the East India Company directors to the Agra Famine in 1838. He offered starving people payment only if they took employment on public works. As it became apparent that the payments were inadequate to feed 2.5 million dependents, Labouchere authorised Treasury loans so that landlords could employ additional workers on their estates. At the same time, he directed the army to guard the food stocks intended for export.[33] With both Merivale and Labouchere at the Colonial Office, Grey found a sympathetic imperial administration backing his intention to use the amaXhosa's starvation as a way of forcing their amalgamation.

The date that Mhlakaza and Nongqawuse had initially promised for the resurrection of the dead passed in August 1856. When the prophecy remained unfulfilled, believers placed the blame on the sceptics who had refused to believe in Nonqawuse's vision. They had let all of the

Xhosa people down by safeguarding their cattle, insofar as they could amidst the lungsickness, by persisting with cultivation, and above all by to continuing to practice witchcraft. Redoubled adherence was called for. By January 1857, desperate believers were sacrificing the remaining cattle in Xhosaland and even the sceptical chiefs were unable to restrain their followers. Sarhili began slaughtering his own cattle and destroying crops, telling Grey that he had no right to interfere. In February, Nongqawuse and Mhlakaza promised for the second time that the dead would arise imminently, as long as all the amaXhosa obeyed. Sandile, paramount chief of the Rharabe Xhosa in British Kaffraria, expelled all those who refused to believe from his Great Place. Mass starvation was already breaking out after the refusal to plant crops during the previous season. As the second resurrection day came and went, Colonel John Maclean, Grey's chief commissioner in British Kaffraria, informed him that 'The present moment presents a most favourable opportunity for introducing a new system for the administration of justice amongst the Kaffirs'.[34]

During the early months of 1857, starvation and emigration into the colony for work, across the Kei and to surrounding African chiefdoms, began the process through which British Kaffraria was significantly depopulated. The Xhosa population was reduced from 105 000 to fewer than 27 000 within a year. Grey responded by arresting Maqoma and other chiefs who had led the amaXhosa in previous wars against the colony, imprisoning them on Robben Island. In Maqoma's case, the initial arrest was on the grounds that he had entered the colony without the requisite labour pass in pursuit of a young woman who had fled from her marriage to the much older chief. He was then sentenced as a recipient of stolen goods from a follower whom he had punished for cattle theft. Grey authorised the magistrate John Gawler to establish a Native police force from Xhosa sceptics to punish the theft of livestock and crops by starving believers. He closed down a charitable organisation, the 'Kaffir Relief Committee', set up by missionaries and sympathetic settlers to feed the starving, on the familiar grounds that it would only encourage indolence and thwart his plan for amalgamation. The amaXhosa must be offered no alternative from applying for passes to find work with settlers.[35] Grey established his own programme of employment for the survivors, putting them to work building roads into the Amatola Mountains, which, he thought, would enable British troops to prevent this natural fortress ever being used again as a haven for guerrilla resistance.

By the end of 1857, further resistance to the colonisation of British Kaffraria was inconceivable. Many of the Gcaleka who remained independent under Sarhili beyond the Kei River, but who had sacrificed their cattle and crops, were also reduced to seeking employment among settlers in the colony. Grey encouraged them by ordering a colonial commando to exact reprisals for Sarhili's leadership of the Cattle Killing 'plot', denuding Gcaleka country yet further. In June 1857, 13 137 starving Xhosa people were sent to the colony as labourers and by February 1858, 22 150 were seeking work there. Grey constructed a system for siphoning off their labour:

> To obtain these ends, and to meet the necessities of their state, it became necessary to collect the famishing creatures in their own districts, there to feed them until they had so far recovered as to be strong enough for the journey, then to send them into the colony, or to the port of embarkation, under some superintendence guarding them as they moved, and when they reached their point of destination in the colony, they had to be supported until masters could be found, who would take them. Sometimes, this was all done by private individuals acting under the authority of the government.[36]

Some of these individuals, like Piet Coots, saw the opportunity to resume slave trading, collecting starving Xhosa people from their homes and selling them to farmers, while James Hart was auctioning off their labour in Graaff-Reinet and Beaufort West.[37] When the imprisoned chiefs of British Kaffraria asked Grey at least to take care of their children, he had them sent to his new school in Cape Town, intending them to become the first generation of amalgamated Xhosa leaders. The school's first cohort included the sons of Sandile and Mhala as well as Maqoma's grandchildren.

Grey now wrote to Merivale and Labouchere: 'Instead of nothing but dangers resulting from the Kaffirs having during the excitement killed their cattle and made away with their food, we can draw very great permanent advantages from the circumstances, which may be made a stepping stone for the future settlement of the country'.[38] By the end of 1857 Grey had capitalised on the crisis to dismantle independent Xhosa society in what became the Ciskei region of the Eastern Cape. Across the river in the Transkei, the Gcaleka remained autonomous, for now.

In 1861 Merivale would add a footnote to the second edition of his *Lectures on Colonisation* to say that the programme of amalgamation had

> been carried out with more success in South Africa than in any other British possession ... on the eastern frontier of the Cape Colony (especially since the strange collapse of the Caffre power, under the influence of scarcity and superstition in 1857–1858), great numbers of natives appear to have taken voluntary service under the settlers, and to have performed it with reasonable steadiness. ... The experiment was superintended by one of those men who seem to possess the rare faculty of entering into the savage mind, and becoming themselves intelligible to it, the governor, Sir George Grey.[39]

The template of colonial governance that Grey had established for the Cape Colony's new African subjects in 1857 was as deceitful and manipulative as his representation of events during that year to Merivale and Labouchere. Ostensibly, it held out the promise of an ultimate equality between black and white in South Africa, as black African subjects who had so long resisted incorporation in the colony would be assimilated to the laws and norms established by white settler society and exposed to the benefits of British medicine, education and even the franchise. The basic demographics of southern Africa were very different from Australasia, however. While Grey might confidently, but mistakenly, expect Australia's Aboriginal people, and perhaps even Māori too, to disappear as distinct entities, with successive generations blending into a numerically superior British settler population, emigration from Europe to southern Africa showed no signs of being sufficient to outnumber its Indigenous peoples.[40] In reality, Grey's amalgamation programme in the Cape meant the allocation of the amaXhosa's land to British settlers, their confinement to specific locations or reserves, and their admittance to settler towns and farms as a cheap labour force regulated by a pass system. Aside from a small African peasantry known as the Mfengu, comprising converted Christian military allies in the frontier wars, who could safely be offered a degree of citizenship under a non-racial, settler self-governing constitution, this package of reserve location, settler employment and pass controlled mobility was the only prescribed route towards an 'amalgamation' in which racial equality was perpetually deferred. As much as any subsequent Akrikaner nationalist leader, Grey can be said to have laid foundations for modern South African apartheid in 1857.[41]

John Bowring and the Second Opium War

As Grey was capitalising on the Cattle Killing during the early months of 1857, two other new imperial men were bringing about a second war to prosecute the British opium trade in China. One of these men, John Bowring, was a product of an increasingly confident British commercial and literary society. The other, Henry Parkes, was part of its lucrative expatriate commercial presence in the Far East. Both Bowring and Parkes found willing supporters among politicians, manufacturers and merchants at home. While Grey was beguiling Labouchere and Merivale with his version of events in southern Africa, Bowring and Parkes' main interlocutors in London were foreign secretary George Villiers, the fourth Earl of Clarendon, and former foreign secretary, now prime minister, Lord Palmerston. These men were all closely connected already.

From the age of thirteen, Bowring had learned a number of languages while working for his father's wool business on the Exeter quayside. As a young man he was a frequent visitor to the Continent, supplying uniforms to the British army during the Peninsular Campaign. After Waterloo, he used his connections in Spain and France to set up a business shipping herring and wine. This put him in the frame for an official commercial mission to France in 1831, on which he was accompanied by future foreign secretary Clarendon. Bowring's business ventures also made him wealthy enough to travel across Europe and Russia acquiring material for a literary career plagued by accusations that he claimed the credit for other people's work. His first publications were translations of Russian poetry. Finding them successful, he published translations and studies of Dutch, Spanish, Polish, Serbian, Hungarian and Czech poetry. Jeremy Bentham befriended Bowring as a result of his literary works and Bowring came to be considered the great man's disciple just as Grey was Carlyle's. Bentham twice saved Bowring from bankruptcy when his business failed, and left him his manuscripts to publish posthumously.[42]

Bowring's companion on the French commercial trip, Clarendon, was appointed minister-plenipotentiary to Spain in 1833, where he worked closely with his own patron and foreign secretary at the time, Lord Palmerston. The next step in Clarendon's career was to take over from Durham as governor-general of British North America in 1839. Like Labouchere at the Colonial Office, Clarendon had then become centrally involved with the Great Irish Famine, as viceroy of Ireland. Despite calling for more resources from England to help deal with the crisis, he declared nonetheless that 'The real Celt is ... almost incapable ... of foreseeing the consequences of his own acts. ... He will ... rather plot than work ... sooner starve ... than prosper by industry'.[43] By 1857, Clarendon had become Palmerston's willing accomplice in plotting for renewed war in China.

Palmerston himself had ascended from the Foreign Office to the prime ministership in 1855, aged seventy, in the midst of the Crimean War, and having twice turned down the offer of the governor generalship of India. Known for his charm, wit and sexual promiscuity, he was a populist who believed in the British mission to 'extend, as far and as fast as possible, civilization'.[44] By 1857 his government had helped to restore the reputation of an aristocratic leadership which had failed to garner any success in the early stages of the risky campaign against Russia. Within the increasingly dilapidated Foreign Office along the street from Number 10, Clarendon was largely guided by his prime minister, conducting a pragmatic foreign policy focused on extending British wealth and influence through free trade.

That agenda was crucial to Bowring's political advancement. Having already developed his literary reputation, he had founded his first election campaign on the platform of free trade, and was elected as Member of Parliament after the 1832 Reform Act. Trade restrictions, he had argued, meant that 'the freedom of the few was necessarily associated with the vassalage of the many'. Bowring claimed his motivation was a youth spent observing the 'crushing of the trade of Exeter ... by privileges and monopolies'. His stand associated him with the radical reformers seeking to lower the price of food on behalf of the poor and in 1838 he addressed the meeting in Manchester which led to the formation of the Anti-Corn Law League. Until the late 1840s, he continued to advocate free trade, both as part of a domestic reform agenda and as an emissary, sent to proselytise it on behalf of the British government in Egypt and in Germany during the Zollverein negotiations. Karl Marx saw him as the personification of the British determination to open up the markets of other nations.[45]

During the 1840s, Bowring distinguished the inherent benefits of free trade in general from Britons' illicit and immoral sale of opium in the Far East. In 1841 this pious writer, politician and official, who also composed a number of well-known hymns, commented that 'Jesus Christ is free trade and free trade is Jesus Christ', since the doctrine is 'intimately associated with religious truth and the exercise of religious principles'. Accordingly, he called for the complete suppression of the opium trade.[46] In 1848, aged fifty-six, however, Bowring's business ventures failed. His position on opium trading shifted when, following his service on a parliamentary commission enquiring into Britain's commerce with China, Palmerston offered him a salary of £1800 as British consul at Canton.

Palmerton's offer was not without its critics. Bowring's fellow Unitarian Harriet Martineau warned that his narcissism rendered him 'no fit representative of Government, and no safe guardian of British interests'. She foresaw that, no matter how much he claimed to identify with the Chinese people, Bowring's vanity would provoke another war with the Qing authorities.[47] Martineau was not alone. Henry Addington, the permanent under-secretary for foreign affairs charged with considering Bowring's appointment, cautioned that 'He would probably be over the Great Wall before we had time to look around us'.[48] Before long Bowring had nonetheless been promoted plenipotentiary and chief superintendent of trade in the Far East, reporting to Clarendon. At the same time he was governor of Hong Kong, reporting, when he could be bothered, to Labouchere and the Colonial Office.

Bowring's potential belligerence would be no deterrent to his appointment as far as Palmerston and Clarendon were concerned. The Treaty of
Nanking, which ended the First Opium War in 1842, had certainly
brought benefits to Britain. The trade in Indian-grown opium through
the treaty ports in China now accounted for some £3–4 million, one-sixth
of the total British revenue from India. Nevertheless, Britain's trade
deficit with China had also grown, due to Britons drinking double the
amount of Chinese tea since the first war had concluded. While the
Treaty of Nanking had conferred Hong Kong to Britain and opened up
China's treaty ports to European traders, it had not gone far enough in
securing Britain's long term goal: driving up Chinese consumption of
British goods and Indian opium.

The opium trade was now reluctantly acceded to by the emperor
Xianfeng, but the Qing authorities had not formally legalised it. What is
more, they were still barring British traders from access to the interior
beyond the treaty ports. This meant that British manufacturers were
denied the enormous Chinese market. British trading agents in the treaty
ports also had to engage Chinese middlemen and pay transit charges
before they could convert the profit derived from opium imports into
Chinese tea bound for Britain. After 1842, British manufacturers had
geared up for a massive expansion of their overseas markets through the
forced opening of China. They had been sorely disappointed. Not only
were there few Chinese customers for London's pianos and Sheffield's
cutlery; even Manchester's worsted and cotton manufactures were
rejected. A great slump had occurred in British trade to China in 1848.
By 1857 British manufacturers, merchants and tea drinkers were all
interested in further prising open China's markets.

Just as importantly, the Qing authorities were also keeping Britain's
diplomatic representatives at arm's length. Xianfeng refused to meet with
any foreign consuls and they were confined to the treaty ports along with
the traders. Within Canton, they were restricted only to the factory area,
prohibited from entering the adjacent walled city, despite periodic British
threats to force open the city gates. For the frustrated manufacturers of
Manchester, such official prohibitions symbolised the archaic Qing
impediments to free trade, which it was the British government's duty
to remove. For Bowring, the prohibition was a cause of intense personal
animosity. He had been preoccupied with it ever since he was first
appointed consul to Canton, when he complained to Palmerston that
the profound insult of being greeted by two local magistrates in the
foreign sector, rather than by the Qing governor Yeh in his residency
within the city walls, had adversely affected his health. Thereafter
Bowring consistently referred to his personal exclusion from Canton as

the 'City Question'. It would play a significant role, driving his actions, in late 1856 and early 1857.

When Clarendon had given Bowring his instructions as plenipotentiary in 1854, foremost among them was renegotiating the Treaty of Nanking. In order of priority he was to: obtain access generally to the whole interior of China; obtain free navigation of the Yangtze River; effect the legalisation of the opium trade, and remove transit duties on foreign goods. As the most diligent historian of the Second Opium War, J. Y. Wong attests, 'These and other conditions were not so much a request for revising the existing terms of the Treaty of Nanking as a demand for a completely new treaty'.[49] If Bowring did find a pretext for war, Palmerston's Cabinet would certainly not be too upset. In fact, by June 1856, having been rebuffed at attempts to get the treaty renegotiated, Palmerston had already set about soliciting a military alliance against China with the USA and France.[50]

Once arrived in Hong Kong, Bowring's *volte face* on the opium trade led him to represent the interests of the British opium traders more vigorously than anyone since the conclusion of the First Opium War. He approved the American Commodore Perry's use of gunboats to open Japan to American imports in 1854 and emulated him in a visit to negotiate free trade with Siam. He turned up in Bangkok in March 1855, leaving his warship the *Rattler* anchored in front of the Siamese capital. When the Siamese court refused to abolish trade restrictions, he threatened to leave the ship permanently stationed there. Bowring gloated in terms similar to Grey's despatches, that the resulting treaty with King Mongkut had 'emancipated [Siam] from her intolerable yoke, – & dragged her from her miseries into the bright fields of hope & peaceful commerce'. Much to the disappointment of his former radical friends at home, the treaty encouraged the importation of Indian opium.[51]

In the summer of 1854, Bowring had seized another opportunity to lever open the Far East's markets, this time in China itself. His chance came about as a result of the Qing Empire's existential crisis, the Taiping Rebellion. This was a challenge on a scale far larger than most Britons could ever have imagined. It had begun in southern China in 1850, when Hong Xiuquan, the self-proclaimed younger brother of Jesus, called for the overthrow of the Manchu Qing dynasty and the wholesale conversion of the Chinese people to a syncretic version of the Christianity. Seen by many in Britain as a positive sign of Western and Christian missionary influence following the success of the First Opium War, the rebellion was fuelled by the humiliation that the Qing government had endured in that war. By the time the rebellion was suppressed in 1864, at least 20 million Chinese had been killed.[52] Taiping rebels had captured Shanghai in

September 1853, leading British and American merchants to cease paying duties to the port's customs authorities. When Qing forces regained
control in July 1854, Bowring forged an agreement whereby Western
merchants would pay the duties in arrears, but only in return for the
creation of a British-led customs inspectorate and the granting of greater
autonomy to the Shanghai foreign settlement.[53]

In 1856 Bowring was presented with his long-awaited pretext, both to
fulfil his official mission to renegotiate the Treaty of Nanking, and to
obtain personal redress for his exclusion from Governor Yeh's Canton
residency. He was greatly assisted by Harry Parkes. Like Bowring, Parkes'
background lay in the rising middle classes of industrialising Britain. He
was the son of a bank clerk turned iron master. Orphaned aged five,
Parkes sailed for China when he was thirteen, to join two sisters who
had already settled with their cousin Mary Gützlaff, who was married to
the missionary and explorer Karl Friedrich Gützlaff. The connection
enabled Parkes to get a job in the office of Henry Pottinger, Bowring's
predecessor as plenipotentiary. Having learnt Chinese, Parkes had joined
the expedition to Nanking which forced the Qing surrender during the
First Opium War, and was present at the treaty signing. He then served in
the consulates of most of the new treaty ports. While in Canton, he had
received the indemnity that the Treaty of Nanking demanded on behalf of
the British government. In Fuzhou, Parkes experienced the resentment
that the humiliating terms of that treaty were generating directly, when he
was pelted with stones by Qing soldiers. In Shanghai he enforced the
punishment of Chinese men who had assaulted British missionaries,
receiving Palmerston's expression of approval. Parkes had accompanied
Bowring on his visit to Siam in 1855 and delivered the treaty to England
for Queen Victoria's signature.

At the time that Parkes supplied Bowring's pretext for war, he was
acting consul in Canton. One of Bowring's continual complaints against
the Chinese authorities concerned their failure to suppress piracy against
merchant ships. In October 1856 a Chinese merchant identified two men
in Canton as pirates who had recently attacked his ship. The men had
since signed on the *Arrow*, a lorcha or schooner with Chinese rigging,
currently anchored mid-river. Chinese marine police boarded the vessel
and arrested its crew of twelve. Far from being pleased with the action,
Parkes and Bowring contrived to engineer a diplomatic crisis out of it.
The *Arrow* was owned by one of the 60 000 Chinese who lived in
Hong Kong but were not considered British subjects. Like many vessels
trading in the region, it had been registered in 1854 under a British flag,
although its crew was entirely Chinese except the Irish 'captain of con-
venience' Thomas Kennedy, who was only nominally the vessel's master.

Kennedy was on a nearby American ship taking breakfast with friends when his crew was arrested.

While the Chinese authorities said that the lorcha was flying no flag, as would have been usual when a ship was in port, Kennedy complained to Parkes that it had been flying the British ensign, and that the flag had been hauled down during the arrest of his crew. The outraged Parkes went immediately to demand the crew's release from a nearby Qing junk and an apology for this insult from the marine police. When he tried to push his way past the guards a minor scuffle broke out and Parkes was pushed by a marine policeman. The enraged acting consul wrote immediately to Governor Yeh demanding public redress for the offence, and to Bowring in Hong Kong, informing him that Britain had been insulted. The Chinese authorities had seized a crew under British protection and, in hauling down the British flag, committed an outrageous breach of their obligations to respect British extraterritoriality.

Upon investigating the *Arrow*'s register, Parkes soon discovered that its British registration had in fact expired in September 1856. Once appraised of this, Bowring wrote privately 'There can be no doubt that after the expiry of the licence, protection could not be legally granted' after all to its Chinese crew. Parkes and Bowring also knew that Kennedy's testimony concerning the hauling down of a British flag was not only improbable given the invariable practice of displaying no flags in port, but disputed by neutral Portuguese sailors who had witnessed the incident from a ship anchored alongside the *Arrow*. However, Bowring had seen his chance. He blatantly lied to Yeh that 'Whatever representations may have been made to your Excellency, there is no doubt that the . . . *Arrow* lawfully bore the British flag under a register granted by me'. Privately, he wrote to Parkes: 'Cannot we use the opportunity and carry the City question? If so, I will come up with the whole fleet. I think we have now a stepping-stone from which with good management we may move on to important sequences'.[54] Parkes demanded that Yeh release the sailors from the *Arrow* with a public apology and also open up the gates of the city, so that Bowring could enter and discuss new terms for permanent access to Yeh's residency.

Yeh was distracted from Bowring's opportunism by a far more significant and immediate issue. The Taiping rebellion had engulfed the entire province of Guangdong. Yeh had been leading the defence of Canton against a Taiping siege and the rebels still threatened to counterattack at any moment. The Qing governor at first responded to the added nuisance of Parkes' demands in a conciliatory manner, hoping to settle the matter by releasing the sailors, including the two suspected pirates, to the British Consulate. What Yeh did not anticipate was Parkes' refusal to receive the

Figure 7.1 View of the British bombardment of the treaty port of Canton during the Second Opium War, Canton, China, 1850s. Getty Images.

sailors on the grounds that they were not given up in the public manner required. Yeh refused to prostrate himself at the feet of the British representative in such a manner, and continued to deny Bowring access to his residency. Instead, he offered to talk with Bowring at a Chinese trader's house outside the city walls.

Bowring rejected the offer as a further personal insult and, without checking with either Clarendon or Labouchere, asked the British admiral at Hong Kong, Michael Seymour, to plan an attack on the four forts guarding the entrance to Canton. Bowring assured the admiral that the *Arrow* was registered British, that the sailors held captive were therefore under British protection, and that the British flag had been torn down when the lorcha was boarded. He wrote to Parkes, 'I doubt not the success of the attack on the forts … and it is now almost to be hoped that [Yeh] will *chercher querelle* [pick a fight], as we are so strong and so right'. Seymour's steamships bombarded the forts and British sailors and marines occupied them on 24 October 1856. Bowring was delighted, telling Parkes, 'Of course the magnitude of our demands grows with the growth of our success'.

Even when faced with this occupying force on his doorstep, Yeh still refused to admit Bowring into the city, fearing that his own subjects would rebel and Canton would be lost to the Taiping if he yielded his tenuous authority to the foreigners. Having involved Seymour, who would be reporting his military action to the Admiralty, Bowring was now obliged to inform Clarendon of the action that he had taken so far. He declared 'that if, instead of being shamefully violated, the engagements entered into by the Chinese authorities had been honourably kept, the present calamities would never have occurred'. In the meantime, Parkes ordered the shelling of Yeh's residence at ten minute intervals throughout the day until such time as he should open the gates (Figure 7.1). Yeh responded by offering thirty dollars for every British head, which was of limited effect given the British occupation of the foreign quarter, where all the British traders resided.[55] Parkes then reinforced the bombardment of the walled city as a whole, disregarding Chinese civilian casualties while complaining that Yeh's bounty was itself the provocation for war.

On 29 October, Parkes joined British marines storming a breach in the city walls to enter the governor's residency at last. Yeh, however had already evacuated his compound for government buildings further into the city, and he still refused to meet Bowring. The plenipotentiary, somewhat peeved at having been beaten into Canton by his deputy, ordered the British steamers to fire 'shot and shell to reach the most distant of the City forts and Government buildings'. During the shelling, and despite the prior destruction of adjacent Chinese houses to create a fire break, the French and American traders' quarters outside the city walls were mysteriously burned to the ground while the British quarters remained intact. Although the fire came to be blamed on the Cantonese, it was certainly convenient for the British, since it encouraged the French and Americans to join the hostilities. Undeterred by the Chinese fleet's attempt to drive away the British steamships, Seymour next attacked and seized the Bogue forts at the mouth of the Pearl River. When this too failed to persuade Yeh formally to accept Bowring's entry to the city, the British steamships were left with nothing else to do but continue sporadically shelling Cantonese civilians while protecting themselves against intermittent rocket attacks from the shore.

As 1857 began the stalemate in Canton was continuing while the situation was being discussed in Britain. The *Times* first heard of the crisis that Parkes and Bowring had engineered from a telegram sent via Trieste on 29 December 1856. Further information from their Hong Kong correspondent was contained in the mail which came overland, arriving on New Year's Day 1857, and the government itself published Admiral Seymour's account of the conflict thus far in the *London Gazette* on 6 January. From these preliminary reports, the *Times* considered the war entirely justified, arguing that to submit to the indignity of the *Arrow*'s seizure would mean forfeiting the advantages gained through the First Opium War and presenting 'Britons to the Chinese as a nation devoid of honour and self-respect'. In the interest 'of humanity and civilization we ought not to let the matter drop'.[56] The *Morning Post* agreed, echoing a popular British belligerence. The Chinese were 'an insincere, distrustful, and arrogant people', who required violence 'before they can be brought to reason or to acknowledge they are in the wrong'.[57] Palmerston of course backed Bowring, describing him 'as "essentially a man of the people", an example of middle-class achievement'.[58]

In Hong Kong, Bowring and his family were finding out that the Chinese were not as grateful as they should be. As Britons debated the merits of war, Chinese civilian residents embarked on a campaign of arson, and arsenic was added to the flour supply of the bakery servicing the British traders and officials.[59] Bowring and his wife, Maria Lewin, were both poisoned and Maria would die, apparently from the effects, after her return to England the following year. While Bowring appealed directly to the governor of Singapore and to the governor-general in India for more troops to defend Hong Kong from what he warned was imminent attack by the Chinese (despite their inability to drive the British steamers away from Canton itself), he hoped that 'Government, Parliament, and public opinion will go with us in this great struggle'.[60] In April he warned that 'the various acts of kidnapping, assassination and incendiarism directed against this colony have been plotted by the Mandarins and have had their direction from Canton'. He had, he claimed, 'irresistible evidence of the restless and busy plotting to imperil the Colony by every foul and nefarious mode of attack, against which nothing but the most active watchfulness – aided by heaven's protection – could have successfully guarded us'.[61]

Unbeknown to Bowring, even as he wrote, the former prime minister Lord John Russell was introducing the first critique of his actions, and more pointedly of Palmerston's support for them, in Parliament. Neither was Bowring to be let off the hook lightly by some of the British colonists in Hong Kong itself. In April 1857, the following doggerel appeared in the *China Times*:

> Was colony ever at such a bad pass

I really can't fancy what next will come it
What with poison, bad mutton, oil dearer than gas
A pretty large *tottle* of ill it will sum to
The taxes increasing, such a state the police in
And coolies refusing to carry our chairs
If you'd know why this was, it was simply because
That horrid Sir John's at the head of affairs![62]

In a counterproductive move intended to prove just cause for war, Palmerston had ordered Bowring's despatches and other correspondence regarding the *Arrow* incident, sent initially to the Foreign Office and then shared with the Colonial Office, to be printed and circulated as a dossier. Although himself a member of Palmerston's Liberal Party, Russell was a dissident, vocal in his criticisms of his successor.[63] Conservatives like Lord Derby and Gladstone gleefully reinforced him when he used the dossier to launch a further attack on the prime minister. Russell pointed out that the plenipotentiary's demand for entry to Canton had aggravated a quarrel over the seizure of the *Arrow*'s crew 'which might otherwise have been amicably settled'. Lord Lyndhurst asked 'Was there ever conduct more abominable, more flagrant, in which ... more false pretence has been put forward by a public man in the service of the British government?' Lord Derby thought that Bowring was obsessed:

I believe he dreams of the entrance into Canton. I believe he thinks of it the first thing in the morning, the last thing at night, and in the middle of the night if he happen to awake. I do not believe he would consider any sacrifice too great, any interruption to commerce to be deplored, any bloodshed almost to be regretted, when put in the scale with the immense advantage to be derived from the fact that Sir John Bowring had obtained an official reception in the yamun [governor's residence] in Canton.

It was Bowring's former radical friend and ally in the pursuit of free trade, Richard Cobden, who led the charge against Bowring and Palmerston in a debate in the House of Commons, held between 26 February and 3 March 1857. Despite his support for the Manchester manufacturers, who had lobbied for further access to Chinese markets, Cobden accused the prime minister of recklessly encouraging his representatives in Canton to find a pretext for renewed war. The Conservative Sidney Herbert who, as secretary at war, had been responsible for sending Florence Nightingale to the Crimean War, alleged that Bowring had simply been waiting for the conclusion of that conflict, anticipating that Royal Navy ships would then be available to back him. The *Arrow* incident was 'auspicious' only because of its timing.[64]

Labouchere did his best to defend his prime minister in the Commons and his governor in Hong Kong, expressing regret that it was sometimes

necessary to use force against nations that were not 'Christian and civilised'. The war was nonetheless in the Chinese people's best interests, he
insisted, since it would undermine a 'tyrannical and cruel Government'.
Clarendon echoed him in the House of Lords: 'I fear that we must come
to the conclusion that in dealing with a nation like the Chinese, if we
intend to preserve any amicable or useful relations with them, we must
make them sensible of the law of force'. Palmerston himself was at least
honest in pointing out that he was obliged to defend the opium trade, no
matter how unsavoury it was, because it helped to balance Britain's trade
deficit with China. Nonetheless, he held, the insult to the British flag on
the *Arrow* constituted a legitimate *casus belli* in its own right. In this he was
supported by Robert Lowe, vice-president of the Board of Trade and
former New South Wales Legislative Council member, who declared that
'brave and honourable men had nailed [the Royal Ensign] to the mast,
and had preferred to go down with it to the depths of the ocean rather than
endure the ignominy of hauling it down in the face of the enemy'. How
dare radicals like Cobden denigrate their patriotic sacrifice? As
Palmerston put it, the problem with Cobden and those who criticised
the new war on China was that 'Everything that was English was wrong,
and everything that was hostile to England was right'.[65]

Cobden was as surprised as anyone when, at the conclusion of the
debate, his motion that the government had failed 'to establish satisfactory grounds for the violent measures resorted to at Canton' was carried
by sixteen votes. Gladstone exulted that the outcome did more 'honour to
the H[ouse] of C[ommons] than any I ever remember'. However, neither
man anticipated Palmerston's reaction. Seeking not only to restore but to
extend his mandate, Palmerston announced the dissolution of Parliament
and called a general election. The prime minister was counting on the
popularity he had acquired through victory in the Crimean War, but more
importantly, Palmerstone sensed that the critical MPs were out of touch
with their patriotic constituents on the issue. Bowring and Parkes had
helped to bring about a crisis in which Britain's imperial relations were
suddenly the overriding issue for a public vote. If ever there was a moment
in the nineteenth century when 'public opinion', at least among the
1 430 000 men out of a population of 28 427 000 entitled to vote, was
tested, this 'Chinese election' of April 1857 was it.[66]

Palmerston's sense of the British electorate's disposition was guided by
the debate on racial difference that had been aired in Britain ever since
emancipation. Even as Britons patriotically claimed the mantle of the
world's greatest liberators during the 1840s, an anti-emancipation backlash had emerged. Many now believed that the evangelicals like Gurney
and Buxton, who had urged both the emancipation of the enslaved and

the protection of Indigenous peoples, had been naïve in their expectations of other races. They had preached that, once liberated from slavery, those of African descent would emulate their British benefactors in industry, while willingly adopting the virtues of their civilisation and religion. They had promised that 1 August 1838 would be a watershed moment, when Britain would show how colonialism could civilise rather than brutalise.[67]

During the 1840s, however, this vision of emancipation had failed to materialise. Indigenous peoples persisted in resisting the attempts of settlers to dispossess them, and of humanitarians to rescue them from their own cultures. As we have seen they were now thought to be doomed to extinction unless Grey's and Merivale's amalgamation plan could rescue compliant individuals among them. The mission industry persisted but with relatively few converts in the regions of settler colonialism and with many colonised people elsewhere intent on producing their own forms of Christianity rather than conforming to the customs that Britons identified with the religion. In Jamaica, sugar production plummeted as formerly enslaved men and women left the plantations to try to reconstitute their dispersed families away from the control of former owners. Indian indentured workers intended to make up the loss, proved less compliant than planters hoped, especially once their conditions were better regulated. Formerly enslaved people seemed not to feel the obligation to continue working industriously on the plantations that their emancipationist benefactors had envisaged.

Just as significant as the loss of labour on Caribbean sugar plantations was the effect of the free trade movement in Britain. In 1846 the Sugar Duties Act abolished the Jamaican plantations' preferential rates on sugar imports and subjected them to cheaper competition from Latin America, where slavery persisted. Thomas Carlyle led the backlash against both the 'naïve' philanthropists and the free trade economists, who, between them, had freed slaves into a state of wage labour while abandoning British colonists in the Caribbean. Continuing his vein of earlier Romanticism, in which he prized feudalism above both the 'cash nexus' of waged labour and the iniquities of slavery, Carlyle argued that emancipation had condemned former slaves to idle pauperism. The Irish, he argued, had been reduced by the same means to 'human swinery', a 'black howling Babel of superstitious savages' during the Famine. In a deliberately provocative article, which Carlyle boasted 'you will not, in the least like', entitled 'Occasional Discourse on the Negro Question', he described the freed slaves of Jamaica 'Sitting yonder, with their beautiful muzzles up to the ears in pumpkins, imbibing sweet pulps and juices; the grinder and incisor teeth ready for every new work; while the sugar crops rot round them, uncut, because labour cannot be hired'.[68]

As Carlyle predicted, his diatribe was not well received within his literary circle in Britain. However, the rancour that it occasioned among intellectuals was not so much the result of his rabid racism but rather his targeting of the 'Exeter hall philanthropists' and what he called the 'dismal science' of free trade economics. Despite the protests of liberal friends like John Stuart Mill, Carlyle's unabashed racism honed a broader British public's sense of disappointment in Africans' ability to become 'civilised'. Together with the stream of racial invective pouring into British homes from colonial newspapers extracted by the British press, in the private correspondence of settlers to their kin at home, and in publications such as the *Memorials of the settlers in the Eastern Cape*, it reinforced the notion that white Britons had a particular, if not unique, claim to that mantle.[69]

One of the most astute observers of this post-emancipation development of British sensibilities on race was the African-American Frederick Douglas. In August 1857, while campaigning to abolish slavery in the USA, Douglas delivered a speech in New York State, timed to mark the anniversary of Britain's formal ending of slavery. Noting that this 'bolt from the moral sky of Britain' had 'made the name of England known and loved in every Slave Cabin, from the Potomac to the Rio Grande', he warned against the ensuing backlash. American slave owners were now shouting themselves 'hoarse in denouncing [British] emancipation as a failure'. Douglas accurately described the new calculus of emancipation's worth:

All our tests of the grand measure have been such as we might look for from slave-holders themselves. They all proceed from the slave-holders' side, and never from the side of the emancipated slaves. The effect of freedom upon the emancipated people of the West Indies passes for nothing. It is nothing that the plundered slave is now a freeman; it is nothing with our sagacious, economical philosophers, that the family now takes the place of concubinage; it is nothing that marriage is now respected where before it was a mockery. . . . It is nothing that the whipping post has given way to the schoolhouse; it is nothing that the church stands now where the slave prison stood before; all these are nothing.[70]

Douglas' speech identified a key reason for the sense of innate British superiority in 1857: the supposed 'evidence' that had emerged after emancipation of shortcomings of people of colour when they refused to conform to British norms. Former slaves of African descent especially had proved unworthy of their freedom because they had turned it to their own ends, rather than obeying the precepts of their British benefactors. Emancipation, it seems after all, was not so much a project of sustained, British-led improvement in the conditions of an imperial labour force as it was a vehicle for Britons' self-congratulation. It was just a shame, so the argument went, that despite British benevolence, people of colour's natural deficiencies still held them back.

Carlyle's racism was more characteristic of Britons' thoughts on racial difference in 1857 than the humanitarian idea of 1838, that all of humanity had the capacity to progress rapidly in Christianity and 'civilisation'. If people of colour would not make the progress that philanthropists had promised willingly, and through demonstrated example alone, perhaps a more forceful approach was required? Although scientific racists, who believed in polygenesis and the innate, biologically determined, incapacity of people of colour to attain the accomplishments of white people, have attracted a lot of scholarly attention, they were never really mainstream. Darwinian ideas of evolution emphasised a common origin for different 'races' and were more compatible with vernacular Christianity, but they certainly did not help the old humanitarian argument that other peoples could attain British accomplishments within a generation or two. Rather, they enabled Britons to bemoan the disappearance of 'weaker races' and perpetually to defer any acceptance of racial equality.[71]

In 1857, Palmerston was well aware of this deep British soil in which the seeds of a new Chinese racial caricature could be sown. Cobden complained that Palmerston 'made greater use of that means of creating an artificial public opinion than any Minister since the time of Bolingbroke'. The prime minister's methods included soliciting the cartoonist George Cruikshank to circulate images of Qing methods of torture and execution. At an electoral rally, Palmerston declared that his opponents may have been able to 'witness with calmness the heads of respectable British merchants on the walls of Canton [a complete fiction], or the murders and assassinations and poisonings perpetrated on his fellow-countrymen abroad', but he for one would not stand for it. He issued a written address to his constituents at Tiverton, which was printed in the *Times* and other evening newspapers and distributed as a flyer across Britain. It began, 'An insolent barbarian, wielding authority at Canton, had violated the British flag, broken the engagements of treaties, offered rewards for the heads of British subjects in that part of China, and planned their destruction by murder, assassinations, and poisons'. Charles Greville's diary recorded his utter disgust at the politician's ability to mislead the electorate with his 'enormous and shameful lying', but Palmerston won a landslide electoral victory nonetheless.

The 'Chinese election' of 1857 was a bombastic assertion of Britons' distinctive right to impose their more advanced 'civilisation' on other peoples. Many of Palmerston's opponents in the Commons debate, including Cobden, lost their seats. All thanks, as the *Daily News* claimed, to 'the excited ignorance of a misinformed public'.[72] Following

Palmerston's electoral vindication, Clarendon continued to build the alliance with the USA and France and even considered one with the perennial enemy, Russia, to wage the Second Opium War.[73] However, before the combined Western assault on China could materialise, the third major imperial crisis of 1857 intervened. British troops on their way to Canton via the Cape and Ceylon were diverted to Bombay, while those earmarked to leave India for China were retained.

We will return to events in China in the next chapter. In the meantime, two of Britain's new breed of colonial governors had behaved remarkably similarly in relation to crises separated by some 7000 miles during the first four months of 1857. Grey and Bowring had deliberately misrepresented emergencies on the frontiers of the empire that were largely of British manufacture. Both had seized opportunities to destabilise other societies and extend British interests. Grey had overcome amaXhosa resistance and allocated more land and cheap, government controlled labour to British settlers during the Cattle Killing, while Bowring was prising open new markets for British opium traders and manufacturers against the backdrop of the Taiping Rebellion. Both had justified their actions on the grounds that greater British control was for the benefit of people who would not or could not be British subjects, and both were supported by the British government and, as far as we can tell, the majority of its electorate.

Further Reading

Lester, A., 'Settler Colonialism, George Grey and the Politics of Ethnography', *Environment and Planning D: Society and Space*, 34, 3, 2016, 492–507.

Peires, J. B., *The Dead Will Arise: Nongqawuse and the Great Xhosa Cattle-killing Movement of 1856–7*, Ravan Press/Indiana University Press/James Currey, 1989.

Wong, J., *Deadly Dreams: Opium and the Arrow War (1856-1860) in China*, Cambridge University Press, 1998.

8   'A Struggle of Life and Death'

Syed Ahmed Khan (Figure 8.1) was born in a mansion in Delhi in 1817. His mother was the daughter of a former Mughal prime minister and his father a nobleman. Despite his family's opposition, he forged a career for himself in the East India Company's judicial branch, helping to ensure some continuity between Mughal and Company forms of governance during the 1840s. He would go on to urge the adaptation of Muslim culture to the British presence in India and be rewarded with a British knighthood.[1] When the Indian Uprising broke out, Khan was the Company's assistant magistrate of Bijnor, some ninety miles north-east of Delhi. His mother and other members of his wider family would be killed during the upheaval and in its aftermath Kahn lamented the vengeful British destruction of Delhi as a great Muslim cultural centre. He was the first Indian meticulously to catalogue the causes of this greatest shock to British imperial complacency.

Khan's explanation of the 1857 rebellion, *The Causes of the Indian Revolt*, was first published in Urdu the following year. His motivation for writing it was his belief that 'an honest exposition of native ideas is all that our Government required to enable it to hold the country with the full concurrence of its inhabitants and not merely by the sword'.[2] The book was read by Charles Canning, son of the former prime minister and now the governor-general of India. Arriving in Calcutta in February 1856, Canning had been a devotee of Macaulay's programme to remake India. He seems not to have heeded his own warning, issued to the Company's directors at his departure banquet in the City of London: 'We must not forget that in the sky of India, serene as it is, a cloud may arise, at first no bigger than a man's hand, but which growing larger and larger, may at last threaten to burst, and overwhelm us with ruin'.[3] In the wake of the Uprising, knowing that Kahn had saved the lives of British colleagues in Bijnor, Canning accepted that the author's intention was to help India's British rulers. He ordered Khan's booklet to be translated and sent to England.

Figure 8.1 Syed Ahmed Khan (left) and his son Syed Mahmood (right).

Among the first recipients of the booklet in London was the new president of the Board of Control, Robert Vernon Smith. A former under-secretary of state at the Colonial Office, Vernon Smith lacked the cha-risma of his predecessor, Hobhouse. His biographer described him as 'a cool, observant man of the world, a steady if rather weak-willed whig who benefited from Palmerston's premiership'.[4] Vernon Smith forwarded Kahn's account to Ross Donnelly Mangles, who had succeeded Lushington as Chair of the East India Company's Board of Directors. Trained at Haileybury, Mangles had first set out for Calcutta in 1820. During Auckland's extended visit to the north-west territories in 1838 he had effectively been in charge in Bengal. Like other company men, he had invested some of the wealth earned in India in the colonisation of Western Australia, where his brother-in-law, James Stirling, had been the first governor.[5] As Company Chairman he too had echoed Macaulay's confi-dent call for the Christian reform and English education of Indians. His son, serving in the Company's army, would receive a Victoria Cross during the violence that was provoked, in part, by that very programme of 'modernisation'.[6] Mangles in turn shared Kahn's account with the

Company directors, while Vernon Smith introduced it to the Cabinet. Khan's booklet would inform the ways that Britain's governing men transformed their administration of the empire in the rebellion's aftermath – to a certain extent.

The Causes of the Indian Revolt

Khan's first priority was to rebut the suggestion, current in Britain, that the Uprising was the result of Muslim elites like himself trying to restore the former Mughal Empire. His explanation also serves to discredit a powerful contemporary distortion. In Britain, the rebellion is popularly held to have been almost exclusively a mutiny of Indian *sepoys*, infantry soldiers who were largely Hindu, and *sowars*, cavalry soldiers who were mainly Muslim, employed in the Company's Bengal army. The stock explanation is that their religious sensibilities were offended by the introduction, in early 1857, of new ammunition cartridges. These were greased with the fat of cows, sacred for Hindus, and pigs, offensive to Muslims. Even the appellation 'Indian Mutiny', rather than Uprising, commonly used in Britain, implies that the violence was a solely military affair.

As Khan acknowledged, the immediate impetus for rebellion did indeed originate among *sepoys* and *sowars*, and there had been previous mutinies confined largely within the Company's garrisons. The label 'Mutiny', however, elides the much broader rebellious coalition that developed in 1857 – one that was sustained for more than a year across a vast swathe of northern India. The Uprising posed a far greater challenge to the governmental framework of British India than a mere soldiers' mutiny. Its repercussions beyond India even called forth a revision of imperial governance at large.

Khan's broad premise was that the rebellion arose through a contingent alliance of Company soldiers, noblemen, clerics, artisans, local officials, minor landlords, merchants and peasants distributed across northern India. He explained that these diverse groups shared an alienation from a Company government, and from the larger part of the expatriate British population in India, that had been mounting for well over a decade. It was the result of their exclusion from decision-making, the Company government's insistence on white Britons' innate superiority and its treatment of Indians, regardless of their relative status, with 'contempt'.[7] Seeds of the rebellion had been sown when Maucaulay and the British Parliament debated the reform of India's governance back in 1833. When they decided that India was best governed by a company of Britons accountable to shareholders and Parliament at home, rather than to certain

Indians themselves, they had prepared the scene for the progressive alienation of the very people upon whom Company governance depended.

Canning's predecessor as governor-general, Lord Dalhousie, shared a considerable part of the responsibility. Dalhousie had been friends with both Canning and William Gladstone when they studied at Christ Church College Oxford. None of these men was plagued by self-doubt. Dalhousie admitted 'We certainly are immensely cocky but then, hang it, we have reason'.[8] As a former president of the Board of Trade, Dalhousie had overseen the British government's response to 'railway mania', inspiring his subsequent enthusiasm for railway building in India, the difference being that there he was 'freed from the limitations imposed by the parliamentary system' and therefore 'able to achieve his own ideal of central railway planning and control'.[9] When appointed governor-general in 1848, he was the youngest ever incumbent, aged just thirty-five. His intention was the same as that of Mangles and then Canning: to enact Macaulay's programme for the reform of Indian institutions, education and culture. In order to achieve such 'modernisation', British authority would have to expand to encompass as much of India as possible under direct Company governance. India's modernisation perfectly complemented Grey's assimilation in the settler colonies.

Dalhousie's self-confidence arose in part from the technological mastery that Britons had demonstrated over the previous two decades. Britain was now the coordinating hub of an unprecedentedly connected world, and Dalhousie and his contemporaries thought of themselves as determining its fate. Screw-propelled steamships had, by and large, displaced paddle steamers. During the 1840s both the British government and the East India Company had invested in more coaling stations, navigation aids, engineering bases, lighthouses and deep water ports around and beyond the empire to support them. Both governmental entities were concerned especially to connect Britain with India more directly, via the Isthmus of Suez. In 1852 the Foreign Office had persuaded the Egyptian Pasha and Ottoman authorities to employ George Stephenson to build a rail line connecting Cairo and Alexandria. Whereas the system of transit across the isthmus negotiated by Campbell in 1838 had entailed horse and cart or camel all the way between Alexandria and Suez, a steam train could now be boarded for at least part of the overland hop.[10]

Dalhousie had been promoting steam travel within India too. Manchester's cloth exporters had agitated for a line from Bombay inland to Thane so that they could access cheaper Indian cotton after the failure of the American harvest in 1846, but the railway opened only in 1853. The first train to navigate its steep and difficult route was watched by millions of Indian subjects. A line constructed in Bengal was also driven by British commercial interests, to bring coal from Raniganj to the Hooghly River near Calcutta.[11] In 1853, Dalhousie's 216 page handwritten 'memorandum' encouraged further investment in India's railways on the grounds that they would propel British enterprise, increase production, and allow the exploitation of India's coal and minerals. Above all they would enable the Company's officials and soldiers to traverse India's terrain more effectively, spearheading the subcontinent's broader transformation.

Canada provided a recent model of what might be achieved. By 1856, the newly opened Grand Trunk Railway had transformed the 'precarious and sometimes even dangerous' winter communication between Quebec, Montreal, Kingston and Toronto. While 'A man starting from Toronto may, if he desires it, reach Quebec in less than 24 hours even in winter. . . . The quantity of freight offered for transport . . . has been at times larger than the present rolling stock . . . enabled them to carry'.[12] Anticipating similar benefits, by the beginning of 1857, the Company was guaranteeing a 5 per cent return for railway investors in India. The Madras Presidency had opened its first line in 1856 and in Bombay, 50 000 Indian labourers were paying a heavy price for the ambitious engineering required to run a railway through the Western Ghats. A British engineer's report complained that as soon as the monsoonal weather was optimal for construction, 'fatal epidemics, such as cholera and fever . . . break out and the labourers are generally of such feeble constitution, and so badly provided with shelter and clothing, that they speedily succumb to those diseases and the benefits of the fine weather are, thereby, temporarily lost'.[13]

Aside from steam travel, a wholly new technology was reinforcing British imperial men's sense of omnipotence. It was now possible for clerks to send a message, coded using a system such as that invented by the American Samuel Morse, via electrical impulses along a telegraph wire. At the receiving end, their counterparts used a mechanical device which made a sound or moved an indicator, enabling the code to be translated back into a written message. When it worked well this new technology of telegraphy could convey short messages within minutes across terrain that could take days or even weeks to traverse by horse or ship. The first successful telegraph line had connected Baltimore and Washington in 1844 and by 1857, cables connected Nova Scotia with Newfoundland in the Canadas and towns within Victoria and New South Wales in Australia, as well as running from Alexandria to Suez.[14] In Malta the governor was overseeing the contract with the Mediterranean (Extension) Telegraph Company to extend the telegraph from Cagliari in Sardinia through Malta to Corfu.[15] The East India Company had

invested in a new college at Stevenage in Hertfordshire to train its tele-
graphers. By 1857 they were communicating across 4250 miles of line
connecting the three presidencies and major garrisons.[16]

A line laid under the English Channel in 1850 meant that the Foreign
Office had become an early adopter of the telegraph, since it could link
into the extensive cable networks being established by the French,
German and Austrian governments. The European network also assisted
the East India Company's communications, since it meant that steamers
from Bombay could deliver letters at Suez which, when carried or telegraphed overland to Alexandria, could be conveyed by French or
Austrian steamer to either Marseille or Trieste. From there, their contents
could be telegraphed direct to Leadenhall Street. Foreign Office diplomats could even communicate directly, if intermittently, with the
Ottoman authorities in Constantinople during the early months of
1857, since the British government had paid for an underwater cable
across the Bosphorus as part of its assistance against Russia.

The Colonial Office was not yet in a position to benefit so much from
the new technology. Even relatively short undersea cables were extremely
unreliable and difficult to repair. The Bosphorus one broke three times
within a year and was abandoned in 1860 and a line laid under the Bass
Strait to link Tasmania with Victoria in 1858 would also fail. Two ships
were attempting to lay the first trans-oceanic cable between Ireland and
the USA in 1857, but it was proving impossible to keep the line open after
the cable snagged three kilometres down on the sea bed. It would not be
until the 1860s that improved cabling allowed the Colonial Office to make
more regular use of telegraphic communication with the far flung Crown
colonies.

In 1857, the government was investing heavily to improve the telegraphic relay system where it could, and to reduce its dependence on
French and Austrian cooperation. The War Office, concerned 'that the
only hindrance to immediate communication between Vienna and
London, is caused by the occupation of the intermediate lines with
international correspondence', was urging that a separate wire be
installed 'on certain lines, hereafter to be agreed upon, devoted to the
English correspondence'.[17] The Treasury was offering guarantees of
interest to telegraph and cable companies, commissioning cables directly
and even subsidising foreign government lines. Plans were under way to
lay a cable stretching either around the Mediterranean or under it and
through the Red Sea to Karachi or Bombay, while another plan was being
considered to connect China and Australia through the Dutch East
Indies.[18] So numerous and chaotic were the various privately sponsored
schemes being promoted that, on Christmas Eve of 1857, the Colonial

Office told the Foreign Office, 'Seeing that numerous schemes of Telegraphic Lines are from time to time brought forward and that the projectors often apply for large and unreasonable privileges long before their plans are ripe or their capacity for accomplishing their designs is proved, Mr. Labouchere has felt it of great importance ... to refer all alike to the Board of Treasury, which has undertaken the function of comparing and examining into the different enterprises that may be submitted for consideration'.[19]

All this technological promise and excitement spurred on Dalhousie's plans for the rapid 'modernisation' of India. Glenelg's 1833 Charter renewal had handed the ambitious governor-general an under-exploited tool in this endeavour. Under its 'doctrine of lapse' the Company was authorised to assume direct government of any princely state where the heir's succession was disputed. This was often the case, although the doctrine had rarely been invoked. Dalhousie saw it as key to a considered programme of territorial consolidation and investment.

Dalhousie admitted that talk of annexations being for the immediate benefit of Indian subjects was 'nothing else than ambitious and hypothetical humbug'. The expansion of direct sovereignty was necessary rather to extend and tighten the Company's grip on the sub-continent, raise more revenue to invest in its 'modernisation', and secure the returns that had been guaranteed to shareholders in Britain. Dalhousie committed the Company to take 'advantage of every just opportunity which presents itself for consolidating the territories which already belong to us, by taking possession of States which may lapse in the midst of them; for getting rid of those petty intervening principalities which may be a means of annoyance, but which can never, I venture to think, be a source of strength'.[20] The programme of annexation began on a small scale with the princely state of Satara in 1848. Its Rajah complained to the Board of Control, that 'in the next Charter of the East India Company' it may as well

be declared, that English morality is no more than a question of latitude and longitude; that in India ... what is virtue and what is vice, what is innocence and what guilt, what truth, what falsehood, shall be determined by the complexion of the agent; the white man, or Company's servant, being always regarded as the embodiment of virtue and truth, incapable of wrong even in his own showing, and alone worthy of belief – the dark man, or native, held up as the personification of vice and falsehood, to be accused only to be condemned, degraded, vilified, punished, imprisoned at will, tortured, beggared, and all in secret and unheard.[21]

Dalhousie did not need to invoke the doctrine of lapse when he annexed the Punjab the following year. Ranjit Singh's kingdom, the key ally of the Company during the 1838 invasion of Afghanistan, was taken under Company control when Duleep Singh, the young successor, was

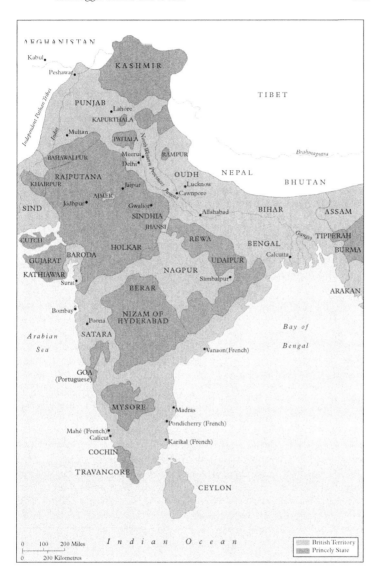

Map 8.1 British India in 1857

deposed. At the same time, Dalhousie confiscated the Koh-i-noor diamond, gaining favour by sending it to Queen Victoria. The Punjab was the most formidable state to have been taken under Company control since the defeat of the Marathas. Its annexation entailed not just the overthrow of a dynasty but the extension of British rule over the majority of Sikhs. Dalhousie recognised that 'until revenues mend' and the territory was pacified, Sikhs themselves would have to have a say in the running of their government alongside the British administrator, John Lawrence. Soldiers in the kingdom's former army would also be offered employment by the Company, making a vital difference when the Uprising broke out (Map 8.1).

Between 1849 and 1852 Dalhousie used the doctrine of lapse as well as other pretexts to annex the states of Jaitpur, Sambalpur, Baghpat, Udaipur and Pegu. In 1853 he explained that the annexation of Nagpur alone 'added 40 lakhs of rupees to the company's annual revenue and 80 000 square miles of valuable territory in central India'. Jhansi, also absorbed in 1853, was too small to add much to the revenue, but 'since it lay in the midst of other British districts its possession . . . would tend to the improvement of the general internal administration of British possessions'.[22] Just as worryingly for India's established elites and the Company's former allies, Dalhousie set about abolishing the titles and privileges of heirs to defunct sovereignties, just in case their persistence raised any doubts about the exclusivity of Company authority. He was overruled by the Board of Control, however, when he sought to abolish the Mughal emperor Bahadur Shah II's title in Delhi.

Dalhousie's intervention in Awadh (which the British called Oudh) proved an annexation too far. The Company had recognised this small Indian state centred on Lucknow and straddling the route from Bengal to the north-west frontier, as independent since 1801. Its nawabs had lent the Company funds to enable the invasion of Afghanistan in 1838 and some of its wealthier subjects even owned Company shares. About 40 000 *sepoys* from the kingdom were serving in the Company's Bengal army. Much as he tried, Dalhousie admitted that he could not 'find a pretext' for annexation under the doctrine of lapse. Instead, he instructed the Company's Resident Agent in the kingdom, James Outram, to prepare a report on misgovernment by its new Nawab, Wajid Ali Shah (whose titles also included the Vizier or guardian of the Mughal Empire). Recognising that his room for political manoeuvre was severely limited by the Company and by his own nobles, Wajid Ali Shah had invested much of his time and resources patronising the arts and writing one of the first plays in Urdu. Outram portrayed him as a 'sensuous lush' and recommended a more intrusive Company oversight.[23] Dalhousie however annexed the entire state.

In early 1856, Wajid Ali Shah appealed to Queen Victoria that Dalhousie had broken with previous understandings to usurp his authority completely and strip his kingdom of all autonomy. Muslim political commentators, including Syed Ahmed Kahn, agreed. When the *sepoys* rebelled in the early months of 1857 recruits from Awadh were prominent among them, and Awadh's aristocrats known as *taluqdars*, now pushed aside with meagre pensions and displaced by the Company's men from Haileybury, were among the first civilians to back them. They were supported by their tenant farmers as well as redundant soldiers from the kingdom's own disbanded army.

Dalhousie is remembered in Britain as the great moderniser of India due to his investments in rail, telegraph and schooling, but he also breached the partly coerced and partly negotiated understanding with Indian elites that had enabled the Company's loose form of suzerainty in the subcontinent during the 1830s. Urged on by Macaulay's conviction of British cultural superiority and the duty to 'civilise', Dalhousie had curtailed ever more presumptively the autonomy of the princely states. Up until the mid 1840s around a third of the subcontinent had still been governed by sovereigns who remained outside of Company control or who retained some independence under the supervision of a Company Resident. But 'in the eight years he was in charge, Dalhousie annexed more than any other single Governor-General, a quarter of a million square miles'.[24]

Perhaps the most infamous of the massacres of Britons characterising the Uprising in 1857 was at Kanpur, which the British called Cawnpore. Here the rebellion was led by Nana Sahib, the adopted heir to Baji Rao II of the Maratha Confederacy. As we saw in Chapter 5, Mangles' predecessor as Company Chairman, Lushington, had helped the Company to overthrow his dynasty. Despite repeated lobbying, successive governors-general including Dalhousie had denied Nana Sahib both a pension and now a title. In June 1857, Nana Sahib led some 12 000 rebel *sepoys* in a three week siege of the British forces in the town before accepting their surrender in return for promising their evacuation along the River Ganges. When fighting broke out along the riverbank the evacuation turned into the massacre of the British soldiers while their wives and children were taken hostage. Once news arrived of British relief forces killing villagers indiscriminately as they closed in on the town, Nana Sahib permitted some of the rebels, including two local butchers, to hack 120 of the women and children to death and throw their bodies down a well. The 'Cawnpore massacre' would become the emblem of the 'Mutiny' in a shocked public imagination, both within Britain itself and in its settler colonies.[25]

Nana Sahib was the disinherited heir to a former Maratha state. When Dalhousie invoked the doctrine of lapse in Jhansi in 1853, another of the most famous rebel leaders, Rani Lakshmibai, had been evicted from her ancestral fort home and her adopted son denied the succession. During the early stages of the Uprising, the Rani of Jhansi, as she is popularly known, initially sought to maintain authority on behalf of the British, but Company officers assumed that she was involved in a spontaneous massacre of British soldiers and so she became a rebel by default. Forming an alliance with Nana Sahib and another of the rebel generals, Tatya Tope, she is believed to have escaped besieging British forces by jumping from the ramparts on horseback carrying her son in her arms, before she was killed in the battle at Gwalior which helped bring the rebellion to an end.

Dalhousie's incessant usurpation of Indian authorities, even if they had already accepted Company oversight, was what drove nobles like Nana Sahib and Rani Lakshmibai to rebel in 1857. But a much more profound and deeper intrusion into the lives of ordinary Indians motivated many more to accept their leadership and turn on the British. Khan explained that the Company's government had come to be seen as a voracious and insatiable extractor of rent, regardless of the suffering that it inflicted.

The cutbacks in Company expenditure after the 1833 charter renewal, combined with the agricultural depression that had exacerbated the Agra famine, had weakened the Indian economy and reduced the Company's income from land tax, even while its British shareholders continued to enjoy their guaranteed dividends. Dalhousie's massive investments in railways and roads had not yet brought significant financial returns. By 1850, the Company's debt stood at £50 million, more than twice its annual income. 'The consequence was an effort to find additional sources of cash, and to do so by squeezing existing Indian hierarchies' as well as through annexing more territory from which to extract rent.[26] By 1857 land tax was being imposed at two-thirds of the total produce in many north Indian villages. Indians of all social classes on the Indo-Gangetic Plain were paying indirectly for British-built railways and British shareholder returns whether or not they could afford it.

Almost as importantly, the elevated tax was being collected in new and alienating ways. Kahn explained that in the 1830s aristocratic governors, *zamindars* and Muslim scholars, across India's diverse patchwork of sovereignties had enjoyed some legitimacy in collecting local taxes. Whether they operated in princely states under Company oversight or on behalf of the Company itself in directly governed territories, these officials were embedded in the communities from which they drew revenue. They tended to be amenable to negotiation on rates and timings. They would waive rent on land for temples, schools and pilgrimage centres and award pensions to certain powerful individuals to secure their consent. The Company officials who had replaced them by 1857, however, understood and cared less about negotiated obligations and inherited arrangements. They had been trained at Haileybury in Mill's Utilitarian philosophy and Ricardo's theories of agricultural rent. For them rent was not a matter of negotiation, but an unearned surplus, the amount of which could be determined formulaically. For most of the Company's Indian subjects, theirs 'was a strange way to govern a - country'.[27] The men who imposed the new taxes were inexplicably inflexible. They saw expenditure on religious symbolism as wastage rather than obligation, and they condemned the judicious waiving of rent as typically Indian corruption. Khan believed that the charging of rent on what had been revenue-free land was the greatest single cause of the rebellion spreading beyond the Company's soldiers.[28]

More broadly, Khan sought to teach the British that the imposition of alien laws and practices, even if intended ultimately to improve the condition of colonised subjects, was widely resented. In the India of 1857, these impositions included initiatives to 'liberate' Indian women from violence at the hands of Indian men and enable their education. Canning had passed the latest such measure, the Hindu Widows' Remarriage Act, in 1856. Providing Hindu women and girls with legal safeguards against the loss of inheritance for remarrying, the act had encountered fierce opposition from Indian petitioners who considered it a flagrant breach of Hindu custom. More concerted attempts by missionaries, officials and army officers to proselytise Christianity were just as provocative to many Indian men as was their dispossession and exclusion from law-making or the threat to their particular controls over women. Britons' cultural arrogance, Khan insisted, had spurred them to govern in ignorance of the true feelings of their more natural allies. Their conviction of moral superiority had also rendered them oblivious to the resentment they were building.

While cataloguing the mounting grievances of various Indian constituencies, Khan was well aware that the opportunity for their effective alliance against Company rule came only when a significant proportion of the Company's own soldiers mutinied. He sought to explain to the British government why they had done so. Khan's argument was, in essence, that Indian men's service in the Company's armies had turned from being a source of pride just two decades beforehand, to one of shame.

During the wars of conquest in the late eighteenth and early nineteenth centuries, the Company's troops, particularly in its Bengal army, had come to think of themselves as an admired elite. Brahmins and Rajputs composed a large proportion of the *sepoys* and service with the army was a family tradition which guaranteed high status and pay in north Indian villages. For Muslim horsemen, service as a *sowar* had come to replace an elevated status as cavalrymen within Mughal armies. An early proclamation from the mutineers of 1857, both Hindu and Muslim, read 'It is we who have conquered the whole territory extending from Calcutta to Kabul for the English, because they did not bring any English army with them from England'.[29] However, Company officials seemed now to evidence little gratitude for these services. The Company had progressively undermined *sepoys'* and *sowars'* status well before the introduction of the greased cartridges proved a tipping point in 1857.

Dalhousie had abolished extra allowances for soldiers who served beyond the presidencies in which they had been recruited. Canning had produced further discontent by approving Dalhousie's drafted General Service Enlistment Act of 1856, which forced new recruits to fight overseas if the Company so ordered. This was despite the understanding, hard earned through a previous mutiny in 1824, that passage over the sea could entail a loss of caste for Hindu soldiers.[30] Although those already serving would not be affected, when their sons joined up, the family as a whole would lose caste. Many of the troops who had fought for the Company in the invasion of Afghanistan had also feared becoming 'outcast to their religion', Hindus having forgone washing before each meal, accepted food prepared by Muslims and worn sheepskin jackets rather than freeze to death, Muslims having fought against co-religionists on behalf of 'infidels'.[31] Following the annexation of the Punjab, Brahmins and Rajputs from the north-west of Bengal resented the increased recruitment of Sikhs.[32] Service in the Company's army had still, by and large, been empowering in 1838, but thanks to the Company's progressively diminishing regard for its soldiers' sensibilities, it was potentially polluting by 1857.

Most fundamentally, Khan explained, the growing British determination to ensure social distance between themselves and their Indian subjects meant that *sepoys*, like other Indians, now found it more difficult to explain and negotiate their grievances with the British officers. No matter how well the officers claimed to 'know' their Indian subalterns, they were never privy to the discussions that they had after duty. This was partly because of the Indian soldiers' long-standing insistence on living in segregated, self-built huts rather than in the barracks of their British counterparts, so that they could see to their own food preparation. But it was also because a new generation of officers from Britain refused to demean themselves by visiting and consulting with their

Indian subalterns when they were off duty. *Sepoys* increasingly presented one face to their officers and another when socialising and complaining in their own languages. By 1857, Khan explained, they 'had no means of protesting against what they might feel to be a foolish measure, or of giving public expression to their own wishes. . . . They misunderstood every act, and whatever law was passed was misconstrued by men who had no share in the framing of it, and hence no means of judging its spirit'.[33] It is remarkable how discriminating rebel *sepoys* and *sowars* seem to have been in the first throes of the mutiny. As British survivors recognised, they tended to spare those officers whom they had come to know and trust while killing those who maintained an air of distant superiority.

The Company armies had begun to replace their Brown Bess rifles with new Lee Enfield ones during the early months of 1857. The Lee Enfield rifles required greased cartridges which would have to be bitten into at one end. A British officer alleged that the rumours of cow and pig fat being used in the grease began when a worker at the Barrackpore arsenal asked a higher-caste *sepoy* for a drink from his canteen. When he was rebuffed he retorted, '"you will soon lose your caste, as ere long you will have to bite cartridges covered with the fat of pigs and cows", or words to that effect'.[34] In March *sepoys* being trained in the new rifles at the same arsenal refused to use the cartridges. Despite the army's reassurance that soldiers would be able to obtain their own grease, thus avoiding any offence to religious sensibilities, rumours spread that the British had introduced the cartridges deliberately to defile both Hindus and Muslims. 'Whether the objection to the cartridges should be attributed to an actual belief that the grease was polluting, or whether group pressure and the fear of being ostracised by friends and kin weighed more heavily, the cartridge issue constituted a unique symbol around which *sepoy* disaffection consolidated'.[35] Those initially refusing to use the cartridges at Barrackpore were arrested and their regiment disbanded, with a proclamation to that effect being read out to all *sepoys* in the Bengal army. As Khan noted, the effect was entirely counterproductive: 'the deepest grief was felt throughout the army. They thought that the refusal to bite the cartridges, the biting of which would have destroyed their caste, was no crime at all; that the men of the disbanded regiment were not in the least to blame, and that their disbandment was an act utterly devoid of justice on the part of the Government. They felt that they had shed blood in its cause and conquered many countries for it, that in return it wished to take away their caste and had dismissed those who had justly stood out for their rights'.[36]

On the following day, 29 March, Mangal Pande, a *sepoy* at Barrackpore, heard that a detachment of British soldiers was disembarking from a steamer nearby. Presumably fearing that they had come to disarm his regiment, he stood resolutely on the parade ground, calling upon his comrades to resist and threatening to shoot the first British officer he saw. That officer was Lieutenant Baugh, who was summoned by the guard duty. Pande immediately fired at Baugh, hitting his horse and bringing him down. Baugh picked himself up and fired back but missed. Pandey then attacked with his sword, wounding Baugh as other soldiers arrived on the scene. The *sepoy* Shaikh Paltu tried to restrain Pande, but the other *sepoys* not only disobeyed the British Sergeant-Major Hewson's order to help Paltu, they hit him, Baugh and Hewson himself with the butts of their rifles, stones and shoes, so as to help Pande break free. The Indian officer in command of the quarter guard, Jemadar Ishwari Prasad, told Hewson that he was powerless to help. At this point the commanding officer, General Hearsey and his two officer sons rode onto the parade ground and threatened to shoot the first man who disobeyed their order to arrest Pande. As the quarter guard advanced finally to obey, Pande tried to shoot himself with his musket but only wounded himself in the chest.[37] With the immediate crisis over, Hearsey had Pande and the Jemadar, Ishwari Prasad, summarily tried and hanged. In a self-fulfilling prophecy, he also had the offending regiment disbanded.

After the incident at Barrackpore, firing practice with the new rifle was resumed, but a wave of arson attacks broke out wherever soldiers were being trained. Cartridges with no grease were introduced, but *sepoys* suspected that the waxy paper itself had been treated with animal fat. On 24 April, six weeks after rumours about the cartridges had first spread, eighty-five of ninety troops ordered to use blank, ungreased cartridges in skirmish practice at the Meerut garrison refused. Their rebuttal was no doubt encouraged by their commander's decision to announce their participation in the drill in the papers, so as to reassure *sepoys* elsewhere that things were back to normal. Regardless of the cartridges used, these men were determined that they would not be the first to incur the wrath of their comrades for breaking ranks. Immediately, the garrison commander had them court-martialled and sentenced to ten years' hard labour. As one British lieutenant later appreciated, the Company's greatest mistake was to turn 'the cartridge question' into 'a test as to which was stronger – the native soldier or the Government'.[38]

On 9 May the British officers in Meerut paraded the arrested *sepoys* in shackles in front of their comrades before leading them off to jail in the town. The mutineers took the opportunity to taunt those who had lost caste and manhood by practising with the new rifles. As the prisoners were led through the town, local prostitutes mocked the *sepoy* escort, declaring that if they were men they would free their proud comrades and telling them they had better 'keep inside the home and put on bangles'.[39] Later that day, friends of the arrested men initiated the Uprising by killing their commanding officer, three other officers and eight British women and children in the cantonment. *Sowars* from the garrison, assisted by the head of police, broke the imprisoned *sepoys* out of jail and joined civilians in the local bazaar attacking the British residents, killing forty of them. The Meerut rebels then marched on Delhi intending to restore the ageing Bahadur Shah II, whose title as Mughal Emperor Dalhousie had failed to remove, and appeal for his leadership of a more general revolt against the Company.

For eleven days, Meerut and Delhi were the only garrisons whose *sepoys* had mutinied, but thereafter the rebellion spread as other constituencies saw their opportunity. Within the next few weeks, around 140 000 *sepoys* from most of the other Bengal army regiments joined the Meerut rebels from other garrisons across northern India, while a diverse set of local leaders like Nana Sahib organised the attack on Britons and their remaining Indian allies across the Indo-Gangetic Plain. During May and June, the rumours of British conspiracies intensified, attracting new recruits. Company officials were thought to be adulterating bread and ghee with ground bones, in order covertly to defile Indians from both main religions. What today we would call fake news spread through informal communication networks beyond the Company's control in the context of systemic distrust of those in charge. For many, the resort to violence mirrored Rani Lakshmibai's experience, occurring only once a vengeful and suspicious British military threatened to punish them for complicity regardless of what they did. As Khan pointed out, the British 'want of confidence' in their own Indian forces led them to try to disarm even loyal and neutral *sepoys* in the quiescent garrisons, persuading some of the soldiers to pick sides against their British officers and the majority simply to desert and head for home.[40] In the epicentres of the rebellion across the Indo-Gangetic Plain neutrality was almost impossible.

Once they had killed their British officers the Meerut mutineers promptly cut the telegraph line to Delhi. Charles Dodd, presumably trained as Telegraph Station Master at the Company's Stevenage college, went out to from the station to check the line the following morning but was intercepted and killed by the rebels heading to the city. His two assistants, William Brendish and J. W. Pilkington, sent a warning along another cable to Ambala, before abandoning their station. When the clerks in Ambala received Brendish and Pilkington's panicked message they telegraphed it in turn to the ports of Karachi and Bombay. The message reached Bombay on 12 May, two days after the Meerut mutiny. There, clerks copied it as a letter and sent it by steamer to Suez. From there, the letter was carried by horse to Cairo. Stephenson's railway then conveyed it rapidly to Alexandria. It was taken aboard a French steamer to Marseille via Malta, transcribed again into code and telegraphed direct to East India House in London.

The alarming news reached the Company directors on 6 June. Letters providing further details of the events at Meerut and Delhi left Bombay on 28 May and were condensed into a telegraph from Marseilles to London on 27 June. A similar telegram arrived at the Foreign Office in Downing Street from Lord Stratford, the British ambassador to the Ottoman Porte, his information having travelled overland via Lahore:

Secret. Native Troops of Bengal army in insurrection from Delhi upwards. State of Matters below Delhi not known at Lahore communication being cut off with Calcutta and Bombay. Massacre of Europeans at Delhi. Insurgents hold the Magazine. Emperor of Delhi proclaimed their head. Little doubt that disaffection has spread throughout the Bengal Army, All the Troops England can furnish ... will be required at Madras and Calcutta.[41]

When the mutiny first broke out, there were some 235 000 Indian Company troops and 29 000 British Company and Queen's troops in India. The Sikh regiments, recently incorporated from the Punjab, were among the few Indian troops whom Company commanders trusted. There were some 15 000 of them, and they were the first to begin the long drawn out process of retaking control of the swathe of northern India from which Britons had fled or within which they were besieged. For the empire's officials in London, the overwhelming priority in early June was to get as many of the 60 000 available white troops from Britain to India as fast as possible.[42] In order to do so the men of the East India Company, the Board of Control, the Colonial Office and the Foreign Office would have to act fast and in concert, not only with each other, but also with private companies and foreign allies. They would have to utilise the recent investments in rail, telegraph, and steamship technology and engage in new forms of diplomacy to secure the rapid passage of the relief army. Their endeavours would presage the restructuring of imperial governance as a whole.

Smuggling an Army

The Company's Political and Secret Committee took the lead in organising the response to the Uprising from London. This was nominally the organ of the Company responsible for political and diplomatic policy, especially in relation to the princely states. Comprising a handful of the senior Company directors and chairs of its other committees, it had emerged during the late eighteenth century 'as the cabinet council of the Company, the most powerful Committee at the India House'.[43] Since the 1833 Charter renewal the Political and Secret Committee had been sidelined by the Board of Control, but during the crisis of 1857, Vernon Smith, president of the Board, appreciated its ability to act more decisively and swiftly than the Court of Directors as a whole. It now comprised only three men – the Company's chairman, Mangles, the deputy chairman and one senior director.[44] The Committee served as a filter for the selective sharing of information known to the government. Mangles and his two senior colleagues would shield sensitive indications of the potential collapse of British power in India from the leaky generality of the Company's directors and shareholders.[45] When the Foreign Office or Colonial Office received intelligence that bore on the situation at hand, they sent copies through the Board to the Political and Secret Committee.

With alarmed messengers scurrying back and forth between the Board of Control in Westminster, the Colonial and Foreign Offices in Whitehall and the Company's Secret and Political Committee in Leadenhall Street, it is not surprising that the Uprising would ultimately set in train a new and more concentrated form of imperial administration. The empire's governing men were forced to join up and activate a planetary-encircling network of communications, transport and people to regain control of India. As a result, they would come both to imagine, and ultimately to govern, the British Empire as a more holistic, global entity. First, though, they had to get British troops to India as fast as possible.

The directors' best estimate of sailing times via the Cape to Bombay was ninety-eight days by sail and sixty-five days by steam, while the Suez route took at best thirty days.[46] The Suez route was clearly preferable even if it meant a reliance on coaling stations that were shared with the French.[47] These were sited in ports falling variously under the authority of the Company itself (Aden), the Ottoman authorities (Mocha Mocha, or Al-Mukha), and the Egyptian Pasha (Cosseir, or Al-Khusayr) (Map 8.2).

Accessing coaling facilities in Ottoman and Egyptian territory was one thing, but transporting an army openly through Egypt presented several problems. There had long been a trickle of Company officers coming and going with the Company's communications between Alexandria and Suez, but there had never been any need to use the route for thousands of soldiers, arms, munitions and possibly horses. In order to gain the assent of the Foreign Office, and not least of the Egyptians themselves,

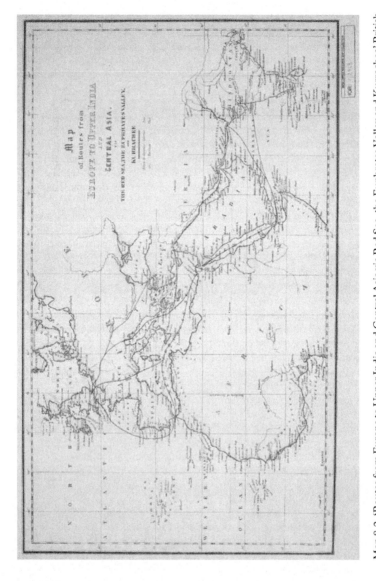

Map 8.2 'Routes from Europe to Upper India and Central Asia via Red Sea, the Euphrates Valley and Kurrachee' British Library.

the Board of Control would have to mediate a snarl of competing priorities and anxieties.

Relations between the British government and the Ottoman Sultan,
Abdülmecid, were friendly after the Crimean War but a large body of
foreign troops traversing Egypt in military order could well undermine
them. British policy towards the Ottoman Empire was focused on maintaining its integrity as a strategic bulwark against rival imperial powers
and especially Russia. This contingent friendliness to the empire as
a whole, however, had to be reconciled with respect for Egypt's relative
autonomy within that empire. The Foreign Office could make arrangements with the Sultan in Constantinople but the Wāli in Egypt,
Muhammad Sa'id Pasha, exercised a degree of autonomy from him, the
precise extent of which the Foreign Office was continually struggling to
understand.[48]

Besides this issue of consent, there were further practical and diplomatic challenges. The Suez Canal, a French initiative, was in its early
surveying stages, and would not be completed until 1869. While the
British built railway between Alexandria and Cairo had become more
reliable, the stretch between Cairo and Suez had not yet been completed.
This segment of the Suez route had an improvisatory infrastructure of
post-houses and horse-drawn van transport, allowing passengers to travel
only during the cooler hours of the morning and evening.[49] As they had in
1838, British passengers to and from India still frequently complained of
being holed up in hot, airless accommodation while they waited at trans-
shipment points in Suez or Cairo for the next train, van or steamer. As it
was, the passage of relatively few Britons along this route could ruffle
diplomatic feathers. William Westgarth, a commissioner returning to
England after investigating the new goldfields in Victoria, travelled across
the isthmus in March 1857, just before the mutiny broke out at Meerut.
Like other Anglophone diarists, he complained of being upon 'thoroughly
Oriental ground, amidst Arabs and innumerable camels'. He thought it
hilarious that English travellers coming home from India ordered 'the
Arab waiters about' calling all of them 'Mahomet' regardless of their true
names. Much to the consternation of Britain's diplomatic representatives
in Egypt, Britons traversing the isthmus would routinely slap as well as
mock and insult the Egyptians who facilitated their passage.[50]

Beyond the overland section between Alexandria and Suez, the geography of the Red Sea provided further challenges to any large-scale
logistical effort. Already a matter of some discussion as traffic increased,
these challenges would now be thrown into more urgent relief. Reports
sent the previous year from the explorer Richard Burton proved
influential.[51] Burton and Lt. John Speke had written to the Royal

Geographical Society (RGS) from Zanzibar, where they were preparing the second phase of the East Africa Expedition, directed at combatting the Indian Ocean slave trade and extending British influence.[52] They went into considerable detail on the naval technology currently available for suppressing slave trading in the region, situating it within local oceanographic and meteorological conditions, noting seasonal variations in ocean currents and prevailing winds, and the requisite drafts of steamers.[53] Burton's further remarks on the ways in which light infantry might be moved most effectively through Suez made the Royal Geographical Society yet another body involved in the suppression of the Indian Uprising, as it passed on his intelligence to Clarendon at the Foreign Office.[54]

A considerable burden of organisation for securing the British army's passage along this fraught route would fall on the obscure figure of Major John Green. Green, about whom little else is known and few historians have written, was a career soldier who fulfilled the double post of East India company agent and acting vice-consul for the Foreign Office at Alexandria. In peacetime, he was responsible for the efficient flow of mails, telegraphs and other communications over the isthmus, their security en route and their efficiency in disembarkation, transit and re-embarkation. From June 1857 though, Green was suddenly the human fulcrum of a transformative geopolitical event.

Green was now expected to produce a digest of all the information that reached him from India in order to guide the response of the various governmental departments in London with a stake in suppressing the Uprising. In September he wrote to Canning at the Foreign Office begging for there to be some arrangement by which the current state of affairs in India could be condensed on his behalf before it reached Egypt. Green explained that 'The means of information at my disposal having been extremely deficient, the messages on more than one occasion have been vague & confused'. This was because 'I am ... entirely dependent as regards telegraphic news from Suez, on the agent of the Transit Administration, who copies statements made up by the Pursers on board the Steamers'.[55] Pursers aboard steamers in Suez harbour now found themselves in the position of interpreting and abstracting intelligence from Indian telegraphs for the imperial government in London's use. Green was acutely aware of the enormously enhanced responsibility of his role. 'The last mail was about to close', he wrote, 'before I proceeded in borrowing a Calcutta Newspaper, & on ... this document only, I had to form in a very limited space of time, the official Bulletin, which was to be circulated to millions at home, & translated into a score of languages, to be commented on throughout Europe'. Meanwhile, and much to the public servant Green's frustration, the *Times'* private correspondent in Egypt 'was framing his Message from files of Papers from every presidency, letters of correspondents purposely written for publication, & others of a more confidential nature, from which he could form a judgement of the various opinions & views of parties on the spot'.[56]

Green's call for a more consolidated packet of news from Bombay was heeded. Henry Anderson, the chief secretary to the Bombay presidency's Secret, Political and Judicial Department, went to extraordinary lengths to prepare fortnightly syntheses of all of the intelligence available to him, to be sent onto Green via the Suez mail.[57] Anderson's enclosures contained a wealth of military reports, returns, judicial papers, maps, intelligence digests and narratives. Once forwarded by Green, only the Board of Control and the Political and Secret Committee in London had automatic right of access to them. Vernon Smith frequently refused the latter's applications to share their information with the Court of Directors.

While Green was responsible for the passage of intelligence in one direction through Suez, he also became critical to the transit of the first detachments of British troops heading the other way. It was Green who negotiated with the Pasha to allow the first small batches of soldiers from Britain to cross the isthmus. The remarkable condition was that they hide their identity as Queen's troops on campaign by pretending to be tourists or the usual colonial transit passengers.

In mid July, the Company's Court secretary wrote to the Army leadership at the Horse Guards reminding the commander-in-chief that in 1846, the practice had been adopted of sending a small group of officers and men via Suez, ahead of the main regiment of the 10th Hussars, who followed around the Cape. This advance party trained locally purchased horses 'for the Effective mounting of the Regiment on its arrival in India'.[58] The suggestion was to adopt the same procedure. Initially, two parties were sent, consisting of a captain, riding-master, vet and nine non-commissioned officers and men. Each of these soldiers was to receive £2 from the Company for civilian clothes in which to traverse the isthmus. Green reassured Foreign Secretary Clarendon that 'the passage through Egypt of the small party of men alluded to is not calculated to attract any particular attention here as being in plain clothes they pass as Officers' servants and other second class Passengers such as it is not unusual to see amongst the transit travellers'.[59]

The initial parties were a success and so several more were sent. As it became clear that they were encountering no difficulties, during August, the Political and Secret Committee and the Board began to plan a larger-scale operation. A Lt. Col. J. G. Fraser, referring to his own extensive logistical experience in Egypt, suggested a workable plan. The arrival of troops in Alexandria would be staggered with that of the mails, so as not to overburden communications links across the isthmus; troops would be disembarked en masse in the morning, given breakfast on the train to Cairo, and then loaded straight onto horse-drawn vans for the desert crossing, to arrive at Suez early the next morning for immediate embarkation. The troops would be in groups of about 200, carefully watched the whole way 'to prevent them communicating with the people of the company'.[60] Fraser envisaged a permanent supply of troops passing to India by this route, to the number of 3000 per year.[61]

It took less than a month for Vernon Smith at the Board of Control and Mangles, Company Chair and head of the Political and Secret Committee, to fall out over the plan. The Company's Court was intent on sending the maximum number of available troops at the first possible opportunity, and did not much care by what means. Vernon Smith too feared losing India to a sustained revolt, but he was also responsible for ensuring that suppression of the Uprising did not compromise British interests elsewhere. The tension between Mangles and Vernon Smith in August and September brought into sharp relief the fragility of the arrangements by which the East India Company and Board of Control were supposed to collaborate in the governance of India. In early September, they broke into an open breach. Frustrated by the pace of arrangements for troop transports, the Company attempted to circumvent the Board by a *coup de main*. In a letter to Vernon Smith, the Company directors wrote that they had consulted with the Pacific and Oriental Steam Packet Company (P&O), which had become major supplier of the Company's opium from India to China, and which had now proposed a timetable and costing for the transport of much greater numbers of troops more swiftly across the Isthmus of Suez. Mangles asked the Board to consider the matter. However, in a separate letter sent the same day, Mangles informed Vernon Smith that the directors had in fact already accepted P&O's tender.[62] Their justification was that Vernon Smith had given his assent in a private conversation.

Vernon Smith's response was immediate and cutting:

It is true that this subject, with very many others relating to the speedy dispatch of troops to India, had been discussed in the conversations which I have frequently had the honour of holding with you since the commencement of the late unfortunate events. But, as no steps had been taken of a formal nature to bring before HM Govt the views of the Court of Directors upon this head, ... [I] of course concluded that they agreed, through you, in the objections urged against them. ... I think it would lead to any end rather than that of the united government of the Court of Directors and the Board, if every proposal that had been broached at our confidential interviews was, in times of great public emergency, to be addressed as [a] scheme submitted to ... the Board.[63]

Vernon Smith noted that, by contracting P&O to ship troops via Suez without the government's, most particularly the Foreign Office's, consent, Mangles and the Company had impeded 'the united action, as well as the good feelings, of the component parts of the government of India'. Something of the Board's difficult position within the diffuse structures of imperial governance had been exposed to public view by this incident. It was not quite master of foreign policy and not quite intermediary; reliant on informal negotiation and relationships of trust to function properly. The structural contradictions between government and Company, which Macaulay had sought to smooth over during the debates about charter renewal in 1833, were now thrown into sharp relief.

Nonetheless, thanks to Green's success in sending small parties of troops through Suez, by late October, the War Office had agreed to send full regiments through Egypt.[64] Vernon Smith's next step was to involve the Foreign Office in the further diplomacy necessary to ensure their passage. Foreign Secretary Clarendon told Vernon Smith and the directors 'that it is of the utmost consequence that the intention to resort to this measure should not be suffered to transpire, and that on the contrary all parties concerned in carrying it out should be strictly cautioned not to allow the nature of the orders given on the subject in any way to become public'.[65] Delicate diplomatic approaches had to be made to the Ottoman authorities to license British troop movements which might appear to Egyptian subjects as an invasion.

Lord Stratford, the British ambassador to the Ottoman Porte, was tasked with securing the assent of Sultan Abdülmecid I in Constantinople, while it fell to Green to manage Muhammad Sa'id Pasha in Cairo. During the autumn these two diplomats and Clarendon in London developed a frequent and meticulous three-way correspondence. Clarendon wrote to Green:

This Govt think it due to the Pasha, who has always evinced so much consideration and attention for their wishes, not to leave him in ignorance of the real character of the large body of passengers who will pass through Egypt with the next mail.... You may add that the men will not remain on shore in Egypt beyond the time absolutely required for their passage through the Country.[66]

To Stratford, he wrote:

Your Lordship will mention this arrangement to the Porte, as Mr Green has been instructed to mention it to the Pasha of Egypt; but as the men pass ostensibly as Civilians, it is scarcely to be expected that the measure will call for forth any observation on the part of the Turkish Govt.[67]

Clarendon was aspiring to pull off something in the nature of an elaborate pantomime: a British army would pretend to pass through Egypt as civilians and the Egyptian and Ottoman authorities would pretend not to notice them. The mail ship carrying the Sultan's letter of assent arrived at Alexandria in early October, and it fell to Green to present it to the Pasha. He reported that:

> I will require a little judgment to communicate the Sultan's letter to the Vice Roy [Pasha] without offending the Vice Roy's dignity, but the written declaration ... enables me, by not hurrying the presentation of this document, to place it in the light of a sanction rather than an order. The exceptional state of things here induces me to use a certain discretion in these proceedings, as it is better that I should take some responsibility on myself, than risk the inconvenience which might result from annoying the Vice Roy at a moment when he might easily retaliate ... without the complete cooperation of the Egyptian Govt it would be impracticable to carry out any measure of this kind, and indeed if the Vice Roy had any disinclination to it, it would be utterly impossible to get over the difficulties that might quietly be thrown in our way.[68]

A week or so later, Green reported that the Pasha had been written to directly by the Sultan, but with a slightly different implication: 'I do not attach any importance to this matter, but it is as well to know that something has been said by the Porte as limiting the number of Troops passed through Egypt'.[69] Throughout the autumn, Green in Cairo, Stratford in Constantinople and Clarendon in London put all of their combined diplomatic talent into testing the temper of the Egyptian and Ottoman authorities, and trying to descry, from outward signs, the inner workings and tensions of this other imperial government so that the British Empire might be sustained in India.

It was not only soldiers whom the Foreign Office helped to convey to India. The Political and Secret Committee required the department's cooperation to obtain cavalry and draught horses too. Most of the horses pressed into the Company's armies were normally purchased from Parsi horse trading families in western India. But these suppliers' loyalty was now suspect and supply lines disrupted. While Green and Stafford were managing the passage of troops through Egypt, the Foreign Office was briefing its consuls in Baghdad and Aleppo to assist Company and Army agents buying horses from the Levant to be sent direct to India. The consul in Aleppo, desperate to be of help, dug up his reports from the end of the Crimean War, in which he had proposed the recruitment of Kurds as irregular cavalry, and advised that a militia too could be raised for swift passage to India. The horses did travel to India, although a Kurdish militia did not.

All the while, British soldiers continued to cross through Egypt in 'mufti'. Throughout the latter part of 1857 and into January of the following year, shipping companies' and the War Office's plans factored in a charge for a civilian overcoat, while equipment and ammunition was disguised as luggage. The journey of these large parties of exclusively male, heavily moustachioed and regimented 'tourists' was recorded, with a dyspeptic eye and a fine sense of irony, by William Howard Russell, the *Times* correspondent who had recently made his name in the Crimea. He passed through in early 1858, and apart from his complaints about 'Oriental' food and accommodation, the impression he gave is of an operation that, though improvisatory, seemed to work efficiently enough. Russell's account was vividly alive to the juxtapositions and displacements of intense colonial and military activity in a small area suddenly invested with geostrategic significance, and of an infrastructure under rapid construction and unexpected strain. He wrote of the troop (ostensibly tourist) train from Alexandria being held up for two hours to make way for the Pasha's private train, which never came (the message was relayed by telegraph to 'some distant station along the line', and then conveyed to the train by foot). Coaling stations along the line were 'helpless, hot, ovenlike erections generally eked out by old Crimean wooden huts, within which may be seen an undoubted Englishman, smoking his pipe'. He noted European and quasi-European food and drink being advertised at various stops, or transported out from Cairo for the passengers and soldiers; local passengers and British soldiers, rather against the Foreign Office's wishes, crammed into crowded trains together; and he lent a Dickensian absurdity to his description of the vans that took the troops the last few miles to Suez as 'Brighton bathing-boxes laid longitudinally on wheels, to which were attached creatures of an uncertain number of legs, resembling very much Scarborough ponies at the end of the season'.[70]

A more straitlaced account was produced by the *Times* in October 1857, as the first large levies began to pass through:

The conduct of the men was most orderly. A lusty chorus, which in several occasions proceeded from the carriages, testified to their good humour; and any petty discomforts of the journey through Egypt were quite unheeded in their satisfaction at travelling 'like gentlemen'.[71]

Many of these troops did not prove so orderly, nor gentlemanly, once sent into combat in India. By the time they arrived, Delhi had been recaptured mainly by Sikh and Muslim *sepoys* from the Punjab and Gurkhas led by the East India Company officer John Nicholson, who executed thousands of rebel soldiers and civilians alike on the way. As one of his British officers noted, 'All the city's people found within the walls of the city of Delhi when our troops entered were bayoneted on the spot, and the number was considerable, as you may suppose, when I tell you that in some houses forty and fifty people were hiding. These were not mutineers but residents of the city, who trusted to our well-known mild rule for pardon. I am glad to say they were disappointed'.[72]

Joining a relief column from Calcutta, the reinforcements from Britain fuelled the 'Devil's Wind', as Indians termed the indiscriminate British retribution enacted across the Indo-Gangetic Plain. Russell's travelling companions joined their Company counterparts in the practice of executing anyone suspected of being a rebel by hanging them or blowing them to pieces after tying them across the mouths of cannons, so that they could neither be cremated nor allowed a proper burial. During the recapture of Lucknow in Awadh, the British troops, most of whom had arrived via Suez, killed some 5000 men, women and children and then proceeded to execute 150 000 civilians and non-combatants. Gordon Highlanders, who had crossed the isthmus around the same time as the *Times* reporter, participated in the final stages of the Uprising's suppression, hunting down Tantya Tope to Narwar and ensuring his execution in April 1859 (Figure 8.2).

These British reprisals were fuelled by stories of the rebellious *sepoys'* rape and murder of British women and children, especially at Kanpur (Cawnpore). When the town was recaptured, British soldiers forced captured Muslim and Hindu rebels to eat pork or beef, and lick the blood of the murdered British women and children from the buildings and floors before their execution. Those troops who arrived via Suez would have been exposed to the British press' hysterically racist reaction to the Uprising, which began as soon as news of the initial mutiny arrived in June.

In *The Perils of Certain English Prisoners*, published in the *Household Words* Christmas edition of 1857, Charles Dickens and Wilkie Collins alluded to the Cawnpore massacre and derided the figure of 'Sambo', a 'double-dyed traitor, and a most infernal villain' representing the archetypal *sepoy*. In October 1857 Dickens had written privately to Baroness Burdett-Coutts, 'I wish I were the Commander in Chief in India. . . . I should do my utmost to exterminate the Race upon whom the stain of the late cruelties rested . . . proceeding, with all convenient dispatch and merciful swiftness of execution, to blot it out of mankind and raze it off the face of the earth'.[73] The *Times* had written of the unspeakable 'violation' of mothers and children in Cawnpore, following which their 'murder was mercy'. When it carried what purported to be an eyewitness account of the mass rape, torture and agonising death of forty-eight English 'females, most of them girls aged 10–14, many delicately nurtured ladies', Karl Marx responded in the *New York Daily Tribune* that the story was actually authored by

Figure 8.2 Outlying picket of the Highland Brigade at the time of the Indian Mutiny in 1857. Engraving from 1858, engraver unknown. Photograph by D Walker. Getty Images.

a 'cowardly parson residing at Bangalore, Mysore, more than a thousand miles ... distant from the scene of the action'.[74] In the aftermath of the rebellion, Canning had reports of wholesale rape of British women and children investigated and found no evidence of it, although hundreds were killed outright by the rebels. When the governor-general attempted to differentiate the punishment of *sepoys* whose mutiny took the form of returning home as non-combatants from those who actively attacked the British, he was derided by *Punch* magazine as 'Clemency Canning'.[75]

Of the approximately 40 000 troops that converged on India from all over the Empire in 1857–8, about 5000 had travelled there directly through Egypt thanks largely to the efforts of Green. By February 1858, troop transports reverted to travelling entirely by the Cape route. Although the suppression of the rebellion would continue into the spring of 1858, the first scramble to mobilise a response from Britain was over.

The attention of London's imperial officials could now turn back to the prosecution of Bowring's war to gain entry to Canton and open China more completely to the opium trade. Canton was attacked with troops released from India and captured on 1 January 1858.[76] In June 1858 the four Treaties of Tientsin forced the Qing authorities to open eleven more ports and allow British, French, Russian and American traders to navigate along the Yangtze River; to open the interior to Westerners and to grant these nations' consuls access to the closed city of Beijing. For good measure, another indemnity was to be paid: 4 million taels of silver to Britain and 2 million to France. When the Xianfeng Emperor sought to resist, the British and French governments resumed the war, which culminated in 1860 with the looting and destruction of the emperor's Summer Palaces. In addition to the concessions already granted in the Treaty of Tianjin, Britain demanded Kowloon on the Chinese mainland adjacent to Hong Kong, the right of British ships to carry indentured Chinese labourers to the Americas, an extra 2 million taels of silver apiece for Britain and France, and the long-awaited legalisation of the opium trade. The decisive victory over the Qing Empire so shortly after the suppression of the Indian Uprising lifted Palmerston to new heights of popularity in Britain.

In the meantime, those who sought to govern the British Empire from London had learned some valuable lessons from their scramble to coordinate a response to the Uprising in India. The logistics of the seemingly simple task of sending troops by the quickest route to India had highlighted the limitations of Britain's disjointed imperial government. The Board of Control had sought to rein in the Company directors' independent contracting of troop movements and limit the information supplied to shareholders, while couriers struggled to ensure the smooth flow of intelligence and direction between the Foreign Office in Downing Street, the Board in Westminster and the Company in Leadenhall Street.[77] The Company's and the Foreign Office's key agent in Alexandria had suffered from a more disjointed communications network than the *Times*' correspondent. The final item in the Company's Political and Secret Correspondence for 1857 is dated 31 December, when troops were still travelling across Egypt. In it, Vernon Smith gave notice that the Board of Control would be seeking to have the East India Company abolished and replaced by a new Indian government department integral to the British government.[78] The various elements of imperial government would from now on be more closely aligned.

Further Reading

Chakravarty, G., *The Indian Mutiny and the British Imagination*, Cambridge University Press, 2005.

Dalrymple, W., *The Last Mughal: The Fall of a Dynasty, Delhi, 1857*, Bloomsbury, 2006.

Nayar, P., ed., *India 1857: The Great Uprising*, Penguin Books India, 2007.

Wagner, K., *The Great Fear of 1857: Rumours, Conspiracies and the Making of the Indian Uprising*, Peter Lang, 2010.

Wilson, J., *India Conquered: Britain's Raj and the Chaos of Empire*, Simon and Schuster, 2016.

9   A New Imperial Government

During the Company's crisis in India, Merivale and Labouchere at the Colonial Office were trying to manage the flow of information, intelligence and guidance to panicking colonial governors elsewhere around the British Empire, many of whom had their own direct correspondents in the Indian presidencies. The first systemic issue was the need for greater surveillance of Indian subjects in other colonies, including those on indentured labour contracts, who might sympathise with, or be inspired by the rebels.

The Uprising in the Indian Ocean

Since the late 1830s, the system supplying and regulating indentured Indian workers and their families had become more sophisticated, with the Colonial Office, the Board of Control and the Indian Presidencies cooperating in its maintenance. It continued to be refined during the Uprising itself. In July 1857, the Colonial Office agreed that planters in British Guyana and then Trinidad could employ their own Indian agents to return to India and recruit workers for their plantations directly, despite evidence of widespread and continuing abuse.[1] In September, Labouchere agreed to liaise with the Board of Control to see whether a Jamaican agent could 'examine personally each Immigrant previous to embarkation [from India]; and ascertain their fitness for Agricultural Labour', after complaints that previous workers had been too old to warrant the costs of their importation.[2]

In the light of the Uprising, however, there was a new concern within the imperial governmental offices that the Indian subjects fanning out across the empire might be infected with mutinous spirit. This anxiety had to be balanced against the continuing need for their labour. The problem of striking the right balance between security and productivity was particularly acute in Mauritius and Ceylon, where the demand for Indian labour had never been greater.

In Mauritius, the governor, James M. Higginson, formerly of the Bengal army, then superintendent general of Indian [First Nation] affairs in Canada and latterly governor of Antigua and the Leeward Islands, had embargoed further labour importation the previous year. This was because recruiters had abused the licensing system for Indian indentured labour, and used it to acquire African captives from Madagascar, where Queen Ranavalona ruled in uneasy alliance with the British.[3] Slave trading under the name of free labour recruitment was continuing, however. In August 1857, for instance, Higginson told Labouchere of Captain Trotter of the Royal Navy's boarding of the English Barque 'Joker' in Boyanna Bay (Madagascar). Trotter found that 'many, if not the whole of the so called emigrant labourers that he found on board, had been slaves up to the moment of their embarkation'. A newspaper in Réunion reported that 'these same labourers had taken advantage of the master of the Joker's absence on shore to revolt, murdering his son and the greater part of the crew, and plundering the vessel'. Nevertheless, Higginson apprehended 'considerable difficulty in obtaining a conviction' for the slave-trading Captain Aps.[4]

All the while that Higginson's embargo pertained, high prices had encouraged the cultivation of sugar cane, which required increasing numbers of unskilled workers. In the Seychelles, administered from Mauritius, plans to construct new roads and other public works were also stymied by the lack of labour. As the administrator at Mahé, wrote, 'so long as Proprietors employ the ex-Apprentices on the Squatting System, as is the case at present, there must always be a scarcity of labour, as the wants of the Black Man are so few and easily obtained from the productiveness of the Soil'.[5] Mauritius' landholders were elated when, soon after the outbreak of the Uprising, in June 1857, Higginson reopened the channels for Indian immigration. Not only that, but 'greater facilities' were now built on Flat Island off Mauritius 'for the safe disembarkation of Coolies when subjected to quarantine'.[6] The planters' demand for labour again largely trumped both the concern that indentured workers might be infected with rebellious spirit and the governor's caution about ongoing abuses of the licensing system.

Steamers carrying the newly recruited labourers to Mauritius arrived in a steady stream throughout 1857, as British troops left the island bound for India. On 10 August alone, six companies of the 33rd Regiment and one company of artillery left for Bombay, with further troops scheduled for despatch the following day. Given 'the urgency of the requisition and emergency of the service for which additional reinforcements were required at Bombay', Higginson acceded to all requests for troops received from India, but he was increasingly concerned that his response 'will certainly leave Mauritius with a garrison reduced considerably below the strength that has been assigned for its requirements, and less than the position and importance of the Colony would entitle it to'.[7] Higginson's successor, William Stevenson, was only partly reassured by an offer from the French governor of Réunion to send troops to assist, should the Indian population of Mauritius rise up in the absence of the British garrison. Labouchere asked the Foreign Office to send 'some fitting acknowledgement/expression of approbation ... to the country of France'.[8]

This combination of heightened security considerations and an influx of Indian labourers prompted an innovative response from Higginson and Merivale. The colony's Legislative Assembly was already debating the introduction of a compulsory government education scheme. The governor and permanent under-secretary now decided to attune the proposal to the imperative of persuading Indian arrivals away from any sympathies with the rebels in northern India. The island's new education system would be used to acculturate the next generation of Indian labourers to their future as colonial subjects in Mauritius. As the Uprising spread across the Indo-Gangetic Plain, Ordinance 21 of 1857, 'for rendering compulsory the education of children in the colony', was debated on virtually every detail in Mauritius' colonial legislature, in the colony's religious community, and in the Colonial Office. The exact nature of the instruction to be offered and the methods by which Indian children in particular would be schooled were considered of great importance.

While some members of the legislature thought that it might be prudent to trial an easier, voluntary system first, Higginson believed that in the circumstances of the Uprising, comprehensive education would have to be compulsory. Exposure to British social and moral ideas was to be conducted in part through religious instruction. When Bishop Collier, leader of the Roman Catholic community, complained that Protestant tuition was taking precedence above Catholic, Merivale concurred that the ordinance ought to be amended so that 'no child should be compelled to attend the government schools if already receiving regular instruction in some other school to be certified as efficient by the Anglican or Roman Catholic Bishop, or by the officiating minister of any other Christian body in the colony to which the school is attached'.[9] However, the Colonial Office's imperative was to ensure that 'an opportunity will be afforded to Indian children to hear the word of God, without offending the religious prejudices of the Coolies'.

The Legislative Assembly voted that tuition be given in the principal administrative language of Mauritius, French, rather than in an Indian language or English. Given the current state of affairs in India, and the diminution of the garrison held in Mauritius, Higginson thought it imperative not to arouse resentment among the newly arrived Indian immigrant population by insisting that they learn a new language, and deferred to the island's planters in the Assembly on the grounds that at least the instruction in French would ensure that labourers were steeped, from an early age, in the linguistic culture of the colony. It was also more pragmatic to employ the larger pool of Francophone teachers in the colony. The final ordinance required that all children in the colony between the ages of six to twelve years attend some kind of government-approved school for three hours per day. Initially both girls and boys were to attend, so as to leave them available for labour the rest of the day, but this requirement was later reduced for girls 'to meet an objection of some weight, grounding on the unusually early physical development, and the precocity of the sexes so remarkable in Mauritius, and the consequent dangers to public morals that might arise from the intercourse between boys and girls of a ripe age'.[10] Mauritius thus introduced compulsory education some twenty years before England, at least in part out of a desire for social order borne of the instability of the Indian Uprising.

Mauritius was not the only colony in receipt of more Indian immigrants at the same time that its garrison was denuded on behalf of the Company. Ceylon's governor, Henry Ward, reported that Indian workers on contracts of indenture were 'now flocking to [the island], in large numbers, the Indian troubles, and the stoppage of the Public Works in the Madras presidency, having thrown an unusually large amount of labour into this market'.[11] At the same time, India's governor-general Canning had appealed directly to him, 'Pray send me every [soldier] that you can spare, and with all possible expedition'. Sending 500 white troops and leaving only 87 in Ceylon, Ward told Labouchere that, 'although the military force now in Ceylon is smaller than that at any former period, and totally inadequate to meet any hostile combination on the part of the natives, – yet it was our bounden duty to run all risks in order to assist the Indian Government, at this most unlooked for crisis'.[12] In June and July 1857, Ward was anxious, but not panicking, about the implications of the rebellion for Ceylon:

in a colony where British capital, to a very large amount, is invested, – with a few wealthy European settlers scattered over distant districts, in the midst of a million and a half of Singhalese and Tamils, – and without even a Ship of War upon the coast, it would be difficult, if not impossible, to resist anything like a general combination against us. On the other hand, the Island is perfectly quiet, and exempt, apparently, from Indian influences. How long it will remain so, it is in vain to ask, since everything depends upon the prompt suppression of the Indian movements at Meerut, and Delhi. . . . For, where there are the same differences of

Race and Creed, there will be the same disposition to combine against the ruling minority; and ... I should be sorry to see [Ceylonese subjects'] loyalty tested by the example of successful Rebellion upon the neighbouring continent.[13]

Ward was slightly less sanguine in September, when he told Labouchere that

A news-room, or club, has been established at Kandy, at which, upon the arrival of every Indian mail, letters, and translations from the Indian papers, are read by the members, who are all Moormen [Muslims], with the exception of one Buddhist Priest, whose presence it is difficult to account for, except upon the political grounds. It is impossible not to connect with this club, the evident organisation of the Moormen, and the secret orders given for their attendance in Kandy. And, though I am not disposed to attach much importance to the boasts of a vain, and talkative, Race, yet ... the language held in the bazaars is 'that the English have lost their power; – that they have no troops, and will be treated in Ceylon as they have been in India; – that the Delhi Raj is to rule the Eastern World; – that the Malays, and Moormen, are all united; – and that, within a few days, there will be real fighting in Kandy'.[14]

Two weeks later, he was reassured again, writing that the rumours of a planned Muslim uprising had been found merely to be 'the embellishments superadded to a few simple facts by the excited imaginations of some of the European residents, who are now ashamed of their own alarm', a reaction excused by 'the natural consequence of events in India, acting upon the minds of a Mahomedan population'. Ward hoped that Labouchere would, 'make due allowance for the exaggerations inseparable from these times, and for the difficulties that a Governor must experience in sifting the information'. India, he pointed out, 'shows that everything is possible, when there is a struggle of Race, and Creed'.[15]

The Uprising Elsewhere

As more troops from Britain arrived in India and suppression succeeded rebellion in late 1857, the Company directors asked the Colonial Office if certain Crown colonies could receive those Indian soldiers and civilians suspected as rebels, who had been captured and convicted to transportation rather than summarily executed. Jamaica's Immigration Commissioners jumped at the opportunity. In the light of a recovering sugar industry, they appealed to the Colonial Office to be sent transported mutineers for work on the plantations.[16] Trinidadian planters formed a committee to request that those *sepoys* found guilty of treachery and rebellion, but not of participation 'in the frightful atrocities that have been perpetrated on women and children', be sent to the island on ten year indentures and made to pay for their own transportation.[17]

In response to a direct request from Canning, who explained that
'Penang or Singapore (our ordinary resource) are too near, and thus
communication with India too easy and constant', George Grey offered
to host Bahadur Shah II, the former Mughal emperor, in exile at King
William's Town, within occupied British Kaffraria. Grey advised, 'I
think it would be better not to call upon the British Parliament to
interfere in the matter, for the Legislature here will readily pass the
necessary law upon the subject, and this will accustom them to legislate
upon matters, which concern the Empire in general, as well as upon
those which regard only their own individual interests'.[18] Ultimately,
however, the transported 'rebels' were all directed to the Company's
prison facilities on the Andaman Islands while the former emperor was
exiled to Rangoon in Burma.[19]

Throughout the year, the uprising in India commanded a large proportion of the Empire's available resources. It was primarily Merivale who
had to reconcile the extraordinary circumstances in the Company's
domain with the need for stability and continuity in the rest of the empire.
Even in Australia, the ripple effect of insecurity and the narrative of 'race
war' was felt during the ensuing months. Settlers in the northern districts
of New South Wales, still engaged in a violent struggle to colonise what
would soon become Queensland, expressed their fears of the morale
boost that the Indian rebellion might give to their black foes and their
determination to assert British supremacy, while a Melbourne newspaper
feared that 'Malay desperadoes and Chinese pirates' would be emboldened to attack the undefended coast.[20] Such panics elsewhere made this
a year of especially careful triage for Merivale's department.

At any other time, for example, Merivale and Labouchere might well
have acceded to the request of the governor of British Guiana, Philip
Wodehouse, for a naval ship to protect British control of the Orinoco
River mouth on the northern coast of South America. The sugar-
producing colony had been formed in 1831 from the merger of the formerly
Dutch colonies of Essequibo, Berbice and Demerara, initially captured
during the Revolutionary, and then again in the Napoleonic Wars.
Wodehouse explained that the discovery of gold deposits on the colony's
uncertain border with independent Venezuela was threatening a contest.
But this tension was mounting in the region at a very inconvenient time. As
Wodehouse's despatch reached Merivale, the Admiralty was scrambling its
available ships to relay troops from Britain to India as swiftly as possible.

The gold was found at Upata, in a mountainous region separating
British and Venezuelan territory. The exact boundary line had been
under dispute for some years. Aside from being one possible boundary
line, the Orinoco was the primary artery from the coast and the only major

waterway into the Upata region and Wodehouse was anxious to ensure proper protection for this strategic holding while the border dispute was being settled. There were implications of the gold discoveries for other British colonies in the region too. Trinidad's governor Robert W. Keate wrote, 'It is hardly likely . . . I think, that the ranks of the gold seekers will be recruited from our indentured labourers, or even from the rural creole population to any great extent; the towns of Port of Spain and San Fernando, and especially the former, could well afford to lose a large portion of their idlers, and could the emigration be confined to them, as I hope it may be, the proximity of the gold district will be a real boon to Trinidad rather than the curse which in some quarters it is feared it may prove'.[21]

When, some twenty years later, diamonds were discovered at Kimberley beyond the Cape Colony's frontier, the colony's uncertain border was simply defined so as to encompass the deposits within British territory by administrative fiat. A similarly neat annexation of the gold on the Venezuelan border was ruled out, however, by the unavailability of troops to realise the possession against potential opposition, and the unavailability of ships to get them there.

Initially, Labouchere sent Wodehouse what information he could glean as to the best way of handling rival 'crown, colony and private individual' claims to gold discoveries, from the colonial governments of Vancouver and New South Wales, which both had relevant and recent experience to draw upon. But then he told Wodehouse, that although it was 'very desirable that in due season a Ship of War should . . . visit the mouth of the Orinoco for the protection of British interests', such action was, at that time, 'not possible'. Merivale advised that a diplomatic approach be pursued in lieu of a military one. The gold itself would be recognised as Venezuelan but British Guiana and the British-controlled Orinoco River would be promoted as the main avenue to the deposits, so that Britons could benefit from the commerce of the gold seekers and merchants.[22]

Given the prevailing mistrust of soldiers of colour prompted by the Uprising, Governor Wodehouse requested that at least a detachment of white British troops be sent to replace the West India Regiment in the colony. Labouchere and Merivale agreed that the Colony would be 'safe if two White Companies were to be sent to it from Barbados or elsewhere, & two or three black companies withdrawn to make room for them. . . . The enlistment of Coloured Creoles should be avoided as much as possible . . . & the recruit should not be stationed more than is necessary in the Colony of which he is a native'.[23]

Even when the Colonial Office received offers of troops for direct service in India during the Uprising, the response varied according to their race. 'It is not deemed desirable to employ Negro troops in the East Indies. It has therefore been determined that no steps should be taken for raising troops from among the coloured population of Canada', Merivale wrote to one Captain Stephens of Collingwood, Canada West, who had offered to raise 'a Regiment of Coloured Troops for service in India'. Neither did the office accept the offer of help from a Deputation of the 'principal Chiefs of the Six Nations' to send warriors to help out the British in India.[24] In contrast, Governor Ward in Ceylon, the Crown colony most directly threatened by the proximity of the Uprising and its connections with India, argued that the worst thing he could do was provoke his Asian troops with any sign of distrust. 'I am anxious, on the contrary, to avoid all distinctions between the European and Native troops or, if any be made, to give the preference rather to the last, who have furnished all the Sentries for the Queen's [governor's] House . . . and will continue to do so, so long as their conduct remains what it is', he wrote.[25]

While the crisis in India led the Colonial Office to advise caution in provoking trouble in South America and elsewhere, this was never going to suit George Grey in the Cape. During the Uprising, Grey turned from being Merivale's model scholar-governor to a thorn in the Colonial Office's side. In June, Grey received a direct appeal to send troops from Elphinstone, governor of Bombay, who explained that 'Telegraphic communications are all interrupted and communication by Post is uncertain, and much valuable time would therefore be lost in awaiting the result of a reference to the Government of India' in Calcutta.[26] Rather than sending the 89th Regiment on from Cape Town to New Zealand where it was expected, Grey unilaterally despatched it to India. He also diverted 92 officers and 1743 men who were on their way to assist Bowring in Hong Kong. By September, affronted that he still had not received any direct communication from Canning in Calcutta, Grey felt that he may have 'gone too far' in his immediate support of the Indian government, and would henceforth 'be cautious what other steps I take until further instructions reach me'. Unable to help himself, however, just two days later, he began 'gradually purchasing horses for the Indian Government' with the intention to 'continue to do so as rapidly as possible'. Despite the demand from India being for only 250 horses, Grey was determined to 'continue to act upon my own discretions, and ship so many horses as I can procure, until I think that the requirements of the public service in India are probably sufficiently met'.

Grey complained that the imperial communication system was simply not up to the job of dealing with a crisis such as that in India. Not only was it difficult to link the Colonial Office–administered Crown colonies such as his with Company-administered India; it was proving impossible to get a coherent message from the government of India itself. The requests that Grey received from the Bombay and Madras presidencies did not align with those from the governor-general in Calcutta, nor with those of the Home Government. Grey complained that while the Government of Bombay applied to him directly for two infantry regiments on 23 September, 'The Supreme Government of India ... did not even ask for one Regiment. The instructions I had received from Her Majesty's Government were to send one Regiment to Calcutta, and one Regiment to Ceylon [to replace its own white troops, now sent to India], and there was a general authority in your despatch of the first of August to take, in conjunction with the authorities in India, such measures in regard to the movement of troops as the interests of the public service might require'.

Through such complaints, Grey was undermining his favoured status at the Colonial Office. By November 1857, a clerk was annotating caustically: 'Governor Sir G. Grey's feelings are hurt, because he has received no direct communication from the Governor General of India respecting the Indian Mutiny – the 1st communication announcing only the employment of Col. Good to purchase horses at the Cape for the Bengal Army – It is under the influence of such feelings that he says he begins to think he may have done too much in assisting the Indian Govt & that he shall now be cautious what other steps he takes; In a despatch, however, (two days later) ... – he promises to continue to exert himself to the utmost in every possible way to aid the Govt of India in the present crisis. ... I think it will be sufficient to acknowledge the receipt of this despatch'.[27]

Unaware of the Colonial Office's increasing impatience with him, Grey continued to blame communicational discrepancies for his deviation from official instructions concerning military deployments. Having initially redirected forces destined for other parts of the empire, Grey disappointed Merivale and Labouchere by dodging their appeals to send soldiers from his own garrison. In November Labouchere urged Grey to

avail yourself of the circumstance of so large a number of troops being assembled in the British Provinces of South Africa to render the utmost assistance ... to the Indian Administration, & pray that you will have been able to despatch considerable additional services to that Country, where seasoned Troops will be especially valuable.

So far in his career, Grey had managed to accumulate a small army of regular British troops to assist his amalgamation projects in both New Zealand and the Cape. Now that he stood to lose his disposable force in the Cape, he explained to Merivale that 'the Empire is large and disjointed, and may, at a moment of great danger be easily involved in the greatest peril. . . . If, at such a time, several distinct portions of the Empire, each without considering what has been elsewhere, place themselves in jeopardy to aid the threatened point, thinking only of it, and danger suddenly appears within their own limits . . . there would be great danger that the Empire might suddenly be broken up. . . . What difficulties we should have been in if, now that Great Britain has stripped herself of Troops, and so large a part of our army is in India, we had had a Kaffir War, a Ceylon Rebellion, and disturbances in Mauritius all, upon our hands, at once'.[28]

Grey had previously assured Merivale and Labouchere of his success in crushing the Cattle Killing 'rebellion' and ensuring the amaXhosa's amalgamation at long last. Now he changed his tune. Reluctantly, he sent a few hundred of his own troops to India while understating how many were left in the Cape and exaggerating the scale of ongoing unrest on the immediate post-Cattle Killing frontier. Grey now professed to Merivale his anxiety that, in his selfless desire to assist another British possession in peril, he had sacrificed the security of the Cape. At a time when the colony 'was embroiled in its own crisis with the native tribes. . . . We have crippled the artillery here by sending every horse from our field batteries', he lamented, and 'we have temporarily almost destroyed the Cape Corps by taking two hundred of the best horses from that force, and this has been done with 70,000 barbarians within our Colonial Borders, exclusive of those in Kaffraria and the neighbouring states . . . [all] that we may efficiently assist our Indian Empire'.[29]

Grey sought to prove his point in February 1858, when four Xhosa chiefs escaped from the prison in King William's Town. He exclaimed that they were now inciting violence against the government, telling their followers

That all the troops had gone to India from England, but were so overpowered by the Indians that all the English troops had left this country for the purpose of assisting their countrymen. That all the horses had been shipped at East London, also the guns, and that the troops had embarked at Port Elizabeth and Cape Town. That it was heard with delight that the Indians are a black race with short hair, and very like the Kaffirs. That it is to be regretted that, whilst their race is overpowering the English in India, the Kaffirs are at the present moment unable to follow up the success, and fall upon the English in this country, and that it was known to his people that Krili [Sarhili] is looking forward to an opportunity and is devising plans for bringing on a war.[30]

In March 1858, Grey was still complaining that 'I cannot close this despatch without observing, in reference to remarks I see have been again made in England upon the subject of the reinforcements I have sent on to India, that it is always lost sight of that, whilst aiding India,

I have been compelled in order to secure the safety of this colony, to carry on very important military operations against a dangerous enemy; that these operations have been invariably successful, that any failure in them would have placed us in a position of great peril, that formerly they would have been carried on by Her Majesty's Troops at a large cost to England, and would have been regarded as a Kaffir War, which they have, in fact, been'.[31]

Neither this account, nor Grey's accounting of soldiers sacrificed from the Cape, however, seems to match other sources. The official reports of the War Department and Colonial Office give troop numbers that are quite different from Grey's. While the governor portrayed a colony selflessly denuding itself of military resources to support the imperial agenda, all the while battling renewed amaXhosa rebellion inspired by Indian *sepoys*, Merivale was beginning to discern a quite different picture: one of a relatively insignificant colony receiving far more than its fair share of imperial resources at a time of crisis for Britain and its empire at large.[32]

The contradiction between Grey's assurances that he had everything under control on the one hand, and his alarmed representation of a state of perpetual emergency requiring large numbers of troops on the other hand, was becoming ever more glaring. Even his admirer Merivale could no longer overlook it. In 1859, the War Office circulated a report examining the distribution of military resources across the Colonial Office–administered sphere of the Empire between March 1857 and March 1858.[33] Particular note was made of inequalities in the numbers and financing of troops among the colonies. While the colony of Victoria paid roughly two-thirds of its own ordinary military expenditure, Canada paid only one-fifth, and the colonies of Nova Scotia, New Brunswick, Tasmania and New Zealand all contributed nothing. The report noted, however, an exceptional 'drain on British resources which has resulted from our undertaking the defence of this [Cape] colony, and ... the inadequacy of the benefits resulting to British interests. As affording a field of emigration, a supply of our wants, or a market for our produce, our connection with the colony has not been, comparatively speaking, of any considerable advantage to us; in fact, the only direct object of Imperial concern, is the use of the road steads [shipping lane harbours] at Table and Simon's Bays'. Including the German Legion of militia settlers recruited to British Kaffraria, Grey had retained at the Cape an army of 10 759 regular troops, costing the British Exchequer a total of £830 687. This was more than one-fifth of the military expenditure across the Empire. If one excluded the 'special class' of strategically placed Mediterranean garrisons, the figure was nearly one-third.

Furthermore, as Thomas Elliot, the former agent general for emigration whom we met in Part I and now Merivale's assistant under-secretary of state, minuted, Grey had manipulated his office into granting an additional and extraordinary £40 000 'for civilising the Kaffirs and averting disputes with the Natives'. Elliot complained that 'It is true that these efforts have given us the satisfaction of being able to say that we have not had a Kaffir War, but nine or ten thousand troops constitute such an army as England seldom has to spare for less favoured spots'. Even before the War Office had finished its report, piecing together the disjointed imperial administration that had allowed such imbalance was emerging as a key British governmental priority.[34]

A New Imperial Government

Palmerston introduced the bill of which Vernon Smith had warned the East India Company Court of Directors on the last day of 1857, in February 1858. Its purpose was to transfer the government of India from the East India Company to the Crown. Palmerton's original proposal built upon the impromptu organisational structure that had overseen the immediate response to the Uprising, with a president of India replacing Vernon Smith's role at the Board of Control and absorbing the functions of the Company's Political and Secret Committee. Palmerston's successor as prime minister, Lord Derby, oversaw the eventual passing of a modified Government of India Act in August 1858. Despite former Company judge Erskine Perry deploring 'that the Bill did not contain a single allusion to the native interests of India', the Act 'left untouched the ... whole rights [of the Company shareholders] as to stock, dividends, the power of requiring redemption of the dividend, and the security fund for the payment of the dividend'.[35] The East India Company was now stripped of both its commercial and governing functions, but as John Stuart Mill, now the Company's chief examiner, explained, its shareholders were protected because their company had, at its 'own expense, and by the agency of their own civil and military servants, originally acquired for this country its magnificent empire in the East'. Indeed it was 'the most beneficent [government] ever known among mankind'.

Contrary to popular belief, then, the East India Company was not dissolved entirely after the Uprising. It remained in existence, its main function simply to continue collecting rent from Indian taxpayers to distribute to its shareholders, now channelled via the new government of India.[36] It was 'a corporate zombie, reduced to the most basic corporate task of all: the distribution of the annual dividend'. Marx commented,

Company directors 'do not die like heroes: they commenced by buying sovereignty and they have ended by selling it'.[37] East India House in Leadenhall Street was sold off and most of the Company's employees given a pension. John Stuart Mill's was a considerable £1500 (and an inlaid inkstand). A clerk was still employed to distribute the dividends and the Company's directors continued to meet in the boardroom of the Red Sea Telegraph Company in Moorgate and later at St Pancras Lane north of the City.

The dividends of 10.5 per cent, first agreed in the 1833 Charter renewal, continued to be paid to British shareholders even though the government of India's debt had grown to nearly £100 million and the annual interest charges were now some £4.5 million. Canning introduced a new Indian income tax to meet the costs and when Charles Trevelyan, the governor of Madras, opposed it, he was recalled. When the East India Company was finally dissolved in 1874, its shareholders were compensated with a generous government buy-out. The East India Stock Redemption Act offered them a range of options so that they could continue to derive income from their investment in the colonisation of India. They could choose to receive £200 worth of 3 per cent government annuities, £200 worth of 4 per cent of India debt, or £200 in cash for every £100 of Company stock they owned.[38] 'In effect, another £12 million of debt was added to the India account, its interest to be covered by the Indian taxpayer, equivalent to over £650 million today'. Through this means Indian taxpayers continued to subsidise British investors until the Second World War.[39]

In the wake of the Uprising, a new British government department was created. The India Office would be headed by a new secretary of state for India, Lord Stanley, while the governor-general, still Canning, became viceroy of India. The secretary of state in London would be advised by a council of fifteen men, the majority of whom were to have had recent experience in India. He could overrule them in secret and urgent matters but was bound to follow their instructions in financial matters. With nine of the fifteen councillors also Company directors, the Council gave the directors a continuing say in the governance of India. As Stanley realised, their wish 'to avoid making needless changes' was fulfilled, since they persuaded Palmerston to be guided 'as much as possible by analogy to existing circumstances'.[40] Their influence only grew once Merivale moved from the Colonial Office to head up the civil service of the India Office, uncharacteristically professing his ignorance of Indian affairs and deferring to the directors' expertise. Just as with the shareholders' dividends, this whole new edifice of imperial governance was to be funded not by British, but by Indian taxpayers.

Within India, Canning heeded Syed Ahmed Khan and sought to conciliate the princely rulers, acknowledging the continuing local power of
Indian elites. He also involved Indians, recruited through new universities
in the three presidency cities, in the lower tiers of the civil service.
Macaulay's and Dalhousie's drive for forced 'modernisation' was eased
and the doctrine of lapse itself allowed to lapse, with princely rulers
accorded the right to adopt their heirs. Before embarking on a tour
among northern India's princely rulers, Canning held a meeting in
Lucknow in 1859, in which he awarded Awadh's *taluqdars* deeds of
ownership to their restored estates. Stanley's successor as secretary of
state for India, former president of the Board of Control Charles Wood,
wrote to him in 1860 that the British would now 'enlist on our side,
and ... employ in our service, those natives who have, from their birth
or their position, a natural influence in the country'. Canning 'showed
great resourcefulness by announcing certain measures not only designed
to pacify India but also to buttress British authority and prestige. Basic to
his plan was the creation and strengthening of a native landed aristocracy
by the delegation of responsibility'.[41] As we will see in Part III however,
these invitations to participate did not mean that Indians were involved in
any of the key decisions of the central government of India.

The restructuring of imperial government after the 1857 Uprising was
not confined to its Indian component. The Uprising in India had revealed
the deficiencies of an imperial governmental edifice which relied upon
messengers scurrying between offices scattered across London, and
which stalled around tensions between Company and government, and
the Colonial Office and East India Company House. The Foreign
Office's delicate diplomacy had been critical to the passage of troops
through Ottoman territory and its personnel too, were frustrated by the
difficulties of coordination. During the multiple crises of 1857, as they
sought to mediate with the Ottoman Sultan and Egyptian Pasha,
Clarendon and his officials had also been preoccupied with Russia.
Even as he sought an alliance with the Tsar against the Qing Empire,
Clarendon was concerned about the Russian government seizing upon of
Britain's predicament in India to advance on its north-western frontier.
John Wodehouse, the British minister-plenipotentiary in St Petersburg
already had his work cut out trying to restore relations with a country with
whom Britain had been in a ruinous conflict only three years previously,
during the Crimean War. He admitted his difficulty in discerning Russian
intentions, describing the Tsarist court and government as impenetrable,
sustained by a notoriously complex and secretive governmental appar-
atus. In August 1857 Wodehouse strove to investigate rumours that
Russia had actively encouraged the Uprising in India. He had little luck.

Aleksandr Mikhailovich Gorchakov, the Russian foreign minister, was mildly offended when Wodehouse made preliminary enquiries. The British plenipotentiary lamented that 'the opportunities of obtaining intelligence at St Petersburg on the proceedings of Russia in the East are ... scanty; especially since the late war'.[42] Clarendon found that the reports from Warsaw, under Russian occupation, were more useful, if also more disturbing, than those from the Russian capital. The consul there, William A. White, explained that the Russians 'do not suppose that we shall be able to restore our authority [in India] for a long time' and that 'there are many men in Russia who are convinced that Asia will some day become the theatre of a bloody struggle between our two Empires ... and with such sentiments they view the dissolution of the Bengal Native Army as immensely in their favour'.[43]

As 1857 drew to a close, Clarendon and the Foreign Office were seeking to impress the need to take this Russian threat to India more seriously on the other governmental departments. Their concern would continue through the following decade, involving an ever more contentious role for the Ottoman Empire as the fragmenting bulwark against Russian expansion. Their anxiety would, as we will see in Part III, explode into warfare again in Afghanistan, in 1879. In the meantime, the Foreign Office, already in search of a new home in London, agreed that a more profound restructuring of imperial governance was called for, so as to enable better integration between its various offices.

King Charles Street

An opportunity to construct a new home for a more integrated imperial governance had already arisen in 1855, when the shabby and over-crowded Downing Street premises of the Foreign Office were condemned. The Crimean War had also revealed the deficiencies of organising a war from multiple offices scattered through London. The secretary of state for the colonies was still, technically, also the secretary of state for war, assisted by separate secretaries at war, who had to liaise with Army headquarters at Horse Guards and the Board of Ordnance during every military operation overseas. This latter department was headquartered at the Tower of London but with its main offices in Pall Mall. The severe problems with the supply of troops in the Crimea prompted the final separation of the functions of the Colonial and War Offices, and the amalgamation of army, ordnance and political leadership in a new War Department. The plan, in 1855, was that this new entity would find a discrete home in Whitehall alongside the relocated Foreign Office in a purposely planned building in King Charles Street.

In an episode known to architectural historians as the 'Battle of the Styles', a farcical architectural competition for the new building ensued. In 1856, Gilbert Scott, an architect of Gothic revival churches, an avid devotee of mediaeval ecclesiastical design and an acolyte of Pugin, one of the architects behind the new Houses of Parliament, entered the competition. He adopted the vogueish Gothic style that he would soon employ for the Midland Grand (now St Pancras) Hotel. He came third, but Palmerston set the results aside, not happy with any of the entries. After Palmerston was replaced by Derby (the first secretary of state for India, Lord Stanley's father) in February 1858, the vocal architectural community in support of the Gothic lobbied successfully for Scott's Gothic design to be adopted.

By then the War Office had found new accommodation in and around the former Board of Ordnance offices in Pall Mall. It was replaced as the Foreign Office's intended neighbour by the newly established India Office. Scott was expected to collaborate with the India Office's own surveyor, Matthew Digby Wyatt. Just as the two men were coming to agreement, in May 1859, Palmerston came back in as prime minister, still resolutely opposed to any new-fangled Gothicism. He insisted that Scott discard his plans in favour of a classical design. Throughout the year, the debate raged in Parliament and the press, with the winners of the original competition joining the prime minister's opposition to Scott's design. Scott attempted to compromise with an Italian-Byzantine design, which Palmerston dismissed as 'neither one thing nor t'other – a regular mongrel affair'.[44]

Scott later recalled that he 'bought some costly books on Italian architecture, and set vigorously to work to rub up what, though I had once understood pretty intimately, I had allowed to grow rusty by twenty years' neglect'. Ultimately, in the wake of the Uprising, he produced a classical design that met with Palmerston's approval. Work began in 1863 and by 1874, the Home and Colonial Offices had joined the Foreign and India Offices arranged around a central courtyard on a plot between Parliament Street and St James's Park, their corridors adjoining.[45] The interiors of the Home and Colonial Offices were utilitarian, but those of the Foreign and India Offices were much grander. The staterooms, an ambassadors' staircase and a grand reception room allowed the Foreign Office to become 'a kind of national palace, or drawing-room for the nation', as Scott's friend Beresford Hope put it.[46]

While Scott would go on to design Glasgow University and the Albert Memorial among other well-known Victorian Gothic structures, the India Office interior was left to Matthew Digby Wyatt. This part of the building is best known for what came to be called Durbar Court, an

Figure 9.1 The Durbar Court, Foreign and Commonwealth Office,
St James Street, London. Getty Images.

interior courtyard originally open to the sky, surrounded by three
storeys of columns, piers and arches of red and grey granite, and
paved with marble that was first used in 1867, appropriately enough
given the building's genesis, to receive the Ottoman Sultan
(Figure 9.1).

Just as the new secretary of state for India's Council was composed
largely of old East India Company men, so Wyatt brought something of
the Company with him to the fabric of the building in which they met. He
designed the interior to include the great doors and door cases, marble
chimneypiece and furniture from the former Director's Court Room at
Leadenhall Street. An overmantle centre panel from East India House
represented Britannia, seated by the sea, receiving the riches of the East
Indies. By the time of our third snapshot of British rule in 1879, the King
Charles Street building had become the home of a fully integrated imperial government.

Further Reading

Anderson, C., *Subaltern Lives: Biographies of Colonialism in the Indian
Ocean World, 1790–1920*, Cambridge University Press, 2012.

Bender, J. C., *The 1857 Indian Uprising and the British Empire*, Cambridge University Press, 2016.

Metcalf, T. R., *The Aftermath of Revolt: India, 1857–1870*, Princeton University Press, 1965.

Porter, B., *The Battle of the Styles: Society, Culture and the Design of a New Foreign Office, 1855–1861*, Continuum, 2011.

Robins, N., *The Corporation That Changed the World: How the East India Company Shaped the Modern Multinational*, Pluto Press, 2006.

Conclusion to Part II: An Empire of Civilisation?

The events which had their genesis around the year 1857 saw some 40 000 amaXhosa starve to death on the borders of the Cape Colony; around 2300 British and allied soldiers and 30 000 Chinese killed in the Second Opium War, and some 3000 British and more than 100 000 Indian soldiers killed in the Indian Uprising and its aftermath. Hundreds of thousands of civilian subjects of colour, whom the colonial authorities never counted, were killed by British forces in the 'Devil's wind' in India and the shelling and ransacking of Chinese towns and cities. What can only be described as British imperial hubris had played a major role in bringing about each of these simultaneous crises. These casualties were the unacknowledged cost of Britain's newly assertive, mid-Victorian, civilising mission – a mission more usually associated with the endeavours of the anti-slavery missionary-explorer David Livingstone, to whom we will return in Part III.

Incessant British settler lobbying for Xhosa land along the eastern frontier of the Cape Colony had been cunningly repackaged by the manipulative George Grey as one component of a well-considered, humane programme for the amalgamation of a people who needed salvation from their wretchedness: a salvation that Grey himself had already gifted the Aboriginal people of Australia and the Māori of New Zealand. In combination with the ravages of a bovine disease introduced from Europe, the loss of land and proven futility of either negotiated or armed resistance had produced such desperation among the amaXhosa that they resorted to an act of self-immolation in hope of spiritual assistance.

Grey's contemporary Bowring, meanwhile, had been primed by Palmerston and Clarendon to seek any opportunity to access China's consumers of opium and producers of tea, even before his personal ire was raised by a denial of access to Canton. Parkes, who was equally offended by the lack of respect to which he felt entitled, gave Bowring his excuse to humiliate the Qing authorities when the Taiping Rebellion rendered them weakest. When the affair of the *Arrow* was revealed to be a trumped up excuse for war, it mattered little to a British electorate aroused into a fit of patriotic loathing of 'Orientals' by Palmerston and his allies.

Confidence in their own ability to modernise for others' benefit, whether they liked it or not, also lay, to a great extent at least, behind the Uprising, in which Britons themselves were victims, in India. Breaking out in May and interrupting preparations for the Second Opium War, it was this crisis which threw the empire as a whole into jeopardy and called forth the restructuring of its government.

What do these overlapping crises of 1857 and the years immediately following tell us about the more systemic and gradual changes in Britain's attempts to rule the world? In particular, what do they indicate of the altered experiences of imperial subjects, rather than the intentions of governing men, since our first snapshot of 1838?

If we take the Indigenous peoples of the settler colonies first, Grey's programme of amalgamation, backed by Merivale at the Colonial Office, had firmly displaced the project of Protection that had been sponsored by George Arthur and James Stephen in the late 1830s. Protectorate and mission stations, the 'nurseries' where Indigenous subjects would be protected from settler encroachment and aggression until such time as they voluntarily joined the ranks of the Christian and 'civilised' world, were, by the 1850s, reserves in which so-called pure-blooded Aboriginal people were confined, while their 'half-caste' offspring were forcibly assimilated as the servants and labourers of white settlers. Canada's notorious Residential Schools and Australia's Stolen Generations were the fruits of these policies of amalgamation, each of them rationalised as being for the ultimate good of the individuals they targeted.

Grey's attempt similarly to amalgamate the black inhabitants of southern Africa encountered the problem of racial demographics. A minority settler society would be overwhelmed by the absorption of people of African descent. South Africa's British colonial governments would experiment instead with policies which mixed the attempted assimilation of a small African elite with the segregation and directed employment of the masses, who remained in managed reserves. We will return to the effects of the later mineral discoveries and industrialisation on these attempts in Part III.

As for the East India Company's Indian subjects, between 1838 and 1857 the screw had been turned ever more tightly. In 1838 they were already being taxed, either directly or indirectly, for the privilege of being governed by the Company's Directors in London. Many of them, however, still experienced the everyday governance of local elites nominally separate from the Company. By the 1850s they were taken for granted as providers of tribute to Company shareholders. After the experiments with indentured workers, they were also, along with Chinese, convenient suppliers of labour to the empire's plantations, partially replacing the apprenticed workers freed in 1838. Under Dalhousie, they were expected to be grateful for new and alien methods of governance, in return for the benefits of railways, which served British investors and manufacturers, schools which acculturated some of them to confined roles in the British administration, and a generally beneficial exposure to British civilisation. The Uprising indicated how many of these imperial subjects felt about their enforced 'civilisation'.

Part III

1879: The Year of Liberalism

10 Liberal Fathers and Sons

Patriotic British historians tell us that the 'progressive Whig agenda' of liberalism, which enfranchised more men, established the rule of law by separating the judiciary from the executive, and ensured the reform of prison, factory and educational conditions in nineteenth-century Britain, 'had to be offered to imperial subjects'. The British government apparently emphasised 'an ideology that sought to provide benefit to those under imperial sway, and this whether they were living in Britain or elsewhere in the empire'.[1] In reality, things were rather more complicated.

Given liberalism's ostensible universalism, it is easy to forget the role that the difference between coloniser and colonised played, both its formulation and its application. The jarring disjuncture between a rhetoric of liberal governance at home and a far more carefully distributed balance of rights and responsibilities across the British Empire, a balance in which race proved critical, is a key theme of our final 'snapshot' of imperial governance in 1879.

James Fitzjames Stephen: Britain, Jamaica and India

In 1865 James Fitzjames Stephen played a leading role in a test case of British liberalism in practice. The son of our central character of 1838, Colonial Office permanent under-secretary James Stephen, James Fitzjames had followed his father into the law. James Stephen described his son in 1846 as having 'more ability than I supposed, i. e. more power doing things. . . . He seems to have great self-reliance & ambition – qualities for which he is certainly not indebted to me'.[2] By the early 1860s Stephen jnr. had published an acclaimed analysis of British law, arguing that its overhaul was a critical part of the reformist utilitarian project. After the book's success, Stephen took on a momentous legal brief, when he accepted an invitation from John Stuart Mill to represent the Jamaica Committee. Mill had convened the committee in order to bring about the

275

prosecution of a British colonial governor for the extra-judicial murder of hundreds of black Jamaican British subjects. In accepting the committee's brief, Stephen would confront the legacy of his father's handling of emancipation in the Caribbean and help define the extent to which liberalism applied to imperial subjects of colour.

As we saw in Part I, in 1838, Stephen's father had insisted that Jamaica's planter-dominated Legislative Assembly adopt a non-racial franchise. Nevertheless, the island's white planters had since managed to exclude all but 2000 of some 450 000 black Jamaican men from the vote. Amidst Colonial Office equivocation, they had prevailed by predicating the franchise on the payment of a poll tax, which only a handful of the formerly enslaved population could afford to pay. The island's black population remained very largely landless, poverty stricken and disenfranchised.

In the early 1860s, cholera and smallpox had devastated black peasant communities who rented land, and in 1864, floods destroyed their crops. Residents of St Ann parish had addressed a petition to the Queen asking for access to Crown lands with low rents, so that they could form a company and sell their own produce. 'The Queen's Advice', actually written by Colonial Office under-secretary Henry Taylor, was widely disseminated around the island. Taylor himself was sympathetic to the petitioners, writing later that 'When a whole generation had grown up under this deprivation, the rebellion of 1865 followed naturally enough'.[3] However, his official response informed the former slaves and their immediate offspring that their 'prosperity ... depends ... upon their working for Wages ... steadily and continuously, at the times when their labour is wanted, and for so long as it is wanted'.[4] Jamaica's sugar plantations had lost markets in the USA during the Civil War, were being priced out of the British market by sugar produced in South American and Cuban slave plantations, and were now also being afflicted by drought. Opportunities for employment on the plantations were more limited than ever.

In early 1865, a number of black people seeking out land to cultivate were convicted for trespass on an abandoned sugar plantation in Morant Bay. A fight broke out in court between supporters of the defendants, including the black Baptist deacon, Paul Bogle and two policemen. The court issued arrest warrants for those involved. On 11 October 1865, Bogle helped lead a group of men and women in an attack on the police station, beating three policemen and taking their weapons. They then marched on the courthouse, gaining supporters on the way. The head magistrate, Baron von Ketelhodt, backed by a handful of local militiamen, ordered them to disperse. When an ever swelling crowd of protesters began throwing stones and attacking the courthouse, the militia opened fire. The protesters then set the court house on fire and killed Von Ketelhodt and seventeen others as they tried to escape. Over the next two days they burned the houses of several local officials and attacked neighbouring estates. This was the beginning of the Morant Bay Rebellion.

Jamaica's governor in 1865 was Edward John Eyre, a former Australian explorer, and a career colonial official whose trajectory had been bound up with George Grey's programme of amalgamation in the settler colonies.[5] Faced with a rebellion which, he claimed, threatened a 'second Haiti', he declared martial law in the Morant Bay district. Eyre's diagnosis of the rebellion aligned with Thomas Carlyle's assessment of black Jamaicans' character in the aftermath of emancipation. The distress which had caused the parishioners to riot had been 'induced by the genial nature of the climate, the facility of supplying their wants in ordinary seasons at comparatively little exertion and their natural disposition to indolence and inactivity, and to remain satisfied with what barely supplies absolute wants'. The riot itself was simply the expression of their tendency towards disorder and violence. Eyre sent in British troops and loyal Maroon allies to hunt down the rebels. Together, they inflicted a terror on the local population more concentrated in scale but similar in intensity to that in India after the Uprising. One of the soldiers admitted 'we slaughtered all before us ... man or woman or child'.[6]

Eyre's forces killed 439 nine black Jamaicans immediately, while magistrates sentenced 354 more, including Bogle, to peremptory execution under martial law. As troops burned down thousands of homes, the magistrates sentenced more than 600 black men and women to flogging, followed by long prison terms. George William Gordon, the parish representative in the Jamaican Assembly, a wealthy businessman and its only mixed race member, had previously written in support of the black petitioners. Eyre now had him arrested for inciting the riot. Gordon was seized in Kingston, but taken to Morant Bay so that he could be tried and executed immediately under martial law. Panicked by the possibility of losing control of the island to a black uprising, Eyre had come a long way since his role as Protector of Aborigines in South Australia.

When news of Eyre's reaction reached the Colonial Office, the permanent under-secretary, W. E. Forster, was both surprised and dismayed at the governor's brutality. With the British press reporting the rebellion and its suppression, prominent liberals were horrified. The legality of declaring martial law, permitting mass killing and transporting Gordon to a place where he could be executed without trial by jury, was questionable under any circumstances. It was especially dubious within a British society that liked to think of itself not only as exemplifying liberal governmental precepts, but also as exporting them through Empire.

Between 1865 and 1867, discussion of the Morant Bay rebellion and its suppression crystallised two related issues. The first was whether British colonial governments were subject to the rule of law, like Britain itself, or were still military autocracies. The second was whether the British Empire was premised on white people's subjugation of people of colour, or on a mission to improve the lives of colonial subjects, regardless of their race. The debate over Eyre' conduct helped Britons to determine quite explicitly whether the benefits of liberal governance really were to be offered to imperial subjects.

As the leading liberal of his day, John Stuart Mill established the Jamaica Committee precisely to test the issue. As well as James Fitzjames Stephen, Mill recruited prominent public figures including Charles Darwin, Thomas Henry Huxley, Charles Lyall, John Bright and Herbert Spencer. The fact that the leading proponents of evolutionary theory, Darwin, Huxley and Lyall, all sided with Mill prompted the *Pall Mall Gazette* to ask whether their 'peculiar views on the development of species have influenced them in bestowing on the negro that sympathetic recognition which they are willing to extend even to the ape as "man and a brother"'.[7] Thomas Fowell Buxton's son, Charles, who now headed the Aborigines Protection Society, was also a member of the Committee, embodying the support of the 'Exeter Hall' lobby. Stephen, determined to uphold the rule of law in Crown colonies just as his father had done, set about trying to prosecute Eyre for 'high crimes and misdemeanours'.

Despite his personal friendship with James Fitzjames Stephen, Thomas Carlyle responded by convening a rival lobby, the Governor Eyre Defence and Aid Committee. It matched Mill's for luminaries, although with more of a literary than a scientific bent. Charles Dickens, Charles Kingsley, John Ruskin, Alfred Tennyson and John Tyndall all joined Carlyle's committee, treating Eyre to a banquet upon his recall to London. The Defence and Aid Committee characterised Eyre as defender of law and order and the victim of a malicious humanitarian campaign. By prosecuting a governor for his defence of vulnerable colonists in desperate circumstances, Mill's committee, they argued, threatened to unleash the unbridled savagery of black colonial subjects against vulnerable white Britons, not just in Jamaica but across the British world. In May 1868, *Punch* relayed their sentiments:

Ye savages thirsting for bloodshed and plunder,
Ye miscreants burning for rapine and prey,
By the fear of the lash and the gallows kept under,
Henceforth who shall venture to stand in your way?
Run riot, destroy, ravage, kill without pity,
Let any man how he molests you beware,
Behold how hard the Jamaica Committee
To ruin are trying to hunt gallant Eyre.[8]

During the late 1860s, Carlyle and his allies won the contest for public opinion. Twice, grand juries refused to indict Eyre, and Stephen's cases against him never proceeded to trial. The Colonial Office was instructed quietly to pension the former governor off. Jamaica's Legislative Assembly dissolved itself so that the colony could be governed directly from London – an action which prevented people of colour from gaining greater influence in the Assembly.

The controversy over Morant Bay in Britain ran in parallel, and occasionally intersected, with protracted discussion of the 1867 Reform Act. Ultimately this doubled the male electorate of England and Wales by granting the vote to all householders and many lodgers in urban areas and reducing the property threshold in the countryside. The British electorate increased from roughly 1 million to 2 million. The *Spectator* summarised the thinking which enabled this simultaneous extension of rights to British working class men and condoning of black Jamaicans' extra-judicial murder:

The upper and middle class of the English people, especially the latter ... are positively enraged at the demand of negroes for equal consideration with Irishmen, Scotchmen, and Englishmen. ... We pardon Eyre because his error of judgment involves only negro blood, which would have otherwise been in our nation's eyes simply unpardonable.[9]

Despite his failure to secure Eyre's prosecution, James Fitzjames Stephen's role as the Jamaica Committee's lawyer had done nothing to dent his prospects. He maintained his friendship with Carlyle and others on the rival Defence and Aid Committee and in fact the episode lent him a new prominence. In 1869 he was appointed legal member of the Indian Viceroy's Council, succeeding to the role formerly held by Thomas Babington Macaulay. By 1879, Stephen was playing a leading role in defining which of Britain's legal principles applied to Indian, rather than black Jamaican, subjects. The three years he spent in Calcutta were 'a sort of second University course' in applied liberalism for Indians.[10]

When Stephen arrived in India he was struck by the tension between two different styles of governance, administered simultaneously in the aftermath of the Uprising. One was closer to the ideals that Britons were developing at home, and that many in the India Office believed should be implemented across the Indian Empire: the separation of executive and judicial powers, so that individuals had recourse to law when abused by government officials. In India this was known as the Regulation system, and it applied, in principle at least, to most of the areas directly governed in the presidencies. The other was the 'Non-Regulation' system that had been developed in the annexed Sind and then the Punjab, and which had been credited with helping to save British India during the Uprising. In this system British district officials combined executive and judicial functions. They were effectively, prosecutors, defenders, judges and juries: the personal embodiment of state authority. Stephen became a significant figure in Indian governance because of the way he merged these two systems according to utilitarian precepts and extended the hybrid result across India.

Stephen's review of the Indian judicial system continued the work begun by his predecessor in the role and great friend, Henry Maine. It was first published in 1872. In it he addressed the question of how 'an efficient rule of law' was to be attained 'without losing the unity, energy, and strength of the Non-Regulation system'. He adapted Jeremy Bentham's writings to conceive of law as part of a broader system of authority, concluding that, while the separation of executive and judicial powers was helpful to the exercise of liberal governance in some circumstances, including Britain's, it was not absolutely necessary. What was more important was that the law worked alongside executive power and to the same ends, while avoiding individual caprice of the kind that Eyre had displayed in Jamaica. 'The question', he wrote, 'is between one kind of law and legal administration and another, not between government by law and government without law'.

The problem with Punjab's system was not so much that its British officials held too much power, it was that the undivided responsibility led them to take on too much work. Stephen held that 'the maintenance of the position of the District Officers is absolutely essential to the maintenance of British rule in India ... any diminution in their influence and authority would be dearly purchased even by an improvement in the administration of justice'. His solution was to leave these British officials in charge of criminal justice, with a revised and simplified criminal code so that they could act more knowledgeably and consistently, but remove from them the administration of civil justice. This would be the responsibility of local magistrates, many of them Indians recruited into service in the aftermath of the Uprising, who would also have the responsibility of rent collection.[11]

In 1878, Stephen wrote to the *Times* explaining that 'there are things which it is much easier for 7 men to do than for 700, and that the direction

of the government of an empire is one of them'. He described his project
as 'the radical change of the ideas and institutions of a vast population
which has already got ideas and institutions to which it is deeply
attached'. The telegraph, by now embedded in everyday Indian administration, with the Persian Gulf cable connecting the India Office directly
with each of the presidencies, allowed Stephen to send his draft legal
codes back and forth between Calcutta and London, obtaining almost
instant ratification. India now became 'a scene of English law-making as it
had not been before'. By the time Stephen left India in 1872, the
Legislative Council in Calcutta had been left 'breathless and staggering,
conscious that they had accomplished unprecedented labours' in drawing
up and implementing entirely new criminal codes across the subcontinent. It was only Hindu and Muslim law dealing with inheritance and
wrongful liability that first Maine's and then Stephen's reforms had left
untouched.[12] In 1879, enforcement of Stephen's law codes was entirely
dependent on Indian policemen, record keepers and magistrates,
employed in a vastly expanded Indian Civil Service and trained in the
universities that Canning had fostered after the Uprising. But Indians
were trusted neither to govern nor to make those laws.

Most fundamentally, the reason that the full extent of Britain's liberal
system could not be applied to India – the reason that it was necessary to
deny Indians self-government and to waive the distinction between
executive and judicial power there – was that Indian subjects were considered fundamentally different from Britons. Stephen himself had first
hinted at this in his seminal *General View of the Criminal Law* in England.
Questioning the utility of swearing a religious oath in court, he noted, 'I
suppose that no one of ordinary common sense would prefer the evidence
of a Chinese or Hindoo, untested by cross-examination, but guaranteed
by an oath . . . to that of an English atheist, tested by cross-examination'.[13]

Following his experience in India, Stephen felt that the combined
executive and judicial power of District Officers allowed justice to be
'plainly dealt out to simple people, unused to the intricacies of legal
proceeding'. 'If it be asked how the system works in practice', he wrote,

I can only say that it enables a handful of unsympathetic foreigners (I am far
from thinking that if they were more sympathetic they would be more efficient)
to rule justly and firmly about 200,000,000 persons of many races, languages
and creeds, and in many parts of the country, bold, sturdy and warlike. . . . The
Penal Code, the Code of Criminal Procedure, and the institutions which they
regulate, are somewhat grim presents for one people to make to another, and
are little calculated to excite affection; but they are eminently well-calculated to
protect peaceable men and to beat down wrongdoers, to extort respect, and to
enforce obedience. . . . If, however, the authority of the Government is once

materially relaxed, if the essential character of the enterprise is misunderstood and the delusion that it can be carried out by assemblies representing the opinions of the natives is admitted, nothing but anarchy, and ruin can be the result.[14]

The *Pax Britannica* of the late nineteenth century – a term which Stephen himself helped to popularise with a treatise on the Roman foundations of British law and order – was founded on this distinction between liberal, utilitarian, British law dispensers and colonised Indian recipients.[15] This, indeed, was the very foundation of the Raj, the post-East India Company British government of India. At the beginning of 1878, Stephen wrote to the *Times* that 'British Power in India is like a vast bridge over which an enormous multitude of human beings are passing, and will (I trust) for ages to come continue to pass, from a dreary land, in which brute violence in its roughest form had worked its will for centuries – a land of cruel wars, ghastly superstitions, wasting plague and famine – on their way to a country ... which is at least orderly, peaceful, and industrious'.[16] At the very time he wrote these words, a heavily indebted Raj was presiding over the worst famine in living memory.

Mahmood Kahn and the Great Famine

The British Indian government's debt and the causes of the famine were interconnected. Rhomesh Chunder Dutt, the Indian Civil Service-trained magistrate and future leader of the Indian National Congress (and University College London historian), would later explain how. European banks' move to the gold standard had caused a collapse of silver prices, on which the Raj based its currency. Although the Indian and British economies were intimately intertwined, the Indian loan market was essentially sovereign, so any risk was borne by the Indian state, and not London financiers. Its main source of revenue was still the rent charged to Indian subjects. The property values upon which rent was based had not been reassessed since the cotton boom of the 1860s, a time when the US South had all but suspended its production and Indian producers had been able partially to fill the gap.[17] American reconstruction brought about an enduring slump thereafter, but the taxes levied by the British government failed to reflect the decline in Indian producers' income. As had been the case with previous famines, the Great Famine of 1877–8 was caused when an environmental trigger – in this case an intense drought resulting in crop failure in the Deccan Plateau – pushed a population already rendered precarious by this restriction of income across the threshold of starvation.[18]

Starting in south and south-western India in 1876, famine spread to the Central and the North-Western Provinces and to part of the Punjab by 1878. As the Legislative council in Calcutta was building Stephen's 'bridge' to a better world, food shortages afflicted 59 million people and caused the death by starvation of around 5.5 million of them.

A new viceroy had arrived in India just as the famine began. Edward Robert Bulwer, first earl of Lytton, was a conservative diplomat and poet (apparently Queen Victoria's favourite), who published under the name of Owen Meredith. Lytton was a forceful and autocratic character who admitted to bearing the scars of the very public and abusive relationship between his parents. His father was the novelist Edward Bulwer Lytton. His mother, Rosina Anne Doyle Wheeler (Bulwer after her marriage), was also a well-known writer, popular for novels which attacked his father.

Lytton's father had begun to commit domestic violence soon after their marriage, while also conducting a series of affairs. After Rosina flirted with a Neapolitan prince, Edward had drawn up an agreement to separate, which demanded that Rosina be parted from the couple's daughter and son, the future viceroy. Lytton's sister, passed by her father from one governess to another, had died soon afterwards. Except for four months in 1858, when he tried and failed to live with his mother in France, Lytton had never seen her again, although he was exposed periodically to his parents' ongoing conflict. Rosina's novels *Cheveley, or, The Man of Honour* (1839) and *The Budget of the Bubble Family* (1840) 'ridiculed Bulwer Lytton's family'. When Bulwer's play, *Not so Bad as we Seem*, premiered in 1851, Rosina wrote to Prince Albert threatening to pelt Queen Victoria with rotten eggs if she attended, and pasted up playbills around Devonshire House advertising the play *Even Worse than we Seem* by 'Sir Liar-Coward Bulwer Lytton, who has translated his poor daughter into Heaven, and nobly leaves his wife to live on public charity'. As Bulwer Lytton embarked on a promising political career at the Hereford hustings in 1858, Rosina burst out of the audience declaring him 'a monster who should ... have been transported to the colonies long ago for mistreating his wife and murdering his daughter'. Edward reacted by having Rosina committed to a private asylum, but a press campaign resulted in her being released within a month.[19]

Lord Derby would later comment of the capricious and opium addicted viceroy, 'When a man inherits insanity from one parent, and limitless conceit from the other, he has a ready-made excuse for almost any extravagance which he may commit'.[20] When Disraeli appointed Lytton to India, he explained to Queen Victoria that he was a man of 'ambition, imagination, some vanity, and much will'.[21] That will was manifested especially in Lytton's adherence to free trade doctrine. He arrived in Calcutta after conducting a series of trade agreements on behalf of the British government within Europe, and with a fixed determination to solve the Raj's debt problem by rendering 'India one of the most advanced free-trading economies in the world'.[22]

Overruling his Executive Council, Lytton immediately repealed duties on cotton imports and reformed the customs and excise system as extensively as Stephen had reformed the law. While some at the India Office thought that this was pushing liberal ideas too far, given the vulnerability of Indians to external market conditions, Lytton was certainly not averse to anti-liberal measures. He prohibited the freedom of the vernacular Indian press as soon as it started to notice his lack of attention to the famine crisis, and ordered that the press and paper of any newspaper publishing 'seditious' content be confiscated. As starvation spread in 1877, Lytton proclaimed the first success of his free trade initiative: a record 320 000 ton of wheat exports to feed Britain.

In 1874, the lieutenant governor of Bengal, Sir Richard Temple, had been criticised for responding to a famine in Bihar by importing grain from Burma. In Britain and in the Australian colonies, his expenditure on charitable relief was reported not so much as preventing loss of life on a much greater scale, but more as indulging idleness and encouraging dependency. When newspapers carried engravings of hundreds of bags of grain and rice left rotting on rail platforms, Temple was disgraced and ridiculed.[23] By 1877, Temple was famine commissioner for the government of India. The new famine presented him with an opportunity to redeem his reputation for judicious government. With Lytton's encouragement, Temple reduced the rations for those employed on government work schemes so that they 'provided less sustenance for hard labour than the diet inside the infamous Buchenwald concentration camp and less than half of the modern calorific standard recommended for adult males by the Indian government'.[24]

Beyond the work camps, which became effectively death camps, Lytton and Temple restricted 'charitable' relief to small children, the elderly and the indigent. Much of the funding for this came not from the Indian government itself but from the first fundraising campaign using photographic images of starving children, mobilised in Britain and the Australian colonies by an appeal from the Colonial Office.[25] In 1877, as far as Lytton and Temple were concerned, 'everything must be subordinated to the financial consideration of disbursing the smallest sum of money'. Commerce alone was the 'universal benefactor' for those in need.[26] When, in early 1877, Temple declared that he had put 'the famine under control', a British journalist commented that it was only because 'one-fourth of the people [are] dead'.[27]

One of the many Indians to pick up on the contradiction between British assertions of their 'bridge to progress' and the reality of mass starvation in 1879, was Syed Mahmood. Mahmood was the son of Syed Ahmed Kahn, whom we met in Part II advising the East India Company how it could have avoided the Indian Uprising (see Figure 8.1). Mahmood had been encouraged by his father to study at Cambridge, where his tutor had been the first professional historian of the British Empire, John Robert Seeley. Upon his return to India, Mahmood would rise through the ranks of the judiciary to become one of the most senior judges enforcing James Fitzjames Stephen's new legal codes. In the 1870s, he was seeking to continue his father's work of mediating between British rulers and Indian subjects. Writing in the *Calcutta Review*, the twenty-nine-year-old Mahmood reminded Lytton's government, just as had his father, that British authority depended on 'native agency, native friendship, native counsels, native valour'. The British had only come to govern India, he insisted, as a result of having being invited by Indians frustrated with the violent instability of the late Mughal regime. They must cease seeing themselves as conquerors and govern 'with the consent of the country'.[28]

Syed Mahmood was part of what, by the late 1870s, was a long tradition of Indian intellectuals' comment on the adaptation of British liberal principles. In the post-Uprising years a 'culture of letters' had developed among Indian elites, who demanded that they too should benefit from their British rulers' much-vaunted liberal achievements, including a free press, freedom of Assembly and the right to criticise government. These, they argued, were vehicles to express their loyalty and their dedication to improving the nation, alongside the British government.[29]

A similar attempt to adopt some of the features of liberal governance was being made by some of India's princely rulers, who governed about a third of the subcontinent under their Resident Agents' oversight. In 1879 Maharaja Sayajirao Gaekwar III, for instance, was in the midst of programme of reform in the state of Baroda. Together with his Dewan or prime minister, Sir T. Madhavarao, he was investing the state's tax revenues in railways connecting with the wider Raj network, the expansion of industry, the founding of the Bank of Baroda and the education and literacy of Baroda's men and women to prepare them for greater participation in government.

However, Sayajiro was not alone in beginning to feel that he couldn't win with the Raj. While applauding his adoption of the principles it preached, Lytton's government was interfering in Baroda's economic policy. In part as a response to the Raj's indebtedness, Lytton had continued a policy of taking many of the princely states' salt pans under direct control. Despite his adherence to free trade when it came to dealing with the famine, he continued to restrict princely states' imports and exports of the staple. All were coerced into paying British excise taxes. By 1879, Madhavarao was lamenting that British Salt Department officials were frustrating his plans for modernisation by ignoring Baroda's self-determination. He complained, 'I feel it is my duty to state that I earnestly, but respectfully, deprecate British officials and British servants entering Baroda territories as a matter of course, making any searches, seizing any persons or seizing any property on the grounds of an infraction of British salt rules, and demanding the extradition of the persons seized for trial and punishment by the British Magistracy'.[30]

Madhavarao called the Raj out upon its own ideas of 'good government' and 'public welfare', noting that Baroda's government could only do what could be 'reasonably expected … consistently with the well-being of its subjects and the integrity of its internal administration'.[31] Impacting most directly upon the mass of India's poorest people, British salt taxation would go on to become the foremost grievance articulated by Gandhi in his first satyagraha campaign.[32]

In 1883, the notorious Ilbert Bill controversy would enable Britons in India to assert their right to trial by a jury of Europeans rather than Indians. In an effort to ameliorate Indians' fury at such explicit judicial racism, Syed Mahmood would be promoted to become the first Indian supreme court, or puisne judge. Within eight years, however, he had been sacked. Mahmood would claim that the erratic, drunken behaviour causing his dismissal was provoked by his constant belittling at the hands of the other, British, judges. The elderly Syed Ahmed Kahn, however, was relieved by his son's dismissal. By 1879, this former ally and adviser to the British Indian government had come to appreciate that Indians, no matter how well qualified, would never be accorded equal treatment under the Raj.

Integrated Imperial Governance

If the supposedly universal liberal doctrines of law and governance were being extended to Indians only in a codified, authoritarian and racially discriminatory way in 1879, what of the broader empire? Had the denial of equality under the law to black Jamaicans in 1865, been superseded by the extension of liberalism's benefits to those administered by the Colonial Office? In principle a more integrated imperial government could have allowed the more uniform implementation of a reformist agenda. The main elements of imperial governance – the Colonial Office, India Office and Foreign Office – were by now all arrayed around the central courtyard of Scott's grand if, somewhat architecturally compromised, building in St James Street.[33] The dysfunction of messengers from the Colonial Office, East India House and Board of Control premises scurrying through London's streets was a thing of the past. If the clerks of the Colonial Office, in receipt of a telegram from a governor, wished to consult with their counterparts in the India Office or Foreign Office, they need only walk along a corridor. In 1867, Wyatt had prepared sketches detailing the India Office wing's new communication system. They gave 'the impression of an intricate neural network' with messenger boxes, bells and speaking tubes its nodes and neurons. The system was 'designed to put the secretary of state in direct contact with other members of the Council and their senior civil servants ... permitting ... "hour by hour" consultation on matters of "the most immediate urgency"'.[34]

The officials in each of these interconnected offices had a more uniform educational background than ever before, based in part on a shared understanding of liberal political economy. In 1854, facing 'the great and increasing accumulation of public business, and the consequent pressure on the Government', the Northcote–Trevelyan report had insisted upon a standardised and meritocratic process for the recruitment of some 16 000 civil servants across all government departments.[35] Northcote and Trevelyan's primary intention was to weed out those 'of indolence of temperament' who had been appointed solely by virtue of their familial and social connections. But another of their ambitions was to 'mitigate the evils which result from the fragmentary character of the Service, and to introduce into it some elements of unity'. By 1879, the effects of their ensuing reforms had filtered through to all the offices of imperial governance. A cadre of young men, with 'discipline' and the 'cultivation of regular habits' staffed all but the higher levels of the service, their understanding 'of history, jurisprudence, political economy, modern languages, political and physical geography' having been examined.[36]

At the India Office, the new under-secretary, Sir Louis Mallet, was determined to 'put an end to the comparatively easy-going days of the Company'. Mallet complained to the secretary of state for India, Lord Salisbury, about the 'laxity' which, twenty years after the Northcote–Trevelyan Report, had been 'allowed to grow up in this office'. He shared Northcote and Trevelyan's view that 'the public service was more important than its servants ... the personality of an official should be vigorously and systematically suppressed' by his impersonal functions.[37] The Colonial Office was also slow to respond, but bowed to pressure from the Treasury to allow the competitive recruitment of its staff in the early 1870s. At the same time, the number of clerks increased from around thirty to sixty-three, reorganised hierarchically into two divisions. The upper division was now devoted entirely to 'intellectual' work within two large geographical departments as well as one general one, the function of which was to consider the needs of the empire as a whole.[38] Contemporaries noted how many of this new cadre had come through Eton school. Their background lent them a 'moveable character' so that they could relocate along the corridors of the St James Street building from one department to another as required, just as Herman Merivale had moved from the Colonial to the India Office in 1859.[39]

Merivale had also left his legacy for the more systematic accumulation of intelligence and data from India. In the early 1870s, Clements Markham, a former Royal Navy explorer who had carried seeds of the cinchona tree from Peru to India so that antimalarial quinine could be made available there, complained to Merivale that, without a separate Geographical Department, the task of governing India through a professional bureaucracy in London was hopeless. His point was proved when the India Office tried to make comparisons about the way that revenue was extracted in different parts of India during the 1860s and found that it lacked any reliable data. Markham told Merivale that, 'in the interests of all departments, there should be a special geographical branch to furnish that local information, without which accuracy is not possible'. When the India Office moved into its new premises alongside the Colonial and Foreign Offices, Markham was permitted to create his new department. Merivale instructed that 'all correspondence on geographical subjects, exploration, the geological surveys, and all annual reports, maps, plans and charts received from India' be sent to him. Copies of Markham's maps were in turn presented to the Royal Geographical Society, the Royal Botanic Gardens at Kew, the Privy Council Office for the use of the Judicial Committee, the War Office, the British Museum and the Radcliffe Camera at Oxford. From 1872 he began editing the *Geographical Magazine* as a source of departmental information.[40]

Markham's vision of a panoptical department that could furnish officials in London with any data on India 'within ten minutes' never came to pass. His proposals were ruled out as simply too expensive by the India Office's Statistics and Commerce committee, but he did significantly contribute to a far more impersonal knowledge base, from which the new corps of bureaucrats could work. At the India Office, this knowledge base came progressively to supplant the personal experience of the old Company men.[41] At the Colonial Office, combined with new communications technology, it partially freed officials from the monopoly of knowledge traditionally exercised by governors on the spot.

Communications from the colonies were being processed not only more rapidly but also more uniformly by the late 1870s. On arrival at St James Street, despatches would be provided with a printed cover-sheet, which performed several functions. It enabled the despatch to be classified with an assigned number, a note as to which other despatches it related to, and a summary of its origin and subject matter. As the despatch moved up through the office's hierarchy, it was stamped on various employees' desks, a string of minutes, usually a paragraph or two long, accumulating on the way. The system enabled secretaries, undersecretaries, assistant undersecretaries and chief clerks to contribute to draft responses, sometimes in an orderly line of precedence and sometimes in something rather more like a back-and-forth colloquy. Each contributor marked their intervention with their initials. The offices of imperial governance now functioned with a workaday intimacy, and a bureaucratic sharing of responsibility that had been lacking in our earlier snapshots.

All of the officials at St James Street also now benefitted, in theory at least, from 'a revolutionary alteration of the base of communications itself'.[42] The advent of steamships had altered the pace and regularity of maritime communication, but it had not fundamentally disrupted the way that James Stephen had organised the Colonial Office's bureaucratic rhythm. As we have seen, this was a rhythm based on the periodic arrival of mailbags from the colonies, their consideration and deliberation and the bundling of responses in mailbags assigned to ships heading for particular colonies. 'The great dividing point was the telegraph'. Just coming into systematic use by the Foreign Office and East India Company around the time of the Indian Uprising, the problems of subsea cabling had, as we have noted, caused a lag in Colonial Office adoption until the 1860s. But by the late 1870s, telegraphic 'abstractions from reality arrived and departed quickly, irregularly, and unpredictably'. The Colonial Office now employed a clerk on night duty in case it was notified of a colonial emergency in real time. Although mailbags of despatches continued to arrive in the office, providing officials with the fuller context for previously telegraphed snippets, the effect of additional and routine telegraphic communication was to increase the productivity of the office's expanded staff.[43] The telegraphic network, however, was still highly uneven, linking some but not all colonies directly to London. Southern Africa in particular was lagging behind, and this would prove crucial to the pattern of events in 1879. Elsewhere, the better connected diplomats and governors now expected responses to urgent queries within hours rather than weeks.

The India Office was well connected by both overland and subsea cable to the Indian presidencies by now, but its staff, as well as those of the Colonial Office, benefitted additionally from the Suez Canal. The old problem of the logistics of transit across the Isthmus of Suez had finally been solved. Now, the problem was how to control this geopolitically vital axis of communication. Despite its being a French – Egyptian collaboration, it was Britain which had the greatest interest in the operation of the canal. By 1875, British ships accounted for around 80 per cent of those traversing it. Disraeli was particularly keen to acquire British government shares in the Suez Canal Company and his opportunity came in 1875 when Ismail, the indebted Khedive of Egypt, sought to sell his 44 per cent share. The British prime minister swiftly intervened, asking Lionel de Rothschild to raise the necessary funds. Just as Nathan Rothschild had assisted in raising the loan for slave owners' compensation payments in 1834, so his son obliged the British government again in 1875. Despite still owning only a minority stake, Disraeli purportedly told Queen Victoria, 'it is settled; you have it, madam!'[44]

Colonial interlocutors with the staff in St James Street were not only better connected in 1879 than they had ever been before; they had also proliferated. In 1862 there had been 1574 senior officials corresponding with the Colonial Office from the Crown colonies. By 1871 there were 2423. This larger, and still growing, pool of senior civil officials was now drawn upon to recruit colonial governors in preference to military and political appointees. By the 1870s, colonial appointments 'resembled a great game of musical chairs' with vacancies increasing 'in Africa, the Malay States and the Pacific' as new protectorates were created and annexations declared.[45]

By 1879, then, there was an entity in St James Street which resembled a unitary 'imperial government'. It was staffed by rigorously recruited bureaucrats who shared certain educational attainments and a view of the world, or as Robinson and Gallagher put it, an 'official mind', shaped by the principles of liberal political economy.[46] These men were better connected to those governing on Britain's behalf in India and in the Crown and self-governing settler colonies, and they shared a similar background with them. In principle, it would have been feasible for this more integrated imperial government to export Britain's liberal dispensation more uniformly around the world. Indeed, many of the officials in London, and many governors too, were proponents of an idealised liberalism and believed in Britain's responsibility to promote it. They believed that the British Empire, which had helped Britons themselves to attain their uniquely advanced political dispensation, stood in stark distinction from the more brutal and authoritarian 'Oriental' empires of the Mughals

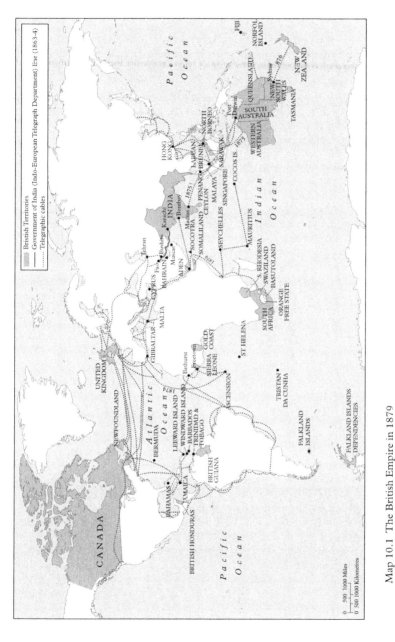

Map 10.1 The British Empire in 1879

Legend:
- British Territories
- Government of India (Indo-European Telegraph Department) line (1863–4)
- Telegraphic cables

Places labelled on map:

CANADA

UNITED KINGDOM
NEWFOUNDLAND
BERMUDA
BAHAMAS
BRITISH HONDURAS
JAMAICA
LEEWARD ISLAND
WINDWARD ISLAND
BARBADOS
TRINIDAD & TOBAGO
BRITISH GUIANA

Atlantic Ocean
Pacific Ocean

GIBRALTAR
MALTA
CYPRUS
BAHRAIN
Teheran
Bushire
Fao
Muscat
ADEN
SOCOTRA
SOMALILAND

GOLD COAST
SIERRA LEONE
Freetown
Bathurst
ASCENSION
ST HELENA
TRISTAN DA CUNHA
FALKLAND ISLANDS
FALKLAND ISLANDS DEPENDENCIES

SOUTH AFRICA
ORANGE FREE STATE
BASUTOLAND
SWAZILAND
S. RHODESIA
MAURITIUS
SEYCHELLES

INDIA
Karachi
Bombay
Madras
CEYLON
PENANG
MALAYA
SINGAPORE
COCOS IS.
NORTH BORNEO
BRUNEI
SARAWAK
LABUAN
HONG KONG

Indian Ocean
Pacific Ocean

SOUTH AUSTRALIA
WESTERN AUSTRALIA
QUEENSLAND
NEW SOUTH WALES
Port Darwin
Sydney
TASMANIA
NEW ZEALAND
NORFOLK ISLAND
FIJI

1875
1874
1871
1876

0   500   1000 Miles
0   500   1000 Kilometres

and Ottomans, and also from the more self-interested empires of France, Germany and the Netherlands, precisely because of its essentially liberal foundations.

This widespread belief – that the British Empire *should* be different – was why, two years beforehand, Disraeli had acceded only reluctantly to Queen Victoria's request to be declared 'Empress of India'. His discomfort was due to the title's association with ancient and Continental empires founded on conquest, plunder and autocracy. The debate over the Queen's new title had prompted British newspapers to hold their noses and apply the word 'imperialism' for the first time to British politics. It denoted something 'un-English and particularly resonant of the tawdry glitter of the regime of Napoleon III'. Britain's politicians, civil servants and colonial appointees had more progressive aspirations. Although the parliamentary bill conferring Victoria's new title was passed, Disraeli's patronage of it temporarily 'shattered [his] authority in the House of Commons', while Lytton's glittering and expensive celebration of it at the Delhi Durbar of 1877 contrasted obscenely with the simultaneous starvation of millions.[47]

When contemporary historians assert that the advantages of British liberalism were disseminated to Britain's imperial subjects, they capture the expressed desire of many of the men governing the empire in 1879. The problem with which they, like Stephen in India, had to grapple in reality, however, was liberalism's transferability to places where British government was not by its subjects' consent. Above all, liberalism was confined and adulterated where subject peoples were considered too backward to manage its responsibilities. This was an issue which pertained closer to home, in Ireland, too. The fissure that would split the Liberal Party within a decade was already developing in the late 1870s as parliamentarians debated the extent to which Catholic Irish men were eligible to govern themselves through home rule. While distinguishing white Irish in other respects from colonial subjects of colour, many Britons believed that they too, were incapable of self-government.[48] In 1879, the Colonial Office was grappling with the same problem across the broader empire, where the rights of millions of colonised people of colour were at issue, with one eye on the Home Office's handling of Ireland (Map 10.1).

One subset of the colonial population was clearly considered eligible for liberalism in full. British settlers (including many from Ireland) in the Canadas, Australasia and southern Africa had been developing the institutions of self-governance since 1838, and most had by now surpassed Britain in the generosity of their franchise. By 1879, elected assemblies with varying, largely property-based, franchises were taking the majority of governmental decisions in most settler colonies, with only nominal oversight from Colonial Office-appointed governors. Indigenous peoples' participation, however, was for the most part denied.

In the Australian colonies Aboriginal people were not necessarily explicitly barred from voting, but it was widely assumed that they would not participate in elections. In instances where Aboriginal men turned up to vote, it was up to local officials to decide upon their eligibility. 'Yellow Jimmy', a so-called half-caste resident of New South Wales, tried to do so in 1859 for instance. He was prosecuted for impersonating a white settler.[49] In the Cape Colony there were enough electors among the Eastern Cape's successful Mfengu and converted Khoisan peasantry to sway the results in six parliamentary constituencies. There was already concern among white electors that any further growth of this portion of the electorate should be limited.[50] In New Zealand, Māori men had been allowed to vote for four 'special' parliamentary seats of their own at the same time that the franchise was extended to working men in Britain, in 1867. In proportion to their population, they should have had fifteen.

In Canada, First Nations men who wanted to vote had to apply for exemption from their 'Indian' status in accordance with the assimilationist policies that Grey and Merivale had sponsored in the 1850s. Even in the long colonised eastern regions, few were willing to make the necessary sacrifices of giving up traditional ways, disassociating from kin and acquiring private property. In the north-west in 1879, the fiercely independent Lakota leader Sitting Bull, who had defeated General Custer at the Battle of Little Big Horn three years beforehand, was living on the Canadian side of the border with some 4000 displaced Sioux. Canada's governor-general, the Marquis of Lorne, feared that the competition for scarce resources, especially with the Buffalo dying out, might cause 'disturbances seriously compromising the two Governments' of Canada and the USA.[51] For his part, Sitting Bull declared that 'I will remain what I am until I die, a hunter, and when there are no buffalo or other game, I will send my children to hunt and live on prairie mice, for when an Indian is shut up in one place his body becomes weak'.[52] While the British and American authorities continued to wrangle over who was responsible for Sitting Bull and on what terms he might return to the USA, the Canadian government continued to try to persuade its own First Nations to become farmers and 'amalgamate' on terms that were unacceptable not only to Sitting Bull, but to the vast majority of its own First Nations.

As in India, distinctions and qualifications defined the Crown colonies' liberal order. The result was ideological dissonance. On occasion, the

Colonial Office would hold firmly that Britain's own liberal governmental principles were universal. In March 1879, for instance, it received a recommendation from the Port Louis Prison Committee in Mauritius. Responding to a 'dangerous spirit of insubordination' on the island, the Committee proposed that public beheading be reintroduced as a form of capital punishment, but specifically for Indians. There were, apparently, special circumstances relating to the 'peculiarities of Indian character' associated with Mauritius' decades of indentured labour settlement, which rendered the racial discrimination reasonable. 'The Indian' in Mauritius, the Chair of the Committee explained, 'is certainly not afraid of death' *per se*. 'He is prepared to die, provided that his identity is not destroyed by any form of mutilation'. Beheading would be 'far more impressive upon the lower classes of the Community' than the hanging currently employed for others in the colony.[53] The permanent under-secretary of state at the Colonial Office, Robert George Wyndham Herbert, responded with disgust. Beheading, he pointed out, was a practice inherited from the French, 'which did not very long survive after our possession' of Mauritius.[54] He instructed that the colony should adopt the system of private execution that was consistent with Britain's own colour-blind judicial order.

Things were not always so clear cut, however. Explicitly or implicitly, racialised punishments continued in British colonies, especially where British settlers made their own law. South Australia had reintroduced public hanging at the scene of the crime, for Aboriginal people but not for settlers, in 1861. Western Australia followed suit in 1875. In May 1879 the Executive Council of New South Wales responded to a public outcry at the death sentence passed on two white youths for rape. Since 1863, thirty-seven men had been sentenced to death for rape in the colony, of whom two had been Aboriginal. Only three men had actually been executed, however, including both the Aboriginal men. The only white man to be executed had murdered his victim after raping her. At the time of the white youths' conviction in 1879, another Aboriginal man named Alfred was also awaiting execution for rape, and the Executive Council decided to hang all three together. A public meeting attracting 3000 liberal colonists adopted a petition 'pleading for the remission of all three sentences, on the grounds that the death sentence for rape had been abolished in the United Kingdom, and that mercy was required in view of the youth of the two Europeans, and the "extreme ignorance" of the "poor wretched aboriginal"'. In response, the New South Wales government granted a postponement of sentence on the white youths to 17 June 1879. Alfred also had his execution postponed, but only until 10 June. As his counsel pointed out, there was a very real danger that the government would concede to the mounting campaign to save the white youths between 10 and 17 June, leaving only Alfred to be executed in the meantime. This was precisely what happened. The tradition of executing only Aboriginal men for the offence of rape, even within an ostensibly colour-blind judicial system, was continued when Alfred was hanged and then the two white youths' sentences were commuted to life imprisonment.[55]

Herbert and Carnarvon: 'Greater Britain' and Confederation

The gap between British metropolitan liberal rhetoric and racist colonial practice ran like a seam through the career of the man who forbade the beheading of Indians in Mauritius. Unlike his predecessors, James Stephen and Herman Merivale, Robert George Wyndham Herbert, permanent under-secretary of the Colonial Office in 1879, had direct experience of colonial governance. He was part of the generation of Etonians 'to capture the civil service "by storm"', starting his governmental career as private secretary to Gladstone.[56] When Queensland had been carved off as a separate colony from New South Wales in 1859, Herbert had emigrated as secretary to its first governor. Queensland's settler men were granted representative government immediately, with a property qualification of £100, and Herbert was dependent for his position upon being elected by them. Not only did he succeed; he soon became the Legislative Assembly's first premier, aged only twenty-eight.

Herbert's tenure as an Australian prime minister was focused on the mutually reinforcing objectives of encouraging further British emigration to the new colony, facilitating settlers' appropriation of Aboriginal peoples' land on the north coast, diversifying the colony's economy and establishing the financial basis for its sound government. Between 1859 and 1866, when he stepped down as premier, thousands of Aboriginal people were murdered in massacres across the colony. They were conducted largely by Native police on behalf of British settlers 'clearing' the land to establish ownership and plantation. In one incident in 1865 alone, about 300 Kullila men, women and children were killed at Ardoch. Aboriginal people resisting or simply obstructing 'settlement' were killed in numbers ranging between seven and seventy in at least twelve different massacres during Herbert's premiership.[57]

It was not only land that Herbert had helped secure for Britons at any price, but also labour. The permanent under-secretary had laid the foundations for the notorious 'Blackbirding' industry. While backing the democratic rights of propertied white men, he accepted that plantation work, including on his own cotton estate, was properly conducted by disenfranchised 'Malays and other black labour'. The trade in Pacific Islander labour for Queensland's northern plantations began under Herbert's premiership in 1863, when Robert Towns seized men from the Loyalty Islands and New Hebrides to grow cotton, supplying part of the global deficit brought on by the US Civil War. Herbert granted Towns large land leases enabling him to found the town and port of Townsville in the far north, where he put Pacific Islanders, generally recruited under false pretences, traded or directly taken captive, to work. French officials in New Caledonia complained to Herbert that the ships sent out to recruit labourers for Queensland kidnapped half the inhabitants of one village under their protection. In 1868, further scandals revealing the extent of this new slave trade forced Herbert's government to pass the Polynesian Labourers Act, requiring the licensing of recruiting ships and the observation of their recruitment by government agents. With the agents sharing in the bonuses paid for 'recruits', the legislation proved largely ineffective.[58]

By 1865, Herbert was 'weary and sick and disgusted with colonial politics', not because of its toll for Aboriginal and Pacific Islander people, but because of the vociferous opposition from those whom he called the 'drunken and unwashed' among disenfranchised settlers. In search of a 'taste of civilisation', he had left Australia to become assistant secretary at the Board of Trade in London, moving to the Colonial Office shortly afterwards. By 1879 his responsibilities included 'political and constitutional questions, general supervision, [and] papers on all subjects before submission to Secretary of State'.[59]

Herbert was strongly influenced in his new role at the centre of imperial governance by two men in particular. The first was the most popular writer on the British Empire of the day, the radical Charles Wentworth Dilke. The son of a baronet, Dilke had inherited substantial property and income from his father, an organiser of the Great Exhibition, and his mother, the daughter of a Madras Cavalryman. After flirting with a career in law, Dilke embarked on a self-funded tour of North America in 1866, which he then extended into a round-the-world trip, with sojourns in New Zealand, Australia, India and Egypt. His rumination on the scope, nature and purpose of the empire was published as *Greater Britain* in 1868. It was proving phenomenally successful at the time Herbert assumed his duties at the Colonial Office. Running through four editions, it would remain in print, and was still widely read by British statesmen, in the early twentieth century.[60]

Dilke perfectly captured late Victorian Britons' sense of themselves as a people of unrivalled achievement, moral purpose and global leadership. As a radical, he was opposed to the remnants of monarchy and oligarchy in Britain and all in favour of the spirit of liberal enterprise that was rapidly transforming the Anglophone colonies overseas and more gradually changing the political order at home. Dilke wrote that he had 'followed England round the world', finding the best of English values in the USA and the settler colonies. His radical liberalism had no room for Indigenous peoples. Noting the demise of Native Americans in the USA, he applauded the fact that 'the Anglo-Saxon is the only extirpating race on earth'. The 'defeat of the cheaper by the dearer peoples' was an essential precondition for the spread of civilisation.[61] As for Britons and their American cousins, although 'I remarked that climate, soil, manners of life, that mixture with other peoples had modified the blood, I saw, too, that in essentials the race was always one. The idea which in all the length of my travels has been at once my fellow and my guide . . . is a conception, however imperfect, of the grandeur of our race, already girding the earth, which it is destined, perhaps, eventually to overspread'.[62]

Despite his upholding of colour-blind law in Mauritius, Herbert shared Dilke's vision of a Greater Britain overseas and, as permanent under-secretary, dedicated himself to implement it. Up until late 1878, he did so in alliance with the second man greatly to influence him after his return to Britain. This was his second cousin and fellow Etonian, the Earl of Carnarvon, who also happened to be secretary of state for the colonies.

A recognised travel writer on the Middle East, Carnarvon had begun his parliamentary career with a speech on the necessity of a strong British Empire. The major preoccupation of his first term as colonial secretary in the mid 1860s had been the confederation of the Canadian colonies, a scheme first proposed by the governor-in-chief of British North America in 1858 with echoes of James Stephen's earlier suggestion. In 1867 Carnarvon had chaired the meeting in London at which a Bill was drafted uniting Canada, Nova Scotia and New Brunswick in a federal dominion under the Crown. The colony would have its own parliament with upper and lower houses on the Westminster model. Carnarvon told the delegates from Nova Scotia and New Brunswick:

Once in the history of England it so happened that we parted from some of our great Colonies with a bad spirit and in a misunderstanding, the evil effects of which were felt for many a long year. . . . This has taught us a useful lesson. . . . It taught us and it taught the [settler] Colonies also – that their interests properly understood are not separate and distinct; but that the more prosperous the Colonies are, the greater will be the strength they confer on the Mother Country.[63]

Together, the cousins Herbert and Carnarvon developed 'a remarkable partnership in policy making for the colonies' during the middle to late 1870s. Taking advantage of the newly integrated imperial departments and their Old Etonians at St James Street, of Herbert's Queensland experience, and of the popularity of Dilke's vision for a *Greater Britain*, they sought to knit the Empire's most reliable components, its settler colonies, closer together and closer to Britain. Self-reliant, Anglophone white men, governing themselves through qualified liberal democracies in Europe, North America, Australasia and southern Africa, would join forces to lead the lagging races of the world towards universal progress.[64]

This vision was shortly to be reaffirmed in what is widely acknowledged as the first coherent history of the British Empire, by Syed Mahmood's former Cambridge tutor, John Robert Seeley. In 1883, Seeley's *The Expansion of England* would prove almost as popular as Dilke's *Greater Britain*. It argued that a federation of Britain and its settler colonies would compose a state the equal in population and power to those of the USA and Russia, but with far greater potential to act as a beacon for liberal civilisation. Whereas Dilke had included India in his *Greater Britain*, however, for Seeley, its predominantly Asian population meant that 'When we inquire ... into the Greater Britain of the future we ought to think much more of our colonial than of our Indian Empire'.[65]

The logical first step towards Herbert's and Carnarvon's vision had already been taken with confederation in Canada. On other continents, however, British settlers remained divided into small and relatively ineffective colonies. Before they could strengthen their alliance with Britain, these fragmented colonies would have to strengthen their bonds with one another. Confederation initiatives similar to Canada's would have to be effected in southern Africa and Australia. Carnarvon's predecessor had dismissed New South Wales' proposal for an Australian Federal Council in 1867, but Herbert would help revive the project in 1880.[66] In the meantime, in late 1878, Carnarvon and Herbert had their sights set on the complicated geopolitical arrangements in southern Africa. It was this region which most preoccupied Herbert and his staff as 1879 began.

Further Reading

Hall, C., K. McClelland and J. Rendall, *Defining the Victorian Nation: Class, Race, Gender and the British Reform Act of 1867*, Cambridge University Press, 2010.

Heuman, G., *The Killing Time: The Morant Bay Rebellion in Jamaica*, University of Tennessee Press, 1994.

Mehta, U., *Liberalism and Empire: A Study in Nineteenth-Century British Liberal Thought*, University of Chicago Press, 1999.

Stokes, E., *The English Utilitarians and India*, Oxford University Press, 1989.

11   Imperialism

In 1874, Colonial Secretary Carnarvon and Permanent Under-Secretary Herbert asked their friend and historian James Anthony Froude to travel to southern Africa to kick-start the confederation of its various colonies. Froude was also a friend of Thomas Carlyle and, along with James Fitzjames Stephen, became executor of his will before writing his biography. In 1865 he had stood aloof from disagreement between Stephen and Carlyle over Morant Bay, preoccupied with making his name as the author of *A History of England*. By 1874, the twelve-volume work was in its fourth edition. Froude's book was based upon the idea that Protestantism had acted as 'a prelude to the release of that energy which would enable Englishmen to conquer and colonize the world'. His second book, *The English in Ireland in the Eighteenth Century*, was more controversial. Although it pointed to the failures of English policy which had generated the Great Famine, its argument was that a better course would have been the more thorough-going displacement of the Irish by the overspill of England's industrialising cities. The Irish themselves were a race 'not fit for self-government'. Only a substantial Protestant English population could have turned Ireland into a settler colony as successful as Canada and the Australasian colonies. Froude had to cut short his book promotion tour of America in 1872 because of the outraged reaction of Irish-American opinion. By the time Carnarvon and Herbert asked him to urge southern Africa's white politicians to consider confederation, he had already 'helped polarize the debate on Irish home rule into a conflict of races'.[1]

An Historian Tries to Confederate

Froude embarked for Cape Town as an independent observer, but with Colonial Office letters authorising him to discuss confederation with the region's political leaders. The colonial polities in the region had multiplied since the late 1830s as a result of the emigration of slaveholding Afrikaner trekkers onto the Highveld beyond the Cape's frontier. The

Colonial Office was now responsible not only for the administration of the Cape Colony, but also of a second southern African colony, Natal. British traders had been permitted to settle on the eastern seaboard, beyond Xhosa and Thembu territory, by the Zulu king Shaka in the 1820s. Trekker emigrants from the Cape had joined them after defeating the Zulu army at the Battle of Blood River in 1838, forming the republic of Natalia. The settlers there had already appealed to Governor D'Urban to be recognised as a separate colony, but D'Urban had informed the Colonial Office that they 'can only be considered as an assembling of British subjects living in a foreign country' whose claim was 'too extravagant to be seriously maintained by any rational person'.[2] However, with its Indian Ocean port named after that governor, the territory had been annexed by the Colonial Office in 1843 (Map 11.1).

Theophilus Shepstone, the son of a missionary who had grown up among the amaXhosa of the Eastern Cape, helped to negotiate the

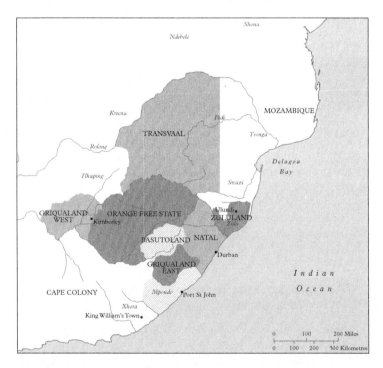

Map 11.1 Southern Africa in 1879.

presence of some 8000 British settlers in the colony with Shaka's successors as Zulu kings. By the 1870s, as Natal's native secretary, Shepstone
had engineered a system of African reserves governed indirectly by chiefs,
which, at first glance, appeared similar to the model of princely states in
India. The key difference was that Shepstone had elevated himself to the
position of supreme chief, dispensing with the need for multiple British
residents and assuming the right to depose any chief who disobeyed him.
Natal's settlers were now able to tap into the reserves for a supply of cheap
labour, while also accessing tens of thousands of indentured workers from
India for the multiplying coastal sugar plantations.[3]

Aside from the two British colonies in the region, two predominantly
Afrikaner republics, first established by the trekkers, remained on the
Highveld: the Transvaal (or South African) Republic, which the
Colonial Office recognised as independent in 1852, and the Orange
Free State, recognised in 1854. To complicate matters further, the
Cape Colony itself had recently expanded to the north, with the annex-
ation of Griqualand West, the site of the largest diamond reserves ever
discovered, around the burgeoning town of Kimberley. When Froude set
sail to begin his mediation between these various colonial polities, Cecil
Rhodes was making his fortune investing in pumping equipment as
Kimberley's diamond mines penetrated deeper into the water table.
The town's extremely rapid industrialisation, premised on the recruitment of low-paid African men migrating from polities across the region,
promised a brighter economic future for Herbert and Carnarvon's
Greater Britain, if only the region's various colonies, republics and
African kingdoms could be combined into a more effective
administration.

Froude's first attempt at confederation was inauspicious. While
romanticising the Afrikaners of the two republics, believing that they
came nearest 'to Horace's description of the Roman peasant soldiers
who defeated Pyrrhus and Hannibal', he totally misunderstood them.[4]
Afrikaners had fought and negotiated with African authorities to carve out
the Transvaal and Orange Free State, beyond Britain's reach, in order to
continue an inter-generational trajectory of expansion onto new lands at
a time when the amaXhosa had blocked further advance to the east. But
they had also emigrated from the Cape Colony in order to retain ownership of enslaved people after emancipation within the British Empire.
When Britain had annexed Natal, most of the trekkers there left for the
Orange Free State rather than live again under British rule. Despite the
payment of compensation, the Orange Free State's leaders were also still
aggrieved by the Cape's recent annexation of the Griqualand West diamond fields and hardly in the mood to re-join the imperial fold.

Froude found that it was not just the Afrikaner republics' representatives who opposed confederation. The Cape Colony's elected Assembly, comprising both Britons and Afrikaners, and recently granted full representative government, saw Froude's intervention as a challenge to its hard won sovereignty. Froude's tour, taking in Cape Town, Durban, Kimberley and Bloemfontein, only served to convince him that, rather than aspiring for a confederated South Africa, Carnarvon was best advised to leave the region's polities to their own devices, retaining only a strategic military presence in Cape Town.

Herbert and Carnarvon, however, were loath to abandon their vision of a more integrated British world. Soon after Froude's return, Carnarvon asked him to try again, this time by attending a conference of the colonies' and republics' leaders that the Colonial Office would arrange in Cape Town. Froude returned there in mid 1875 only to find that the Cape Colony's prime minister, John Charles Molteno, had already taken umbrage at Carnarvon's failure to consult about the conference. Froude then compounded the offence with a high-handed speech at a public dinner which alienated even the Colonial Office's appointed governor, Henry Barkly.[5] The conference was abandoned and Carnarvon was left to try again the following year, this time hosting a conference in London. He began by nominating Froude as the representative of Griqualand West, a decision which, even before the other states refused to take part, alienated the region's own representatives.

Herbert and Carnarvon persisted. In March 1877, they agreed upon the appointment of Sir Henry Bartle Frere, not only as the new governor of Cape Colony, but also as high commissioner for South Africa. Frere's sway would extend to Natal and, ultimately, they hoped, the Afrikaner republics and all the independent African polities located inconveniently between and around them. Carnarvon introduced a South African Confederation Bill in the House of Lords on 23 April, but even before he could launch it, and before Frere could reach Cape Town, Herbert excitedly informed him that the first concrete step towards confederation had been taken. From Natal, Shepstone had written to the Colonial Office that the Transvaal's neighbouring Afrikaner government had collapsed after a failed attempt to conquer the African Pedi Kingdom on its northern fringes. Shepstone had been able to step in and annex the republic on behalf of Britain.

Sir Henry Bartle Frere's Remarkable Career

Henry Bartle Frere, the man appointed to build confederation where Froude had failed, had graduated top of his year at the East India

Figure 11.1 Sir Henry Bartle Frere. Photograph by John Watkins/ Hulton Archive. Getty Images.

Company's Haileybury College (Figure 11.1). His first employment was as a writer in the Bombay civil service. He would later narrate his passage to India across the Isthmus of Suez in dramatic fashion, replete with 'hair-raising adventures in an Arab dhow' and near-starvation en route.[6] His subsequent careering across the British Empire knitted together many of the places and themes visited in each of our prior snapshots, and during his lifetime he became emblematic of the Empire in Britain. His career also highlighted some of the most glaring contradictions between the rhetoric of a liberal empire at home and its practice overseas.

In the late 1830s and early 1840s, as the question of the potential emancipation of enslaved people in India was being overcome by inertia, Frere was taking responsibility for gathering the funds which kept the Company solvent and supplied its shareholders with dividends by leading a reformation of the Bombay presidency's revenue survey and assessment system. In 1842, he was promoted to private secretary to George Arthur, the innovator behind the Protectorate of Aborigines whose exploits in Honduras, Van Diemen's Land and Upper Canada we traced in Part I, and who was by now governor of Bombay. Within two years Frere had married Arthur's daughter, Catherine. By 1847, he was the Company's Resident in Satara, one of the first states to be subject to Dalhousie's doctrine of lapse (to which he objected). From there, he moved to Sind, where, as chief commissioner, his overtures to polities beyond the north-west frontier aggravated the contest with Russia and, as we will see, helped to pave the way for the Second Afghan War.[7]

Within the annexed province of Sind, Frere has become known for his installation of a postal system based on Britain's, which was subsequently adopted across India. It is often proclaimed as one of the enduring, positive, legacies of British rule. Frere's swift action during the Uprising, sending troops to support Lawrence in the Punjab, earned him the thanks of both Houses of Parliament and a knighthood. His promotion of literacy in the Sindhi language was rewarded with member-ship of the Viceroy's Council in 1859, and in 1862, he succeeded his father-in-law as governor of Bombay. Again, Frere sought to use his authority for modernising, liberal projects. He is remembered in Mumbai as the driving force behind extensive infrastructural and educa-tional investments, including the Deccan College at Pune, and a specialist college to instruct Indians in civil engineering. The city's growth under his supervision led to his being appointed to the secretary of state for India's Council of India when he returned to London in 1867.

Frere's imperial career began to transcend India in 1872, when the Foreign Office commissioned him to travel to Zanzibar. However, this was not his first engagement with East Africa. While governor of Bombay, Frere had hosted the famous missionary-explorer David Livingstone as he prepared for his expedition to find the source of the Nile. Frere seconded a number of Bombay army *sepoys* to accom-pany the expedition and, in January 1866, sent it under way to Zanzibar in a Bombay government steamer. Livingstone had then famously disappeared, at least as far as the British public were con-cerned, until 1871, when the American journalist Henry Morton Stanley found him just about alive on the shores of Lake Tanganyika and uttered his famous query 'Dr Livingstone I presume?' Since then, Livingstone and Morton had drawn fresh British attention to Zanzibar's role as an entrepôt for the Indian Ocean slave trade, with around 20 000 enslaved people shipped from the island to mainland East Africa every year. Amidst the publicity of Stanley's book, *How I Found Livingstone*, the explorer was becoming 'a symbol of what the British – and other Europeans –

wished to believe about their motives as they took over tropical Africa in the late nineteenth century'.[8]

At the same time that Livingstone was being elevated into an icon of the three Cs – Christianity, Commerce and Civilization – Frere was lending his weight to his renewed anti-slavery campaign. Both a high churchman and a member of the Anti-Slavery Society, Frere had long condemned what he called the 'fashion of looking down on all men who differed from us in colour or in race'. He also bemoaned the British public's general ignorance of the East African slave trade.[9] Livingstone's fame gave Frere further fuel. In March 1872, he was the star speaker at an Anti-Slavery Society meeting at the Surrey Chapel. Invoking the original struggle of Thomas Fowell Buxton and his generation against Atlantic slavery, Frere 'exhorted the present supporters of the anti-slavery movement to imitate their predecessors and to be up and doing'. In May he addressed a much larger gathering at the Friends Meeting House in London and by the time he gave his third address at Mansion House in the City of London, he had the *Times* on board, campaigning for new measures to honour Livingstone's heroism by abolishing the Indian Ocean slave trade.

Although much of this slave trade was financed by British Indian subjects in Bombay, the popular British outrage mobilised by Livingstone and Frere was becoming focused on Zanzibar's sultan, Barghash bin Said. The Foreign Office also happened to have a grievance against the sultan since he had recently challenged British control of the region by backing an Islamic revivalist movement, which circumscribed the activities of Indian as well as European and American traders.[10] This convergence of a popular British lobby against Zanzibari slave trading and strategic interests led the Foreign Office to ask Frere, in August 1872, if he would put his campaigning to practical use as the new British envoy to the sultan. Frere was given the autonomy to draw up his own instructions. In November 1872, 250 people assembled for dinner at the Royal Geographical Society to send him on his way. The *Times* declared that it stood ready to bear any expense to put down the Zanzibari slave trade, and it was emulated by nearly all of the other major British newspapers.[11] As Frere was being carried to Zanzibar on this tide of goodwill, members of the Anti-Slavery Society at home set off on a public speaking tour of the midlands and the north, to keep the issue at the forefront of the British public's mind.

When he arrived in Zanzibar in January 1873, however, Frere found a sultan emboldened by a French promise of support for his independence. In a foretaste of what was to come in southern Africa, he acted immediately, prior to any consultation with the Foreign Office, ordering the Royal Navy to seize any slave ships sailing between Zanzibar and the

African coast. He then threatened Barghash with a total blockade. Given the popular support for his objectives, the Foreign Office felt obliged, belatedly and somewhat reluctantly, to approve of his forceful actions. Against fierce local opposition, the sultan was forced to close the slave market in Zanzibar, end the import and export of enslaved people, and ban British subjects, including Indians, from owning enslaved people. Arab slave owners, however, were left in possession of their 'property'. The promised French support never materialised.

Having fulfilled Livingstone's anti-slavery legacy on behalf of the British people in East Africa, Frere engaged next with slavery's persistent West African variants. This time he served the Colonial Office rather than the Foreign Office, and Carnarvon in particular. In 1872, the office had sought to consolidate Britain's fragmentary governmental entities on the West African coast – a policy in accord with the much larger objective of confederation in the settler colonies. This included the purchase of the Dutch Gold Coast with its port of Elmina, and its incorporation within the British Gold Coast. However, Elmina was also the powerful Ashanti kingdom's sole remaining trade outlet on the coast, and a key source of its revenue. In early 1873 Kofi Karikari, the Ashanti king, ordered his army to attack the British at Elmina in an attempt to reclaim the port.

Sir Garnet Wolseley, a man whose path would cross with Frere's again in 1879, was despatched to repel the attack and then invade the Ashanti kingdom itself. Thanks largely to Henry Morton Stanley's reporting of his campaign, Wolseley achieved celebrity as Gilbert and Sullivan's 'Modern Major-General' when his British and black West Indian troops advanced on and destroyed the Ashanti capital Kumasi, laying a telegraph cable as they went.[12] In 1874, Wolseley required Kofi Karikari to pay a war indemnity, keep the inland trade routes open, and halt the practice of human sacrifice. Policing the treaty, however, meant that the Colonial Office was ineluctably drawn into responsibility for an ill-defined British 'protectorate' stretching well inland from the Gold Coast. While Wolseley's victory was being celebrated in the illustrated British newspapers, the Colonial Office was trying to figure out how to govern this protectorate, in which domestic slavery was still practised, during the renewed peak in British anti-slavery concern.

In November 1873, the *Times* reported that not only was domestic slavery still condoned, even within the directly governed Gold Coast, but slave-dealing was being practised just outside the British-run coastal forts. British magistrates in the colony were returning runaway slaves to their owners in the protectorate, and even Wolseley's corps of porters for the assault on Kumasi had comprised in part enslaved women. The Anti-Slavery Society and the Aborigines Protection Society now campaigned vigorously for Carnarvon to intervene in the same way that Frere had done in Zanzibar. Henry Holland, the Colonial Office's legal adviser, initially reassured Carnarvon that the Gold Coast government had no legislative or executive authority over the 'protected states' of the interior. Carnarvon sought to postpone consideration of the issue by warning the House of Lords that local slave owners might well demand compensation if the British intervened. Within a month, however, he had changed his tune, deciding to prohibit slavery in the Gold Coast and take action against the interior slave trade.

What compelled the change in policy was the increasing pressure of an electorate engaged once more, as it had last been in the early 1830s, with the suppression of slavery as a unifying national project. Disraeli's government needed to assuage anti-slavery concern in Britain, and that would entail exercising some further kind of authority over African polities in the new protectorate. It was now up to Herbert and his Colonial Office officials to develop a more explicit understanding of what a British West African protectorate actually meant. Through 1874, Herbert had played a critical role in evolving this ambiguous tool of imperial governance. In July he advised that the Gold Coast and Lagos become a united Crown colony, under a single governor and Legislative Council, called 'the Gold Coast Colony'. This new, enlarged entity was empowered to enact laws and ordinances for 'territories adjacent', as well. In August, Holland drew up a draft proclamation, approved by Herbert and signed by Carnarvon. It itemised the 'primary sectors of economic, social and administrative change (including slavery) over which the colonial government would be authorised to expand its authority in the hinterland'. Based upon it, Carnarvon ordered the immediate prohibition of the slave trade, with the recommendation that in the course of time this should be supplemented by 'the extinction of slavery itself'.[13]

Next, Carnarvon turned to the hero of Zanzibar, Frere, for advice on implementing the prohibition. Frere counselled that attention be paid to the history of emancipation. Reminding Carnarvon and Herbert of India's anomalous position during the debates of the 1830s, Frere suggested that the Colonial Office follow the East India Company precedent. Simply withdrawing legal recognition of slave ownership without any further intervention to suppress the practice had allowed for 'no disturbance of labour relations', Frere said. 'Where the slaves were content they went on serving. ... There was no excitement and no occasion for compensation'.[14] Carnarvon passed on Frere's suggestion to the Gold Coast's governor Strahan, who had actually already begun negotiating an emancipation ordinance with the main chiefs in the protectorate.

By the late-1870s Frere had become a kind of management consultant for the British Empire. Long credited with the improvement of Sind and the modernisation of Bombay, he now had the added lustre of being Britain's main anti-slavery crusader in Africa. Although many of the cast of characters in this book had event-filled careers played out on the global stage of the British Empire, Frere's stands out. A proponent of liberal education, civic investment, modernisation and anti-slavery, he would shortly share responsibility for two of the bloodiest of Britain's imperial wars, fought simultaneously some 8000 miles apart in southern Africa and Afghanistan. In the meantime, however, he provoked a third: the ninth and final frontier War against the amaXhosa of the Eastern Cape.[15]

In October 1876, it was Frere to whom Herbert and Carnarvon resorted once more in their continuing attempts to achieve South African confederation. They promised him a '*special*' appointment, rather than an ordinary governorship. He would be equipped with far more power than Froude had been, not only as high commissioner, but also as commander-in-chief of all British military forces in the region. After all their setbacks, the men who ran the Colonial Office were resolved to force the issue of confederation by whatever means necessary. Frere's gubernatorial salary was supplemented by an imperial grant of £2000 and he was promised a peerage if he succeeded in effecting the merger of the region's polities.

Before he could capitalise on Shepstone's opportunistic annexation of the Transvaal, however, Frere was diverted by an opportunity to extend British control over another part of the region: the lands of the Gcaleka Xhosa, Nongqawuse's people who had suffered so much during the Cattle Killing of 1857, and which lay in the Transkei, a region which, along with Mpondo territory, separated the Cape from Natal.

Despite the devastation of the late 1850s, the Gcaleka Xhosa had not yet been absorbed into the Cape colony like their kin the Rharhabe across the Kei River. In August 1877 though, amidst a severe drought, a fight broke out between Gcaleka Xhosa and Mfengu men at a wedding ceremony. In its wake, Gcaleka men attacked a Cape Colony police outpost manned by Mfengu. Although Molteno's settler government in Cape Town wished to refrain from any further destabilising conflict on its frontier, Frere saw the incident as an opportunity to intervene in pursuit of confederation. Conquering Gcaleka territory once and for all would fill in one of the obdurate gaps preventing unified British government of the entire region. The Transkei could then either be occupied by British settlers or governed indirectly, either in the way that Frere had overseen

Satara on behalf of the East India Company or according to the precedents of protectorates established recently in West Africa and the Pacific.

Frere began by summoning Sarhili, still the paramount chief of Gcalekaland, to discuss the surrender of his autonomy. In the light of past experience, Sarhili declined the invitation, fearing arrest and imprisonment. Frere then declared that the Xhosa paramount was deposed and war declared. Molteno and the Cape Assembly immediately objected, seeing no need to become embroiled in a war of Carnarvon's and Frere's making. In some respects the 1878 frontier war was a reversal of the 1834 war, when local, settler pressure for land and conquest had dragged the reluctant Colonial Office into a frontier conflict. Now it was the Colonial Office, with Frere as its representative, drawing settlers into a conflict beyond the lands that they claimed, in pursuit of a much more extensive imperial vision.

Molteno made Frere promise that British troops would fight only defensively, if and when Sarhili's forces attacked the frontier. It was the Eastern Cape's colonial commandos which fought the Gcaleka when they did try a pre-emptive attack. The colonial forces defeated the amaXhosa within three weeks, after which Sarhili asked for peace. Molteno's ministers, John X. Merriman and Charles Brownlee, joined Frere's war council to decide upon the British response. These Cape Colony representatives were willing to accept the amaXhosa's surrender and leave the Transkei autonomous under Gcaleka authority, but this was unacceptable to Frere. The opportunity to remove one of the bastions of remaining African sovereignty standing in the way of confederation was too good to miss.

With the Cape government complaining not only that it had to fight a war on behalf of the Colonial Office's vision, but that it was also expected to fund it, Frere pressed ahead with an order that all African peoples in the region should be disarmed. After the colony's own black militia deserted, Frere used British troops to occupy the Transkei and enforce the edict. Sarhili's forces, roused to fight again, crossed into the colonised Ciskei to join with the Rharhabe Xhosa, many of whom were also now in rebellion against disarmament. During the second half of 1877 the combined Xhosa forces succeeded in sacking Mfengu and other frontier settlements and cutting the British supply lines. The outraged Molteno demanded that the Cape government be allowed to re-arm its black soldiers in order to restore control. Frere responded by appealing to Carnarvon to dissolve the Cape's elected Assembly, while employing frontier militia and rearmed Mfengu against the Gcaleka. When British troops entered the Amatola Mountains, where Maqoma had held out in previous frontier wars, in March 1878, they were ambushed repeatedly until, finally, a well-organised system of mounted units pursuing scorched earth tactics saw to the amaXhosa's surrender.

By mid 1878, Frere had destroyed the last independent Xhosa chiefdoms, subjecting the Gcaleka to British authority through Resident Agents backed by British troops, but only at the expense of suspending the Cape Colony's representative government. He certainly could not be criticised for lack of effort in fulfilling Carnarvon's vision of a Greater Britain, although he seemed to have forgotten that self-governing associations of white settler men were its very bedrock. It is not surprising that Disraeli wrote scathingly of Carnarvon (nicknamed 'Twitters' because of a nervous tick): 'if anything annoys me more than another, it is our Cape affairs, where every day brings forth a new blunder of Twitters'.[16]

At the beginning of 1878, the Cape's Assembly was reconstituted under a new prime minister leading a more amenable minority government. Gordon Sprigg was an Eastern Cape settler who had previously supported Molteno. However, with the war against the Gcaleka under way, he had switched sides to support Frere's disarmament bill. With a more compliant colonial government in place, Frere's next obstacle was the still powerful Zulu kingdom on Natal's northern, and the Transvaal's eastern, border.[17]

Before he could open his new front in the struggle for confederation, however, Frere lost his staunchest political support in London. In January 1878, just as Frere was writing that he had found a new ally in Sprigg, Carnarvon resigned from the Colonial Office. It took Frere over a month to realise, since Cape Town was still not connected to London by telegraph. Although a line had opened to Simonstown in 1860 and a land line connected the Cape and Natal by 1878, the Eastern And South African Telegraph Company was founded only in 1879 to extend a cable to Britain. Only in April was the demand from the Cape Assembly that the terminus be Cape Town rather than Durban dropped, and the terms agreed.[18] It would not be until late December 1879 that the company completed a branch cable from the Red Sea line at Aden, via Zanzibar to the Portuguese-held Lorenzo Marques, to Durban. In the meantime, the Colonial Office telegraphed urgent messages as far as Madeira, where they could catch up with ships which had departed England some four days beforehand. Thereafter they were dependent on steamer transport all the way down the African coastline to Cape Town.[19] This turned out to be too late to allow for the coordination of all the moving parts in the southern African region that the Colonial Office so desperately needed in 1879.

Between Frere sending notice of Sprigg's loyalty and Herbert receiving it a month later, Carnarvon had stood down as secretary of state for the colonies because of the 'Eastern Question', which bedevilled governmental coordination in London throughout Frere's tenure in southern Africa. Carnarvon's successor, and Herbert's new boss, would adhere far less tenaciously to the vision of a Greater Britain, and be more reticent to pay the necessary price for it. He would also struggle to direct Frere using a communications system that lagged well behind most other parts of the empire.

Soon after inheriting Carnarvon's plan and Frere as its instrument, the new secretary of state for the colonies, Michael Hicks Beach, told Disraeli, 'I cannot really control him without a telegraph'. Given Frere's determination, and perhaps his own adviser Herbert's enthusiasm for confederation, Hicks Beach added, 'And I don't know that I could with one'.[20]

The 'Eastern Question' and Southern Africa

Carnarvon had resigned on 23 January 1878, after a fierce disagreement with Disraeli. The prime minister may already have been fed up with 'Twitters' blunders' in southern Africa, but it was not actually the policy of confederation that caused the rift. It was the longer standing Foreign Office policy of supporting the Ottoman Empire against Russia. In Palmerston's day, the strategy had garnered popular support. Pursuing it initially as foreign secretary, Palmerston had emerged triumphant as prime minister in the wake of the Crimean War. By the beginning of 1878, however, the Ottoman Empire was looking like a very different kind of ally, while Russia was a resurgent power, fuelled by the same kind of racial self-belief that was prevalent in Britain.

British political life in the late 1870s was convulsed by the complexities of the government's disposition towards the Ottomans, by now generally referred to more narrowly as the Turks. The issue had gained its own title: the 'Eastern Question'. At its heart was whether Britain should continue to support a government in Constantinople which was not only heavily indebted, but also believed to be persecuting Christians, just so as to prevent the spread of Russian influence.

In return for Britain and France's support during the Crimean War, the Ottoman Porte had been persuaded to grant Christians equal rights with Muslims across its empire, but Ottoman provincial authorities continued to discriminate in practice when it came to obligations such as military service and taxation. When the Turkish suppression of a Maronite Christian revolt in Lebanon led to the killing of thousands of Christians in 1860, Britain and France had intervened to insist on reforms including the appointment of a Christian governor. Six years later, Orthodox Christian insurgents in pursuit of Crete's union with Greece alleged that Muslims had slaughtered Christians there too. Ottoman troops supported Cretan Muslims in massacring the insurgents. The Duke of Argyll, explaining the complexities of the Eastern Question for British readers in 1879, noted that such events created the 'vague but ... settled and general impression that the Sultans were not fulfilling the "solemn promises" they had made to Europe; that the vices of the Turkish government were ineradicable; and that whenever another crisis might arise affecting the "independence" of the Ottoman Empire, it would be wholly impossible to afford to it again the support we had afforded in the Crimean war'.[21]

Support for the Ottoman Empire had become more contentious in Britain as a result of these reports of Christian oppression, and through the repeated characterisation of the empire as the 'sick man of Europe'. In the meantime, however, the perceived threat from Russia had only increased. While the 'Great Game' continued to be played on the northern fringes of the Raj and in Central Asia, fear of Russia was concentrated especially in the Balkans. There, Russian writers and politicians were promoting a pan-Slavic, Christian Orthodox affinity against Muslim Ottoman rule. German unification under Bismarck had provided Russia with a powerful ally in its attempts to regain influence after the territorial losses of the Crimean War, most notably through the resurrection of its Black Sea fleet. Russia was supporting Slavic nationalist movements against fragile Turkish control in the Balkans just as a severe drought, followed by flooding in Anatolia, forced the Porte to declare bankruptcy in 1875.

The Turkish government's attempt to raise taxes in order to clear the debt helped provoke an uprising in Herzegovina in July 1875, which spread into Bosnia and Bulgaria. When Bulgarian rebels attacked Turkish troops, they combined with Muslim militias to massacre at least 30 000 Bulgarians. While Froude was trying to negotiate a Greater Britain in southern Africa, reports of the mutilation of babies and children and the mass rape of women were generating a 'wave of moral outrage' against the Turkish authorities in Britain.[22]

In 1876, Disraeli's Conservative government, including Carnarvon, was still supporting the Porte in order to prevent Russian control of the Balkans, despite the Turks' increasing unpopularity among the electorate. Galvanised to come out of semi-retirement, Gladstone waded in on behalf of the Liberals, publishing his sensational *Bulgarian Horrors and the Question of the East*. The book was primarily an attack on Disraeli for withholding information on the scale of Turkish atrocities from the British public and preventing parliamentary debate of them. 'We learn with astonishment and horror', Gladstone lamented, that

we have been involved, in ... moral complicity with the basest and blackest outrages upon record within the present century ... crimes and outrages, so vast in scale as to exceed all modern example, and so unutterably vile as well as fierce in character, that it passes the power of heart to conceive, and of tongue and pen adequately to describe them. These are the Bulgarian horrors; and the question is, what can and should be done, either to punish, or to brand, or to prevent?

A by-product of Gladstone's attack on Disraeli was his sponsoring of a new racism against Turks. 'Let me endeavour very briefly to sketch, in the rudest outline, what the Turkish race was and what it is', he wrote:

It is not a question of Mahometanism simply, but of Mahometanism compounded with the peculiar character of a race. They are not the mild Mahometans of India, nor the chivalrous Saladins of Syria, nor the cultured Moors of Spain. They were, upon the whole, from the black day when they first entered Europe, the one great anti-human specimen of humanity. Wherever they went, a broad line of blood marked the track behind them; and, as far as their dominion reached, civilisation disappeared from view. They represented everywhere government by force, as opposed to government by law.[23]

By the end of 1877, Carnarvon had become deeply uncomfortable supporting Disraeli and the Ottomans. His own vision of British settler confederation might have led already to the subjugation of the Gcaleka Xhosa and it was about to provoke war with the amaZulu, but he shared Gladstone's view that it was 'the Turk' who 'represented force as opposed to the law'. The colonial secretary also believed that another war with Russia would be disastrous. 'There are very few people now who look back upon [the Crimean War] with satisfaction', he argued, 'and I am confident that there is nobody insane enough in this country to desire a repetition of it'.[24] When Disraeli reprimanded him for breaking ranks, Carnarvon apologised, but as the European powers' combined attempts to negotiate independence for the Balkans failed, and as Russian forces declared war on Turkey and advanced towards Constantinople, Disraeli's decision to despatch the British fleet in support of the Turks proved Carnarvon's final straw. Together with Lord Derby, the foreign secretary, he resigned.

From Disraeli's perspective, sending the Royal Navy as a deterrent worked. In July 1878, Russia entered into a settlement at the Berlin Congress by which the Ottoman Porte would recognise Romania's, Serbia's and Montenegro's independence and Bulgaria's autonomy within the empire. The British Colonial Office gained control of Cyprus as a further deterrent to Russian ambitions in the Balkans, and almost immediately considered sending some of the 'surplus', impoverished population of Malta there.[25] However, in the meantime, the 'Eastern Question' had thrown its pursuit of confederation into disarray.[26] Detached from Carnarvon and isolated from direct telegraphic communication, Frere was now effectively a loose cannon in southern Africa. Hicks Beach may have been cautious, and one of his first despatches warned Frere that he was reluctant to send any more troops for southern African wars, but his South African high commissioner continued enthusiastically to pursue the unification and extension of British governance. With up to three months elapsing before replies to despatches were received, and Frere's reputation for impulsive self-direction, Herbert could rest assured that his cousin Carnarvon's confederation endeavours would not be halted immediately.

Before we return to Frere and southern Africa, however, we need to trace the simultaneous implications of the 'Eastern Question' for the Colonial Office's neighbour, the India Office.

The 'Eastern Question' and Afghanistan

As a key adviser on its council, Frere had left his legacy in the India Office before heading to southern Africa. Seemingly oblivious to the lessons of 1838–9, Frere led a policy of intervening among rulers beyond the East India Company's territory in order to deter them from making alliances with Russia. He advised that a British mission should again be established in Kabul. Its job would be identical to that of Alexander Burns in 1838: to persuade Afghanistan's Amir to resist any further Russian encroachment through Central Asia. In doing so, Frere had helped to revive the tension on India's north-western frontier.

By the time Frere was in southern Africa, and just as the Russo-Turkish War in the Balkans was ending to Disraeli's satisfaction, the Russians had sent their own, rival, mission to Kabul. Disraeli had appointed Lord Lytton viceroy when the Russian advance on Constantinople was still under way, telling Queen Victoria that, if necessary, he would be 'a good instrument for [the] purpose' of waging war against Russia through India. After the Berlin Congress had concluded the Balkan conflict, the prime minister still feared that Britain's diplomatic success could immediately be countered by Russian advances on India. The fear now seemed to be borne out by the Russian mission.

In late 1878, as Frere was starting to depart from Hicks Beach's intentions in southern Africa, Lytton was cultivating his relationship with the India Office, but ignoring the advice of his Council in Calcutta. In Lord

Cranbrook, the secretary of state for India, Lytton found a compliant ally. Cranbrook told the new viceroy, 'I often wish that I had seen something of the vast region which I am called upon to administer but I must make the best use I can of the knowledge of others'. When Lytton described his Calcutta councillors as a 'collection of old fogies with all the ignorant prejudices of retired Anglo-Indian', Cranbrook obligingly bemoaned their lack of 'cordiality of feeling'.[27] Assisted by the direct telegraphic link that Frere lacked in southern Africa, Lytton was able to gain the avid support of Cranbrook and Disraeli, and the rather more reluctant acquiescence of Lord Salisbury as foreign secretary, for Frere's former 'Forward Policy'. Afghanistan would be cultivated once again as a British client state.[28] From this base, Lytton proposed that his Indian government could sponsor revolts among the Central Asian Muslim polities, which would 'shake down the Asiatic power of Russia at its very centre, raise the Khanates in its rear, and swiftly sweep it altogether out of Central Asia'.[29]

The British and Indian governments may have been agreed on their goals, but the Afghan Amir, Sher Ali Khan, was proving less than enthusiastic. In 1873, Lytton's predecessor had made the Amir promises of support that had failed to materialise and Sher Ali saw no reason why this new, expedient, intervention against the Russians would turn out any differently. By the summer of 1878, as Bismarck was chairing the negotiations between Britain, Russia and the other European imperial powers in Berlin, Lytton was getting impatient at Sher Ali's repeated rebuffs. Promising to break Afghan Amirs 'like reeds' and fulminating against the 'vile Russians', he dismissed the reservations of Disraeli's more cautious Cabinet members as 'puling nonsense'. Salisbury had lodged a protest with the Russians about their unsolicited mission to Kabul and wanted to hear their response before taking the next step. In the meantime, however, Lytton demanded that Sher Ali accept a British mission headed by Neville Bowles Chamberlain, a former East India Company officer and veteran of the first British occupation of Kabul.[30]

Sher Ali warned Lytton that he would refuse to receive Chamberlain's party, but the veteran officer set off for Afghanistan nonetheless. In September 1878, after an embarrassing stand-off, the Amir's men forced the British mission to turn back from the entrance to the Khyber Pass. When Lytton telegraphed the India Office with this news, Cranbrook and the Cabinet were placed in a difficult position. Salisbury was furious with Lytton for forcing the Amir's hand and bringing about an unnecessary challenge to British prestige. Disraeli too, was concerned that the 'snub' delivered to Chamberlain would take 'much to wipe away', but was more sanguine at the prospect of avenging it. It was really only the timing of Lytton's actions that caused the prime minister some annoyance.

Just as Palmerston had backed Bowring's impulsive provocation of the Second Opium War, so, once the initial overtures to the Amir had failed, Disraeli, Cranbrook and Salisbury all came into line supporting Lytton's plan for forceful action against Sher Ali. When the Amir wrote to Lytton complaining of the 'threatening ... harsh and breathless haste' of the viceroy's demand that he receive Chamberlain, the Cabinet permitted Lytton to prepare another full scale British invasion of Afghanistan. In late 1878, Lytton issued Sher Ali with an ultimatum demanding his apology and official reception of Chamberlain's mission. The Second Anglo-Afghan War began when the deadline expired on 21 November.

By the beginning of 1879, then, the British government was presiding over the aftermath of a great famine in India while simultaneously occupying Afghanistan – exactly the scenario of forty years beforehand. Meanwhile, Frere was bringing about his second war of confederation, against the amaZulu in southern Africa. For a nation that favoured liberalism over imperialism, this was paradoxical indeed.

Further Reading

Guy, J., *The Destruction of the Zulu Kingdom: The Civil War in Zululand, 1879–1884*, University Kwazulu Natal Press, 1999.

Klein, I., 'Who Made the Second Afghan War?' *Journal of Asian History*, 8, 2, 1974, 97–121.

Seton-Watson, R. W., *Disraeli, Gladstone, and the Eastern Question: A Study in Diplomacy and Party*, W. W. Norton, 1972.

Thompson, L. M., *The Unification of South Africa, 1902–1910*, Clarendon Press, 1960.

Carnarvon's successor as colonial secretary, Michael Hicks Beach, was another old Etonian and 'an uncompromising tory squire and high-churchman'.[1] His reputation for aloofness and intolerance earned him the nickname 'Black Michael', and he was never very popular with colleagues other than his lifelong friend, Randolph Churchill. Despite taking no trouble to hide his disdain for the 1867 Reform Bill, Hicks Beach's reputation for administrative efficiency led Disraeli to appoint him chief secretary for Ireland in 1874. When Carnarvon resigned and Hicks Beach inherited Frere's confederation project in January 1878, it still seemed likely that Britain was heading for a new war with Russia. Disraeli left his new secretary of state for the colonies in no doubt that, after 'Twitters' blunders', it was imperative to restrain Frere from further costly military interventions in southern Africa. In the meantime, however, Frere was steamrolling the latest obstacle to his confederation plan – an insurrection in Griqualand West.

Politics in the annexed Griqualand West district, containing Kimberley's diamond fields, was complex and fraught in 1878. The British immigrants, mostly engaged in mining, and their financial backers in London, vied for control with independent Setswana-speaking chiefdoms, the Afrikaners of the Transvaal and Orange Free State and Griqua polities. The Griqua were Afrikaans-speaking settlers of mixed Afrikaner, Khoikhoi, San and enslaved Malay and Indonesian heritage, who had moved across the Cape Colony's northern frontier over the last fifty years. They had negotiated recognition as sovereign polities from successive Cape governments. In 1873, however, the Colonial Office had recognised Griqualand West as a discrete British colony, appointing the former secretary to the governor of Jamaica, and veteran of the Morant Bay suppression, William Owen Lanyon, to the governorship in 1875. Lanyon described his new posting as the most 'hideous and disgusting' place he had ever seen.[2]

As Disraeli's reforms were enfranchising working men and improving their conditions in Britain, Griqualand West was becoming a laboratory for the creation of a racially defined working class, excluded from any access to government and subject to ever greater control by employers. Lanyon facilitated British mining interests' forging of a modernised, systematised and bureaucratised form of racial discrimination, which would find its apotheosis in apartheid. In 1876, Lanyon decreed that all Africans entering the diamond fields were required to carry a pass. Masters and Servants Laws required African men to work for white employers in order to obtain one. So as to guard against diamond theft, claim-holders were accorded the right to search African employees' bodies and property at any time. By 1879 around 20 000 African mineworkers were housed around Kimberley in open compounds with barrack-type accommodation, enclosed by corrugated-iron fences. Compound gates guarded by mine-owners' security personnel regulated their movement to and from the 'locations', where other Africans lived in shanty conditions outside the town.[3] Still, thousands of African men from the surrounding chiefdoms continued to circulate between their homesteads and the mines for annual contracts of work, many of them intent on purchasing guns with their earnings.[4]

In July 1877, Frere pressured Molteno's Cape government to annex Griqualand West as a further step towards confederation. Tswana chiefdoms bordering the diamond fields correctly feared for their autonomy, sending messengers and forging alliances with the Gcaleka Xhosa, who were already engaged in the final struggle for their own independence in the Eastern Cape, and with the Bapedi, who supplied many of the migrant mine workers to Kimberly and had just defeated the Transvaal's Afrikaners. During the ensuing revolt, colonial forces intercepted messengers returning from the Zulu kingdom too.

The independent African polities of the Highveld had clearly acquired 'imperial literacy': in this case an understanding of Frere's confederation project and its implications for African sovereignty across the entire region.[5] Along with other societies facing imperialist threats, their leaders were engaging in complex calculations about which alliances would best preserve their polity's autonomy. Strategic alliance with the British against Indigenous foes and rivals was one option, deployed as we have seen by Mfengu in the Eastern Cape. The amaSwazi would soon ally with the British too, against the Bapedi. For some, such an alliance was still the lesser of two evils. However, the possibility of broader realignment against the more consolidated threat of Frere's confederation drive was now being actively considered. Much to the consternation of Frere himself, it appeared that some of the Highveld Batswana and Basotho were reaching out to Nguni chiefdoms to create new, albeit provisional, anti-imperial alliances.

Within Griqualand West itself, Griqua leaders known as captains were ready to join any combined African revolt, since the Land Court established by the Cape Colony to decide on contested claims after annexation (and led by Andries Stockenström's son), had displaced some of them in favour of both Batswana and Afrikaners. In May 1878, Griqua, Batswana, Kora, San, Bapedi and dislocated amaXhosa combined to launch attacks on Afrikaner farmers, initiating the Griqualand West rebellion. During the first major battle with colonial forces hastening back from fighting the amaXhosa in the Eastern Cape, more than thirty of the rebels were killed.[6]

The Griqualand West rebellion raged through the remainder of the year amidst rumours that a black alliance, mirroring the scale of Frere's confederation plan, was intent on killing all the whites in the district. Before Herbert and Hicks Beach knew of it in London, Frere had ordered its suppression by any means. Criticism of the ensuing massacre of rebels' wives and children in November 1878, would be aired in Britain only the following year, by which time Frere had moved on to his next target, the amaZulu.[7]

The suppression of the Griqualand West rebellion, together with an uprising among Griqua bands who had settled in Griqualand East, in 1878–9, effectively saw to the end of Griqua landholding in southern Africa. It helped to produce a dispossessed working class of mixed descent that was now labelled 'Coloured'. This newly minted 'race' was to be excluded from white privileges and positioned just above Africans in the consolidating and extending racial hierarchy that would be codified under apartheid.[8]

More immediately, the crushing of Griqua and African resistance in southern Africa's emerging industrial heartland cleared the way for Frere's next steps towards confederation. It also provided a clearer, specifically southern African rationale for Carnarvon's confederation project as a whole: the unitary government regulation of a vast system connecting migrant workers from conquered African chiefdoms with white-controlled industrial centres like Kimberley. Frere foresaw that such a system would, at last, render southern Africa an economic asset for the empire, rather than a continual drain on its resources.[9] Remodelled as an integrated industrial economy, the region could become a counterpart to India within the global Greater Britain. African reserves would take the place of the princely states, and British shareholder profits would flow from large-scale mining instead of rent.

In July 1878, Frere persuaded the Mpondo chief Nqwiliso to cede Port St John to the Cape Colony in return for being recognised as an independent ruler. Lying between the newly conquered Gcaleka Xhosa and

Natal, this acquisition filled another of the gaps in the region's patchwork of sovereignties. The annexation would provide the confederated South Africa with another Indian Ocean port, balanced by the appropriation of Walvis Bay on the Atlantic. In September 1878, as Lytton was preparing for war in Afghanistan, Frere was heading to Natal to plan for the next landmark in his remarkably bloody trajectory across the empire: the absorption of the Zulu kingdom, the most powerful still standing in the way of a confederated region, and incidentally, a vast reserve of potential migrant labour for the mines.[10]

Frere found three main excuses for attacking the amaZulu. The first was a border dispute between Cetshwayo's kingdom and what had, until its recent annexation, been the independent Transvaal Republic. In February 1878, Frere tasked Henry Bulwer, the lieutenant governor of Natal, who also happened to be the Indian governor-general Lord Lytton's nephew, to prepare a report on the dispute.[11] Unlike his uncle, Bulwer sought to avoid war. He found largely in favour of the amaZulu, basing his conclusion on the fact that the Transvaal had not been able to produce any evidence of what they claimed had been the former Zulu king Mpande's cession of the land. This was not, however, the answer that Frere required. Shepstone wrote to him, 'The fact that [Bulwer's judgement] is adverse is difficulty enough but the worst part is its insulting tone and the cynical language towards the Transvaal people'. Frere did not want to be seen as overturning Bulwer's independent finding, but he was able to add the stipulation that Cetshwayo must either leave the seventy-five Afrikaners who had settled in the disputed strip on their lands, or pay them compensation for removal. More insidiously, he also insisted that Cetshwayo accept a British Resident Agent to enforce the terms.[12] At the Colonial Office, the manoeuvre was belatedly interpreted as Frere giving the amaZulu sovereignty over the land, but 'the country itself to 80 or 90 Boers'.[13]

The story of the brutal treatment of two Zulu women gave Frere his second pretext for war. In July 1878, two of the Zulu chief Sihayo's wives fled his control into Natal. Sihayo's brother led parties of men across the border to seize them and bring them back to Zululand, where they were executed. Cetshwayo apologised to Bulwer for the transgression but refused to hand over the culprits for trial in the colony. Frere swiftly told Bulwer, 'it will be necessary to send to the Zulu King an ultimatum which must put an end to pacific relations with our neighbours'.[14] Shortly afterwards, the high commissioner found his third *casus belli*. Two Natal surveyors, Messrs Smith and Deighton, investigating the Tugela River, had been detained briefly by Zulu men, who believed they had crossed onto the amaZulu side without permission. Frere wrote to Hicks Beach telling him that, although quickly released, the British subjects had been 'roughly treated and threatened for some time'.[15] Just as in Canton in 1856, the rough treatment of British subjects provided a pretext for a long-intended imperial war.

At St James Street Hicks Beach was gradually becoming aware of, and alarmed by, Frere's provocations of the Zulu king. Obliged to respond to the high commissioner's warnings of bloodthirsty Zulus threatening Natal's vulnerable settlers, he reluctantly acceded to sending extra troops to Durban. However, he told Frere, 'It is the desire of Her Majesty's Government not to furnish means for a campaign of invasion and conquest, but to afford such protection as may be necessary at this juncture to the lives and property of the colonists. . . . I can by no means arrive at the conclusion that war with the Zulus should be unavoidable, and I am confident that you, in concert with Sir H. Bulwer, will . . . avoid an evil so much to be deprecated as a Zulu war'.[16]

Frere waited until 14 October 1878 to write privately to Hicks Beach informing him that he intended to press further demands upon Cetshwayo in an ultimatum. As a steamship was conveying his notification up the African coast, he summoned the Zulu king to a meeting to reveal the boundary commission's findings.[17] On 11 December 1878, before Hicks Beach had had time to convey his response to the idea of an ultimatum, Frere presented Cetshwayo with Bulwer's report on the boundary dispute and his own additional conditions. But he also surprised the Zulu king with a set of new demands. These were premised on the notion that, because Shepstone had travelled with colonial soldiers to attend Cetshwayo's coronation ceremony in 1873 to recognise him as King of the Zulu, Cetshwayo was not a fully independent sovereign. Frere maintained that it was the British who had installed him, just as they had many of the princely leaders in India. As with the new protectorate in West Africa, the British high commissioner had a right of interference 'on behalf of the Zulu people, to secure for them that measure of good government which we undertook to promise for them'.[18]

Cetshwayo was told that he had until 10 January 1879 to surrender Sihayo's three sons and brother, and pay a fine of 500 head of cattle for his delay in handing them over, along with another hundred head for the ill treatment of Smith and Deighton. He would also have to surrender a Swazi chief to whom he had given land, and who was proving a thorn in the side of the Transvaalers. Humiliating in themselves, these were Frere's relatively minor demands. He threw in some far more drastic ones. Cetshwayo was told that he must disband his army and discontinue the Zulu military system, based on age-group cohorts of men known as amabutho, inaccurately likened by the British to regiments. He must abandon his control of amabutho-based marriage arrangements, give freedom to missionaries to convert Zulu subjects and, of course, accept a British Resident Agent to oversee the kingdom's future governance.[19]

It seems inconceivable that Frere intended anything other than a provocation to war. His ultimatum insisted essentially that Zululand be rendered a subordinated reserve, along the lines of a princely state, or perhaps a protectorate, but with even less control for the king over his subjects. While Frere awaited the results of his ultimatum, he continued to plan for the shape that a reformed Natal Legislative Assembly would take once it joined the confederated Union of South Africa.[20] Hicks Beach could only read belatedly of Frere's action on 2 January 1879. His response came far too late:

> The communications which had previously been received from you had not entirely prepared [the Colonial Office] for the course which you have deemed it necessary to take. . . . I took the opportunity of impressing upon you the importance of using every effort to avoid war. But the terms which you have dictated to the Zulu king . . . are evidently such as he may not improbably refuse, even at the risk of war; and I regret that the necessity for immediate action should have appeared to you so imperative as to preclude you from incurring the delay which would have been involved in consulting Her Majesty's Government upon a subject of so much importance.[21]

On 9 January 1879, a day before Cetshwayo's deadline expired, Frere told the Colonial Office of his plans to absorb British Kaffraria, the newly conquered Gcalekaland and even the still independent Basutholand beyond, into his unified South Africa. The Colonial Office considered the despatch only on 1 March. Herbert commented, 'Sir B. Frere thinks that the time has come for dealing with the whole of Kaffraria from the Kei to Natal, including Griqualand East & Basutoland. . . . But I do not gather what exactly he wishes us to do. . . . It would seem . . . preferable to wait until the assembling of Colonial Delegates to render whether any terms of Confederation can be agreed upon, and then to bring under their consideration the whole question of the native territories not now under any Colonial Government . . . – including Zululand – with a view to ascertaining distinctly what responsibilities the Colonial Governments are prepared to accept in regard to those territories, and which of them must be declared British property'.[22]

By then, though, Frere's invasion of Zululand, and thus the whole confederation project, had already encountered a disastrous setback. The secretary of state's earlier admonition to refrain from provoking war with the amaZulu had barely left London by the time Frere had amassed the troops sent for Natal's defence, for his long planned attack. On 11 January 1879, a day after the expiration of his deadline, and having had no response from Cetshwayo, Frere ordered Lord Chelmsford to launch a meticulously planned invasion of 18 000 British, colonial and Natal African troops, divided into three columns, into Zululand.[23]

Aftermaths

Herbert and Hicks Beach heard of the loss of nearly 1700 men of the central British column at Isandhlwana, which had occurred on 22 January 1879, the following month. Ironically Frere had written to them on the day of the battle to express his support for a telegraph cable connecting southern Africa with the Red Sea line as soon as possible.[24] The over-confident Chelmsford had neglected properly to defend the column's main camp while he set off with an exploratory party, and it had been surprised by a large Zulu army. The news came as a great shock to the British public.[25] With Chelmsford forced to abandon his initial invasion plan, Hicks Beach was now obliged either to send reinforcements or suffer ignominy.

News of the defeat at Isandhlwana rippled throughout the empire. Before the War Office could formally requisition further troops from Ceylon, the governor of St Helena had despatched his own reinforcements to Chelmsford, who noted his disappointment that the neighbouring Cape Colony had responded with far less alacrity.[26] In Mauritius, Governor Frederick Napier Broome overruled his commanding officer to despatch much of his garrison to Natal as soon as he heard of the disaster in early March. Although the military commander was worried about 'the Criminal Tendencies of the lower classes of the population, ... the possibility of a rising on the part of the Indians, and ... the sympathies of the Mozambiques [Africans from the Portuguese colony immediately to the north of Zululand] and Indians with our enemies in South Africa and Afghanistan', Broome justified the action by referring to the way that his predecessor had sent troops to India during the Uprising.[27] A Mauritius Aid Society was formed for the benefit of the British wounded and sick in southern Africa, with more than 1400 pounds subscribed. Even during the Indian Uprising, Mauritius 'was not so thoroughly denuded of [its own] troops' in pursuit of the larger imperial cause.[28]

As Cetshwayo refrained from pressing home his advantage, ordering his army not to invade Natal, Frere was allowed time to request the despatch of seven further regiments direct from Britain, while continuing to plan for the permanent occupation of Zululand once the struggle was won. In a despatch written on 5 March, the high commissioner indicated the scheme that he had in mind for a Zululand incorporated in a confederated region. It adverted once again to his Indian experience. He requested that the Colonial Office mediate with the India Office and War Office to send him *sepoys* from India with which to garrison occupied Zululand. Frere wrote,

There are objections of race and colour, which would be obstacles to an experiment anywhere but in the neighbourhood of Natal, where Indian Coolies are already present in considerable numbers; but Sepoys would probably be found very useful in garrison between the Drakensberg and the sea, anywhere from the Kei northwards to the Limpopo . . . Sepoy Regiments do not suffer either in health or discipline from being cut up into small detachments as European Regiments do . . . for a very moderate allowance of hutting money, they provide their own quarters, and do not require permanent barracks, and . . . the pioneer regiments do an immense deal of useful engineering work. . . . When the strength of the Zulu Army is once broken, and the people relegated to their natural pastoral and agricultural avocations, it would take a very small force of Sepoys to keep 400,000 of them in order with the aid of a good Zulu police. I have Zululand in view rather than Natal, in the above observations; but if any Indian authority would consider the force necessary to keep in order a million of men of the most martial races in India, he would probably name a garrison very much smaller than anything yet contemplated for Natal and Zululand combined.

Once discharged, Frere continued, the imported *sepoys* could join the ranks of the Indian indentured workers occupied on Natal's sugar plantations and in the colony's trade, 'though a Madras Sepoy would probably find himself more at home at once among the Indian Coolies than Sepoys from other parts of India'. As for the existing Indian population of the colony, 'that . . . material is generally much inferior to the Indian Sepoy of the same race – the ordinary Sepoys are the finest of the population, while the ordinary coolies who emigrate, are often the poorest and weakest'.

The delayed Colonial Office response was lukewarm. While referring the matter to the War Office to contain the relative costs of maintaining Indian and British garrisons overseas, information which might be ascertained from the dual garrisons of Malta, its clerks noted that Frere was, yet again, inappropriately by-passing Bulwer in Natal. Hicks Beach himself was more scathing, minuting that, given the recent experience of defeat at their hands, 'the Zulu or Kaffir is, man for man, better than the Sepoy – and that therefore this experiment might be dangerous'.[29]

The nail in the coffin for Frere's scheme was advice from the India Office that the terms on which *sepoys* might accept service in South Africa 'would certainly require a considerably higher rate of pay than the Government of India give for Indian service, even across the seas'. This led Lord Cranbrook to doubt 'whether the charges would fall so far short of those of British Troops as would compensate for the difference in value of the two classes'.[30]

All this remained speculative, of course, until the disaster at Isandhlwana could be reversed and the amaZulu defeated. Chelmsford set off from Natal to relieve the second invasion column, besieged at Eshowe, on 29 March. At the same time the remaining column from the initial invasion, properly dug in, was able to kill 3000 amaZulu at the Battle of Khambula. By June, Chelmsford was in a great hurry to finish the war before his replacement, Garnet Wolseley of Ashanti War fame, could reach Natal. Before he could do so, there was another high-profile casualty of Frere's confederation plan: the prospect of a Bonaparte ever acceding again to the leadership of France.

Napoléon Eugène Louis Jean Joseph Bonaparte, the Prince Imperial and only child of the Emperor Napoleon III of France and his wife, Eugénie de Montijo, had received sanctuary in England after his father was dethroned by the Franco-Prussian War. Following his father's death in 1873, Bonapartists had declared him Napoleon IV, Emperor of the French in exile. The Prince Imperial was a popular figure in Britain, especially among those who opposed the Third Republic that supplanted him. Having trained at the Royal Military Academy, Woolwich and served with the Royal Artillery, he was keen to see action in Zululand, intending to carry into battle the sword that the original Napoleon had worn at Austerlitz. With Queen Victoria lobbying on his behalf, Chelmsford was obliged to include the Prince in the second invasion force, but ensure that he was kept out of harm's way. On 31 May, however, his supervising officer, Lt. Col. Harrison, agreed to let the Prince Imperial scout ahead on the path of advance. Setting off the next morning with just six others, before his full escort could be assembled, he was surprised and killed by a group of Zulu warriors while resting at an abandoned kraal.

Chelmsford reported to Frere that 'the six Basutos who had been detailed to go with him did not turn up & the Prince himself refused to wait for them, saying that the six Europeans were amply sufficient. – Had these Basutos been with him they would have acted as scouts when the Prince off-saddled & would have prevented his being surprised'. The commander of the British forces was also now concerned about his own reputation, writing, 'I suppose my enemies in the English Press will make a raid upon me again & endeavour to turn the whole blame upon my shoulders. I have always felt that it was somewhat unfair to saddle me with the responsibility which naturally would be attached to such a charge, but I had to accept it with all the rest. I did my best to prevent the Prince from assuming undue risks, but unless I had kept him tied to my side, which would have been irksome to both of us, I could not ever be sure that he was not doing something foolish and risky'.[31] Chelmsford was also keen to offer reassurance to Frere about the latter's son, who was also serving with him: 'I will not allow your boy to run any risk which is not shared by us all', he wrote. 'We all like him very much & I feel sure that the experience he will gain in his 1st Campaign will be of lasting benefit to him during his whole military career'.[32]

When the small group of Zulu men ambushed the Prince Imperial, they unwittingly altered the future dynamic of European politics, prompting Disraeli's famous utterance, 'A very remarkable people, the Zulu. They defeat our generals; they convert our bishops; they have settled the fate of a great European dynasty'.[33] With the Prince Imperial's death as well as the disaster of Isandhlwana to atone for before Wolseley could arrive, Chelmsford and Frere spurned Cetshwayo's offer to negotiate a surrender and attacked his royal kraal at Ulundi on 4 July 1879. Bristling with Gatling machine guns, recently tested by the US army against the Cheyenne, a British square mowed down the repeated Zulu charges, killing up to 6000 Zulu men with the loss of only ten Britons. The battle brought Frere's bloodiest war of confederation yet to an end.

As the killing was continuing throughout the first half of 1879, Frere and the Colonial Office were tussling over its causes and the high commissioner's behaviour. At St James Street, it was not so much Herbert or Hicks Beach who engaged directly with Frere's missives, but the Colonial Office's southern Africa specialist, Under-Secretary Edward Fairfield. He commented, 'There does not appear to be anything ... to relieve Sir B. Frere from the crime administered to him on the 19th of March for committing the country to war without the sanction of Her Majesty's Government'. As soon as news of the January invasion reached the office, Fairfield minuted that Frere had 'exceeded his functions and trumped the prerogative of the Crown and the Cabinet in commencing an offensive war, for which there was no immediate and overwhelming necessity'. 'Sooner or later this War (which was again in the name of the Gospel)', he wrote, 'will end in the extermination of the persons intended to be benefitted'. The potential consequences extended well beyond the high commissioner's purview. Frere was guilty of 'derailing the whole financial arrangements of this Government and locking up a great part of the military force of the country at a time when for ought he knew, there might have been far more urgent necessity for it elsewhere'.[34] There was, of course, precisely such a concurrent necessity in Afghanistan.

Frere defended his actions, arguing the following month that 'it would have been useless to expect to wait the two months for a reply from Her Majesty's Government, without some fresh manifestation of Zulu impatience or without an outbreak of discontent in the Transvaal or elsewhere'.[35] Reminded of the boundary dispute, Fairfield then suspected that 'this war has been undertaken to please the Boers'.[36] Frere's attempt to blame the weather for his haste also backfired. He suggested that he had to act swiftly since the river frontier was impassable during the rainy months. Fairfield reasoned that if the river was impassable to the British forces then it would also be impassable to the amaZulu. With no imminent threat to the colonists of Natal across the Tugela River, Frere could have waited for instructions from Hicks Beach before declaring war. Furthermore, the senior civil servant pointed out, it was Frere's own ultimatum and its deadline which set the schedule for invasion, not any new behaviour of Cetshwayo. Fairfield's minute for Hicks Beach concluded that 'Sir B. Frere might have put the matter before the Government in time to have obtained their assent to his advancing into Zululand in January, and yet have left it open to them to veto the measure in time'.[37]

Fairfield's exasperated sense that Frere had failed to appreciate the conditions in which the imperial government as a whole found itself in late 1878 and early 1879, runs throughout his minutes. Even in August 1879, Frere was still advocating not only confederation, but also new constitutional arrangements for the empire as a whole, through which the confederated settler colonies around the world might take part in a restructured imperial government. His vision for how the consolidated dominions might work alongside Britain 'is part of the question of the Relations of Colonies with the Sovereign and the Empire which so few apply their minds to consider at all', he argued. It was now time 'to give Earl Beaconsfield [Disraeli] that opportunity, which he looked forward to … of considering practically the question of consolidating the Empire'. Frere had his own suggestion of how it might be done, based yet again on his Indian experience: 'by the constitution of a consultative council, like the Council of India, responsible to the Secretary of State and to the colonies they represented, for the information and advice given, and capable of adding weight to his decisions, or those of the Imperial Parliament on Colonial questions'.[38]

Carnarvon's ambitious, transformative project of confederation for a Greater Britain, however, had been put on the back burner by more immediate challenges to Britain's global role. The Eastern Question was reshaping British politics as it saw off Carnarvon himself, while Lytton's impulsive but not unwelcome aggression in Afghanistan was stretching imperial as well as Indian resources. To Fairfield it seemed that Frere's experiences in India and Zanzibar, and his role as Foreign and Colonial Office troubleshooter, had inspired an arrogant self-confidence, and a dismissive attitude towards the opinions of London-bound officials and politicians. The only reason that Hicks Beach did not recall Frere was that Disraeli overruled him, fearing a loss of face.

While the Colonial Office was becoming exasperated with Frere, Lytton was preoccupying the India Office with the second British occupation of Afghanistan. Just as in 1838, the initial invasion of British and Indian soldiers across the Khyber and Bolan passes, a month before the invasion of Zululand, had gone well for the viceroy. It was certainly more successful than Chelmsford's invasion plan. Sher Ali Kahn fled Kabul after his forces suffered a series of defeats, and the Amir died in exile in February 1879. Lytton installed Sher Ali's son, Mohammad Yaqub Khan, as his new client Amir, henceforth to be 'advised' by the British Resident on the model of the Indian princely states. Describing Afghanistan not as a protectorate, but rather as India's natural 'scientific frontier', Lytton, backed by Disraeli, confidently aspired to integrate the two territories with new railway and telegraph lines.

On 26 May 1879, a week before the Prince Imperial was killed in Zululand, Yakub Khan signed the Treaty of Gandamak in the village marking the last stand of the British retreat of 1842, chosen by the British as an appropriate place for the restoration of pride. While ceding frontier districts to India and opening up the country to free trade, the treaty left the Amir with nominal sovereignty over the rest of Afghanistan. But Yaqub Kahn was now obliged 'to conduct his relations with Foreign States in accordance with the advice and wishes of the British Government'. Lytton withdrew his troops and proclaimed the success of his (and formerly Frere's) 'Forward Policy'.

The man who signed the Treaty of Gandamak on behalf of Lytton and the India Office was the colourful Major Pierre Louis Napoleon Cavagnari. Born in France, he was the son of General Adolphe Cavagnari, an Italian officer who had served with Napoleon I, and Caroline Montgomery of County Down in Ireland. Having been naturalised as a British citizen, he had trained as an officer in the Bengal army shortly after the Uprising. He had fought during the Uprising in Awadh and was promoted assistant commissioner in the Punjab and then deputy commissioner of Peshawar. As an adviser to Lytton, Cavagnari was all in favour of the Forward Policy, not least because it was a vehicle for him to make a name for himself. Lytton assigned him to accompany Chamberlain in the first attempt to foist a British mission on Sher Ali Kahn, and he was now a natural choice of British representative for the treaty negotiation with his successor.

Once Cavagnari was assigned to take up his residence in Kabul, he reportedly told his friends that 'the chances were four to one that he would never return'.[39] He entered Kabul on 24 July, twenty days after Frere and Chelmsford had finally defeated the Zulu kingdom at Ulundi, and moved into the Amir's residential complex, the Bala Hissar. Just as

Macnaghten had done in 1839, Cavagnari assured Lytton and the India Office that there was popular support in Kabul for the new Amir and his British allies. Lytton exulted that the Afghans 'will like and respect us all the more for the thrashing that we have given Sher Ali and the lesson we have taught Russia'.[40] By the end of July, it seemed that both of the imperial wars of 1879 were over, that British prestige had been reclaimed in Africa and Asia, and that the officials of the Colonial and India Offices at St James Street could finally pause for breath. Within six weeks, however, Cavagnari and all the members of his Kabul mission were dead and Zululand was in a state of civil war.

In September 1879, three Afghan military units arrived in Kabul from Herat and Balkh, demanding that they be paid for their services now that the new Amir had effectively surrendered to British demands. Turned away by the British mission, they joined with local residents enraged by the British presence to force their way into the Bala Hissar, killing Cavagnari and his guards.[41] With Yaqub obliged to abdicate in the face of widespread Afghan resentment at his capitulation to the British, Lytton ordered a second invasion so as to mete out the 'roughest and readiest kind of justice'. General Frederick Roberts led British troops into Kabul again in October and set about burning the capital to the ground, blowing up the Bala Hissar and killing any Afghan suspected of assisting the insurgents. He was following to the letter Lytton's instructions: 'Every Afghan brought to death by the avenging arm of British power, I shall regard as one scoundrel the less. ... Remember it is not *justice* ... but *retribution* that you have to administer'.[42]

As Roberts led a victory parade through the ruined city (having expelled a journalist who sought to inform the liberal British public of his actions), Lytton set about trying to find a substitute compliant Amir. Roberts' army relieved the British besieged at Kandahar and fought Afghans led by Ayub Kahn, a contender for the role of Amir, at the Battle of Maiwand in July 1880, suffering the loss of 1000 British and Indian men. The Afghan insurgents were not finally overcome until late 1880, after Lytton had spent over £14 million in the two occupations, the partial construction of the frontier railway and payments to Afghan allies.[43]

In southern Africa meanwhile, Wolseley took command in August 1879. In the aftermath of the Battle of Ulundi, Cetshwayo was captured and sent initially to Cape Town (see Figure 12.1). Together with Swazi allies, British forces then succeeded where the Transvaal Afrikaners had failed by launching yet another invasion of the Pedi kingdom. Sekhukhune, the Bapedi king, had reluctantly accepted incorporation in the British-annexed Transvaal under Shepstone in 1877 but in early 1878, he was attempting to expel Afrikaner farmers and impose his

PUNCH, OR THE LONDON CHARIVARI.—September 27, 1879.

A BLACK "WHITE ELEPHANT."

John Bull (puzzled). "HE'S COST ME ENOUGH TO CATCH HIM! AND NOW I'VE GOT HIM, WHAT AM I TO DO WITH HIM?"
The Great F-rini (with alacrity). "MIGHT I SUGGEST THE AQUARIUM?"

Figure 12.1 'A Black White Elephant', Joseph Swain, 1879. This cartoon from *Punch*, or the *London Charivari*, 27 September 1879, shows John Bull wondering what to do with the captured Cetshwayo. The man tapping his shoulder is Mr Farini, a showman who often displayed colonised people of colour for the amusement of the British public. Photograph by The Cartoon Collector/Print Collector. Getty Images.

rule over Africans on the eastern side of the Lulu Mountains. By the middle of the year, Sekhukhune had brought most of the small African polities in the area under his control and was communicating with the diffident Cethswayo about combined resistance to Frere's confederation plan. During the prelude to Frere's ultimatum to Cetshwayo, fighting had already been occurring between well-armed Bapedi and colonists from the Transvaal and Kimberley, aided by amaZulu recruited to the Transvaal police. Chelmsford was attempting to deal with the conflict as a side issue from the planned invasion of Zululand.

British troops had initially been committed against Sekhukhune's mountainous stronghold in October 1878 but, failing in their first attempt to take it, they had been withdrawn for the invasion of Zululand. Although Wolseley arrived in southern Africa too late to defeat the Zulu, he could at least finish off the campaign against the Bapedi. Having offered Sekhukhune the option of accepting British rule with a garrison stationed to police him, Wolseley sent 1400 British infantry, 400 mounted colonists, and about 10 000 Africans, mainly Swazi allies, to attack the Bapedi in November 1879. Most of the uncounted thousands of Pedi defenders were killed, including women and children holed up in caves, while Sekhukhune himself lost three brothers and eight of his children before surrendering. The British lost thirteen men but some 500 of their allies among the Swazi warriors, who bore the brunt of the fighting, were killed in the assault. Frere wrote that 'Sir Garnet Wolseley seems to me to deserve great credit for determining to make the attack at once, and, still more, for his dispositions, which, as far as I can judge, left nothing to be desired in thorough thoughtfulness or completeness, and nothing could be better than the decision, punctuality, and courage with which every movement seems to have been executed'.[44]

With Hicks Beach now restricting Frere to the governorship of the Cape, Wolseley succeeded him as the new high commissioner for Natal, the Transvaal and Zululand with orders to pause the pursuit of confederation. From late 1879, rather than occupying Zululand with Indian *sepoys* as Frere had contemplated, he would try to divide and rule a Zululand balkanised into thirteen chiefdoms headed by compliant chiefs and supervised by a Resident Agent. Wolseley proved unable, however, to prevent former Cetshwayo loyalists and rivals from fighting over the remnants of the kingdom, prompting the resentful Frere to write to Hicks Beach that he had implemented a policy of 'divide and don't rule'.[45]

In 1881, Cetshwayo would write to Gladstone, now prime minister, 'Make me happy, and make me a stronger friend than ever of the English. Put me back with some good and discreet men, if you do not trust me'.[46]

By the time Gladstone succeeded Disraeli and Cetshwayo was returned to power under British supervision in 1883, however, Cetshwayo's followers had been undermined. Backed by Afrikaner mercenaries, Cetshwayo's rival, Zibhebhu, attacked him at his new royal kraal near Ulundi, and massacred his supporters. Cetshwayo died at Eshowe soon afterwards.

The verdict of Frances Colenso, daughter of the campaigning Bishop of Natal, on the Anglo-Zulu War and its aftermath, was damning and influential among liberals in Britain:

Here official fiction, under the able management of Sir Bartle Frere, wrought up a situation – peaceful as far as the Zulus were concerned . . . into the appearance of urgent necessity for an army of defence. This, being granted by England, was speedily employed for offence, and brought about one of the most needless and disastrous campaigns that ever disgraced our British arms – a campaign in which honour was reaped, with very few exceptions, only by the dead, though honours have, in modern fashion, been sprinkled far and wide amongst survivors. . . . There are few now . . . who will maintain that the British invasion of Zululand in 1879 was either just, necessary, or 'expedient', even in the modern sense of that word.[47]

By the time Colenso wrote, the Transvaal was independent of Britain again, its Afrikaner farmers, or Boers, having overthrown Shepstone's annexation. At the same time, the Basotho kingdom successfully resisted Wolseley's attempt at disarmament and incorporation. Despite Frere's continued best efforts from the Cape, further efforts at the unification of South Africa were stymied until after the gold rush in Johannesburg and the South African War of 1899–1902. The unification of South Africa would take place in 1910, amidst the combined efforts of both Afrikaner and Briton to restore white control. Within it a system of segregation would be developed to enable the controlled flow of African labour from reserved remnants of formerly independent chiefdoms to the rapidly industrialising cities, just as Frere had hoped.[48]

In the meantime, an anonymous missionary wrote to Frere and, via him, the Colonial Office, to warn of the legacy that two years of continual warfare against African chiefdoms in pursuit of confederation had left for the new South Africa:

The effect of the late war is more alienation than subjection, much less any closer tie between the races. . . . There is a more widespread and hopeless feeling of distrust, on the part of the natives, than before – this may be more prominent at present than it soon will be, but I fear it will remain as one of the results of the war[s]. . . . The feeling I refer to is not written in newspapers nor spoken in public meetings. But it is there. Colonial society at present is strangely blind to its own interests and very far from being moved by Christian principle – There is a deeper alienation between the natives and the whites, between the natives & the Government.[49]

In Afghanistan, Lytton's task was to find a replacement for Yaqub Kahn as Britain's proxy ruler. The man that he persuaded the India Office to support, Abdur Rahman, was the exiled nephew and former rival of the deposed Sher Ali and the grandson of the Amir whom the British had first supplanted back in 1838 and later supported, Dost Mohammad. Ironically the newly favoured Amir had been living under Russian protection in Central Asia. He proved compliant with the British only to a certain extent. Using the threat of re-mobilising tribal leaders against the British, he insisted on renegotiating the terms of the Treaty of Gandamak, so as to remove the condition that he govern alongside a British Resident. With large British monetary subsidies, he tolerated British supervision specifically of his relations with Russia, only through Muslim Indian agents.

Abdur Rahman had been inspired by his time in exile to replicate the Russian Tsar's centralised and autocratic rule, overturning the decentralised 'tribal federalism' that had long characterised Afghanistan. His priority was to disempower potential opponents among Afghanistan's tribal leaders. He became known as the 'iron Amir' for his ruthless determination to do so.[50] Opponents were stripped of their wealth, land and control of religious endowments, prompting forty rebellions over the next two decades and a reign of terror. Gradually instituting a pervasive network of spies, Abdur Rahman was able to execute around 100 000 potential opponents during his two decades of rule. Set on isolating his regime as much as possible from both British and Russian interference, he also blocked British plans to connect Afghanistan with India by rail and telegraph, leaving the country with very little infrastructure.[51] This was the ally that liberal Britain was obliged to prop up in its determination to keep hold of India.

At the same time, access to India courtesy of another British ally was under threat, thanks in part to the wars in Zululand and Afghanistan. By 1879, the newly assertive Khedive of Egypt, Ismail Pasha, had incurred enormous debts to British and French financiers as a result of the building of the Suez Canal, massive infrastructural projects and a war against Ethiopia. As we have seen, in 1875 he had sold his share of the Suez Canal Company to Disraeli's government in an attempt to pay off some of that debt. 'The irony of the situation was that Egypt had embarked on its development schemes to secure independence from Ottoman and European domination. Yet with each new concession, the government of Egypt made itself more vulnerable to European encroachment'.[52]

As a result, Ismail had been reduced to a constitutional sovereign with British and French ministers running his finances. Without the blows endured at Isandhlwana and Kabul, Disraeli later informed Queen

Victoria, the Khedive would probably have remained content with this state of affairs, and been able to suppress internal opposition to British interference. But with British power stretched and prestige dented after the setbacks in each of the concurrent imperial wars, from March 1879, the Khedive began passively to support an Egyptian revolt against British and French control. The British and French governments responded by applying pressure on the Ottoman Sultan to depose Ismail. By the end of June 1879 he was in exile near Naples, and his son had reinstated the Anglo-French ministers. It was the simultaneous wars in Zululand and Afghanistan which, according to Disraeli, had therefore forced the British and French governments into a more forceful and direct control of Egyptian governance by the end of 1879.[53]

There were immediate political consequences of the simultaneous wars in Afghanistan and Zululand in Britain too. In late 1879, campaigning began for the 1880 general election. Gladstone had already seized upon the Bulgarian massacres to discredit Disraeli's approach to the Eastern Question. He now galvanised the Liberal Party to capitalise on the opposition encountered by the Forward Policy in Afghanistan and the confederation project in southern Africa.

Gladstone's path-breaking campaign to win the Midlothian parliamentary seat from the Tories and secure a general election victory was based upon a series of speeches attacking these colonial misadventures, but without casting doubt on the legitimacy of Britain's empire as a whole. In a speech at Leeds, he declared, 'While we are opposed to imperialism, we are devoted to the empire'. His rhetoric was that of the liberal, benevolent empire in which patriotic Britons still like to believe. The Midlothian campaign 'presented his commitment to a world community, governed by law, protecting the weak. His vision of the ideal world order combined universalism and inclusiveness; he appealed to group feeling, the sense of concern for others, rising eventually to the larger picture of the unity of mankind'.

In November 1879, in a series of addresses, Gladstone asserted that both amaZulu and Afghans had a natural right to defend themselves from aggression. Of the Afghan War he said, 'And when, going forth from their villages they had resisted, what you find is this, that those who went forth were slain, and that the village was burned. ... The women and the children were driven forth to perish in the snows of winter. ... To think that the name of England, under no political necessity, but for a war as frivolous as ever was waged in the history of man, should be associated with consequences such as these?' Gladstone appealed to the British electors to 'Remember the rights of the savage, as we call him. Remember that the happiness of his humble home, remember that the sanctity of life in the hill villages of Afghanistan among the winter snows, is as inviolable in the eye of Almighty God as can be your own'. He concluded by setting out the principles by which Britons could have their global power, but with a clear conscience: 'The first thing is to foster the strength of the Empire by just legislation and economy at home. My second principle of foreign policy is this: peace ... you should avoid needless and entangling engagements. ... The foreign policy of England should always be inspired by the love of freedom'.[54]

Gladstone's rhetoric helped unify the Liberal Party and gain him a decisive electoral victory in 1880. His government ended Disraeli's Forward Policy and settled for Russian influence up to the border with Afghanistan but no further. Lytton resigned along with Disraeli, but not before he had sought to remind Britons that the future of the empire depended not so much on their benevolent intent as on their ability to display 'the courage and determination of their forefathers'.[55]

Further Reading

Delius, P., *The Land Belongs to Us: The Pedi Polity, the Boers, and the British in the Nineteenth Century Transvaal*, Ravan Press, 1983.

Laband, J., *Zulu Warriors: The Battle for the South African Frontier*, Yale University Press, 2014.

Lee, J., *Afghanistan: A History from 1260 to the Present*, Reaktion Books, 2018.

Robson, B., *The Road to Kabul: The Second Afghan War, 1878–1881*, Spellmount, 2007.

Conclusion to Part III: A Liberal Empire?

It has always been easier to define liberalism by what it is not rather than what it is. Never a coherent programme of governance, it emerged in modern Europe and its offshoots as an expression of the rights of individuals against arbitrary, absolutist governance. Rights of Assembly, representative government, free trade and trial by an independent judiciary had, initially, to be won in Britain through radical agitation. By no coincidence, this occurred at the very time that its governing elites were consolidating a vastly expanded empire in the wake of the Revolutionary and Napoleonic Wars. During our first snapshot of that empire's governance, in 1838, a liberal order was just emerging in Britain, the new prosperity gained from colonialism being as much a part of that process as the Reform Act of 1832 or the agitation against the Corn Laws. By the mid nineteenth century, British liberals believed in free trade as an economic principle, and as the appropriate response to colonial famines, first in India, then in Ireland and the Cape Colony. The 1867 Reform Act consolidated liberal governance in Britain by extending the franchise again, at the same time that arbitrary rule over black people in Jamaica was condoned. In the mid 1870s, a new feature was added to Britain's liberal dispensation as Disraeli's 'One Nation Tory' government intervened in housing, working conditions and the education of the workforce.

By 1879, the more uniformly recruited officials governing the empire from a consolidated headquarters at St James Street were agreed that Britain's was the best of all possible political dispensations. When it came to empire though, it was again easier to define what liberal governance would not be, rather than what it would be. The British Empire would not be characterised by the supposed tawdry glitter of the French empire, the brutality of the Spanish, the ruthlessness of the German, the despotism of the Russian, the backwardness of the Qing, or the decadence of the Ottoman. Nor, however, could it be governed on the same principles as Britain itself. Liberalism was appropriate for Britons, at home and overseas, but only to a certain extent for colonised subjects of colour. Imperial subjects needed certain cultural and educational correctives before liberal governance could ever work its progressive magic among them.

By the 1870s, many Indians had been persuaded of the advantages of Britain's liberal political dispensation. Inspired by the doctrines of Bentham, Mill and Macaulay, men like Syed Mahmood Kahn were seeking to become active participants, assisting British viceroys in the governance of their own country. The reforms led by the Benthamite James Fitzjames Stephen, however, just like the adaptations to civil rights that Stephen's father had overseen with emancipation, permitted only a limited role for Indians in governance. Like his father, Syed Mahmood Kahn became disillusioned by the ways in which the supposedly universal principles of British liberalism were in practice racially circumscribed. Rather than adapting liberal principles so as to mitigate the worst effects of famine, for instance, reformers like Stephen adapted them so as to recombine executive and judicial powers, which had been so carefully disarticulated in Britain. The viceroy, Lytton's, own liberalism was equally selective. A fundamentalist adherent of free trade as a panacea for economic ills, even in the face of the starvation of 5.5 million subjects, he was not so enthusiastic about a free press or free speech.

After the attempts to impose British civilisation on imperial subjects by force in the 1850s had largely been rejected, the progress of liberal governance in Britain proceeded hand in hand with the firmer conviction of white racial supremacy. The policy most aggressively pursued by Carnarvon and Herbert at the Colonial Office in 1878–9, confederation, was predicated on Dilke's vision of a *Greater Britain*, comprising associations of white, self-governing, Anglophone men girdling the earth. Women and people of colour were to be this global polity's subjects rather than its citizens. Furthermore, the realisation of confederation, a precondition for this vision, would require staggering levels of violence.

The violence enacted to sustain and expand the British Empire in the nineteenth century may not have been on the scale of the Taiping Rebellion and its suppression in China, and, other than in suppressing the 1857 Uprising, Britons may not have perpetrated individual massacres on the scale of the Ottomans' Bulgarian atrocities, but British killing was both extensive and prolonged. Even without recounting the casualties of two occupations of Afghanistan and two Opium Wars, tens of thousands of amaXhosa, Griqua, Batswana, Bapedi and amaZulu were killed in 1878–9 alone, in order to bring Greater Britain about in southern Africa. As the most recent *Cambridge History of South Africa* observes, 'The scale of warfare conducted all over southeastern Africa during [Frere's] high commissionership dwarfed all previous conflicts in the region. Only the colonial habit of blaming all wars on African aggression and later historians' tendency to treat the history of southern Africa on a region-by-region basis have prevented these conflicts from getting the label they deserve: the first British War for Southern African Unification (1877–82)'.[1]

There were certainly beneficiaries of British liberal governmental principles among colonial subjects of colour, just as St James' Street officials intended, in 1879. Indians sentenced to execution in Mauritius would not, at least, be publicly beheaded. Relatively small numbers of Indigenous men could exercise the vote alongside the vast majority of white settler men in the self-governing colonies, and enslaved peoples benefitted from the anti-slavery crusades of Livingstone, Frere and Carnarvon in East and West Africa. Wealthier Indian businesspeople could also use the railways that Dalhousie had admitted building for Britons' benefit, while tens of thousands more gained employment in the Indian government's expanded bureaucracy. Reconciling liberal aspiration with reality, however, was a thorny issue for those at the coalface of colonial governance in London. Even a revitalised cadre of eager, liberal, often Eton-educated men, some of whom had the best intentions to render the British Empire a force for good, found it impossible to realise an empire of liberalism when colonial legislatures enacted racially discriminatory law and when threats to British prosperity, or to the maintenance of British rule itself, required more authoritarian measures or the recruitment of authoritarian allies.

Wherever the basic premise of British control was secure, and whenever British public opinion or political invective was mobilised against governmental hypocrisy, liberalism could gain qualified purchase in imperial governance. However, liberal rhetoric would never override basic economic or geopolitical self-interest. Where trade-offs were necessary the interests of white Britons always came first. The cementing of factory and public health reform in Britain ran alongside the coercive recruitment of Pacific Islanders' labour for new cotton plantations, such as the one formerly owned by the Colonial Office's permanent under-secretary, in Australia and the Pacific, and the extension of the Indian indentured labour system for sugar production in Natal and Fiji. In 1879, Fiji's governor was still debating with the Colonial Office the merits of allowing indentured Pacific Islanders access to their own wages in cash, rather than having the Agent General for Immigration spend them on the workers' behalf.[2]

The officials of St James' Street, simultaneously preoccupied with trying to rein in a governor set on provoking war in southern Africa and managing the latest invasion of Afghanistan, might encourage reforms to these systems of labour exploitation, but they could not fundamentally improve their subjects' conditions. Where the extension of 'an ideology that sought to provide benefit to those under imperial sway' might jeopardise control of empire itself, as on India's north-western frontier, liberal principles were set aside entirely.[3] If it took alliances with a ruthless and autocratic Afghan Amir to preserve British rule in India, then so be it.

The British Empire by 1879 was governed by an entity of split personality. It was (and still often is) imagined as a non-racial and essentially progressive liberal force for global improvement. It certainly invested heavily in steamship, railway and telegraph technologies, which yielded unprecedented global connectivity, and in the construction of legal and educational infrastructures around the world. These features led, as Ferguson argues, to a more integrated global economy.[4] But the British Empire, like any other, was simultaneously violent, discriminatory and rapacious: characteristics witnessed by millions of its incorporated subjects overseas and overlooked by most of those at home. In India, 'Lytton's viceroyalty highlighted that contradiction between the words and the actions of British imperialism which was to provide the animus behind the eventual foundation of the Indian National Congress in 1885'.[5] In Afghanistan, 'what the British gained' from the Second Afghan War 'was the everlasting bad will of Afghans'.[6] In southern Africa, a series of 'small wars' for the British Empire were wars of societal annihilation and subjugation for African people, which enabled the aberration of apartheid until the end of the twentieth century. For all Gladstone's opposition to Disraeli's former imperialism after 1879, the need to preserve an empire that now had a foothold in Egypt and a far greater stake in Africa would continue to require distinctly illiberal techniques and allies. Its legitimation among contemporary Britons continued to be based not so much on the benefits that empire brought to people of colour, as on a sense of their deep seated inferiority to white people. Disavowal of what actually went on in the colonies was, and is, the only way for Britons to reconcile the liberal idea, and the more self-interested practice, of their empire.[7]

Appendix: Cast of Characters

1838

Ajayi (Bishop Samuel Crowther), 'liberated African' and Bishop of West Africa

George Eden, earl of **Auckland**, Governor of Bengal and Governor General of India

George Frederick **Angas**, agent for West Indian slave owners and compensation beneficiary who invested in the colonization of South Australia

George **Arthur**, lieutenant governor of Upper Canada, former superintendent of Honduras and lieutenant governor of Van Diemen's Land

Alexander **Burnes**, East India Company soldier, translator and spy, envoy to Amir of Afghanistan

Thomas Fowell **Buxton**, MP and leader of the antislavery and then humanitarian lobbies

Charles **Buller**, MP, journalist, critic of James Stephen and the Colonial Office, Wakefieldian

Patrick **Campbell**, East India Company agent in Alexandria, responsible for passage across the Isthmus of Suez

Francis **Cockburn**, governor of the Bahamas

Sir Benjamin **D'Urban**, governor of the Cape Colony

Charles **Elliot**, plenipotentiary representing the British traders in Canton

Thomas **Elliott**, Agent General for Emigration at the Colonial Office

John, thirteenth Lord **Elphinstone**, governor of Madras

Sir John **Franklin**, lieutenant governor of Van Diemen's Land and Arctic explorer

Robert **Godlonton**, editor of the *Graham's Town Journal* and British settler spokesman in the eastern Cape Colony

Charles Grant, Lord **Glenelg**, Secretary of State for the Colonies and former President of the Board of Control

Robert **Grant**, governor of Bombay and Lord Glenelg's younger brother

Anna **Gurney**, humanitarian campaigner, writer, Anglo-Saxon scholar and maritime live-saver

Hintsa, paramount chief of the Rharhabe Xhosa, killed by Harry Smith's column in 1835

John Cam **Hobhouse** (Baron Broughton), President of the Board of Control

Thomas **Hodgkin**, Quaker reformer, medical researcher and founder of the Aborigines Protection Society

James Deacon **Hume**, Huskisson's successor at the Board of Trade and proponent of free trade

William **Huskisson**, former President of the Board of trade and briefly Colonial Secretary who had promoted free trade

Robert **Wilmot-Horton**, governor of Ceylon, emigration theorist and former Colonial Office permanent under-secretary

Sir Richard **Jenkins**, Deputy Chair of the East India Company Directors

James Henry **Johnston**, East India Company captain who developed steam route between Britain and India via Suez

Kahkewaquonaby/Peter Jones: Mississauga convert, activist and leader of the Credit River community

Akbar **Kahn**, Dost Mohammad's son and leader of the resistance against the British occupation of Kabul

Sir James **Lushington**, Chair of the East India Company Directors

Thomas Babington **Macaulay**, Secretary to the Board of Control during the 1833 East India Company Charter renewal and later famous historian

Alexander **Maconochie**, author of *Report on the State of Prison Discipline in Van Diemen's Land*, private secretary to Sir John Franklin

George **Maclean**, agent to the African Committee, Sierra Leone

Dost **Mohammad**, Amir of Afghanistan overthrown by the invasion of 1839

Maqoma, Ngqika Xhosa chief and leader during Sixth Frontier War in the Cape Colony

William Hay **Macnaghten**, advisor to Auckland in the occupation of Afghanistan

Sir Evan John Murray **MacGregor**, the Scottish clan chief and governor of Antigua and Bermuda

Sir William **Molesworth**, chair of committee recommending end to convict transportation and assignment in Australian colonies

William **Nicolay**, governor of Mauritius, former governor of Dominica and St Kitts

Dr John **Philip**, Director of the London Missionary Society, Cape Colony

James **Read**, LMS missionary at Bethelsdorp and then the Khoisan Kat River settlement in the Cape Colony

Ranjit **Singh**, Maharaja of the Punjab

Sir Harry **Smith**, military commander and later governor of the Cape Colony, commander during the Sixth Frontier War

Lionel **Smith**, governor of Jamaica

James **Stephen**, Permanent Under-Secretary of the Colonial Office

Alfred Ward **Stephens**, editor and proprietor of the *Sydney Herald* and campaigner for responsible government in New South Wales

Andries **Stoeffels**, Khoi-Khoi Christian convert who testified before the Aborigines Committee

Joseph **Sturge**, reformer and campaigner for immediate end to apprenticeship

Dwarkanath **Tagore**, Indian businessman, pioneer of steam investment in India and philanthropist

Jan (Dyani) **Tzatzoe**, Xhosa chief and Christian convert who testified before the Aborigines Committee

Edward Gibbon **Wakefield**, emigration theorist and publicist

James **Williams**, apprenticed former slave in Jamaica and author of *A Narrative of Events since the First of August, 1834*

1857

John **Bowring**, governor of Hong Kong and Plenipotentiary to China

Charles **Canning**, governor general of India

George Villiers, the Earl of **Clarendon**, Foreign Secretary

James Ramsay, Lord **Dalhousie**, governor general of India, 1848–56

Frederick **Douglas**, African American antislavery activist

George **Grey**, governor of the Cape Colony, former explorer and governor of South Australia and New Zealand, and ethnographer

Syed Ahmed **Khan**, Company official, author of *The Causes of the Indian Revolt* and Muslim scholar

Henry **Labouchere**, Secretary of State for the Colonies, former Chief Secretary for Ireland

Rani **Lakshmibai**, the Rani of Jhansi, leader during the Indian Uprising whose adopted son was disinherited by Dalhousie

Ross Donnelly **Mangles**, Chairman of the East India Company Court of Directors

Herman **Merivale**, Permanent Under-Secretary at the Colonial Office, author of *Lectures on Colonization*

Mhlakaza, Nongqawuse's uncle, who helped disseminate and empower her prophecies

Nongqawuse, fifteen-year-old Xhosa girl whose prophecies underpinned the Great Xhosa Cattle Killing

Lord **Palmerston**, Prime Minister and former Foreign Secretary

Henry **Parkes**, British consul in Canton

Nana **Sahib**, adopted heir to Baji Rao II of the Maratha Confederacy and leader of the rebels in Kanpur (Cawnpore) during the Uprising

Wajid Ali **Shah**, nawab of Awadh (Oudh) overthrown by Dalhousie shortly before the Uprising

Robert **Vernon Smith**, President of the Board of Control

1879

Napoléon Eugène Louis Jean Joseph **Bonaparte**, French Prince Imperial killed by Zulu warriors in second British invasion of Zululand

Herbert, Henry Howard Molyneux, **Earl of Carnarvon**, Secretary of State for the Colonies

Sir Pierre Louis Napoleon **Cavagnari**, British envoy to Afghanistan

Cetshwayo, Zulu King removed after Anglo-Zulu War

Frederic Augustus Thesiger, Baron **Chelmsford**, commander of the British forces during wars against the amXhosa, Bapedi and amaZulu

Romseh Chunder **Dutt**, lecturer and critic of British policies in India

Sir Henry Bartle **Frere**, South African High Commissioner and former East India Company official and imperial trouble-shooter

James Anthony **Froude**, historian who attempted to negotiate South African confederation

Charles Wentworth **Dilke**, travel writer, politician and author of *Greater Britain*

Gathorne Hardy, Earl of **Cranbrook**, Secretary of State for India

Robert George Wyndham **Herbert**, Permanent Under-Secretary at the Colonial Office and former premier of Queensland

Abdur Rahman **Kahn**, Afghan Amir installed by British, known as the 'Iron Amir'

Sher Ali **Kahn**, Afghan Amir displaced by Lytton's Forward Policy

Syed Mahmood **Kahn**, judge and critic of British governance in India and Syed Ahmed Kahn's son

Yaqub **Kahn**, the Amir whom Lytton hoped to co-opt in Afghanistan.

Edward Robert Bulwer, first earl of **Lytton**, Viceroy of India

Sekhukhune, Bapedi paramount

Theophilus **Shepstone**, Native Commissioner in Natal and administrator of the Transvaal

James Fitzjames **Stephen**, law reformer in India and James Stephen's son

Garnet **Wolseley**, General who led British forces in the Ashanti War, the Anglo-Zulu War's latter stages and the Anglo-Pedi War

Notes

CO refers to Colonial Office files kept at The National Archives, Kew
IOR refers to India Office Records kept at the British Library. These include the
records of the East India Company.

INTRODUCTION

1. See A. Curthoys, 'We've Just Started Making National Histories and You Want Us to Stop Already?', in A. Burton, ed., *After the Imperial Turn: Thinking with and Through the Nation*, Duke University Press, 2003, 70–89.
2. C. Hall, 'Introduction: Thinking the Postcolonial, Thinking the Empire', in C. Hall, ed., *Cultures of Empire: Colonizers in Britain and the Empire in the Nineteenth and Twentieth Centuries: A Reader*, Manchester University Press, 2000; K. Wilson, ed., *A New Imperial History: Culture, Identity and Modernity in Britain and the Empire, 1660–1840*, Cambridge University Press, 2004; M. Sinha, *Colonial Masculinity: The 'Manly Englishman' and the 'Effeminate Bengali' in the Late Nineteenth Century*, Manchester University Press, 1995; C. Hall, *Civilising Subjects: Metropole and Colony in the English Imagination 1830–1867*, Polity, 2002; A. Burton, *Burdens of History: British Feminists, Indian Women, and Imperial Culture, 1865–1915*, University of North Carolina Press, 2000. At the same time, John MacKenzie was initiating a vein of enquiry on the ways that Britons themselves identified as an imperial people. J. M. MacKenzie, *Imperialism and Popular Culture*, Manchester University Press, 1989.
3. In this they were inspired by a more literary tradition of postcolonial writing associated with Edward Said, Homi Bhabha and Gyatri Spivak. See D. Kennedy, 'Imperial History and Post-Colonial Theory', *Journal of Imperial and Commonwealth History*, 24, 3, 1996, 345–63.
4. A. Lester, *Imperial Networks: Creating Identities in Nineteenth Century South Africa and Britain*, Routledge, 2001; T. Ballantyne, *Orientalism and Race: Aryanism in the British Empire*, Palgrave Macmillan, 2002. Lester's work drew in particular upon the 'new imperial history' of Catherine Hall, which focused on the relationship between Britain and empire: C. Hall, *White, Male and Middle Class: Explorations in Feminism and History*, Polity, 1992.

5. See T. Banivanua Mar, *Decolonisation and the Pacific: Indigenous Globalisation and the Ends of Empire*, Cambridge University Press, 2016.
6. See for example the structure of L. James, *Rise and Fall of the British Empire*, Abacus, 1995; N. Ferguson, *Empire: How Britain Made the Modern World*, Penguin, 2018.
7. J. Gallagher and R. E. Robinson, 'The Imperialism of Free Trade', *Economic History Review*, 2nd series, 6, 1, 1953, 1–15; R. Robinson and J. Gallagher with A. Denny, *Africa and the Victorians: The Official Mind of Imperialism*, 2nd ed., Macmillan, 1981, xvii. See also J. S. Galbraith, 'The "Turbulent Frontier" as a Factor in British Expansion', *Comparative Studies in Society and History*, 2, 2, 1960, 151; R. Robinson, 'Non-European Foundations of European Imperialism', in E. R. Owen and B. Sutcliffe, eds, *Studies in the Theory of Imperialism*, Longman, 1972, 117–42.
8. P. J. Cain and A. G. Hopkins, *British Imperialism: Innovation and Expansion 1688–1914*, Longman, 1993, 5.
9. Cain and Hopkins, *British Imperialism*, 15.
10. T. Ballantyne, *Orientalism and Race: Aryanism in the British Empire*, Palgrave, 2002, 2.
11. D. Fieldhouse, 'Can Humpty-Dumpty Be Put Together Again? Imperial History in the 1980s', *The Journal of Imperial and Commonwealth History*, 12, 2, 1984, 10, 18, 22.
12. CO 537/155, Military, Confidential General & Original Correspondence; Memorandum (vol. pp. 350–53), T. Frederick Elliot, 28 January 1860.
13. Quoted by J. Darwin, *The Empire Project: The Rise and Fall of the British World System, 1830–1970*, Cambridge University Press, 2011, 268.
14. J. Black, *Imperial Legacies: the British Empire around the World*, Encounter Books, 2019, 168.
15. Ferguson, *Empire*.
16. Black, *Imperial Legacies*, 168.
17. Ferguson, *Empire*, 3–5.
18. Black, *Imperial Legacies*, 10.
19. This is not to mention the starvation of millions of Indians (5.5 million in 1878–9 alone) exacerbated by British free trade policies or the killing of thousands of Indigenous peoples resisting British colonisation in the settler colonies.
20. CO 179/132, *Natal* (vol. pp. 119–20), No. 7418, War Office to Colonial Office, 8 May 1879.
21. CO 537/155, Memorandum, Thomas Frederick Elliot, 28 January 1860.
22. CO 54/329, *Ceylon* (vol. pp. 387–97), No. 6925 Ward to Labouchere, 26 June 1857.
23. CO 54/517, *Ceylon* (vol. p. 268), No. 44–4292, Longden to Hicks Beach, 4 February 1879.
24. CO 137/221, *Jamaica* (vol. pp. 148–51), Legislative No. 3636, Smith to Glenelg, 15 November 1837.
25. Ferguson, *Empire*, 5.

26. J. C. Beaglehole, 'The Colonial Office, 1782–1854', *Australian Historical Studies* 1, 3, 1941, 170–89.

27. *Catalogue of the Printed Books of the Library of the Colonial Office*, Eyre and Spottiswood, 1896.

28. Charles Buller, 'Responsible Government', 1839, https://archive.org/details/McGillLibrary129131 4915. Buller's description provided the model for Dickens' 'Circumlocution Office' in Little Dorrit.

29. The modern Lloyds of London building stands on its site, appropriately enough given both organisations' underpinning of Britain's nineteenth-century maritime dominance.

30. CO 167/198, Mauritius, No. 101, Nicolay to Glenelg, 10 October 1837. Colonial Office to Maberly, 27 January 1838; Colonial Office to Nicolay, 26 January 1838.

31. Cambridge University Library, Add 7511, James Stephen's diary, 1 January 1846.

32. Cambridge University Library, Add 7888, II/122, f. 57, Letters from James Stephen to his wife, 30 March 1841.

33. On a regular basis throughout the year, William Cabell of the Board of Control would inform James Stephen that 'Mr. Charles Dick Wittenoon is again about to proceed to Malta through France in charge of Despatches for India and to bring back the Official Despatches expected by the January Mail from India'. CO 158/103, 3795, Malta, Cabell, India Board (EI Board) to Stephen, 24 December 1838.

34. P. Swaab, 'Lamb, Charles (1775–1834), Essayist', in *Oxford Dictionary of National Biography*, www.oxforddnb.com/view/10.1093/ref:odnb/97801986 14128.001.0001/odnb-9780198614128-e-15912; A. P. Kaminsky, *The India Office, 1880–1910*, Mansell, 1986.

35. D. Howlett, 'Jenkins, Sir Richard (1785–1853), East India Company Servant', in *Oxford Dictionary of National Biography*, www.oxforddnb.com/view/10.1093/ref:odnb/9780198614128.001.0001/odnb-9780198614128-e-14733.

36. A. Shaw, 'Stephen, Sir James (1789–1859), Civil Servant', in *Oxford Dictionary of National Biography*, www.oxforddnb.com/view/10.1093/ref:odnb/9780198614128.001.0001/odnb-9780198614128-e-26374.

37. Cambridge University Library, Add 7888, II/122, f. 73, Letters from James Stephen to his wife, 1816–45, 21 February 1842.

38. P. Knaplund, *James Stephen and the British Colonial System: 1813–1847*, University of Wisconsin Press, 1953.

39. G. Martin, 'Grant, Charles, Baron Glenelg (1778–1866), Politician', in *Oxford Dictionary of National Biography*, www.oxforddnb.com/view/10.1093/ref:odnb/9780198614128.001.0001/odnb-9780198614128-e-11249.

40. Stephen to Mrs. Austin, Feb. 12, 1839, in C. E. Stephen ed., *The Right Honorable Sir James Stephen: Letters with Biographical Notes by his Daughter, Caroline Emelia*, John Bellows, 1906, 56.

41. Shaw, 'Stephen'.

42. Shaw, 'Stephen'.

43. The loss of the American colonies was caused, in part, by the connections across the British Empire as a whole. The British government's attempts to prop up the stock price of the East India Company after the South Sea Bubble crash, by granting it a monopoly over the American tea market, was what prompted the Boston Tea Party.

44. E. E. Williams, *Capitalism and Slavery*, University North Carolina Press, 1994.

45. C. Jeppesen, 'East Meets West: Exploring the Connections between Britain, the Caribbean and the East India Company, c.1757–1857', in K. Donington, R. Hanley and J. Moody, eds, *Britain's History and Memory of Transatlantic Slavery*, Liverpool University Press, 2016, 102–28.

46. See S. Doherty, L. Ford, K. McKenzie, N. Parkinson, D. Roberts, P. Halliday, Z. Laidlaw, A. Lester and P. Stern, 'Inquiring into the Corpus of Empire', *Journal of World History*, forthcoming.

47. See E. J. Evans, *The Great Reform Act of 1832*, 2nd ed., Routledge, 1994, 1; see also Michael Brock, *The Great Reform Act*, Gregg Revivals, 1973; Philip Harling, *The Waning of Old Corruption: The Politics of Economical Reform in Britain, 1779–1846*, Clarendon Press, 1996; Boyd Hilton, *A Mad, Bad and Dangerous People? England 1783–1846*, Clarendon Press, 2006; Jonathan Parry, *The Rise and Fall of Liberal Government in Victorian Britain*, Yale University Press, 1993; John Cannon, *Parliamentary Reform, 1640–1832*, Cambridge University Press, 1973; Peter Mandler, *Aristocratic Government in the Age of Reform: Whigs and Liberals, 1830–1852*, Oxford University Press, 1990. For a more contextualised approach to domestic political reform, see Arthur Burns and Joanna Innes, eds, *Rethinking the Age of Reform: Britain 1780–1850*, Cambridge University Press, 2003.

48. T. Ertman, 'The Great Reform Act of 1832 and British Democratization', *Comparative Political Studies*, 43, 8/9, 2010, 1006–10. See also Hilton, *A Mad, Bad and Dangerous People*.

49. *Mirror of Parliament*, 22 November 1830, 310–11, quoted E. A. Smith, 'Grey, Charles, Second Earl Grey (1764–1845), Prime Minister', in *Oxford Dictionary of National Biography*, www.oxforddnb.com/view/10.1093/ref:od nb/9780198614128.001.0001/odnb-9780198614128-e-11526.

50. Brock, *The Great Reform Act*, 19–20, 34, 310–13; C. Schonhardt-Bailey, 'Specific Factors, Capital Markets, Portfolio Diversification, and Free Trade: Domestic Determinants of the Repeal of the Corn Laws', *World Politics*, 43, 4, 1991, 545–69.

51. See Cain and Hopkins, *British Imperialism*, 50–61.

52. Mandler, *Aristocratic Government in the Age of Reform*, 151.

53. Harling, *The Waning of Old Corruption*; Parry, *The Rise and Fall of Liberal Government*; Hilton, *A Mad, Bad and Dangerous People*; D. Turley, *The Culture of English Antislavery, 1780–1860*, London, 1991. MPs representing the East India Company's investors were also mounting growing objections to trade preferences for Caribbean sugar over that grown in India: M. Taylor, 'Empire and Parliamentary Reform: The 1832 Reform Act Revisited', in Burns and Innes, *Rethinking the Age of Reform*, 295–311.

1 SETTING THE SCENE FOR EMANCIPATION

1. www.slavevoyages.org/voyage/search.
2. www.ucl.ac.uk/lbs/project/context/.
3. N. Draper, *The Price of Emancipation: Slave-ownership, Compensation and British Society at the End of Slavery*, Cambridge, 2010.
4. Hansard, Vol. 42, House of Commons Debate, 'Abolition of Negro Apprenticeship', 29 March 1838, 40–108.
5. CO 23/100, *Bahamas*, No. 28, Cockburn to Glenelg, 15 January 1838.
6. Quoted A. Major, '"The Slavery of East and West": Abolitionists and "Unfree" Labour in India, 1820–1833', *Slavery and Abolition*, 31, 2010, 501–25.
7. D. Kooiman, 'Conversion from Slavery to Plantation Labour: Christian Mission in South India (19th Century)', *Social Scientist*, 19, 8/9, 1991, 57–71.
8. A. William, *The Law and Custom of Slavery in British India, in a Series of Letters to Thomas Fowell Buxton, Esq.*, Weeks, Jordan, 1840, 10–11.
9. M. Jasanoff, *Liberty's Exiles: The Loss of America and the Remaking of the British Empire*, Harper, 2012; S. Schama, *Rough Crossings: Britain, the Slaves and the American Revolution*, Vintage, 2009.
10. Quoted Major, 'The Slavery of East and West', 503.
11. Wilmot-Horton was Lord Byron's cousin and was thus acquainted in the early part of his career with the poet's friend John Cam Hobhouse, president at the Board of Control in 1838. It was Wilmot-Horton who had destroyed Byron's memoirs in order to protect the family's reputation.
12. Quoted C. S. M. Wickramasinghe, 'The Abolition of Colonial and PreColonial "Slavery" from Ceylon (Sri Lanka)', *Cultural and Social History*, 7, 2010, 315–35.
13. CO 54/156, *Ceylon*, No. 144, Wilmot-Horton to Glenelg, 21 February 1838.
14. Quoted in Carter, 'The Transition', 120.
15. CO 167/198, *Mauritius*, No. 125, Nicolay to Glenelg, 5 March 1838.
16. S. A. Crowther, 'The Narrative of Samuel Ajaya Crowther', 1837, in P. D. Curtin, *Africa Remembered: Narratives by West Africans from the Era of the Slave Trade*, University of Wisconsin Press, 1968.
17. In early 1838, Stephen expressed his dismay when a number of captives freed from a Portuguese slave ship were enlisted in the Bahamas. The governor at the time was Francis Cockburn, who had fought in South America and the Iberian Peninsula before taking on the Americans in the war of 1812. He had helped establish thousands of British emigrants in Upper Canada and Quebec before his appointment as superintendent of British Honduras from 1830 to 1837, after which he had transferred to the Bahamas. Following his report of the captured Portuguese slave ship, Glenelg told him that 'the welfare of the captured Africans and the interest of the Bahama Islands would both be best committed by returning them as settlers instead of permitting their enlistment as soldiers'. Pointing out that this opinion was 'at variance with that which prevails within the Colony', Cockburn grudgingly conceded that military recruitment would be avoided

in future. CO 23/100, *Bahamas*, No. 45, Official Reply from Colonial Office to Lieutenant Colonel Cockburn, 12 March 1838; No. 34, Cockburn to Glenelg, 15 January 1838.

18. B. Everill, *Abolition and Empire in Sierra Leone and Liberia*, Palgrave Macmillan, 2013.

19. Quoted in S. Schwarz, 'Reconstructing the Life Histories of Liberated Africans: Sierra Leone in the Early Nineteenth Century', *History in Africa*, 39, 2012, 175–207.

20. CO 267/150, Correspondence Number: Slave Trade, No.1, Disbrowe, The Hague, to Palmerston, Foreign Office, 7 February 1838. James Stephen comment on CO 267/150, No. 288, Joseph Reid, W. M. Hutton, and J. G. Nicholls (Gold Coast Committee) to Grey, 24 February 1838.

21. Shortly after Maclean's initial correspondence with Stephen in late 1837, Maclean's new wife, Letitia Elizabeth Landon, was found dead next to an empty bottle of prussic acid in the couple's quarters in the Cape Coast Castle. During the ensuing scandal, the British press insinuated that Maclean's African common-law wife was responsible for Letitia's murder, and the Gold Coast leaped to the attention of the British public for the first time since the abolition of the slave trade.

22. A. Maconochie, *Report on the State of Prison Discipline in Van Diemen's Land, etc.: Presented to both Houses of Parliament by Command of Her Majesty*, William Gore Elliston, 1838.

23. When the undiplomatic Maconochie's report was published, it proved so scathing of the governing establishment with whom Franklin now had to work in Van Diemen's Land that the new governor dismissed him. Maconochie was kept out of the way as governor of the Norfolk Island penal settlement for re-offenders, which he tried to turn into a model reformatory. By the 1840s James Stephen had had enough of his 'much ill-timed and superficial preaching', but his system of rehabilitation through the award of 'marks' for good behaviour, resulting in earlier release from indeterminate sentences, would, in the end, prove influential in penal reform in both Britain and the USA.

24. CO 267/150 G. Maclean to Nicholls, 26 February 1838.

25. CO 30/22/3B, *Van Diemen's Land*, Franklin to Glenelg, 9 December 1837.

26. By the time of his appointment to the lieutenant governorship of Van Diemen's Land, Franklin already was a celebrity in Britain. He had been on his uncle Matthew Flinders' ship *Investigator* as it circumnavigated Australia, fought in the Battle of Trafalgar and led a party sent to explore the Arctic for a north-west passage between the Pacific and Atlantic oceans. After losing eleven of the twenty men in his party, he was rescued from starvation only through the assistance of Inuit people, but returned home in 1822 a hero. His wife Lady Jane Franklin's transparent zeal for political reform in Van Diemen's Land, sympathy for convicted women transportees and own exploratory adventures (she would be the first woman to travel overland from Port Phillip to Sydney), occasioned outrage among the men of his government, who felt that Franklin should remind her of her proper place. Franklin's famous disappearance on

a third Arctic exploratory voyage in 1845 was occasioned because Stephen and the Colonial Office had seen his Australian governorship as a failure and declined to reappoint him.

27. CO 30/22/3B Franklin to Glenelg, 9 December 1837.

2 MANAGING EXPECTATIONS

1. CO 137/221, *Jamaica*, No. 231, Smith to Glenelg, 7 February 1838.
2. Comments of J. Stephen on CO 137/221, Jamaica: Dispatches, No. 231, 7 February 1838.
3. Anne Chambers, *The Great Leviathan, The Life of Howe Peter Browne, second Marquess of Sligo, 1788–1845*, New Island, 2017.
4. CO 137/221, *Jamaica*, No. 216, Smith to Glenelg, 20 December 1837.
5. CO 167/198, *Mauritius*, No. 123, Nicolay to Glenelg, 18 November 1837.
6. Even in Jamaica, as we will see in Part II, the planter dominated assembly managed, in the years after emancipation, to raise the franchise qualification so as to exclude the vast majority of people of colour after all.
7. J. Williams, *A Narrative of Events, since the First of August, 1834, by James Williams, an Apprenticed Labourer in Jamaica*, ed. D. Paton, Duke University Press, 2001.
8. Hansard, 'Abolition of Negro Apprenticeship', 40–108.
9. I. Gross, 'Parliament and the Abolition of Negro Apprenticeship 1835–1838', *The English Historical Review*, 96, 1981, 565.
10. CO 23/102, *Bahamas*, Comments of Grey on No. 41, Cockburn to Glenelg, 26 March 1838.
11. For a very different assessment of the 'success' of immediate emancipation, see N. Lightfoot, *Troubling Freedom: Antigua and the Aftermath of British Emancipation*, Duke University Press, 2015.
12. CO 28/122, *Barbados*, No. 22, McGregor to Glenelg, 15 March 1838.
13. Comments of J. Stephen on CO28/122, No. 289, MacGregor to Glenelg, 7 February 1838.
14. Letter from J. Stephen to Gladstone, 18 April 1838, quoted in Gross, 'Parliament and the Abolition of Negro Apprenticeship', 566.
15. CO 28/122, *Barbados*, No. 12, MacGregor to Glenelg, 26 January 1838.
16. Comments of J. Stephen on CO 28/120, Barbados: Despatches, No. 12, 26 March 1838.
17. CO 28/120, *Barbados*, No. 291, MacGregor to Glenelg, 10 February 1838.
18. Hansard, 'Abolition of Negro Apprenticeship'.
19. There were already signs that they would emigrate altogether. A. Johnson, 'The Barbados Emigration War', Conference Paper, 'After Slavery? Labor and Migration in the Post-Emancipation World', 27 June 2016.
20. CO 28/122, *Barbados*, Comments of J. Stephen on No. 22, MacGregor to Glenelg, 15 March 1838.
21. CO 318/141, Circular, Glenelg to Colonial Governors, 2 April 1838.
22. Quoted A. Tyrrell, *Joseph Sturge and the Moral Radical Party in Early Victorian Britain*, Christopher Helm, 1987.

23. R. N. Ghosh, 'Malthus on Emigration and Colonization: Letters to Wilmot Horton', *Economica, New Series*, 30, 117, 1963, 47.

24. *The Spectator*, 4, 1831, 207.

25. Preface, *A Letter from Sydney, the Principal Town of Australasia*, ed. Robert Gouger, Shackell and Baylis, 1829.

26. T. Ballantyne, 'The Theory and Practice of of Empire Building: Edward Gibbon Wakefield and "Systematic Colonization"', in R. Aldrich and K. MacKenzie, eds, *The Routledge History of Western Empires*, Routledge, 2014, 92–3; P. Wakefield, *Reflections on the Present Condition of the Female Sex; with Suggestions for its Improvement, Joseph Johnson, 1798*, 2, and *Excursions in North America, Described in Letters from a Gentleman and His Young Companion to their Friends in England*, Darton and Harvey, 1806, 83.

27. E. G. Wakefield, *England and America*, London, 1833, Vol. II, 33, quoted in J. Lydon, 'A Secret Longing for a Trade in Human Flesh: The Decline of British Slavery and the Making of the Settler Colonies', *History Workshop Journal*, forthcoming.

28. Settlers did press Aboriginal children to work for them in the 1840s. P. Hetherington, *Settlers, Servants and Slaves: Aboriginal and European Children in Nineteenth-Century Western Australia*, University of Western Australia Press, 2002.

29. CO 537/22, Glenelg to Wilder, 26 April 1837.

30. M. Ray, 'Elliot, Sir Thomas Frederick (1808–1880), Civil Servant', *Oxford Dictionary of National Biography*, 2008. www.oxforddnb.com/view/10.1093/ref:odnb/9780198614128.001.0001/odnb-9780198614128-e-41086.

31. CO 48/197, Comments of J. Stephen on No. 362, Elliot to J. Stephen, 14 March 1838.

32. CO 158/114, *Malta: Commissioners of Inquiry*, 'Emigration to Jamaica', from the *Jamaican Standard*, forwarded 16 April 1837.

33. CO 201/262, 'Comments of J. Stephen' on No. 83, Bourke to Glenelg, 1 February 1838.

34. Prinsep had witnessed Chinese workers recruited to Van Diemen's Land beforehand. A. Woollacott, *Settler Society in the Australian Colonies: Self-Government and Imperial Culture*, Oxford University Press, 2015, 57. See also Lydon, 'A Secret Longing'.

35. CO 201/262, *Emigration* (vol. pp. 149–58, No. 85, Bourke to Glenelg, 8 September 1837, Encl. Final Report of the Committee on Immigration (Indian and British) into New South Wales and Minutes of Evidence (vol. pp. 164–79).

3 POLITICAL FREEDOM

1. He certainly grew impatient with governors who lacked a sense of priority. In early 1838, as he was ploughing through the Caribbean governors' returns on the cessation of apprenticeship, he was somewhat surprised by the governor of St Helena's urgent request that he commission and ship out a new coat of arms for the island's Sessions Hall. Stephen's usually neat annotation

descended into an exasperated scribble: 'surely some painter can be found in the place to supply an Arms?'

2. Another of the missives that Stephen and Glenelg batted away at this time was from Mauritius, where Governor Nicolay was appealing for the British Treasury to fund an observatory. The case he made included the observation that, 'With regard to the amount of the expense which will be necessary ... it will not probably be much ... For I believe an Astronomer, if a good one and tho'ro'bred, will sleep all day & watch the stars all night, being more like a ghost than a man, & returning to bed when he thinks he scents the morning air. So that he requires little more than what is requisite to afford him shelter and victual, & his amusements are his duties & by there his wants are bounded'. CO 167/198, Mauritius, No. 97, Nicolay to Glenelg, 25 September 1837.

3. A. Greer, '1837–38: Rebellion Reconsidered', *Canadian Historical Review*, LXXVI, 1, 1995, 1–18.

4. F. Ouellet, 'Papineau, Louis Joseph', in *Dictionary of Canadian Biography*, vol. 10, University of Toronto/Université Laval, 2003.

5. Ouellet, 'Papineau'.

6. F. H. Armstrong and R. J. Stagg, 'Mackenzie, William Lyon', in *Dictionary of Canadian Biography*, vol. 9, University of Toronto/Université Laval, 2003.

7. W. L. Mackenzie, *The Celebrated Letter of Joseph Hume, Esq., M.P., to William Lyon Mackenzie, Esq., Mayor of Toronto*, G. P. Hull, 1834.

8. Letters from Stephen to his wife, 1816–45, Cambridge University Library, Add 7888, II/122, no. 11, 10 November, 8 December 1837.

9. CO 42/274, *Lower Canada*, Gosford to Glenelg, 30 November 1837.

10. CO 42/274, *Lower Canada*, Gosford to Glenelg, 23 December 1837.

11. CO 42/277, *Lower Canada*, Creighton to Buchanan, 19 December 1837.

12. M. L. Harris, 'The Meaning of Patriot: The Canadian Rebellion and American Republicanism, 1837–1839', *Michigan Historical Review*, 23, 1, 1997, 33–69.

13. In December 1837, Gosford had written with some relief to Gleleg that the president of the USA 'has ... instructed the public authorities of the frontier states to be attentive to all movements of a hostile character contemplated or attempted within their districts, and to prosecute without discrimination all violaters of those laws of the United States which have been enacted to preserve peace with foreign powers, and to fulfil the obligations of treaties with them'. CO 42/274, *Lower Canada* Gosford to Glenelg, 23 December 1837. Many of the Patriots were infuriated by their government's appeasement of the British at the same time that it was supporting slave-holding Texans fighting against republican Mexico.

14. Quoted P. Burroughs, *The Canadian Crisis and British Colonial Policy*, Hodder & Stoughton, 1972, 92.

15. Quoted A. G. L. Shaw, *Sir George Arthur 1784–1854 – Superintendent of British Honduras, Lieutenant-Governor of Van Diemen's Land and of Upper Canada Governor of the Bombay Presidency*, Melbourne University Press, 1980, 229.

16. Quoted Shaw, *Sir George Arthur*, 197.

17. Quoted Boyce, *Van Diemen's Land*, Black Inc., 2009, 146.

18. H. Reynolds, *Fate of a Free People*, Penguin, 2004.

19. Quoted Reynolds, *Fate of a Free People*, 146.

20. Quoted Shaw, *Sir George Arthur*, 227.

21. T. B. K. Hutchings, 'The Emigrant and the Noble Savage: Sir Francis Bond Head's Romantic Approach to Aboriginal Policy in Upper Canada, 1836–1838', *Journal of Canadian Studies*, 39, 1, 2004, 115–38.

22. Hutchings, 'The Emigrant and the Noble Savage', 120.

23. Z. Laidlaw and A. Lester, eds, *Indigenous Communities and Settler Colonialism: Land Holding, Loss and Survival in an Interconnected World*, Palgrave, 2015.

24. Hutchings, 'The Emigrant and the Noble Savage', 121.

25. D. B. Smith, 'Jones, Peter', in *Dictionary of Canadian Biography*, vol. 8, University of Toronto/Université Laval, 2003.

26. Lieutenant Governor Peregrine Maitland would have preferred if Jones had converted to Anglicanism rather than Methodism, and the colony's Family Compact would later try unsuccessfully to bribe him away from nonconformity with a higher salary.

27. When Jones visited England again in 1845, he would complain that audiences came only to revel in the exotic Kahkewaquonaby, dressed in 'odious' native clothes, and were not at all interested in Peter Jones, the 'civilized Indian' that he had become. Smith, 'Jones'.

28. Jones himself became increasingly disaffected with his Methodist brethren in Canada as men from Britain were appointed to senior positions above him, some of whom, fluent only in English, were even given the task of translating the Bible into Ojibwe (a project which Jones himself had already considerably furthered). Nonetheless, he became the Canadian correspondent for the Aborigines Protection Society's publication *The Colonial Intelligencer or Aborigines' Friend*.

29. Quoted Shaw, *Sir George Arthur*, 230.

30. C. Read and R. J. Stagg, eds, *The Rebellion of 1837 in Upper Canada*, Ontario Heritage Foundation, 1985, lxxx.

31. Hutchings, 'The Emigrant and the Noble Savage', 116.

32. G. Martin, 'Lambton, John George [nicknamed Radical Jack], First Earl of Durham (1792–1840), Politician', in *Oxford Dictionary of National Biography*, www.oxforddnb.com/view/10.1093/ref:odnb/9780198614128.001.0001/odnb-9780198614128-e-15947.

33. Martin, 'Lambton, John George'.

34. Martin, 'Lambton, John George'.

35. J. Henderson, 'Uncivil Subjects: Metropolitan Meddling, Conditional Loyalty, and Lord Durham's 1838 Administration of Lower Canada', PhD dissertation, York University, 2010.

36. H. Spencer, 'Buller, Charles (1806–1848), Politician and Wit', in *Oxford Dictionary of National Biography*, www.oxforddnb.com/view/10.1093/ref:odnb/9780198614128.001.0001/odnb-9780198614128-e-3913; H. Lysons-Balcon, 'Buller, Charles', in *Dictionary of Canadian Biography*, vol. 7, University of Toronto/Université Laval, 2003.

37. We owe Buller something of a debt. His proposal that parliamentary papers be archived and made publicly available in 1838 eventually led to the establishment of The National Archives.
38. Quoted Shaw, *Sir George Arthur*, 225.
39. H. T. Manning, 'Who Ran the British Empire 1830–1850?', *Journal of British Studies*, 5, 1, 1965, 88–121.
40. Martin, 'Lambton, John George'.
41. Durham Report, British Parliamentary Papers vol. 2, 1839, 23.
42. The forty-nine-year-old Stephen and Jane Catherine had three sons and one daughter in 1838, having lost another daughter in infancy. We will encounter one of the sons, James Fitzjames, in Part III, transforming the law of British India in the 1870s.
43. On behalf of his friend Wakefield, Buller continued, 'Those who have suggested any improvement in the system existing in our Colonies, or proposed to found new colonies on a new principle, know to what a complete science the officials of the Colonial department have brought their mode of repelling all such invasions of their domain'.
44. Charles Buller, Responsible government for colonies, available online at htt ps://archive.org/details/McGillLibrary-129431-4915.
45. Buller has a river and gorge named after him in New Zealand and Mount Buller in Victoria, Australia. His 'illegitimate' daughter, Theresa Reviss married into foreign aristocracy, became a well-known society figure in Calcutta, and was assumed by many to be the model for Thackeray's character Becky Sharp in *Vanity Fair*.

4 SETTLER LIBERTIES

1. A. Lester, *Imperial Networks: Creating Identities in Nineteenth Century South Africa and Britain*, Routledge, 2001.
2. Smith was the celebrated British hero of the Battle of Aliwal in the First Anglo-Sikh War of 1845. Acquiring a baronetcy, along with the thanks of both houses of Parliament and the East India Company, he was then known formally as 'Sir Harry Smith of Aliwal'. All this may have gone to his head. When he returned to the Cape Colony to take command of the reconquered frontier amaXhosa in 1847, he declared himself their supreme chief, inkosi inkulu, and ordered great meetings at which he lined up his troops and artillery and humiliated the chiefs by making them kiss his boots. He then made them choose either a staff of war or one of peace, which he had planted in the ground. Not content with this, he attempted to strike awe among his new subjects, pointing dramatically at a wagon full of gunpowder with a pre-lit fuse, so that it exploded apparently at his magical gesture. He told the mute Xhosa audience that he would do the same to them if they disobeyed him. Smith managed to convince himself that his Xhosa subjects believed him a god-like figure, embodying omnipotent but ultimately benevolent British power. It would come as a rude shock when the distinctly un-awed amaXhosa rose in revolt again in 1850. Smith, who was visiting a frontier fort at the time, was forced to flee, disguised as

a civilian woman. N. Mostert, *Frontiers: Evolution of South African Society and Its Central Tragedy, the Agony of the Xhosa People*, Jonathan Cape, 1992; Lester, *Imperial Networks*; R. Vetch, 'Smith, Sir Henry George Wakelyn [Harry], Baronet, of Aliwal (1787–1860), Army Officer and Colonial Governor', in *Oxford Dictionary of National Biography*, www.oxforddnb.com/view/10.1093/ref:odnb/9780198614128.001.0001/odnb-9780198614128-e-25810.

3. Maqoma's resistance to colonial expansion did not end in the 1834–5 war. We will return to him too, in Part II. After leading amaXhosa resistance in the war of 1850–52 he was imprisoned on Robben Island for twelve years. When he then attempted to resettle on his former land, he was banished to the island again, and he would die there in 1873.

4. CO 48/185 (167) Court of Inquiry into Hintsa's Death, 30 August 1836. What became of Hintsa's body thereafter is disputed. Smith stated that he was sickened by the mutilation and ordered that the body be left in the bushes for Hintsa's followers to bury respectfully. But many among the amaXhosa believe that Hintsa's head was removed and taken to Britain, which was certainly the fate of other amaXhosa killed in the war. In 1996 Nicholas Tilana Gcaleka, a descendant of King Hintsa, travelled to Scotland to repatriate what he claimed was Hintsa's skull. The contemporary Xhosa king and council did not accept that it was genuine however, and refused to bury it.

5. A. Ross, *John Philip, 1775–1851: Missions, Race and Politics in South Africa*, Mercat Press, 1986.

6. R. Ross, 'Philip, John (1775–1851), Missionary', in *Oxford Dictionary of National Biography*, www.oxforddnb.com/view/10.1093/ref:odnb/97801986 14128.001.0001/odnb-9780198614128-e-22104.

7. The cousins Anna and Sarah Maria lived together on a cottage on the family's Northrepps estate in Norfolk and were known locally as the 'Cottage Ladies'. They referred to each other as 'Partners'.

8. In 1825, Gurney published *On Means of Assistance in Cases of Shipwreck*, and she edited *The Fisherman's Friendly Visitor and Mariner's Companion*. In 1830 she persuaded Trinity House to have a lighthouse installed off Happisburgh, still called the Gurney Light.

9. H. Brookman, 'Gurney, Anna (1795–1857), Old English Scholar', in *Oxford Dictionary of National Biography*, www.oxforddnb.com/view/10.1093/ref:odnb/9780198614128.001.0001/odnb-9780198614128-e-11759.

10. Quoted E. Elbourne, *Blood Ground: Colonialism, Missions, and the Contest for Christianity in the Cape Colony and Britain, 1799–1853*, McGill-Queen's University Press, 1991, 307.

11. Quoted J. G. Pretorius, *The British Humanitarians and the Cape Eastern Frontier, 1834–1836*, Government Printer, Pretoria, 1988, 197, 207.

12. State Archives, Cape Town, GH 1/22, Glenelg to D'Urban, 26 December 1835.

13. Court of Inquiry into Hintsa's Death.

14. CO 48/185 (167), Opinion of Court of Enquiry.

15. Quoted Pretorius, *The British Humanitarians*, 127.

16. Zoe Laidlaw, 'Aunt Anna's Report': The Buxton Women and the Aborigines Select Committee, 1835– 37', *The Journal of Imperial and Commonwealth History*, 32, 2, 2004, 18, 31.

17. Report from the Select Committee on Aborigines (British settlements); with the minutes of evidence, appendix and index, House of Commons, 1837 (425), evidence of Rev. John Philip, 555.

18. E. Elbourne, 'Sara Baartman and Andries Stoffels: Violence, Law and the Politics of Spectacle in London and the Eastern Cape, 1809–1836', *Canadian Journal of African Studies/La Revue Canadienne des Etudes Africaines*, 45, 3, 2011, 549.

19. R. S. Levine, *A Living Man from Africa: Jan Tzatzoe, Xhosa Chief and Missionary, and the Making of Nineteenth-Century South Africa*, Yale University Press, 2011.

20. Elbourne, *Blood Ground*, 288.

21. Elbourne, 'Sara Baartman', 555.

22. Report from the Select Committee, evidence of John Tzatzoe, 571.

23. Report from the Select Committee, evidence of Col. Wade, 417, 579. Stoeffels and Tzatzoe never gave up while in Britain. In speech after speech at provincial towns and cities across England and then in Scotland, both men insisted on speaking of land loss and injustice, as well as of the redeeming power of the Bible and of literacy. Back in the Cape, however, Tzatzoe would renounce his alliance with the colony to fight for amaXhosa independence in the 1846–7 and 1850–52 wars.

24. 'Report from the Select Committee, 16.

25. The Aborigines Committee's recommendation would soon be superseded. Joseph Barrow Montefiore gave a different version of the *Elizabeth* story to a Select Committee of the House of Lords, which reported at the end of 1838. This committee was established in the wake of the Aborigines Committee report, specifically to recommend on governmental regulation of the Britons already in New Zealand, and to weigh up the New Zealand Company's proposals. Montefiore, who had stayed on the *Elizabeth* while Tama-i-hara-nui was being held captive before his murder, testified that the incident certainly did not indicate powerless Māori being corrupted by nefarious British traders. 'The white man possesses no power at all, for if the New Zealanders [Māori] chose they could annihilate the whole of the Europeans in one day'. Furthermore, the behaviour of Captain Stewart was by no means representative of the traders there. In fact it was deeply frustrating to the majority of legitimate traders, who were pursuing a mutually lucrative relationship with the Māori (which also happened to be rendering missionary influence more marginal). Montefiore's evidence reinforced the finding of the House of Lords Committee that an extension of sovereignty was needed in New Zealand, preparing the way for the Treaty of Waitangi and the declaration of British sovereignty in 1840: 'Report from the Select Committee of the House of Lords Appointed to Enquire into the Present State of the Islands of New Zealand and the Expediency of Regulating the Settlement of British Subjects Therein', 1838, 65.

26. Report from the Select Committee, 47–8, 76, quoting Rev. Whewell's sermon before the Trinity Board.
27. P. Edmonds and Z. Laidlaw, '"The British Government Is Now Awakening": How Humanitarian Quakers Repackaged and Circulated the 1837 Select Committee Report on Aborigines', in S. Furphy and A. Nettelbeck, eds, *Aboriginal Protection and Its Intermediaries in Britain's Antipodean Colonies*, Routledge, 2020, 38–57.
28. Buxton, quoted Laidlaw, 'Aunt Anna's Report', 107.
29. Robert Godlonton, *A Narrative of the Irruption of the Kafir Hordes into the Eastern Province of the Cape of Good Hope, 1834–5*, Godlonton and Meurant, 1836, 70; R. Godlonton, *Memorials of the British Settlers of South Africa*, Godlonton, Grahamstown, 1844, 56–7.
30. CO 48/173, *Cape*, No. 71, D'Urban to Glenelg, 9 October 1837.
31. F. Watson, ed., *Historical Records of Australia*, 1st ser., 21, 1924, 127.
32. CO 201/262, *New South Wales* Bourke to Glenelg, 11 September 1837.
33. https://archive.org/details/MassacreOfAustralianAborigines/page/n5. See L. Ryan, 'Settler Massacres on the Port Phillip Frontier, 1836–1851', *Journal of Australian Studies*, 34, 3, 2010, 257–73.
34. R. Millis, *Waterloo Creek : The Australia Day Massacre of 1838, George Gipps and the British Conquest of New South Wales*, University of New South Wales Press, 1995.
35. Quoted G. Mellor, *British Imperial Trusteeship, 1783–1850*, Faber and Faber, 1951, 292–3.
36. Extracted by Aborigines Committee from Despatch to Lord Goderich, 6 April 1833.
37. Report from the Select Committee, 56.
38. Mitchell Library 572.990/1, J. Dredge, *Brief Notices of the Aborigines of New South Wales, Including Port Phillip, in Reference to Their Past History and Present Condition*, James Harrsion, 1845, 20.
39. Whether that property included their land was never clarified in Port Phillip, although the protectors earlier appointed to South Australia had a soon-to-be -forgotten instruction to protect Aboriginal proprietary rights in land. A. Nettelbeck, *Indigenous Rights and Colonial Subjecthood: Protection and Reform in the Nineteenth-Century British Empire*, Cambridge University Press, 2019.
40. https://c21ch.newcastle.edu.au/colonialmassacres/detail.php?r=1706.
41. P. Whithycombe, 'The Twelfth Man: John Henry Fleming and the Myall Creek Massacre', in J. Lydon and L. Ryan, eds, *Remembering the Myall Creek Massacre*, University of New South Wales Press, 2018.
42. A. Atkinson and M. Aveling, *Australians, 1838*, Fairfax, Syme & Weldon Associates, 1987, 393.
43. *Australian Aborigines' Protection Society: A portion of the report of the public meeting, held on Friday, Oct. 19th, 1838, in the Hall of the Mechanics' School of Arts, containing the speech of G. A. Robinson*, Noyes & Son, 1865.
44. Quoted L. Arkley, *The Hated Protector: The Story of Charles Wightman Sievwright, Protector of Aborigines, 1839–42*, Orbit Press, 2000, 105.
45. *Sydney Herald*, 14 November 1838.

46. *Sydney Herald*, 19 November 1838.
47. R. Broome, *Aboriginal Victorians: A History since 1800*, Allen and Unwin, Crow's Nest, 2005, xviii.
48. Broome, *Aboriginal Victorians*, 54. Mitchell's returning route left a clearly defined track – 'the Major's Line' – 'which survived for years to guide a stream of overlanders entering Victoria from the north'. J. M. Powell, *The Public Lands of Australia Felix: Settlement and Land Appraisal in Victoria 1834–91 with Special Reference to the Western Plains*, Oxford University Press, 1970, xxv.
49. A. Lester and N. Vanderbyl, 'The Restructuring of the British Empire and the Colonization of Australia, 1832–1838', *History Workshop Journal*, 2020, dbaa017, https://doi.org/10.1093/hwj/dbaa017.
50. T. Banivanua Mar, 'Imperial Literacy and Indigenous Rights: Tracing Transoceanic Circuits of a Modern Discourse', *Aboriginal History*, 37, 2013, 1–28.
51. The meticulous research of Lyndall Ryan has shown that massacres were 'responsible for the deaths of more than 11 per cent of the known Aboriginal population' in the District between 1836 and 1851. Introduced diseases were responsible for most of the rest, although the two causes were interlinked since the killing of those who could acquire food and displacement from country undermined the immunity of the remainder. Ryan, 'Settler massacres'.
52. P. Edmonds, *Urbanizing Frontiers: Indigenous Peoples and Settlers in 19th Century Pacific Rim Cities*, University of British Columbia Press, 2010, 129.
53. B. Attwood, *'My Country': A History of the Djadja Wurrung 1837–1864*, Monash University, Department of History/Dja Dja Wrung Aboriginal Association, 1999, 15.
54. State Library of Victoria, *Diary of the Late James Dredge, from September 1 1839 to October 8 1843, Typed by Miss D. MacDougall from the original manuscript lent by Mrs A. C. Dredge, Aug–Sept. 1935*, 5.
55. Quoted J. Mitchell, *In Good Faith: Governing Indigenous Australia through God, Charity and Empire, 1825–1855*, ANU Press, 2011, 46.
56. I. Clark, ed., *The Journals of George Augustus Robinson, Chief Protector, Port Phillip Aboriginal Protectorate*, vol. 2, Heritage Matters, 1998, 104.
57. Quoted Arkley, *The Hated Protector*, 4.
58. *Port Phillip Gazette*, 17 August 1839.
59. *Port Phillip Gazette*, 14 March 1840.
60. Quoted Arkley, *The Hated Protector*, 63.
61. Arkley, *The Hated Protector*, 280, 320.
62. Quoted H. C. Madden, 'The Loddon District Aboriginal Protectorate', La Trobe University honors thesis, 1976, 36.
63. H. N. Nelson, 'Parker, Edward Stone (1802–1865)', in *Australian Dictionary of Biography*, National Centre of Biography, Australian National University, http://adb.anu.edu.au/biography/parker-edward-stone-4363/text7093.
64. E. Morrison, *A Successful Failure, a Trilogy: The Aborigines and Early Settlers*, ed. Geoff Morrison, Graffiti, 1965, 158.
65. Morrison, *A Successful Failure*, 23

66. Madden, 'The Loddon District', 23. Parker's son later wrote, 'After we had been settled [at Neereman] a few weeks, one fine morning a squatter came with his men, nine in all, mounted and fully armed, expecting to find us all killed by the blacks, but to their surprise they found us all well. The leader, addressing Father stated that he was quite at a loss to know how Father and his family had lived in the midst of these savages'. Morrison, *A Successful Failure*, 309.
67. Quoted Madden, 'The Loddon District', 17.
68. Quoted Madden, 'The Loddon District', 25–6.
69. Morrison, *A Successful Failure*, 310.
70. *The Daylesford Express*, 9 April 1864, spoke of the 'disgraceful state of the cemetery' where 'the Aboriginal savages and the white settlers are all packed together in this charnel house'. In the 1960s, the station's cemetery was unique in Victoria for being 'racially mixed'. Morrison, *A Successful Failure*, 215.
71. Report from the Select Committee, 14–15.
72. Quoted Arkley, *The Hated Protector*, 289.
73. A. G. L. Shaw, *A History of the Port Phillip District: Victoria before Separation*, Melbourne University Press, 1996, 127.
74. Atkinson and Aveling, *Australians, 1838*, 367.
75. R. Wood, 'Frontier Violence and the Bush Legend: The *Sydney Herald*'s Response to the Myall Creek Massacre Trials and the Creation of Colonial Identity', *History Australia*, 6, 3, 2009, 25.
76. Milliss, *Waterloo Creek*, 381.
77. Quoted Arkley, *The Hated Protector*, 205.
78. Molesworth encouraged tenants from his estate at Pencarrow to emigrate among the first settlers to New Zealand and charged his gardener with sending back plants and shrubs. Among them was the first British import of the *Araucaria* conifer, the more popular name of which derived from the barrister Charles Austin's comment that the 'tree would puzzle a monkey'. P. Burroughs, 'Molesworth, Sir William, Eighth Baronet (1810–1855), Politician', in *Oxford Dictionary of National Biography*, www.oxforddnb.com/view/10.1093/ref:odnb/9780198614128.001.0001/odnb-9780198614128-e-18902.
79. Hansard, 3, 41, 6 March 1838, 479. Shortly before his death in 1855, Molesworth himself would serve briefly as colonial secretary.

5 FREE TRADE, FAMINE AND INVASION

1. A. Howe, 'Huskisson, William (1770–1830), Politician', in *Oxford Dictionary of National Biography*, www.oxforddnb.com/view/10.1093/ref:odnb/9780198614128.001.0001/odnb-9780198614128-e-14264.
2. Howe, 'Huskisson'.
3. B. Hilton, *The Age of Atonement: The Influence of Evangelism on Social and Economic Thought, 1795–1865*, Oxford University Press, 1991.
4. Bizarrely, one result of these had been that the American colonists were supposed to send the goods they traded with compatriots in the neighbouring

West Indian colonies via London. In practice such rules were widely circum-vented in any case by a lively smuggling trade.

5. Howe, 'Huskisson'.
6. Standing on the line on which the engine was advancing, he dithered before trying to climb out of its way into the King's carriage, standing on an adjacent line.
7. H. Parris, 'Hume, James Deacon (1774–1842), Civil Servant and Free-Trader', in *Oxford Dictionary of National Biography*, www.oxforddnb.com/vi ew/10.1093/ref:odnb/9780198614128.001.0001/odnb-9780198614128-e-14145.
8. MacGregor would die in exile in France in 1857 after filing misleading accounts and drawing loans which he could not repay, as chairman of the Royal British Bank. H. Parris, 'MacGregor, John (1797–1857), Civil Servant and Free-Trader', in *Oxford Dictionary of National Biography*, www .oxforddnb.com/view/10.1093/ref:odnb/9780198614128.001.0001/odnb-9 780198614128-e-17521.
9. Quoted H. V. Bowen, *The Business of Empire: The East India Company and Imperial Britain, 1756–1833*, Cambridge University Press, 2009, 260.
10. Bowen, *The Business of Empire*, 265.
11. Bowen, *The Business of Empire*, 290.
12. Bowen, *The Business of Empire*, 154–5.
13. In fact its monopoly was already being widely circumvented as American merchants bought wool and cloth from British manufacturers for importation to China.
14. Joseph Hume, later Mackenzie's main ally in the Upper Canadian revolt and devotee of Wakefield, was simply pleased to see the end of the Company's monopoly on trade and preferred it over an entity like the Colonial Office for government.
15. Quoted C. Hall, *Macaulay and Son: Architects of Imperial Britain*, Yale University Press, 2012, 206.
16. Hansard, 10 July 1833, vol. 19, cc479–550.
17. Hansard, 10 July 1833, vol. 19, cc479–550.
18. After his performance in the Commons, Macualay wrote to his sister that he had 'made the best speech, by general agreement, that I ever made in my life'. Hall, *Macaulay and Son*, 213.
19. M. Allbrook, *Henry Prinsep's Empire: Framing a Distant Colony*, ANU Press, 2014.
20. Hansard, 10 July 1833, vol. 19, cc479–550.
21. W. Thomas, 'Macaulay, Thomas Babington, Baron Macaulay (1800–1859), Historian, Essayist, and Poet', in *Oxford Dictionary of National Biography*, www.oxforddnb.com/view/10.1093/ref:odnb/9780198614128.001.0001/od nb-9780198614128-e-17349.
22. E. T. Stokes, 'Bureaucracy and Ideology: Britain and India in the Nineteenth Century', *Transactions of the Royal Historical Society*, 5, 1980, 145.
23. The Company's resident agent in Travancore was Zachary Macaulay's brother and Thomas Babington's uncle, Colin Macaulay.

24. The Peshwa's adopted son, Nana Sahib, would become one of the leaders of the Rebellion in 1857.
25. D. Howlett, 'Jenkins, Sir Richard (1785–1853), East India Company servant', in *Oxford Dictionary of National Biography*, www.oxforddnb.com/view/10.1093/ref:odnb/9780198614128.001.0001/odnb-9780198614128-e-14733.
26. G. Martin, 'Grant, Charles, Baron Glenelg (1778–1866), Politician', in *Oxford Dictionary of National Biography*, www.oxforddnb.com/view/10.1093/ref:odnb/9780198614128.001.0001/odnb-9780198614128-e-11249.
27. P. J. Marshall, 'Eden, George, Earl of Auckland (1784–1849), Politician and Governor-General of India', in *Oxford Dictionary of National Biography*, www.oxforddnb.com/view/10.1093/ref:odnb/9780198614128.001.0001/odnb-9780198614128-e-8451.
28. J. C. Marshman, *The History of India from the Earliest Period to the Close of Lord Dalhousie's Administration*, Longmans, Green, Reader & Dyer, 1867, www.ibiblio.org/britishraj/Marshman3/chapter33.html.
29. E. Eden, *'Up the Country': Letters Written to Her Sister from the Upper Provinces of India*, Richard Bentley, 1867.
30. S. Sharma, 'The 1837–38 Famine in U.P.: Some Dimensions of Popular Action', *The Indian Economic & Social History Review*, 30, 3, 1993.
31. C. A. Bayly, *Rulers, Townsmen and Bazaars: North Indian Society in the Age of British Expansion, 1770–1870*, Oxford University Press, 1998, 339.
32. Despite the Company's remaining monopoly of opium production.
33. By contrast, they would remember the next major famine 1860–61 as having the 'pleasant' aspect of 'greater order' among its victims. Sharma, 'The 1837–38 Famine in U.P.'.
34. Bayly, *Rulers, Townsmen*, 359.
35. Sharma, 'The 1837–38 famine in U.P.'.
36. At least it was until Ranjit Singh's death and the ensuing the Anglo-Sikh War of 1846, in which, as we have mentioned, Harry Smith became the hero of Aliwal.
37. C. Murray, *Sikunder Burnes: Master of the Great Game*, Birlinn, 2017.
38. K. Prior, 'Macnaghten, Sir William Hay, Baronet (1793–1841), Administrator in India', in *Oxford Dictionary of National Biography*, www.oxforddnb.com/view/10.1093/ref:odnb/9780198614128.001.0001/odnb-9780198614128-e-17705.
39. Part of the price that Shah Shuja paid Ranjit Singh for his support was the Koh-i-Noor diamond, taken to England after the subsequent British conquest of the Punjab.
40. W. Dalrymple, *Return of a King: The Battle for Afghanistan*, Bloomsbury, 2012.
41. Quoted Dalrymple, *Return of a King*, 142.
42. Auckland was also commemorated in the naming of the new British colony of New Zealand's major settlement.
43. Marshman, *The History of India*.
44. Quoted J. A. Norris, *The First Afghan War, 1838–1842*, Cambridge University Press, 1967, 384.
45. Marshall, 'Eden, George, Earl of Auckland'.

46. While Auckland suffered from a stroke, Dost Mohammad returned from exile to resume and extend his rule of Afghanistan, broadly in alliance with the British.

6 STEAM AND OPIUM

1. The first steam railway in India opened in 1853.
2. D. Dewar, *Bygone Days in India*, John Lane, 1922.
3. IOR E/4/754, *Despatches to India and Bengal*, No. 5, Marine Dept, 'Re: Reply to general letter 12th July 1837 (No. 19) and Secretary's Letter 15th March 1837 (No. 30)', 7 March 1838.
4. J. H. Wilson, *On Steam Communication between Bombay and Suez, with an Account of the Hugh Lindsay's Four Voyages*, Bombay, 1833.
5. IOR B/195, *Court Minutes*, pp. 522–61, 7 February 1838; IOR B/242, *Court Dissents*, pp. 364–75, No. 538, 21 February 1838.
6. IOR B/195, *Court Minutes*, pp. 375–403, 10 January 1838; IOR B/195, *Court Minutes*, pp. 522–61, 'Col. Patrick Campbell, EIC agent at Alexandria, 11 November 1837, with copy of a letter from Boghas Bey about a coal store-house for steamers at Cosseir, noting that no coals have yet arrived from England,' 7 February 1838.
7. Although coal mining had been developed by Company officers on a small scale on the Damodar River, large-scale investment would be spurred only by the railway developments of the 1850s.
8. IOR E/4/753, *Despatches to India and Bengal*, pp. 797–804; 13 February 1838, Marine Department, India, No. 1 of 1838. 'Re: Circular on Steam Navigation'.
9. These are taken from all Courts in January, and B/195 – Court Minutes, 344–74 – Court meeting 5 January 1838 to IOR B/195, 498–521. Court minutes. 30 January 1838.
10. IOR B/195, *Court Minutes*, pp. 522–61. 7 February 1838; IOR B/195, *Court Minutes*, pp. 375–403. 10 January 1838; IOR B/195, pp. 522–61, 7 February 1838; IOR B/195, pp. 562–92, 13 February 1838; IOR B/195, pp. 593–634, 13 February 1838.
11. IOR E/4/754, Despatches to India and Bengal (2nd vol.), pp. 11–36, No. 5, 'Re: Reply to general letter 12th July 1837 (No. 19) and Secretary's Letter 15th March 1837 (No. 30)', Marine Dept, 7 March 1838.
12. In 1845 the superiority of the new screw propelled steamships over existing paddle technology was confirmed by the Royal Navy's tug of war between the screw propelled *Rattler* and paddle steamer *Alecto*.
13. J. F. Richards, 'The Indian Empire and Peasant Production of Opium in the Nineteenth Century', *Modern Asian Studies*, 15, 1, 1981, 59–82.
14. T. Chung, 'The Britain-China-India Trade Triangle (1771–1840)', *Indian Economic History Review*, XI, 1974, 426–7.
15. Chung, 'The Britain-China-India Trade Triangle'.
16. The Indian silver rupee was by now the medium for the entire Indian Ocean trading zone.
17. Chung, 'The Britain-China-India Trade Triangle'.
18. Chung, 'The Britain-China-India Trade Triangle'.

19. Throughout the ensuing Opium War, Cantonese loyalty to the emperor remained ambivalent at best.
20. J. Lovell, *The Opium War: Drugs, Dreams, and the Making of Modern China*, Picador, 2011.
21. Lovell, *The Opium War*, 36–7.
22. https://cyber.harvard.edu/ChinaDragon/lin_xexu.html.
23. Chung, 'The Britain-China-India Trade Triangle'.
24. B. Semmel, *The Rise of Free Trade Imperialism: Classical Political Economy the Empire of Free Trade and Imperialism, 1750–1850*, Cambridge University Press, 1970, 151.
25. Semmel, *The Rise of Free Trade Imperialism*, 153.
26. Quoted Semmel, *The Rise of Free Trade Imperialism*, 152.
27. Quoted Semmel, *The Rise of Free Trade Imperialism*, 152.
28. K. Marx, 'Free Trade and Monopoly', *New York Daily Tribune*, 25 September 1858, quoted in N. Robins, *The Corporation That Changed the World: How the East India Company Shaped the Modern Multinational*, Pluto, 2006, 162.
29. *The Times*, 30 March 1840.
30. See Lovell, *The Opium War*.

CONCLUSION TO PART I: AN EMPIRE OF FREEDOM?

1. Hansard, 10 July 1833, vol. 19, cc479–550.

7 SETTING THE SCENE: HUBRIS AND CRISIS

1. This is a different George Grey to the former Colonial Office under-secretary of 1838, who was home secretary in 1857.
2. J. B. Peires, 'The Central Beliefs of the Xhosa Cattle-Killing', *Journal of African History*, 28, 1, 1987, 43.
3. See A. Lester, *Imperial Networks: Creating Identities in Nineteenth Century South Africa and Britain*, Routledge, 2001; R. Price, *Making Empire: Colonial Encounters and the Creation of Imperial Rule in Nineteenth-Century Africa*, Cambridge University Press, 2008.
4. Still the most best and most comprehensive account of the amaXhosa's wars of resistance is Mostert, *Frontiers*.
5. Quoted T. Stapleton, 'Reluctant Slaughter: Rethinking Maqoma's Role in the Xhosa Cattle-Killing (1853–1857)', *The International Journal of African Historical Studies*, 26, 2, 1993, 345–51.
6. Quoted Peires, 'The Central Beliefs', 53.
7. J. B. Peires, *The Dead Will Arise: Nongqawuse and the Great Xhosa Cattle-killing Movement of 1856–7*, Ravan Press/Indiana University Press/James Currey, 1989. For controversy over the identification of Mhlakaza as Goliat, see S. Boniface Davies, 'Raising the Dead: The Xhosa Cattle-Killing and the Mhlakaza-Goliat Delusion', *Journal of Southern African Studies*, 33, 1, 2007, 19–41; J. B. Peires, 'Cry Havoc! Thoughts on the Deconstruction of Mhlakaza', *Journal of African Studies*, 67, 2, 2008, 233–55.

8. Today the interpretation that the prophecies were orchestrated by the British colonial authorities in order to prompt the collapse of amaXhosa independence is common. Given the outcome, such an interpretation is not surprising.

9. This is Stapleton's argument in 'Reluctant Slaughter'.

10. Peires, 'The Central Beliefs', 44.

11. J. Rutherford, *Sir George Grey K. C. B.. A Study in Colonial Government*, Cassell, 1961, v.

12. J. Belich, 'J. Grey, Sir George (1812–1898), Colonial Governor and Premier of New Zealand', in *Oxford Dictionary of National Biography*, www .oxforddnb.com/view/10.1093/ref:odnb/9780198614128.001.0001/odnb-9 780198614128-e-11534.

13. L. Dale, 'George Grey in Australia, New Zealand and South Africa', in P. Hulme and R. McDougall, eds, *Writing, Travel and Empire*, I. B. Tauris, 2008, 147.

14. Quoted J. M. R. Cameron, 'Agents and Agencies in Geography and Empire: The Case of George Grey', in Morag Bell, ed., *Geography and Imperialism, 1820–1940*, Manchester University Press, 1995, 26.

15. Quoted Cameron, 'Agents and Agencies', 32.

16. Ultimately it was proven to exist, although Grey's description of its potential for settlement was exaggerated.

17. *South Australian Register*, 15 March 1843. Thanks to Johanna Skurnik, whose research on Arrowsmith's mapping of the British Empire informs this section.

18. *Geelong Advertiser*, 2 December 1848.

19. Cameron, 'Agents and Agencies', 32.

20. G. Grey, *Report on the Best Means of Promoting the Civilization of the Aboriginal Inhabitants of Australia*, reproduced in Russell to Gipps, 25 August 1840, NSW Legislative Council Votes and Proceedings 1839–42, 1/MAV/FN4/ 0867, State Library of New South Wales.

21. D. I. Salesa, *Racial Crossings: Race, Intermarriage, and the Victorian British Empire*, Oxford University Press, 2011, 108.

22. H. Merivale, *Lectures on Colonization and Colonies Before the University of Oxford in 1839, 1840 and 1841*, vol. 2, Longman, Orme, Brown, Green and Longmans, 1861, 499.

23. James Stephen had retired in 1848. In 1857 he was among those teaching a new generation of East India Company officials at Haileybury, where he occupied Malthus' old chair. Merivale was his immediate successor.

24. After his spell at the Colonial Office, Merivale would move into Macaulay's former East India Company realm as permanent under-secretary in the new India Office. L. Stephen, 'Merivale, Herman (1806–1874), Civil Servant and Economist', in *Oxford Dictionary of National Biography*, www.oxforddnb.com/v iew/10.1093/ref:odnb/9780198614128.001.0001/odnb-9780198614128- e-18593.

25. CO 42/610, 7147. *Canada* (vol. pp. 201–2), Eyre, to Labouchere, 11 July 1857; Merivale Ans. 5 August.

26. National Archives of South Africa, Cape Town, GH 23/26, Grey to Colonial Secretary, 22 December 1854.

27. See A. Lester, 'Settler Colonialism, George Grey and the Politics of Ethnography', *Environment and Planning D: Society and Space*, 34, 3, 2016, 492–507.
28. In the meantime Grey came to an understanding with Keppel that they would both keep the matter quiet and Keppel promised to be absent from Cape Town as much as possible. Keeping his word, Keppel departed for a lengthy cruise of the South Atlantic and Indian Oceans. No sooner was he out of port, Grey, secure in the knowledge 'that months must pass before Keppel could make any reply', told the secretary of state of the 'affair' and managed to get Keppel demoted to the Royal Navy's 'inferior' Brazil station. In a covert letter to Keppel, Eliza compared herself to a vine plant that clings unknowingly to a strut that cannot support her, but it is not clear whether she meant Grey or Keppel. B. J. Dalton, 'Sir George Grey and the Keppel Affair', *Historical Studies: Australia and New Zealand*, 16, 1974–5, 192–215.
29. J. Milne, *The Romance of a Pro-Consul: Being the Personal Life of the Right Hon. Sir George Grey, KCB*, Chatto and Windus, 1899. It was in his correspondence with Grey that Darwin used the phrase 'origin of species' on one of the first occasions. S. Grant, 'God's Governor: George Grey and Racial Amalgamation in New Zealand, 1845–1853', PhD dissertation, University of Otago, 2005, 66.
30. Belich, 'Grey, Sir George'.
31. Quoted Helen Bradford and Msokoli Qotole, 'Ingxoxo enkulu ngoNongqawuse (A Great Debate about Nongqawuse's Era)', *Kronos* 20, 2008, 85. At the time of the cattle killing Gqoba was learning to build wagons at the Lovedale mission station.
32. The Canadian rebellions had proved the political undoing of former secretary of state for the colonies Glenelg. Never able to escape the lampoon of him asleep after that cabinet dinner, when he resigned in 1839, Lord Stanley asked, 'Who is to have Glenelg's nightcap?' G. Martin, 'Grant, Charles, Baron Glenelg (1778–1866), Politician', in *Oxford Dictionary of National Biography*, www.oxforddnb.com/view/10.1093/ref:odnb/9780198614128 .001.0001/odnb-9780198614128-e-11249.
33. The other George Grey, the man who had been Glenelg's deputy as under-secretary at the Colonial Office in 1838, had worked alongside Labouchere during the Irish Famine, as home secretary. He believed that it was not the British government's responsibility to alleviate the plight of the starving, but that of local landowners. His main response to the famine had been to tighten the laws allowing suppression of unrest during the crisis. D. Smith, 'Grey, Sir George, Second Baronet (1799–1882), Politician', in *Oxford Dictionary of National Biography*, www.oxforddnb.com/view/10.1093/ref:odnb/97801986 14128.001.0001/odnb-9780198614128-e-11533.
34. Stapleton, 'Reluctant Slaughter', 354–5.
35. J. B. Peires, 'Sir George Grey versus the Kaffir Relief Committee', *Journal of Southern African Studies*, 10, 2, 1984, 145–69.
36. CO 48/388, *British Kaffraria* (vol. pp. 24–8A), No. 7, Grey to Labouchere, 2 February 1858.

37. Peires, *The Dead Will Arise*, 272.
38. Quoted Peires, *The Dead Will Arise*, 269.
39. H. Merivale, *Lectures on Colonization and Colonies Delivered before the University of Oxford in 1839, 1840, and 1841*, Longman, Green, Longman and Roberts, 1861, 510–11.
40. After his momentous posting to the Cape, Grey would return to New Zealand and resume his efforts to amalgamate the Māori, most notably by prosecuting the war contemplated by his predecessor against the Kīngitanga (Kingite) movement in the early 1860s, and confiscating some 486 500 hectares of Māori land in its wake. Grey's predecessor, Thomas Gore Browne, had first warned the Colonial Office of 'the election of a King', heralding new, combined, Māori resistance to British settlement, in June 1857, while Grey was capitalising on the Cattle Killing. He wrote that it might 'become the greatest political difficulty we have had to contend with since the establishment of the British Government in these Islands'. CO 209/142, 61, *New Zealand* (vol. pp. 240–43), No. 61, Gore Browne to Labouchere, 23 September 1857, Gore Browne to Labouchere, 3 August 1857; translation of a letter addressed to the New Zealand Government by the Chief Hoani Papita and others, of Rangiaohia, Upper Waikato (vol. pp. 80–85): A True Copy: by Henry Morris, 25 June 1857.
41. See A. Lester, E. Nel and T. Binns, *South Africa Past, Present and Future*, Prentice Hall, 2000.
42. G. Stone, 'Bowring, Sir John (1792–1872), Politician, Diplomatist, and Writer', in *Oxford Dictionary of National Biography*, www.oxforddnb.com/view/10.1093/ref:odnb/9780198614128.001.0001/odnb-9780198614128-e-3087.
43. Quoted D. Steele, 'Villiers, George William Frederick, Fourth Earl of Clarendon (1800–1870), Politician', in *Oxford Dictionary of National Biography*, www.oxforddnb.com/view/10.1093/ref:odnb/9780198614128.001.0001/odnb-9780198614128-e-28297.
44. D. Steele, 'Temple, Henry John, Third Viscount Palmerston (1784–1865), Prime Minister', in *Oxford Dictionary of National Biography*, www.oxforddnb.com/view/10.1093/ref:odnb/9780198614128.001.0001/odnb-9780198614128-e-27112. Palmerston was accused of sexual assault by one of Queen Victoria's maids in waiting.
45. D. Todd, 'John Bowring and the Global Dissemination of Free Trade', *The Historical Journal*, 51, 2008, 373–97.
46. P. Bowring, *Free Trade's First Missionary: Sir John Bowring in Europe and Asia*, Hong Kong University Press, 2014, 19.
47. D. Logan, *Harriet Martineau, Victorian Imperialism, and the Civilizing Mission*, Routledge, 2016, 173–4.
48. Quoted J. Wong, *Deadly Dreams: Opium and the Arrow War (1856–1860) in China*, Cambridge University Press, 1998, 85.
49. Wong, *Deadly Dreams*, 262.
50. The French government was driven most immediately by a desire to avenge the Chinese killing of a French missionary, but both the French and the Americans also wanted to open up China's markets to their manufacturers

and traders. The Americans wanted to impose additional demands for freedom of thought and expression and the reform of Chinese government.

51. Bowring's most successful of many books was *The Kingdom and People of Siam*, published in two volumes in 1857. Stone, 'Bowring, Sir John'. Bowring's son had become a partner in the largest opium trading firm in the region, Jardine Mattheson & Co., and in the Hong Kong press Bowring was accused of furthering the firm's interests.

52. J. D. Spence, *God's Chinese Son: The Taiping Heavenly Kingdom of Hong Xiuquan*, Reprint ed., W. W. Norton, 1996.

53. The Taiping rebellion was also enabling British traders to play an increasing role in the recruitment and shipping of Chinese workers on indentured labour contracts overseas. Bowring himself intervened to commute the sentences passed on some Chinese workers, possibly recruited under false pretences, who took over a British ship bound for Havana. CO 129/63, *Hong Kong* (vol. pp. 5–9), No. 64, Bowring to Labouchere, 10 April 1857.

54. The whole story is told in forensic detail by Wong, *Deadly Dreams*, from which these and other quotes are taken.

55. The effect of Yeh's call to arms was the killing of a British marine and sailor when they strayed outside the fort in Macau and an attack on a postal steamer travelling from Canton to Hong Kong, in which eleven Europeans, including the Spanish vice-consul at Whampoa, were killed, both of which events took place in December. The British response to the killing of the two servicemen was to burn down the entire village where the event occurred.

56. *The Times*, 2 January 1857, 6. Wong notes that *The Times*' new editor, John Delane, met with Palmerston at William Molesworth's house in 1855 to come to a new understanding whereby the former would gain access to government sources and the latter would benefit from a cessation of the paper's criticism. 'To keep Delane on side, Clarendon ... once declared to the editor that "whether they [telegrams] come by night or by day, I have ordered that they shall always go first to *The Times*"'. Wong, *Deadly Dreams*, 153–73.

57. *Morning Post*, 2 January 1857.

58. Steele, 'Palmerston'.

59. The dose was high enough to induce vomiting, thus saving the lives of most victims. The baker, Cheong Ah-lum, was tried but acquitted through lack of evidence. Bowring nevertheless 'required him to find securities himself in one thousand dollars and two sureties in five hundred dollars each that he would absent himself from this Colony for the space of five years. Such sureties were perfected on July 31st and he was that day discharged from custody and left the island the same night'. CO 129/64, *Hong Kong* (vol. p. 61), No. 120, Bowring to Labouchere, 5 August 1857.

60. Quoted J. W. Norton-Kyshe, *History of the Laws and Courts of Hong Kong*, T. Fisher Unwin, 1898, 423–4. The danger of the telegraphic relay of coded messages across Europe was revealed when the word 'hong', meaning a European factory outside Canton, was misread by the *Morning Post* as 'Hong Kong', leading the paper to believe that the colony had indeed been attacked. Wong, *Deadly Dreams*.

61. CO 129/63, *Hong Kong* (vol. p. 15), No. 66, Bowring to Labouchere, 14 April 1857.
62. *China Mail*, 21 April 1857. Shortly afterwards, the same newspaper reported that indentured labour recruiters had been allowed to get away with the imprisonment of Chinese workers awaiting transhipment. Bowring complained to Labouchere that 'the Hong Kong Press without any exception is so untrustworthy that I have been again and again urged (even by the Representatives of foreign powers) to suppress its mendacity by a censorship or by some other despotic action. I hold its general character in great indifference and contempt and should often have proceeded against it by criminal information were I not convinced that nothing would better serve its policy and that by noticing I should give importance to its misrepresentations and its slanders'. At the Colonial Office, Thomas Elliot annotated the despatch: 'This is a strange despatch from Sir John Bowring. One of the local newspapers reported a gross case of unlawful imprisonment and oppression of some Chinese, and a very inadequate sentence by the Chief Justice. Sir John Bowring admits that the statement was quite true, sends home a report which confirms it in every respect, and then proceeds to a general invective against the Press, and says that its mendacity has made him seriously think of establishing a censorship'. CO 129/64, *Hong Kong* (vol. pp. 142–4), No. 131, Bowring to Labouchere, 25 August 1857, Elliot note dated 4 November.
63. Having been in the forefront of the campaign for electoral reform in 1832, Russell had continued to urge a further widening of the franchise. Palmerston was resisting. Russell had dismissed Palmerston as secretary of state for foreign affairs in 1851.
64. *Hansard*, 26 February 1857. Herbert's argument would have been reinforced had he known that, in June, the Colonial Office would respond to the Mexican seizure of a British vessel carrying mahogany through purely diplomatic means, via the Superintendent of British Honduras. Furthermore, in November, the Colonial and Foreign Offices agreed to do the same regarding the American seizure of a British vessel on the Great Lakes, declaring that 'H.M. Govt would regret to be instrumental in pursuing a claim on the Government of the United States unless there was strong & sufficient reason to believe that it had good foundation'. CO 123/95, Ino. Carmichael & Co., Mathé to Berkely, 8 June 1857, 52; Superintendent Frederick Seymour, Belize, to Martinez, Esq., Consul for the Republic of Mexico, 8 June 1857; CO42/611, 10084, Foreign Office to Colonial Office, 3 November 1857.
65. *Hansard*, 3 February–21 March 1857.
66. See M. Taylor, *The Decline of British Radicalism, 1847–1860*, Oxford, 1995, 269–79.
67. See Hall, *Civilising Subjects*, for an extended treatment of this argument.
68. The article was first published in 1849 in *Fraser's Magazine* and republished in 1853 as 'Occasional Discourse on the N****r Question'. The version reprinted in America under the title 'West India Emancipation' can be found in the University of Michigan's 'Making of America' Database and at https://cruel.org/econthought/texts/carlyle/carlodnq.html.

69. R. Godlonton, *Memorials of the British Settlers of South Africa*, Godlonton, 1844.
70. Douglas noted that 'it is remarkable that the highest services rendered the anti-slavery cause in both countries, were rendered by women. Elizabeth Herrick [Heyrick], who wrote only a pamphlet, will be remembered as long as the West India Emancipation is remembered, and the name of Harriet Beecher Stowe can never die while the love of freedom lives in the world'. Heyrick had argued for immediate emancipation rather than just the abolition of the slave trade in 1807 and thereafter until her death in 1831. https://rbscp.lib.rochester.edu/4398.
71. For more on this, see S. Qureshi, *Peoples on Parade: Exhibitions, Empire, and Anthropology in Nineteenth-Century Britain*, University of Chicago Press, 2011.
72. *Reynolds's Newspaper* was also not a Palmerston fan: 'What a truly melancholy exhibition! The foremost nation of all the Old World rushing, and screaming, and swearing, and shouting in mad hysterical hallelujahs, the praises of a man whose principal characteristic was an unconquerable disposition to jest at national calamities, and whose greatest recommendation was a species of boasts'. *Reynolds's Newspaper*, 22 March 1857. This footnote was written on the day that Boris Johnston became the British prime minister.
73. Officially, the USA refused Britain's offer of an alliance since it had signed a treaty of neutrality with the Qing authorities in 1856. However, the USS *San Jacinto* would assist the British and French bombardment of Chinese forts in 1859. Russia would also seize the opportunity to negotiate appropriation of a large chunk of the Manchurian coast, including the site where Vladivostok was later constructed.

8 'A STRUGGLE OF LIFE AND DEATH'

Title quote is from E. B. Lytton, future colonial secretary, quoted in J. C. Bender, *The 1857 Indian Uprising and the British Empire*, Cambridge University Press, 2016, 2.
1. F. Robinson, 'Ahmad Khan, Sir Saiyid [Syed Ahmed Khan] (1817–1898), Muslim Leader in India', Oxford Dictionary of National Biography, www.oxforddnb.com/view/10.1093/ref:odnb/9780198614128.001.0001/odnb-9780198614128-e-47667.
2. S. Ahmed Khan, *The Causes of the Indian Revolt*, Medical Hall Press, 1873.
3. T. Metcalf, 'Canning, Charles John, Earl Canning (1812–1862), Governor-General and First Viceroy of India', *Oxford Dictionary of National Biography*, www.oxforddnb.com/view/10.1093/ref:odnb/9780198614128.001.0001/odnb-9780198614128-e-4554.
4. W. Williams, 'Vernon, Robert [formerly Robert Vernon Smith], First Baron Lyveden (1800–1873), Politician', *Oxford Dictionary of National Biography*, www.oxforddnb.com/view/10.1093/ref:odnb/9780198614128.001.0001/odnb-9780198614128-e-25898.

5. Malcolm Allbrook, *Henry Prinsep's Empire: Framing a Distant Colony*, ANU Press, 2014.

6. K. Prior, 'Mangles, Ross Donnelly (1801–1877), East India Company Servant and Politician', *Oxford Dictionary of National Biography*, www.oxforddnb.com/view/10.1093/ref:odnb/9780198614128.001.0001/odnb-9 780198614128-e-17934.

7. Khan, *The Causes*, 14.

8. D. Howlett, 'Ramsay, James Andrew Broun, First Marquess of Dalhousie (1812–1860), Governor-General of India', in *Oxford Dictionary of National Biography*, www.oxforddnb.com/view/10.1093/ref:odnb/9780198614128 .001.0001/odnb-9780198614128-e-23088.

9. E. Stokes, *The English Utilitarians and India*, Oxford University Press, 1989, 250.

10. The entire rail route from Suez to Alexandria would be completed in 1858.

11. Here, the first transit had been delayed until 1855 because an expensive clerical error in Britain led to the locomotives being sent to Australia instead of Calcutta. C. Wolmar, *Blood, Iron and Gold: How the Railways Transformed the World*, Atlantic Books, 2009.

12. CO 42/610, *Canada* (vol. pp. 143–55, No. 93-6049, Head to Labouchere, 16 June 1857.

13. It is estimated that 25 000 Indian labourers, referred to dismissively as 'coolies' by the British engineers, died in the construction of the Ghat inclines alone. A. Burton, *On the Rails: Two Centuries of Railways*, Aurum, 2004, 135.

14. Victoria's system alone conveyed 35 792 messages in 1857.

15. CO 158/182, *Malta*, No. 7532, Pennefather to Labouchere, 1 August 1857. In December, a colonial office clerk who signed himself 'G', annotated that 'a Message from Malta to London by Electric Telegraph took only 3 hours & 10 minutes – & that the return message would only have taken 2 hours & 20 minutes if "Corsica" had not continually given "Cagliari" the signal "wait". The personification of the countries as senders of telegraphs is amusing': 182–1666, Malta, Reid, to Labouchere, 22 December 1857.

16. The Indian telegraph system was based on the American one but with the cables strung between stronger iron posts set farther apart to protect against monkeys, and with the wires suspended higher above the ground to allow the passage of elephants. Neither precaution would prevent *sepoy* mutineers cutting the lines in 1857 and converting sections of cable into ammunition slugs for their rifles. http://distantwriting.co.uk/companiesandforeigntraffic .html.

17. CO 537/155, Military Confidential General & Original Correspondence (vol. pp. 302-36), Report to the Minister for War, Major M.A. Biddulph, R.A., Director of Telegraphs in the Black Sea: 'Telegraphic Communications from Constantinople through Vienna to England and generally on the Submarine Telegraph Service in the East', printed: August 1856, War Department.

18. At the beginning of 1857 the Treasury was moving slowly, considering two rival consortia's proposals to connect London and India directly. The European and Indian Company, an offshoot of a railway enterprise, envisioned an overland line, circling around the Mediterranean and connecting the Austrian network

with the Company's Karachi station via Constantinople. The Red Sea and Indian Telegraph Association was awaiting the Treasury's response to its request of a financial guarantee for a route via Suez and under the Red Sea. The Treasury would develop a much greater sense of urgency once 'an empire was obviously at stake' in the summer of 1857. The British and reformed Indian governments backed the Red Sea route and the line was completed in 1860, although it ultimately failed and no direct message was ever sent along it. Direct communication to India would have to wait until the Persian Gulf cable was laid in 1864. Cell, *The Colonial Office*, 223.

19. CO 201/500, Official Draft Reply (vol. pp. 151–2), Colonial Office to Foreign Office, 24 December 1857.
20. D. Howlett, 'Ramsay, James Andrew Broun, First Marquess of Dalhousie (1812–1860), Governor-General of India', in *Oxford Dictionary of National Biography*, www.oxforddnb.com/view/10.1093/ref:odnb/9780198614128 .001.0001/odnb-9780198614128-e-23088.
21. Rango Bapujee, Rajah of Sattara, *A Letter to the Right Hon. J. C. Herries, M.P., President of the Board of Control*, G. Norman, 1852, www.csas.ed.ac.uk/muti ny/Part1Texts.html.
22. Howlett, Ramsay, James Andrew Broun, First Marquess of Dalhousie.
23. J. Wilson, *India Conquered: Britain's Raj and the Chaos of Empire*, Simon and Schuster, 2016, 235.
24. Wilson, *India Conquered*, 233.
25. A despatch from South Australia's governor conveying its settlers' sympathy for 'the sufferings and wrongs of their fellow subjects in India' prompted Merivale to deliberate whether such intimations of support should be sent on to Queen Victoria. Some research by the Colonial Office's clerks revealed that similar expressions from the North American and West Indian colonies, received well before those from Australia, had not been shown to the Queen, and so it was concluded that neither should this one. Somewhat bizarrely, the South Australian Legislative Assembly accompanied its expression of sympathy with a request that trophies seized from the Russians during the Crimean War be donated to the colony in return for its earlier support for wounded British soldiers and their families: CO 13/97, Correspondence Number: 220–3362, South Australia (vol. pp. 94–5), MacDonnell to Labouchere, 10 February 1858; 210–3352, South Australia (vol. pp. 8–9), MacDonnell to Labouchere, 22 January 1858.
26. Wilson, *India Conquered*, 230.
27. C. Bates, Commemorating 1857, from C. Bates, *Subalterns and Raj: South Asia since 1600*, Routledge, 2007, www.csas.ed.ac.uk/mutiny/history.html.
28. Mukherjee, *Awadh in Revolt*.
29. Wilson, *India Conquered*, 240.
30. When Burma was first being conquered in 1824, the issue of passage across the Bay of Bengal had played a part in prompting *sepoys* to mutiny at the Company's garrison at Barrackpoor near Calcutta. One hundred and eighty of them had been shot dead in a panicked response from British officers that was later condemned in Britain.

31. K. Wagner, *The Skull of Alum Bheg: The Life and Death of a Rebel of 1857*, Hurst, 2017, 56–8.
32. Gurkhas had also been recruited from Nepal since 1816.
33. Khan, *The Causes*, 14.
34. N. A. Chick, *Annals of the Indian Rebellion, 1857–58*, Sanders, Cones, 1859, 30.
35. Wagner, *The Great Fear of 1857*, 219.
36. Khan, *The Causes*, 51–2.
37. Wagner, *The Great Fear of 1857*. The name Pande came to be associated with the Mutiny as a whole in Britain and the children's toy and TV character Andy Pandy was based upon a caricature of the sepoy.
38. Quoted S. David, *The Bengal Army and the Outbreak of the Indian Mutiny*, Manohar, 2009, 103.
39. Wagner, *The Great Fear of 1857*, 219.
40. Khan, *The Causes*, i–vi.
41. IOR L/PS/3/54, Political & Secret Home *Correspondence*, No. 251, Stratford to Clarendon, 28 June 1857, Dated from Corachee [Karachi], 20 May, Lahore, 15 May, Bagdad, 8 June.
42. Despite the urgency, Labouchere decided to decline the offer from Andrea Zir, one of the many Italian refugees from the Risorgimento wars living in exile in Malta, to raise an army of '3000 men, chiefly old soldiers ... from Sicily for the service of the Queen'. Zir was apparently 'connected with the theatre ... and has been more than once admonished by the Police to behave better in that place of public entertainment'. The War Office's reply was a curt 'Her Majesty's Government has no intention of enlisting foreigners for service in Her Majesty's Army'.: CO 158/182, *Malta*, No. 8735, Pennefather to Labouchere, 8 September 1857; No. 9211, War Office to Merivale, 5 October 1857.
43. C. H. Philips, 'The Secret Committee of the East India Company, 1784–1858. II', *Bulletin of the School of Oriental and African Studies*, 10, 3, 1940, 699–716, 708.
44. M. Moir, *A General Guide to the India Office Records*, British Library, 1988.
45. The Home Correspondence of the Political and Secret Committee's records is remarkable for the number of erasures and crossings-out, and the amount of care given to judicious wording.
46. Both routes were believed to place a strain on soldiers' health. At Suez, soldiers awaiting embarkation were exposed to a port 'unequipped' by climate and infrastructure to house large numbers of British soldiers. The sheer duration of the Cape voyage was also seen as a challenge to health, although a Company memorandum sardonically dismissed this as a vestigial attitude, noting that a regiment of 900 men, with some officers' wives, sent via the Cape had increased its number, through births on the voyage, to 910 by the time of its arrival in Bombay: IOR L/PS/3/56, *Political & Secret Home Correspondence*, pp. 785–82, Memorandum, Clerk.
47. Steam power had brought a greater imperative for the British and French empires to cooperate. For instance, in August 1857, Colonel Riky, Commanding the 48th Regiment, asked the governor of Gibraltar to express 'for himself and every individual in the corps, the deep sense of gratitude they

entertain for the great kindness and respect which they received from the French Authorities at Algiers, on the occasion of the 'Abeona', Steam Transport, in which the Regiment was embarked, being obliged to put into that port on her passage from Malta, in consequence of her machinery being much injured'. Governor Marshall Randon of French Algeria had directed the Commander of the French Frigate 'Cacique' to take the 'Abeona' in tow to Gibraltar: CO 91/234, *Separate*, No. 152, Fergusson to Panmure, 23 August 1857.

48. The Foreign Office was also vying with the French government to influence the Egyptian Pasha. Helen Anne B. Rivlin, 'The Railway Question in the Ottoman-Egyptian Crisis of 1850–1852', *Middle East Journal*, 15, 4, 1961, 365–88.

49. F. Harcourt, 'The High Road to India: The P&O Company and the Suez Canal, 1840–1874', *International Journal of Maritime History*, 22, 2010, 19–72.

50. W. Westgarth, Victoria and the Australian gold mines in 1857: with notes on the Overland Route from Australia, via Suez, London, 1857, 434–5.

51. IOR L/PS/3/54, Hammond to Clerk, 25 May 417.

52. We will return to this in Part III.

53. IOR L/PS/3/54, *Elphinstone*, pp. 419–37, Burton to Nordenshaw, Secretary to the RGS, 18 December 1856.

54. IOR L/PS/3/54, *Elphinstone*, pp. 419–37, Burton to Nordenshaw; IOR L/PS/3/54, p. 417, Hammond to Clerk, 25 May.

55. IOR L/PS/3/56. Green added that, when he had a chance, he would also read the Indian newspapers that were sent through the mail.

56. IOR L/PS/3/56.

57. These are labelled the 'Mutiny Enclosures' in the India Office files at the British Library.

58. IOR L/PS/3/55, *Political & Secret Home Correspondence*, Melville to Yorke, 18 July 1857.

59. IOR L/PS/3/55, *Political & Secret Home Correspondence* p. 327, Green to Clarendon, 19 August 1857.

60. It is unclear here whether 'company' is a slip for 'country' or whether Fraser means that the troops would have to be prevented from communicating with other British travellers crossing the isthmus; clearly, both could be the case, although the stricture does cast some doubt on how surreptitious such a scheme could really hope to be.

61. IOR L/PS/3/55, Fraser to the Company, 18 July 1857.

62. IOR L/PS/3/55, Mangles and Currie to Vernon Smith, 9 September 1857.

63. IOR L/PS/3/55, Vernon Smith to the Chairs, 17 September 1857.

64. IOR L/PS/3/56, Storks (War Office) to Clerk, 26 October 1857.

65. IOR L/PS/3/55, Hammond to Clerk, 24 July 1857.

66. IOR L/PS/3/55, Clarendon to Green, 16 September 1857.

67. IOR L/PS/3/55, *Political & Secret Home Correspondence*, pp. 685–86, Clarendon to Stratford, 22 September 1857.

68. IOR L/PS/3/56, Green to Clarendon, 12 October 1857 (copy); Green to Clarendon, 9 October 1857.

69. IOR L/PS/3/56, *Political & Secret Correspondence*, pp. 384–86, Green to Clarendon.

70. William Howard Russell, *My Diary in India in the Year 1858–59*, Routledge, 1860, 27, 36, 37.

71. *Times*, 29 October 1857.

72. C. Herbert, *War of No Pity: The Indian Mutiny and Victorian Trauma*, Princeton University Press, 2008.

73. P. Scheckner, *An Anthology of Chartist Poetry: Poetry of the British Working Class, 1830s–1850s*, Fairleigh Dickinson University Press, 1989, 53.

74. *Times*, 25 August 1857; K. R. Beckman, *Vanishing Women: Magic, Film, and Feminism*, Duke University Press, 2003, 33–4.

75. *Punch*, 24 October 1857.

76. Governor Yeh was exiled to Calcutta, where he starved himself to death while a British–French alliance maintained control of his city.

77. To say nothing of the Colonial Office's role in the suppression of the Uprising, which we will come to in the next chapter.

78. D. Williams, *The India Office, 1858–1869*, Hoshiarpur, 1983, 7–8; see also D. Williams, 'The Council of India and the Relationship between the Home and Supreme Governments, 1858–1870', *English Historical Review* 81, 36, 1966, 56–73.

9 A NEW IMPERIAL GOVERNMENT

1. Labouchere was informed by the governor of Trinidad that 'both the Master & the Medical Officer in charge complain that the allowance of rice is insufficient, and that the biscuit does not agree with the Coolies' on the ships coming from India. Sixty out of 228 migrants on board the 'Scindian' had died en route. In British Guiana, Governor Wodehouse reported in July 1857 that, although forty-nine Indian immigrants had died on the voyage from Calcutta in the ship 'Burmah', 'I did not think it necessary, after all that has taken place lately, to order any special investigation'. CO 295/195, *Trinidad* (vol. pp. 47–8), No. 56, Keate to Labouchere, 8 July 1857; CO 111/317, *British Guiana*, Wodehouse to Labouchere, 7 July 1857.

2. CO 137/334, *Jamaica* (vol. pp. 428–32), No. 21, Darling to Labouchere, 25 September 1857.

3. In 1857, Ranavalona's son, Rakoto, and her French confidant, Laborde, conspired with the French shipping merchant Joseph Lambert to usurp her. Hearing of the plan, Ranavalona expelled the conspirators. Higginson warned the Colonial Office that they might arrive in Mauritius, bringing the British authorities into the affair. His despatch prompted a Colonial Office official to note, 'It was fortunate for Mr. Lambert & his friends that in the opinion of Ranavalona ... cutting in pieces was too good for them, & that a sense of the unsatisfactory nature of that expiation, concurring with a prudent policy, induced her simply to send them away'. Labouchere asked Higginson to send a supportive letter to the Madagscan Queen and to interfere no further in the affair. CO 167/389, *Mauritius*, Confidential - No. 9788, Higginson to Labouchere, 29 August 1857; correspondence between Rainikilaka, Officer of the Palace of Madagascar, and Governor

Higginson; K. Laidler, *Female Caligula: Ranavalona, the Mad Queen of Madagascar*, Wiley, 2005.

4. CO 167/389, *Mauritius*, No. 8836, Higginson to Labouchere, 2 August 1857.
5. CO 167/389, *Mauritius*, 'Report upon the Condition and prospects of the Seychelles,' From Victoria Town, Mahé, Seychelles to Higginson, 10 July 1857.
6. CO 167/389, *Mauritius*, Humphry Sandwith, Colonial Secretary to the Secretary to the Government of India, 25 July 1857.
7. CO 167/389, *Mauritius*. Higginson to Labouchere, 10 August 1857.
8. CO 167/389, *Mauritius*, Confidential – No. 11143, Stevenson to Labouchere, 5 October 1857. Comment – J/B 9 December.
9. CO 167/389, *Mauritius*, 'Draft Letter from Colonial Office to Governor William Stevenson', 31 December 1857.
10. CO 167/389, *Mauritius*, Higginson to Labouchere, 4 August 1857.
11. CO 54/330, *Ceylon*, Military Confidential – No. 9446, Ward to Labouchere, 14 September 1857.
12. CO 54/329, *Ceylon* (vol. pp. 387–97), No. 6925, Ward to Labouchere, 26 June 1857.
13. CO 54/329, *Ceylon* (vol. pp. 199–210), No. 91, Ward to Labouchere, 6 June 1857. Ward reported the 'absurd predictions' circulating 'in the Bazaars, [that] in the present state of the East ... the cessation of British rule, which is to occur within 60 days, is to be followed by a division of the Island between the Moormen and the Cinghalese, – the latter taking the Interior, – the former, the Maritime Provinces'. CO 54/329, *Ceylon* (vol. pp. 449–57), No. 7515, Ward to Labouchere, 11 July 1857.
14. CO 54/330, *Ceylon*, Military Confidential – No. 9446, Ward to Labouchere, 14 September 1857.
15. CO 54/330, *Ceylon*, Military Confidential – No. 9817, Ward to Labouchere, 27 September 1857.
16. CO 137/334, *Jamaica* (vol. pp. 384–87), No. 14, Darling to Labouchere, 5 and 7 September 1857; draft reply 17 October 1857.
17. CO 295/196, *Trinidad* (vol. pp. 371–80), No. 113, Keate to Labouchere, 6 November 1857.
18. CO 48/384, *Cape* (vol. pp. 279–83), Confidential – No. 304, Grey to Labouchere, 11 November 1857.
19. See C. Anderson, M. Mazumdar and V. Pandya, *New Histories of the Andaman Islands: Landscape, Place and Identity in the Bay of Bengal, 1790–2012*, Cambridge University Press, 2018.
20. J. Mitchell, 'Great Difficulty in Knowing Where the Frontier Ceases': Violence, Governance, and the Spectre of India in Early Queensland', *Journal of Australian Colonial History*, 15, 2013, 43–62; A. Woollacott, *Settler Society in the Australian Colonies: Self-Government and Imperial Culture*, Oxford University Press, 2015, 168, 179–90.
21. CO 295/195, *Trinidad* (vol. pp. 77–9), No. 61, Keate to Labouchere, 8 July 1857.
22. CO 111/316, *British Guiana*, No. 5924, Wodehouse to Labouchere, 9 June 1857; Colonial Office to Wodehouse, 1 July 1857.

23. CO 111/318, *British Guiana*, No. 11410 War Office to Merivale, 16 December 1857; 'Mr. Merivale. 16 Dec. See 10423 & 10697'. Merivale also received a 'return of the number of troops, distinguishing white & black, & their proportion to the population at present time in the colonies of B. Guiana, Barbados, Trinidad & Jamaica respectively'.

24. CO 42/610, *Canada* (vol. p. 441), No. 104–11571, to Labouchere, 4 December 1857; Draft Reply, Colonial Office to Head, 2 January 1858; R. J. Pennefather, Superintendent General, Indian Department, Toronto, to Head, 1 December 1857.

25. CO 54/329, *Ceylon* (vol. pp. 387–97), No. 6925, Ward to Labouchere, 26 June 1857. However, Ward added, 'But after the examples that we have seen in India, of Regiments hanging the emissaries of disaffection one hour, and being in open mutiny the next, I should be sorry to see the predominant power, in this Island, left for any lengthened period, in the hands of a Native Force. They will know it; they will presume upon it; – discipline will be relaxed; – and sooner or later the Government will be forced to connive at abuses, on the part of its armed servants, for the want of means to repress the abuse, or lose the services of the only Force upon which it can at present rely'.

26. CO 48/384, *Secret Department* (vol. pp. 226–31), No. 702, E. Elphinstone, J. G. Lumsden, & A. Malet, to George Grey, 29 June 1857.

27. CO 48/384, *Cape* (vol. pp. 6–9), No. 141–10686, Grey to Labouchere, 22 September 1857, SB comments, 26 November 1857.

28. CO 48/384, *Cape*, Grey to Labouchere, 5 November 1857.

29. At the same time, he complained that 'the accounts, which have … been received of the revolting atrocities committed by the mutineers in India, have created such a feeling in this colony that no Sepoy Regiments could now be received here, until I have had an opportunity of consulting the Colonial Parliament upon the subject'. CO 48/384, 147–11342, Cape (vol. pp. 72–3), Grey to Labouchere, 3 October 1857.

30. CO 48/384, *British Kaffraria* (vol. pp. 42–51), No. 9, Grey to Labouchere, 11 February 1858.

31. CO 48/388, *Cape* (vol. pp. 119–24A), No. 18–3948, Grey to Labouchere, 9 March 1858.

32. The Colonial Office had already reluctantly had to defend Grey from an accusation in Parliament that he had a history of accumulating British military forces in his colonies, with at least six Regiments being deployed against the Maori during Grey's tenure in New Zealand: CO 48/384, Separate – 404, Cape (vol. pp. 272–4), Grey to Labouchere, 7 November 1857, Comments (vol. p. 276), HM 15 January 1858.

33. CO 537/155 *Military Confidential General & Original Correspondence* (vol. pp. 344–49), 'Military Expenditure in the Colonies,' 1859.

34. CO 537/155, Elliot, Memorandum, Colonial Office, 28 January 1860.

35. Hansard 24 June 1858, House of Commons third reading of Government of India (No. 3) Bill.

36. Although the Company directors did continue to manage the tea trade on behalf of the British Government and supplied the colony of Saint Helena.

37. N. Robins, *The Corporation That Changed the World: How the East India Company Shaped the Modern Multinational*, Pluto Press, 2006, 164–7.
38. Hansard, 7 July 1858.
39. Webster, *Twilight*.
40. D. Williams, 'The Council of India and the Relationship between the Home and Supreme Governments, 1858–1870', *The English Historical Review*, 81, 318, 1966, 56–73.
41. T. R. Metcalf, *The Aftermath of Revolt: India, 1857–1870*, Princeton University Press, 1965, 172.
42. IOR L/PS/3/55 (from Microfilm IOR NEG 38561), *Political and Secret Home Correspondence, Vol. 2*, pp. 411–14, Wodehouse to Clarendon, 27 August 1857.
43. IOR, L/PS/3/56, *Political and Secret Home Correspondence, Vol 3*, pp. 267–70, White to Clarendon, 2 October 1857.
44. G. Stamp, 'Scott, Sir George Gilbert (1811–1878), Architect', in *Oxford Dictionary of National Biography*, www.oxforddnb.com/view/10.1093/ref:od nb/9780198614128.001.0001/odnb-9780198614128-e-24869.
45. See B. Porter, *The Battle of the Styles: Society, Culture and the Design of a New Foreign Office, 1855–1861*, Continuum, 2011.
46. Stamp, 'Scott, Sir George Gilbert'.

10 LIBERAL FATHERS AND SONS

1. J. Black, *Imperial Legacies*, Encounter, 2019, 148.
2. Cambridge University Library, Add 7511, James Stephens' diary, 1 January 1846.
3. C. S. S. Higham, 'Sir Henry Taylor and the Establishment of Crown Colony Government in the West Indies', *The Scottish Historical Review*, 23, 90, 1926, 94.
4. G. Heuman, *The Killing Time: The Morant Bay Rebellion in Jamaica*, University of Tennessee Press, 1994, 54–5.
5. Eyre had been a protector of Aborigines in South Australia and Grey's lieutenant governor in New Zealand. For his remarkable trajectory across the empire, see J. Evans *Edward Eyre: Race and Colonial Governance*, University of Otago Press, 2005, and C. Hall, *Civilising Subjects*, 23–66.
6. Heuman, *The Killing Time*, 54, 139.
7. Quoted B. Semmel, 'The Issue of "Race" in the British Reaction to the Morant Bay Uprising of 1865', *Caribbean Studies*, 2, 3, 1962, 11.
8. Quoted Semmel, 'The Issue of "Race"', 5.
9. Quoted Semmel, 'The Issue of "Race"', 14.
10. Quoted J. A. Colaico, *James Fitzjames Stephen and the Crisis of Victorian Thought*, Macmillan, 1983, 120.
11. E. Stokes, *The English Utilitarians and India*, Oxford University Press, 1989, 293.
12. C. Ilbert, 'Sir James Stephen as a Legislator', *Law Quarterly Review*, 10, 1894, 222–4.

13. J. F. Stephen, *A General View of the Criminal Law of England*, Cambridge University Press, 2014. John Stuart Mill, another East India Company employee, may have stood out for his campaigning for the rights of British women but he too 'accepted with little question the view that Indians were similarly immature and incapable of self-government'. J. Pitts, *A Turn to Empire: The Rise of Imperial Liberalism in Britain and France*, Princeton University Press, 2006, 8.
14. Quoted Stokes, *The English Utilitarians and India*, 297–8.
15. J. F. Stephen, *Liberty, Equality, Fraternity*, Holt & Williams, 1873. In 1883 Stephen would play a prominent role in the crisis over Home Rule in Ireland, which led the Liberal Party to split. Adverting to his Indian experience, he argued that it was quite legitimate to deny Irishmen self-governance on the same grounds that Indians were denied it: their backwardness compared to a population of Britons who could, by now, be trusted with a share of governance.
16. *The Times*, 4 January 1878.
17. British settlers in Queensland and Fiji also supplied the global cotton deficit, some of them utilising captive Pacific Islander labour and drawing the Colonial Office into the declaration of new protectorates in the Pacific.
18. R. C. Dutt, *Famines and Land Assessments in India*, K. Paul, Trench, Trübner, 1900.
19. M. Mulvey-Roberts, 'Lytton, Rosina Anne Doyle Bulwer [née Rosina Anne Doyle Wheeler], Lady Lytton (1802–1882), Novelist', in *Oxford Dictionary of National Biography*, www.oxforddnb.com/view/10.1093/ref:odnb/97801986 14128.001.0001/odnb-9780198614128-e-17316.
20. M. Davis, *Late Victorian Holocausts: El Nino Famines and the Making of the Third World*, Verso, 2001, 31.
21. I. Klein, 'Who Made the Second Afghan War?', *Journal of Asian History*, 8, 2, 1974, 99.
22. D. Washbrook, 'Lytton, Edward Robert Bulwer, First Earl of Lytton [pseud. Owen Meredith] (1831–1891)', in *Oxford Dictionary of National Biography*, https://doi.org/10.1093/ref:odnb/17315.
23. W. M. Kennedy, 'The Imperial Politics of Death: Australian Responses to India's Famines, 1874–1902', unpublished paper.
24. Davis, *Late Victorian Holocausts*, 38.
25. C. Twomey, 'Framing Atrocity: Photography and Humanitarianism', *History of Photography*, 36, 3, 2012, 255–64.
26. *Sydney Morning Herald*, 31 March 1877, quoted Kennedy, 'The Imperial Politics of Death'.
27. Washbrook, 'Lytton'. It was not just the Indian government that proved reluctant to provide relief, however. The following year, the rains failed in parts of Ceylon, a Crown colony under Colonial Office administration. When its governor, James Robert Longden, reported that district officials had used public funds to provide both relief works and grain for those unable to work, the secretary of state, Michael Hicks Beach, added a note to the draft reponse, 'And add a caution, with regard to the distribution of relief to them unable to work, that great care should be exercised in this

matter, so as to ensure that work shall be exacted from all them who are able to give it. Let me see draft'. CO 54/518, *Ceylon* (vol. p. 307), No. 113–6554, Longden to Hicks Beach, 22 March 1879, annotation, Sir M. H. B. 16 May 1879.

28. Quoted Wilson, *India Conquered*, 308–10.

29. D. E. Haynes, *Rhetoric and Ritual in Colonial India: The Shaping of a Public Culture in Surat City, 1852–1928*, Oxford University Press, 1992, 97; C. A. Bayly, *Recovering Liberties: Indian Thought in the Age of Liberalism and Empire*, Cambridge University Press, 2012.

30. Baroda Archives (BA), *Huzur Political Series*, File 260/6, Sir T. Madhavrao to P. S. Melville, 1879.

31. BA, *Huzur Political Series*, File 260/6, Sir T. Madhavrao to P. S. Melville, 1879.

32. While Syed Mahmood was drafting his *Calcutta Review* piece, the military accounts employee Vasudev Balwant Phadke left his wife to form a revolutionary army in the Mahrashtra forests. Early in 1879, Phadke's followers were raiding villages around Pune demanding that government officials' salaries be cut and threatening to attack Europeans. The rebellion would continue until June, when Phadke was captured and transported to Aden. Within six years, Pune Sarvajanik Sabha would form the basis of the Indian National Congress. Wilson, *India Conquered*, 344–6.

33. The India Office had moved into the building in 1867, having stayed at East India House in Leadenhall Street until its demolition in 1861 and then occupied the building which afterwards became the Westminster Palace Hotel.

34. G. Bremner, 'Nation and Empire in the Government Architecture of Mid-Victorian London: The Foreign and India Office Reconsidered', *The Historical Journal*, 48, 3, 2005, 729.

35. Charles Edward Trevelyan had been a senior East India Company employee in Calcutta. As assistant secretary to the Treasury, convinced by free trade doctrine, he then played a critical role in withholding famine relief during the Great Irish Famine. Stafford H. Northcote was legal secretary to the Board of Trade.

36. www.civilservant.org.uk/library/1854_Northcote_Trevelyan_Report.pdf.

37. D. Williams, 'Clements Robert Markham and the Geographical Department of the India Office 1867–77', *The Geographical Journal*, 134, 3, 1968, 343–52.

38. J. W. Cell, *British Colonial Administration in the Mid-Nineteenth Century: The Policy-Making Process*, Yale University Press, 1970, 25, 31.

39. www.civilservant.org.uk/library/1854_Northcote_Trevelyan_Report.pdf.

40. Williams, 'Clements Robert Markham'.

41. P. Mitchell, K. J. Boehme and A. Lester, '"The Centre of the Muniment": Archival Order and Reverential Historiography in the India Office, 1875', *Journal of Historical Geography*, 63, 2019, 12–22.

42. Cell, *British Colonial Administration*, 25.

43. Cell, *British Colonial Administration*, 41–3.

44. R. Aldous, *The Lion and the Unicorn: Gladstone vs Disraeli*, W. W. Norton, 2007, 263.

45. C. Newbury, 'Patronage and Professionalism: Manning a Transitional Empire, 1760–1870', *The Journal of Imperial and Commonwealth History*, 42, 2, 2014, 193–214.
46. R. Robinson and J. Gallagher with A. Denny, *Africa and the Victorians: The Official Mind of Imperialism*, 2nd ed., Macmillan, 1981.
47. Aldous, *The Lion and the Unicorn*, 265. Lytton's Durbar included 'a week-long feast for 68,000 officials, satraps and maharajas: the most colossal and expensive meal in world history'. Davis, *Late Victorian Holocausts*, 28.
48. In 1879, Isaac Butt, leader of the Home Rule League, who had been launching parliamentary filibusters to obstruct governmental business, died. His successor, William Shaw, was leading the party. The following year, Charles Stuart Parnell took over, leading the call for limited self-government for Ireland. Gladstone's support for home rule split the Liberal Party in 1886, leading to a Liberal Unionist Party faction, which eventually merged with the Conservatives.
49. N. Gabrielle Parkinson, 'Impersonating a Voter: Constructions of Race, and Conceptions of Subjecthood in the Franchise of Colonial New South Wales, c. 1850–1865', *The Journal of Imperial and Commonwealth History*, 47, 4, 2019, 652–75.
50. It was, by a raised property bar, in the 1890s.
51. CO 42/756, *Canada*, No. 78–5593, Lorne (Governor-General of Canada) to Hicks Beach, 20 March 1879, Enclosure: Report of Committee of the Privy Council of Canada, 17 March. Consisting of a Dept of the Interior Memo; 8507, Lorne to Hicks Beach, 12 May 1879. Accordingly, Lorne instructed that 'the movements of all Indian tribes, on the Boundary line, [be] carefully watched by half-breeds [since] the Minister of the Interior prefers to take that class of men for this service, lest the employment of the North West Police Force should afford to the United States Government further excuse for the policy they have adopted of throwing the responsibility of the actions of these Indians on the Canadian Government'. No. 6413 Lorne to Hicks Beach, 10 April 1879.
52. CO 42/757, *Canada*, No. 133–8397, Lorne to Hicks Beach, 30 April 1879, Enclosure: Report from Inspector J. M. Walsh of the North West Mounted Police, Wood Mountain, North West Territories, 25 March 1879. Sitting Bull was advised that he could not persist in a traditional lifeway in Canada and should return to the Sioux reservations in the USA. He did so in 1881. In the meantime, Walsh reported that 'the paramount difficulty which constantly present itself' to the assimilation of First Nations along the border 'arises from the scarcity of food; the Buffalo which forms the staple of consumption amongst the Indians of British North America is diminishing rapidly in numbers and their migration Northward into Canadian territory had ... latterly been arrested (as far as it could be) by United States Troops stationed along the Border, and whilst our Indians and Half Breeds are prohibited by the United States Military Authorities from going South of the Boundary in pursuit of the animal necessary to feed themselves and their families no restriction has ever been placed by the Canadian Authorities when the Buffalo herds come Northwards upon United States Indians coming into

our territories in pursuit of the game in which all are so much interested. It is true that the American Government undertake to feed their Indians if they remain on the Reservations provided for them within the United States but in fact they come North and chase the buffalo in our Country, diminishing the food supply of our Indians and Half Breeds. The Canadian Government is making great exertions to settle their Indians and to induce them to become herdsmen, and to cultivate land and raise supplies of food for themselves, but in the meantime and until this is accomplished Half Breeds and Indians alike depend upon the chase, particularly of the Buffalo for sustenance'. CO 42/757, First Nations Affairs, No. 138–16262, Lorne to Hicks Beach, 26 September 1879.

53. CO 167/581, *Mauritius*, No. 170-6782, Napier Broome to Hicks Beach, 'Prison Committee: Minute on the Public Execution of Criminals,' 31 March 1879.

54. CO 167–581, *Mauritius*, Minutes on 'No. 170,' 28 April 1879.

55. A. Curthoys, 'Race and Ethnicity: A Study of the Response of British Colonists to Aborigines, Chinese and Non-British Europeans in New South Wales, 1856–1881', PhD thesis, Macquarie University, 1973, 206–8.

56. P. Gordon, 'Herbert, Henry Howard Molyneux, Fourth Earl of Carnarvon (1831–1890), Politician', in *Oxford Dictionary of National Biography*, www.oxforddnb.com/view/10.1093/ref:odnb/9780198614128.001.0001/odnb-9780198614128-e-13035.

57. https://c21ch.newcastle.edu.au/colonialmassacres/map.php; J. Richards, *The Secret War: A True History of Queensland's Native Police*, Queensland University Press, 2008.

58. James Fitzjames Stephen's cousin Alfred Stephen, the Chief Justice of the New South Wales Supreme Court, found in 1869 that one of the slaving ships captured by the Royal Navy in Fiji had been seized illegally. With no evidence taken from the enslaved islanders, this member of the Stephen family ordered the Royal Navy to pay reparations to the ship's owner. See T. Banivanua Mar, *Violence and Colonial Dialogue: Australia-Pacific Indentured Labor Trade*, University of Hawai'i Press, 2007.

59. E. Fairfield, *The Colonial Office List for 1879: Comprising Historical and Statistical Information Respecting the Colonial Dependencies of Great Britain*, Kessinger, 2010.

60. At Cambridge, Dilke became friends with yet another member of the influential Stephen family. Leslie Stephen was son of James and younger brother of James Fitzjames, author, literary critic, and first editor of the *Dictionary of National Biography*.

61. Dilke's liberalism was laced through with racism. He linked the inherent inferiority of Africans to the availability of the banana. This was 'the most dangerous crop – you could live on it, raw or fried, but do nothing constructive with it. Thus it offered the fatal prospect of a soft life in a soft climate'. R. Jenkins, *Dilke: A Victorian Tragedy*, Bloomsbury, 1996, 28.

62. C. W. Dilke, *Greater Britain A Record of Travel in English-Speaking Countries during 1866–7*, J. B. Lippincott and Macmillan, 1869, preface.

63. P. Gordon, 'Herbert, Henry Howard Molyneux, Fourth Earl of Carnarvon (1831–1890), Politician', in *Oxford Dictionary of National Biography*, www .oxforddnb.com/view/10.1093/ref:odnb/9780198614128.001.0001/odnb-9 780198614128-e-13035.

64. For the perpetuation of these ideas, see M. Lake and H. Reynolds, *Drawing the Global Colour Line: White Men's Countries and the International Challenge of Racial Equality*, Cambridge University Press, 2008.

65. J. R. Seeley, *The Expansion of England*, repr. University of Chicago Press, 1971, 15–18.

66. In 1889 he was still exhorting that 'the solidarity of the Empire will be improved by Australian federation, which will get rid of the now dangerous nuisance of 7 ministries getting up quarrels with Downing Street in order to draw off attention from their corrupt and bad home policy'. BL, Add. MS 60795, Herbert to Carnarvon, 30 October 1889. By 1900 Herbert was back at the Colonial Office under Chamberlain and dealing with the final achievement of Australian confederation. He was also proposing tariffs to protect the newly consolidated British-settler world, which was at odds with earlier liberalism's free trade ethos. L. Trainor, *British Imperialism and Australian Nationalism: Manipulation, Conflict, and Compromise in the Late Nineteenth Century*, Cambridge University Press, 1994.

11 IMPERIALISM

1. A. Pollard and W. Thomas, 'Froude, James Anthony (1818–1894), Historian and Man of Letters', in *Oxford Dictionary of National Biography*, www.oxforddnb.com/view/10.1093/ref:odnb/9780198614128.001.0001/od nb-9780198614128-e-10202.

2. CO 48/173, *Cape*, No. 75–172, D'Urban to Glenelg, 28 October 1837.

3. D. Welsh, *Roots of Segregation: The Native Policy in Colonial Natal, 1845–1910*, Oxford University Press, 1972.

4. Pollard and Thomas, 'Froude'.

5. J. Martineau, *Life and Correspondence of Sir Bartle Frere*, J. Murray, 1895, 172–3.

6. J. Benyon, 'Frere, Sir (Henry) Bartle Edward, First Baronet (1815–1884), Colonial Governor', in *Oxford Dictionary of National Biography*, www .oxforddnb.com/view/10.1093/ref:odnb/9780198614128.001.0001/odnb-9 780198614128-e-10171.

7. Benyon, 'Frere'.

8. A. Roberts, 'Livingstone, David (1813–1873), Explorer and Missionary', in *Oxford Dictionary of National Biography*, www.oxforddnb.com/view/10 .1093/ref:odnb/9780198614128.001.0001/odnb-9780198614128- e-16803.

9. *Anti-Slavery Reporter*, 30 March 1872, quoted R. J. Gavin, 'The Bartle Frere Mission to Zanzibar, 1873', *The Historical Journal*, 5, 2, 1962, 139.

10. As both Muscat and Zanzibar were coming under greater Islamic revivalist influence, and as the Ottoman Empire shifted its focus from the Balkans

southwards to the Arabian Peninsula, the imperial departments at St James Street became locked 'in a complex of quarrels which caused a virtual breakdown in government policy toward the area for several years'. Gavin, 'The Bartle Frere Mission', 129.

11. 'The surprising thing about this … was that eighteen months before, in the summer of 1871, the national newspapers had been equally unanimous in their indifference and opposition to the campaign against the East African slave trade'. Gavin, 'The Bartle Frere Mission', 143.

12. Wolseley had fought in Burma, the Crimean War, the Indian Uprising, the Second Opium War and the crushing of the Métis Red River rebellion in Canada before the Ashanti campaign. Whilst serving in Canada, he had visited General Lee during the US Civil War and written in support of the Confederacy. When the supply of locally contracted African carriers ran out on the march to Kumasi, he ordered the black soldiers of the West India Regiments to carry the white British soldiers' supplies as well as their own. M. Bennett, 'The West India Regiments in the Anglo-Ashanti War, 1873–74', www.bl.uk/west-india-regiment/articles/the-west-india-regiments-in-the-anglo-ashanti-war-1873-74.

13. R. E. Dumett, 'Pressure Groups, Bureaucracy, and the Decision-making Process: The case of Slavery Abolition and Colonial Expansion in the Gold Coast, 1874', *The Journal of Imperial and Commonwealth History*, 1981, 9, 2, 198.

14. Dumett, 'Pressure Groups', 199.

15. Frere's view of the global strategic significance of Britain's possessions along the perimeter of the Indian Ocean, from Afghanistan in the north to the Cape in the south, would provide inspiration for Halford Mackinder's later geopolitics. F. V. Emery, 'Geography and Imperialism: The Role of Sir Bartle Frere (1815–84)', *Geographical Journal*, 150, 1984, 342–50.

16. Marquess of Zetland, *The Letters of Disraeli to Lady Bradford and Lady Chesterfield*, Ernest Benn Ltd, 1929, vol. 2, 189.

17. L. M. Thompson, *The Unification of South Africa, 1902–1910*, Clarendon Press, 1960.

18. CO 48/492, *Cape* (vol. pp. 169–74), No. 2527, Crown Agents to Colonial Office, 22 May 1879.

19. In May 1879, one of the Colonial Office clerks commented, 'If any telegrams are to be sent to Sir B. Frere or Sir G. Wolseley [in the Cape Colony] they must go today in order to catch last Thursday's mail at Madeira'. AAP 9 June, annotation on CO 48/490, *Cape* [italics] (vol. pp. 54–5), No. 9189, Frere to Colonial Office, 19 May 1879.

20. M. Pugh, 'Beach, Michael Edward Hicks, first Earl St Aldwyn (1837–1916), Politician', in *Oxford Dictionary of National Biography*, www.oxforddnb.com/view/10.1093/ref:odnb/9780198614128.001.0001/odnb-9780198614128-e-33859.

21. G. D. C. Argyll, *The Eastern Question from the Treaty of Paris 1836 to the Treaty of Berlin 1878 and to the Second Afghan War*, Strahan, 1879, 122.

22. Twomey, 'Framing Atrocity', 256.

23. W. E. Gladstone, *Bulgarian Horrors and the Question of the East*, J. Murray, 1876, 9–10.
24. Gordon, 'Herbert, Henry Howard Molyneux'.
25. CO 158/252, *Malta*, No. 14–1764, Governor A. Borton to Colonial Office, 30 January and 20 March 1879.
26. The treaty signed in Berlin satisfied none of the empires invested in the Balkans and sowed some of the seeds for the First World War.
27. S. N. Singh, *The Secretary of State for India and His Council*, Munshi Ram Manohar Lal, 1962, 44. Lytton's frustration was caused by the Council's opposition to his censorship of the Indian press.
28. Cranbrook was known for his reluctance to tolerate public demonstrations and his emphasis on tough policing, especially in the wake of the Fenian attacks in 1867. J. Parry, 'Hardy, Gathorne Gathorne, First Earl of Cranbrook (1814–1906), Politician', in *Oxford Dictionary of National Biography*, www .oxforddnb.com/view/10.1093/ref:odnb/9780198614128.001.0001/odnb-97 80198614128-e-33356. Prior to succeeding Derby as foreign secretary, Salisbury had been secretary of state for India. In that role he had told Lytton 'if England was to remain supreme ... she must' tolerate 'the political role of the Indian princes, and of participation by Indians in the administration, but ... that if the number of well-educated Indians ... should increase, the government would face the indecent and embarrassing necessity of closing that avenue to them'. P. Smith, 'Cecil, Robert Arthur Talbot Gascoyne, Third Marquess of Salisbury (1830–1903), Prime Minister', in *Oxford Dictionary of National Biography*, www.oxforddnb.com/view/10.1093/ref:odnb/978019861 4128.001.0001/odnb-9780198614128-e-32339.
29. Disraeli quoted Klein, 'Who Made the Second Afghan War?', 103.
30. Chamberlain (no immediate relation to the later colonial secretary) had been wounded six times during the first British occupation of Afghanistan and gained further recognition for bravery during the Indian Uprising. Klein, 'Who Made the Second Afghan War?'

12 IMPERIAL WARS AND THEIR AFTERMATHS

1. M. Pugh, 'Beach, Michael Edward Hicks, First Earl St Aldwyn (1837–1916), Politician', in *Oxford Dictionary of National Biography*, www.oxforddnb.com /view/10.1093/ref:odnb/9780198614128.001.0001/odnb-9780198614128- e-33859.
2. Lanyon would succeed Shepstone as administrator of the Transvaal in 1878. There, knowing of his Caribbean experience and pointing to his relatively dark skin, Boers referred to him as a 'West Indian bastard' and a 'Kaffir'. R. Stearn, 'Lanyon, Sir (William) Owen (1842–1887), Army Officer and Colonial Official', *Oxford Dictionary of National Biography*, www.oxforddnb.com/view/10.1093/ref:odnb/9780198614128.001.0001/o dnb-9780198614128-e-16060.
3. Within a few years, consolidated mining companies like De Beers ended this freedom of movement by enclosing the compounds within wire mesh fences and preventing workers from leaving during the duration of their contract. 'This

completed the total isolation of African workers in a world of their own'. R. Turrell, 'Kimberley's Model Compounds', *The Journal of African History*, 25, 1, 1984, 61.

4. The alternative means of acquiring firearms was less palatable: exchanging precious cattle with itinerant British, Afrikaner and Griqua arms dealers. P. Delius, *The Land Belongs to Us: The Pedi Polity, the Boers, and the British in the Nineteenth Century Transvaal*, Ravan Press, 1983.

5. The productive phrase 'imperial literacy' is borrowed from T. Banivanua Mar, 'Imperial Literacy and Indigenous Rights: Tracing Transoceanic Circuits of a Modern Discourse', *Aboriginal History*, 37, 2013, 1–28.

6. Some of the Griqua and also some amaZulu fought alongside the whites.

7. The white men accused of the massacre at Koegas were acquitted by settler juries, but the only black culprit, Zoutaar, was sentenced to five years' imprisonment with hard labour. Frere would also be criticised for allowing colonial volunteers to force the indenture of African women and children during the rebellion. I. B. Sutton, 'The End of Coloured Independence: The Case of the Griqualand East Rebellion of 1878', *Transafrican Journal of History*, 8, 1/2, 1979, 181–200.

8. At the same time, Natal settlers' recruitment of Indians indentured to work on the colony's coastal sugar plantations was generating a large South African Indian population which would, under apartheid, constitute a fourth legally inscribed racial group, positioned below whites and above Coloureds and Africans. See A. Lester, E. Nel and T. Binns, *South Africa Past, Present and Future: Gold at the End of the Rainbow?*, Prentice Hall, 2000.

9. S. Marks and S. Trapido, eds, *The Politics of Race, Class and Nationalism in Twentieth-Century South Africa*, Longman, 1987.

10. J. Guy, *The Destruction of the Zulu Kingdom: The Civil War in Zululand, 1879–1884*, University Kwazulu Natal Press, 1999.

11. Bulwer had previously been secretary to the British ambassador with the Ottoman Porte in Constantinople and governor of the Malay colony Labuan.

12. J. Martineau, *The Life and Correspondence of the Right Hon. Sir Bartle Frere, bart., G.C.B., F.R.S.*, John Murray, 1895, 241.

13. CO 48/489, Fairfield, Minutes on 'Confidential No. 3217', 1 March 1879.

14. British Parliamentary Papers, C. 2220, No. 105, Frere to Hicks Beach, 30 September 1878.

15. British Parliamentary Papers, C. 2222, No. 111: Frere to Hicks Beach, 6 October 1878.

16. F. E. Colenso, *History of the Zulu War and Its Origin, Assisted by Edward Durnford*, Chapman & Hall, 1880, 258–60.

17. The letter arrived at the Colonial Office on 16 November.

18. Bulwer had reservations: 'The part taken by the Natal Government in the installation of the present Zulu King marks a certain departure from the previous policy, but no practical hold was then established, either upon the King or upon the nation, nor was any attempt made to establish one'. Nevertheless, he came into line behind Frere, equivocating that 'The course of events during the last two years has so altered the position of British authority in South Africa, it has so multiplied our responsibility, and the political and military situations have

become such that the relations of the Zulu Government with us, and the condition of the Zulu country, can no longer with safety be left as they are. It has now become a matter of positive necessity to do something'. CO 48/487, *Cape* (vol. pp. 537–39), No. 313, Bartle Frere to Colonial Office, 12 December 1878, enclosed Minute (vol. pp. 540–85) from Sir Henry Bulwer.

19. CO 48/487, Cape (vol. pp. 537–39, No. 313, Bartle Frere to Colonial Office, 12 December 1878, enclosed Minute (vol. pp. 540–85) from Sir Henry Bulwer.

20. CO 48/487, *Cape* (vol. pp. 622–23), No. 323, 323–1339, Cape (vol. pp. 622–3), Bartle Frere to Colonial Office, 20 December 1878.

21. Colenso, *History of the Zulu War*, 260–62.

22. CO 48/489, *Cape* (vol. pp. 44–6), No. 9a–3231, Bartle Frere to Colonial Office, 9 January 1879. Annotated comments, Herbert and Hicks Beach.

23. J. Laband, *Zulu Warriors: The Battle for the South African Frontier*, Yale University Press, 2014.

24. CO 48/489, *Cape* (vol. pp. 133–35), No. 23, Bartle Frere to Colonial Office, 22 January 1879.

25. The Rev. Kilvert for instance, recorded that, while he was attending a conference at the local Drill Hall on 11 February (a place where he had previously heard Bartle Frere deliver a speech on church matters), devastating 'News came … of the terrible disaster inflicted by the Zulus on the 24th regiment at Rorke's Drift, S. Africa': F. Kilvert, *Kilvert's Diary 1870–1879: Selections from the Diary of the Rev. Francis Kilvert*, ed. W. Plomer, Vintage Books, 2013, 345. A breakaway component of the Zulu army attacked the supply base and hospital at Rorke's Drift the following day and was repulsed, enabling the salvaging of some military pride and immortalisation in the film *Zulu*.

26. CO 179/132, Lord Chelmsford, Lieutenant General Commanding in South Africa, Pietermaritzburg to Secretary of State for War, 2 March 1879.

27. CO 167/581, *Mauritius*, No. 129, Napier Broome to Hicks Beach, 9 March 1879. One of Herbert's senior clerks was dubious about the wisdom of Broome's action, noting on the despatch that 'large bodies of troops were rapidly being dispatched from England, which would reach the seat of War almost if not quite as soon as troops from Mauritius' and that 'the paucity of the … Mauritius Contingent made the expedition almost seem useless as an addition to the strength of the English reinforcements; at best, the chance of their arriving in advance of the English troop ships was reduced to the fine point of a day or two; added to that, negotiations for the hire of the French Mail Steamer for the voyage failed, and accordingly the Artillery and Company of the 88th had to go in a sailing vessel'. Annotation GWR, 30 April.

28. CO 167/582, 10, Bowen to Hicks Beach, 22 April 1879.

29. CO 48/489, *Mauritius*, No. 10, Frere to Colonial Office, 5 March 1879, annotations HC and JB 18 April, Hicks Beach 21 April.

30. CO 48/492, *Cape* (vol. pp. 303–16), No. 66–6147, from India Office to Colonial Office, 17 June 1879.

31. Frere first informed the Colonial Office of the Prince's death on 9 June, and the message was received on 3 July, with Herbert deciding that the Queen must be the first to be informed. CO 48/490, *Cape* (vol. pp. 96–8), No. 169, Frere to Colonial Office, 9 June 1879. Chelmsford also noted that the Prince

'was riding his tallest horse, on to which he had always great difficulty in mounting. He was killed owing to his inability to climb up into the saddle' quickly enough.

32. CO 48/490, *Cape*, Copy of Letter (vol. pp. 117–18) from Lord Chelmsford, Camp near Itelegi Mountain, Zululand to Frere, 2 June 1879.

33. J. A. Froude, *The Earl of Beaconsfield*, J. M. Dent & Sons, 1914, 213. The reference to converted bishops was because John Colenso, Bishop of Natal, had collaborated with his Zulu friend and convert, William Ngidi, in an isiZulu translation of the Bible. The adaptations made to Colenso's own theology during the course of Ngidi's questioning provoked accusations of heresy in Britain, not least from the famous cultural critic Matthew Arnold. J. Guy, 'Class, Imperialism and Literary Criticism: William Ngidi, John Colenso and Matthew Arnold', *Journal of Southern African Studies*, 23, 2, 1997, 219–41; J. A. Draper, ed., *The Eye of the Storm: Bishop John William Colenso and the Crisis of Biblical Inspiration*, Cluster, 2003.

34. CO 48/489, *Cape* (vol. pp. 152–55), Confidential – No. 3217, Frere to Colonial Office, 26 January 1879, Fairfield, Minutes, 1 March 1879.

35. CO 48/489, *Cape*, Confidential – No. 3217, Frere to Colonial Office, No. 61, 1 March 1879.

36. CO 48/489, *Cape*, Confidential – No. 3217, Minutes on No. 61, 4 April 1879.

37. CO 48/489, *Cape* (vol. pp. 152–55), Confidential – No. 3217, Frere to Colonial Office, 26 January 1879, Fairfield, Minutes, 1 March 1879.

38. CO48/490, *Cape* (vol. pp. 438–46), No. 241, Frere to Colonial Office, 19 August 1879.

39. G. Boase and J. Lunt, 'Cavagnari, Sir Pierre Louis Napoleon (1841–1879), Army and Political Officer in India', in *Oxford Dictionary of National Biography*, www.oxforddnb.com/view/10.1093/ref:odnb/9780198614128 .001.0001/odnb-9780198614128-e-4916.

40. Quoted J. Lee, *Afghanistan: A History from 1260 to the Present*, Reaktion Books, 2018, 366.

41. The parallel with the fate of Alexander Burnes in 1841 was picked up in the British press: *Pall Mall Gazette*, on 8 September 1879, cited Z. Aslami, 'The Second Anglo-Afghan War, or The Return of the Uninvited', in D. F. Felluga, ed., *BRANCH: Britain, Representation and Nineteenth-Century History*, extension of *Romanticism and Victorianism on the Net*, http:// www.branchcollective.org/?ps_articles=zarena-aslami-the-second-anglo-afghan-war-or-the-return-of-the-uninvited.

42. Quoted Lee, *Afghanistan*, 371–2.

43. B. Robson, *The Road to Kabul: The Second Afghan War, 1878–1881*, Spellmount, 2007.

44. H. W. Kinsey, 'The Sekhukhune Wars Part II', *Military History Journal*, 2, 6, 1973; Delius, *The Land Belongs to Us*.

45. J. Benyon, 'Frere, Sir (Henry) Bartle Edward, First Baronet (1815–1884), Colonial Governor', in *Oxford Dictionary of National Biography*, www .oxforddnb.com/view/10.1093/ref:odnb/9780198614128.001.0001/odnb-9 780198614128-e-10171.

46. F. E. Colenso, *The Ruin of Zululand: An Account of British Doings in Zululand since the Invasion of 1879*, vol. 1, William Ridgway, 1884, 253.
47. Colenso, *The Ruin of Zululand*, xiv–xv. The 'sprinkling of honours' refers especially to the unprecedented number of Victoria Crosses awarded to the defenders of Rorkes Drift in the aftermath of Isandhlwana.
48. See Lester et al., *South Africa Past, Present and Future*.
49. CO 48/489, *Cape* (vol. pp. 330–32), Confidential – No. 6183, Frere to Colonial Office, 12 March 1879, Extract of letter from Missionary (vol. pp. 333–5), minutes HC 18 April, who noted, 'Sir Bartle Frere, however, does not agree with all that the writer states'; Herbert, 18 April; Hicks Beach, 18 and 21 April. Hicks Beach noted, 'I should hope the writer's opinion is not well founded'. Herbert responded, 'I fear it may be'.
50. Lee, *Afghanistan*.
51. Z. Aslami, 'The Second Anglo-Afghan War'.
52. E. Rogan, *The Arabs*, Penguin, 2011, 101. Just as the interruption to the global supply of cotton during the US Civil War had at first advantaged and then disadvantaged Indian producers, so it did Egyptian too. Ismail's lavish expenditure was premised in part on the boom to cotton export that occurred when supplies from the US South were interrupted, but continued after their resumption had undercut Egyptian profits from the trade.
53. Parry, 'Disraeli'. In turn, during the mid 1880s, that control of Egypt would draw General Gordon into an idiosyncratic attempt to curtail the Mahdist revolt in Sudan. The reluctant imperialist Gladstone was obliged to embark on the Disraeli-esque venture of sending Garnet Wolseley to the rescue again, belatedly despatching a British relief column to Khartoum.
54. https://liberalhistory.org.uk/history/the-midlothian-campaign/.
55. W. F. Monypenny and G. E. Buckle, *The Life of Benjamin Disraeli, Earl of Beaconsfield: 1837–1846*, Vol. 2, John Murray, 1929, 393.

CONCLUSION TO PART III: A LIBERAL EMPIRE?

1. N. Etherington, P. Harries and B. K. Mbenga, "From Colonial Hegemonies to Imperial Conquest, 1840–1880", in C. Hamilton, B. K. Mbenga and R. Ross, eds, *The Cambridge History of South Africa, vol. 1, From Early Times to 1885*, Cambridge University Press, 2009, 383.
2. CO 83/19, *Fiji*, No. 14, Des Voeux to Hicks Beach, 5 February 1879, annotation E. W. 3 June 1879.
3. J. Black, *Imperial Legacies*, Encounter, 2019, 148.
4. N. Ferguson, *Empire: How Britain Made the Modern World*, Penguin, 2018.
5. Washbrook, "Lytton".
6. M. Hassan Kakar, quoted Lee, *Afghanistan*, 383.
7. See S. Hall, *Familiar Stranger: A Life between Two Islands*, Penguin, 2018.

Index

Printed in Great Britain
by Amazon